Cinema

and

Painting

~

CINEMA

AND

PAINTING

~

How Art

Is Used

in Film

~

ANGELA

DALLE

VACCHE

University of Texas Press

AUSTIN

Earlier versions of Chapters 1, 3, 4, 6, 7, and 8 were previously published as

"A painter in Hollywood: Vincente Minnelli's *An American in Paris,*" *Cinema Journal* 32:1 (Fall 1992), pp. 63–83.
"Eric Rohmer's *The Marquise of O*: Painting Thoughts, Listening to Images," *Film Quarterly* 46: 4 (Summer 1993), pp. 2–15. © 1993, the Regents of the University of California (by permission).
"Jean-Luc Godard's *Pierot le Fou:* Cinema as Collage against Painting," *Literature/Film Quarterly* 23:1 (1995), pp. 39–54.
"F. W. Murnau's *Nosferatu:* Romantic Painting as Horror and Desire in Expressionist Cinema," *Post-Script: Essays in Film and the Humanities* 14:3 (Summer 1995), pp. 25–37.
"Kenji Mizoguchi's *Five Women around Utamaro*: Film between Woodblock Printing and Tattooing," *East-West Film Journal*, January 1994, pp. 24–51.
"Alain Cavalier's *Thérèse:* Still Life and Close-Up as Feminine Space," *Film Criticism* 17:1 (1992), pp. 3–25.

(∞) The paper used in this publication meets the minimum requirements of American National Standard for Information Sciences—Permanence of Paper for Printed Library Materials, ANSI Z39.48-1984.

Library of Congress Cataloging-in-Publication Data

Dalle Vacche, Angela, 1954–
 Cinema and painting : how art is used in film / Angela Dalle Vacche.
  p.   cm.
 Includes bibliographical references (p.) and index.
 ISBN 0-292-71582-X (cloth). — ISBN 0-292-71583-8 (pbk.)
 1. Art and motion pictures.   2. Art in motion pictures.   3. Painting and motion pictures.   4. Motion pictures—Aesthetics.   I. Title
PN1995.25.D36 1996
791.43`657—dc20   95-32441

~

To Aaron Spencer

~

Contents

~

List of Illustrations   *ix*

Acknowledgments   *xiii*

INTRODUCTION   A Thematic and Intertextual Approach
1

CHAPTER 1   Vincente Minnelli's *An American in Paris:*
Painting as Psychic Upheaval
13

CHAPTER 2   Michelangelo Antonioni's *Red Desert:*
Painting as Ventriloquism and Color as Movement
43

CHAPTER 3   Eric Rohmer's *The Marquise of O:*
Painting Thoughts, Listening to Images
81

CHAPTER 4   Jean-Luc Godard's *Pierrot le Fou:*
Cinema as Collage against Painting
107

CHAPTER 5   Andrei Tarkovsky's *Andrei Rublev:*
Cinema as the Restoration of Icon Painting
135

CHAPTER 6   F. W. Murnau's *Nosferatu:*
Romantic Painting as Horror and Desire in
Expressionist Cinema
161

CHAPTER 7   Kenji Mizoguchi's *Five Women around Utamaro:*
Film between Woodblock Printing and Tattooing
197

CHAPTER 8   Alain Cavalier's *Thérèse:*
Still Life and the Close-Up as Feminine Space
221

Notes   *247*

Bibliography   *267*

Index   *293*

~

Illustrations

~

FIGURE 1   A set from *An American in Paris* based on the painting
            Pont-Neuf, by Pierre-Auguste Renoir.   25

FIGURE 2   A set from *An American in Paris* based on paintings
            by Henri Rousseau.   25

FIGURE 3   *The Football Players,* by Henri Rousseau.   26

FIGURE 4   A set from *An American in Paris* based on the painting
            Montmartre, by Maurice Utrillo.   28

FIGURE 5   A set from *An American in Paris* based on Raoul Dufy's
            serpentine outlines.   29

FIGURE 6   Prehistoric art in *An American in Paris.*   30

FIGURE 7   *The She-Wolf,* by Jackson Pollock.   32

FIGURE 8   Gene Kelly as the dancer in Toulouse-Lautrec drawing
            Chocolat Dancing at the Achilles Bar, in *An American in Paris.*   33

FIGURE 9   *Eiffel Tower with Trees,* by Robert Delaunay.   37

FIGURE 10   A street from *Red Desert* with an atmosphere reminiscent
            of Giorgio De Chirico's paintings.   52

FIGURE 11   The industrial landscape of Antonioni in *Red Desert,*
            between prehistory and the cosmos.   59

FIGURE 12   Monica Vitti as diva, in *Red Desert.*   61

FIGURE 13   *Periferia Industriale,* by Mario Sironi.   67

FIGURE 14   *Sackcloth,* by Alberto Burri.   68

FIGURE 15   *Painting,* by Alfred Otto Wolfgang Schulze Wols.   70

FIGURE 16   *Corps de Dame: Blue Short Circuit,* by Jean Dubuffet.   71

FIGURE 17   *Hostages Black Background,* by Jean Fautrier.   73

FIGURE 18   *Painting,* by Nicholas de Staël.   74

FIGURE 19   *Abstraction,* by Pierre Soulages.   75

FIGURE 20   Monica Vitti as Giuliana in *Red Desert.*   76

FIGURE 21   *The Nightmare,* by Henry Fuseli.   91

FIGURE 22   Edith Borckhardt as Giulietta, in *The Marquise of O.*   91

FIGURE 23   *The Oath of the Horatii,* by Jacques-Louis David.   95

FIGURE 24   *Madame Récamier,* by Jacques-Louis David.   95

FIGURE 25   *Young Woman Sewing by Lamplight,*
            by Georg Friedrich Kersting.   96

FIGURE 26   *The Paternal Curse,* by Jean-Baptiste Greuze.   98

FIGURE 27   *The Bolt,* by Jean-Honoré Fragonard.   98

FIGURE 28   *Storming the Citadel,* by Jean-Honoré Fragonard.   99

FIGURE 29   The Count pursuing the Marquise, in *The Marquise of O.*   99

FIGURE 30   *Garden Terrace,* by Caspar David Friedrich.   100

FIGURE 31   The Marquise reflecting on her pregnancy in the
            peacefulness of the park, in *The Marquise of O.*   101

FIGURE 32   *The Death of Sardanapalus,* by Eugène Delacroix.   102

FIGURE 33   Anna Karina and Jean-Paul Belmondo as fugitive lovers,
            in *Pierrot le Fou.*   115

FIGURE 34   *Drowning Girl,* by Roy Lichtenstein.   121

FIGURE 35   *Girl before a Mirror,* by Pablo Picasso.   124

FIGURE 36   *The Roumanian Blouse,* by Henri Matisse.   125

FIGURE 37   Anna Karina pushing a pair of scissors toward the camera,
            making explicit Jean-Luc Godard's iconophobic vocation,
            in *Pierrot le Fou.*   131

FIGURE 38   *Saint George,* icon.   139

FIGURE 39   *The Face of Christ Not Made by Human Hands,* icon.   142

FIGURE 40   *The Annunciation,* icon.   151

FIGURE 41   *Suprematist Composition: Red Square and Black Square,*
by Kazimir Malevich.   *155*

FIGURE 42   *The Isle of the Dead,* by Arnold Böcklin.   *169*

FIGURE 43   *The Monk by the Sea,* by Caspar David Friedrich.   *172*

FIGURE 44   Ellen as a Rückenfigur, in *Nosferatu.*   *173*

FIGURE 45   The shrine in the forest, in *Nosferatu.*   *173*

FIGURE 46   *The Cross in the Mountains,* by Caspar David Friedrich.   *174*

FIGURE 47   The opening view in *Nosferatu.*   *176*

FIGURE 48   *The Red Tower in Halle,* by Ernst Ludwig Kirchner.   *176*

FIGURE 49   The heavy door of the vampire's castle, in *Nosferatu.*   *177*

FIGURE 50   *The Churchyard,* by Caspar David Friedrich.   *177*

FIGURE 51   Biedermeier decor, in *Nosferatu.*   *183*

FIGURE 52   *Woman before the Setting Sun,* by Caspar David Friedrich.   *185*

FIGURE 53   The real estate agent Knock as a scarecrow, after turning
into a scapegoat, in *Nosferatu.*   *185*

FIGURE 54   The crowd as a moving strip of photographic negatives,
in *Nosferatu.*   *186*

FIGURE 55   *Before the Mirror,* by Georg Friedrich Kersting.   *192*

FIGURE 56   The vampire at sunrise, in *Nosferatu.*   *195*

FIGURE 57   *An Oiran (A Courtesan),* by Kitagawa Utamaro.   *213*

FIGURE 58   Utamaro paints the body, in *Five Women around Utamaro.*   216

FIGURE 59   Painting the body and becoming invisible, in
Ugetsu monogatari.   *216*

FIGURE 60   Introspective clothing, in *Thérèse.*   *227*

FIGURE 61   Candles, in *Thérèse.*   *227*

FIGURE 62   *Woman with a Parrot,* by Edouard Manet.   *232*

FIGURE 63   *Shoes,* by Vincent van Gogh.   *233*

FIGURE 64   Thérèse as Joan of Arc, in *Thérèse.*   *237*

FIGURE 65   *The Young Virgin,* by Francisco de Zurbarán.   *238*

FIGURE 66   *Christ the Redeemer,* by Quirizio da Murano.   *241*

FIGURE 67   Catherine Mouchet as Thérèse falling ill, in *Thérèse.*   *243*

FIGURE 68   *Woman Looking at a Table,* by Wolfgang Heimbach.   *243*

~

Acknowledgments

~

The writing of this book has been supported by a one-year Morse Fellowship from Yale University. I have also received great encouragement from Dudley Andrew at the University of Iowa and Joanna Hitchcock at the University of Texas Press.

While I was analyzing films and researching art historical sources, I repeatedly turned to my colleagues in art history for advice. In particular, I wish to thank Emily Braun, Walter Cahn, Esther Da Costa-Meyer, Ann Gibson, and Mimi Yiengpruksawan.

The development of this book has also been possible thanks to the love and companionship of my friends Maria Brodsky, Jennifer Church, Susan Edwards, Glenn Elliott, Hani Kablawi, Mary Paganelli, Jill Poller, Suzy Reynolds, and Masha Vorobiov. This book is dedicated to Aaron Spencer to acknowledge his love and support.

I wish to thank Jürgen Heinrichs, Jeff Leib, and Annie Heminway for their help with the bibliography and with French accents. I am also grateful to my editors, designer, and indexer for their excellent help: Wendy Wipprecht in New Haven, Connecticut, and Lorraine Atherton, Lois Rankin, Ellen McKie, and Linda Webster in Austin, Texas.

Finally, I wish to thank the Whitney Humanities Center at Yale University for two A. Whitney Griswold faculty grants that have enabled me to pay for the illustrations.

~

Cinema

and

Painting

~

While some may feel that film does not belong to the history of art, the fact is that filmmakers often use paintings to shape or enrich the meaning of their works. Thus the history of art is *in* film, even though, by evoking high art and creativity, rather than technology and mass culture, painting for the cinema constitutes a forbidden object of desire. This relation of love and hate between cinema and painting is further complicated by the tendency of art history to be evoked well beyond the boundaries of a text or the intentions of a filmmaker. It takes more than a study of the sources of a film to reveal the beauty of the encounter between cinema and painting; one must imagine all the possible elements of visual culture that a film, just by virtue of its circulation, has the power to attract into the textual orbit. It is that internal richness and outbound energy that I strive to convey in this book, by opening up film studies to the history of art and by trying to encourage other colleagues to join me in the new field of comparative arts. In short, my effort in this book stems from the belief that art history as a discipline cannot afford any longer to ignore film studies, for the advent of the cinema has forever changed the meaning of the word "art" and the meaning of the word "history."

By looking at eight films produced under different historical circumstances and in different cultural contexts, each directed by strong creative personalities, I ask: what happens to the paintings used or alluded to in these texts, and how do these films define painting as the realm of high art, creativity, and femininity, setting it against popular culture or industrial technology? Precisely because each film I examine offers a different definition of painting as art in film, my approach is thematic; the title of each chapter is meant to spell out the director's attitude toward painting. With Vincente Minnelli, for example, painting in *An American in Paris* (1951) is so compelling and subversive that it goes hand in hand with psychic upheaval, whether beneficial or harmful; for Michelangelo Antonioni, however, painting in *Red Desert* (1964) is both unsettling and irresistible, so that the director transfers the burden of creativity to the female protagonist.

Just as painting translates itself into different themes ranging from psychic upheaval to feminine sensitivity in the films I examine, the whole category of art emerges in a variety of manifestations across my case studies. In *An American in Paris,* Minnelli explores many views of art: as decoration, neurosis, temporary utopia; as a source of economic power; and as a mark of foreignness, elitism. In F. W. Murnau's *Nosferatu* (1922) and in Kenji Mizoguchi's *Five Women around Utamaro* (1946), art is meaningful as long as it prevails over the laws of the marketplace. In *Pierrot le Fou* (1965) and *Thérèse* (1986), art is implicated in the establishment, whether this means aesthetic tradition or patriarchy; thus collage and still life, because of their historical reputation as subversive or marginalized genres, offer Jean-Luc Godard and Alain Cavalier a standpoint from which to challenge a wide range of dominant values, from fixed gender roles to the separation of art and life.

For Andrei Tarkovsky in the film *Andrei Rublev* (1966), art is a form of prayer and of communal energy. By contrast, in *The Marquise of O* (1975), art fosters a series of vices that Eric Rohmer denounces by developing a film style that opposes artifice, vanity, and self-indulgence, even as his pictorial images disclose the strength of temptation. Finally, for Antonioni, to practice art means to be caught in the struggle between experimentation and nostalgia. In short, the cinema's use of art in innumerable ways suggests that, even though my book focuses on painting as the most problematic but also the most alluring of art forms, all the films I examine must summon all sorts of sources in order to define art as a category.

This is the case because, by blurring the distinction between high art and popular culture, the cinema has always had a tendency to challenge not just painting in isolation but rather the whole system of the arts, thus disclosing the possibility of new configurations, hierarchies, alliances, and hostilities. In *An American in Paris*, for instance, while Minnelli associates painting with extreme expressions of creativity and emotion, he also turns to dance to stress communal values that reinsert the single artist within a national tradition. In *Red Desert* the contrast is not between solipsistic painting and communal dancing; rather, architecture, with its allegiances to mass culture, public space, and industrial technology, allows Antonioni to align painting with a feminine vision at odds with the values of rationality and efficiency but open to inner rebirth and new avenues of self-expression.

My approach is also intertextual. A broad category of analysis with overtones that range from narrative to stylistic detail, intertextuality for me includes the borrowing of images from art history to inflect the meaning of a text, the rejection of painting to stress the unique features of film, the insertion of cinema in broadly shared visual cultures and national traditions, and, finally, the power filmmaking has to redefine art history. Thus intertextuality enables thematic contrasts, iconographic similarities, and historiographic commentaries. In a sense, as broad as it may be, my definition of intertextuality shuttles between two extremes in the way film sees itself in relation to other arts: either film is plagued by a cultural inferiority complex and therefore obsessively cites other art forms, or it is self-confident enough to move beyond this state of dependency and arrive at the point where it can teach something new to art historians. To highlight this second extreme, I will present as my final case study the daring film *Thérèse*, by Alain Cavalier. Far from being overwhelmed by the history of painting, this film teaches us to look at the tradition of domestic genre painting with a still-life component in a new way.

My method also assumes that since the cinema is engaged in a dialogue with the other arts, the films under analysis can be read as allegorizations, self-conscious meditations on what is at stake in the encounter between painting and cinema, art and technology, tradition and modernity. This allegorical or metacinematic dimension is especially apparent in Murnau's *Nosferatu* and Mizoguchi's *Five Women around Utamaro*. *Nosferatu* thrives on Murnau's familiarity with the legacy of German Romantic landscape painting and also on the director's awareness that the invention of the cinema shortly preceded the development of art history as an academic discipline—a discipline to which he was exposed while a university student as well as through personal contact with members of the Expressionist avant-garde.

If the self-consciousness of *Nosferatu* is based on the generation to which Murnau belongs—the men and the women who lived through the transition from the nineteenth to the twentieth century, from the achievements of Romanticism to the displacements of Expressionism—likewise *Utamaro* owes its ability to reflect on the nature of the cinema to the timing of its creation during a traumatic historical moment: Japan's defeat in World War II and the subsequent occupation by American forces. *Utamaro* comments on the nature of the cinema in relation to the arts of woodblock printing and tattooing by overlaying definitions of artistic creativity with issues of national and religious identity.

Like the theme of painting as tradition and creativity, the battle of the sexes—or, if you will, the social construction of gender roles—is a preoccupation that informs all my case studies. Put another way, my analyses assume that artistic production in the cinema entertains a dialogue not only with mechanical but also with sexual reproduction. Most importantly my attention to the iconography of sexual difference is meant only to enhance our understanding of the power relations between cinema and painting, and is not an attempt to say something new about male and female identities on the screen.

Some readers may wonder if my intensive intertextual approach risks weakening my interpretation of individual films. My answer to this legitimate concern is that it is *the film* in all its aspects—genre, production history, reception, historical context, auteur—that channels, contains, and gives meaning to intertextual citations. While I acknowledge the art historical point of view, I am writing about what happens on the screen. The cinema is the protagonist of my book, and art history is considered only in relation to it. Film, in short, has the last word.

Besides relying on intertextuality, all together my chapters raise questions about influence and intentionality—two categories that have been traditionally hard to tackle because, like architecture, filmmaking is an industrial art characterized by collaborative authorship.

Influence and intentionality, for instance, are hard to prove in *An American in Paris*. Minnelli's primitivist notion that creativity involves psychological upheaval has affinities with Jackson Pollock's equivalence of painting with dancing. Both the brilliant director of Hollywood musicals and the painter with a masculine, aggressive public image sought a renewal of the self through a fusion of the arts. We have no record that either artist made statements about the other, but we can still account for the weakness of Minnelli's happy ending for *An American in Paris* by recalling the popular perception of Pollock's visceral approach to art-making. This is to say, in the fifties Pollock's laconic, intense persona must have pushed the boundaries of heterosexuality to the point where it threatened to slip into homoeroticism. Even if Hollywood appropriated Pollock's charisma to construct stars like Marlon Brando and Montgomery Clift, it certainly expected Minnelli to trade off the exhilaration of painting in Paris for a weak heterosexual romance with a rather insipid French girl. Thus, in my analysis of *An American in Paris,* I cannot speak of direct influence or conscious intentionality but only of meaningful cultural constraints or affinities, which the parallel of Pollock and Minnelli helps to illuminate, regardless of any recorded contact between the two.

Mizoguchi's *Five Women around Utamaro* is another extreme example, in which neither direct influence nor conscious intentionality seems applicable. Because *Five Women around Utamaro* is about the life of the artist, the connection between him and Mizoguchi is so obvious that influence and intentionality can exist only in their most excessive form: total identification. It is as if the Japanese filmmaker were telling a story about his own life and his own relationship to art. As a result of this overpowering congruence of the artist in the film and the artist making the film, we feel free to look outside the text, into the shared folklore of the national culture.

When I was at work on Murnau's use of art history in *Nosferatu,* I was able to reinforce my speculations on influence and intentionality with documents located in the archives of the University of Heidelberg; however, in my readings of Rohmer's *Marquise of O,* Antonioni's *Red Desert,* Godard's *Pierrot le Fou,* Tarkovsky's *Andrei Rublev,* and Cavalier's *Thérèse,* I have availed myself of the directors' published statements on painting and the arts in general—while always recognizing that the content of interviews is either fragmentary or implicated in the marketing process. Hence I read between the lines of my sources and often bring to the discussion art historical references that the films themselves, regardless of the directors' expressed intentions, seem to integrate into their textual space.

My book is structured like a necklace upon which eight different beads, so to speak, are strung on a thematic-intertextual red thread. Hence I must comment on the order of my chapters and on my choice of films. I start with Minnelli's *American in Paris* and follow it with Antonioni's *Red Desert* because by setting them next to each other I want to suggest how much common territory can be found between a European "art film" and an MGM Hollywood musical. This order makes it possible to see the European art film as a special genre that only deviates from or simply alters, but does not subvert, the Hollywood mode. Antonioni's reaching out to painting in film is as unsettling as Minnelli's. Whether creativity is set in the rigid context of the American industry or in the looser European milieu, it always and inevitably destabilizes male identity. *An American in Paris* and *Red Desert* both qualify as art films, but I have not constructed my case studies to emphasize the parallels between them. Each is conceived as a self-contained unit. Too many cross-references and comparisons would cloud the richness of the images, which are already multifaceted and have many levels of meaning.

Toward the end of this book, I discuss Mizoguchi's *Five Women around Utamaro* in a chapter that further develops issues of gendered identity and artistic creativity and thus returns me to where I started, but with this difference: the whole discussion has been based on the elision, not the exhibition, of art historical citations. Mizoguchi's disinclination to cite Utamaro's (or anyone else's) artwork, even as he develops a theoretical position on the nature of the filmic image, is both an effective ending point for the book and a way of reopening all the questions it raises.

After my discussion of *An American in Paris* come three chapters on Antonioni's *Red Desert*, Eric Rohmer's *The Marquise of O*, and Jean-Luc Godard's *Pierrot le Fou*, which I have grouped together because in these three directors' work, the dialectic of word and image characterizes the encounter of cinema and painting. In *Red Desert*, the words are by far less daring than the pictorial images, yet the female protagonist's visual sensitivity is limited by the alignment of her speech with a masculine perspective. While in *Red Desert* word and image are as difficult to reconcile as man and woman, for Rohmer, in *The Marquise of O*, literature and painting are categories that can be rearranged or broken down by attributing a plastic edge to words and by endowing images with an introspective aura. In Rohmer's film, the images that achieve the nuances of written speech and the use of language as an object of sensuous contemplation contribute to a steady, predictable oxymoronic logic; by contrast, with Godard the translation of the verbal into the visual and the visual into the verbal has a compulsive quality that well conveys the random proliferation of competing, unstable signs.

The dialectic of word and image and the playing out of artistic creativity within the scenario of sexual difference are two themes that are common to Antonioni's *Red Desert* and Jean-Luc Godard's *Pierrot le Fou*, a breathless philosophical essay on how collage works and what it can tell us about subjectivity in modern life. By adopting collage as his medium against painting, which he sees as obsolete, Godard assumes an iconoclastic, avant-garde stance that clearly contrasts with the conservative orientation and iconophilic project of Tarkovsky's *Andrei Rublev*. In this film, the director aims to use the cinema to restore the emotional power of religious icon painting in our modern world, which, he feels, has lost its spiritual values.

While in the films examined so far the encounter of cinema and painting redefines gender roles, expands the dialectic of word and image, and shows what creativity means to different filmmakers, in chapter 6 and chapter 7—on Murnau's *Nosferatu* and Mizoguchi's *Five Women around Utamaro* respectively—I dwell on the tension between art and technology. As a character, Nosferatu the vampire stands for Murnau's ambivalence about his historical position between cinema and painting. In a similar way, Mizoguchi situates his medium between the competing poles of mass appeal and forbidden artistry, mechanical reproduction and manual labor, that are respectively occupied by woodblock printing and tattooing—a tactic that also enables him to express his divided allegiance between East and West as well as his struggle with the cinema, which he views as being simultaneously a form of patriarchal oppression and a liberating force.

My book's final chapter is devoted to *Thérèse* because this film allows me to discuss what the cinema, instead of only borrowing or repressing paintings, can teach art history about itself. If I wanted to retitle the book so as to describe my sense of the encounter between cinema and painting, I would choose something like *The Magic Mirror* or *Screen as Arabesque*, for cinema does not merely reflect back to art history the image it received, but through intertextual activity it rearranges all its outlines, boundaries, and priorities. Thus I am offering my readers a brand-new, cinematic *lens* through which to view the older and more established discipline of art history.

Having explained the sequencing and the key issues of my chapters, I should now comment on my choice of films. Most readers will wonder why I have not included a chapter on Peter Greenaway, since this director's work is heavily concerned with the relation between film and the other visual arts, the dialectic of word and image, the tension between high and low culture, and the parallel between artistic and sexual activity. My answer is that precisely because a single Greenaway film, *The Belly of an Architect* (1987), explores all the issues I raise in my book, I have chosen to deal with other directors in order to spread my inquiry across many different personalities, instead of collapsing everything into one case study. To those who want to know what place Greenaway might have had in this book, I will say that he would have served as a summary of my first seven chapters, for *The Belly of an Architect* relies on a type of intertextuality in which film is more preoccupied with defining itself than with redefining art history.

My choice of films also reflects my attempt to introduce into film studies an awareness of different genres of painting and their relevance to the cinema. For example, the chapter on Murnau's *Nosferatu* is meant to make the reader think about the links between Romanticism and Expressionism, between landscape painting and subjectivity; Cavalier's *Thérèse,* a film I greatly admire, encourages us to pay attention to the connection of still life and the close-up, particularly in the way both art forms use domestic objects to explore gender roles. Furthermore, were we to compare these two films in a more direct fashion, we would quickly realize that they both draw upon art historical traditions, intent upon challenging what was formerly considered the highest and most central of genres: history painting.

My chapter on Godard and collage addresses the end of painting as art, and *Pierrot le Fou* is a film about the impossibility of portraiture in modern life, because this genre stands for a belief in a coherent and unified subjectivity. Besides *Pierrot le Fou,* two more films in my book shy away from portraiture: Tarkovsky's *Andrei Rublev* and Mizoguchi's *Five Women around Utamaro.* Yet these directors' rejection of portraiture is not based on a modernist crisis but rather on religious and social philosophies that do not equate individualism with mastery or physiognomy with identity.

Finally, my choice of films has also been determined by availability on video, and this is why I have not been able even to consider Raoul Ruiz's *Hypothesis of a Stolen Canvas* (1978) as a candidate for a case study.

Needless to say, my eight case studies are not the first attempts to discuss the dialogue between cinema and painting. In *Moving Pictures,* Anne Hollander searches through the history of art for the kinds of paintings that anticipated what cinema later on did with movement. The cinema, Hollander argues, is a mass medium, yet its pictures move each one of us in a secret and highly individual manner, so that the paintings that best pave the way for this psychological impact are from Northern Europe, where Protestantism favored an intensely private apprehension of images.[1]

While Hollander feels that the tradition of Northern European art is responsible for the birth of the moving image, I would argue that throughout the history of art, starting with the flickering shadows on the wall of Plato's cave, we can find innumerable instances of a protocinematic imagination. As soon as we acknowledge cinema's tendency to borrow from all sorts of art forms and to employ many different visual sources within the same film, we have to conclude that Hollander's belief in one single, direct genealogy risks narrowing the richness of the encounter between cinema and painting. Hollander's work would rather teach us about which kinds of paintings anticipated the cinema than about the various ways in which cinema addresses painting. It is precisely this second direction of inquiry—from film to painting instead of painting to film—which I set out to explore.

Because Jacques Aumont in *L'oeil interminable* has no interest in citing paintings in film, it should come as no surprise that I reach conclusions different from the French scholar's on at least three topics we both discuss: Cavalier's *Thérèse*, color in film (my example is Antonioni's *Red Desert*), and Godard's relation to painting (which I examine by using *Pierrot le Fou*). To begin with, Aumont sees *Thérèse* as a failure, because it would like to be "painting" when it cannot or should not be. My intertextual reading of *Thérèse*, however, shows that the film teaches something valuable about the destabilizing power of still life and the multifaceted nature of the close-up.[2]

Although Aumont offers a convincing explanation of how film technology dictates that filmmakers and painters have to work with color in completely different ways, in my analysis of *Red Desert* I want to expand on the current belief that Antonioni uses color as a way of making "abstract painting" in film. I contend that he uses color to depict and analyze a scenario of death and rebirth in *Red Desert.* As a nonverbal element of the mise-en-scène, an element invested with a poignancy that well fits the polarities and upheavals inherent in the death of an old order and the birth of a new one, color in *Red Desert* makes up "the text of muteness" that Peter Brooks argues is typical of melodrama.[3] In other words, the historical trauma and psychological rebirth in *Red Desert* are so extreme that words cannot express them; only the silence of colors can convey the intensity of these changes. Thus color *is* movement in a film made like an abstract painting, for it charts the interface of public and private shifts.

Besides making a case for *Red Desert* as a melodrama concerned with historical upheavals and psychological transformations, my chapter on Antonioni intends to explain that his allegiance to both painting and architecture is predicated on the battle of the sexes, and to argue that Antonioni's visual ventriloquism through his female protagonist, Monica Vitti, is both experimental and exploitative in that while he uses his actress's eyes to work innovatively with color in film, her power resides more in the eloquent muteness of the images she shares with the director than in anything she says.

Thus, what I gain by reading *Red Desert* intertextually and in a melodramatic key is an expansion of the themes commonly associated with color: not only painting and abstraction but also the power of silence and femininity. It is precisely this broader thematic understanding of what color means in *Red Desert* that, in contrast to Aumont's technological preoccupations, enables me to assess how innovative Antonioni's film truly is.

Instead of concentrating on surface similarities and notions like influence, Aumont argues for an ongoing dialogue, a continuing relationship between cinema and painting that plays itself out in the norms of visual representation, in the historical changes of the "eye." Thus, for Aumont, the relationship between painting and cinema is not one of influence and borrowing but of joint participation in culture. Yet, since the cinema is the *lens* I use to look at art history, Aumont's metaphor of an eye is somewhat at odds with his intense historical consciousness.

Aumont's notion of the eye as a continuous but always incomplete system is both a problematic and provocative formulation; in addition, it matches the French theorist's definition of Godard's cinema. Yet precisely because Aumont refuses to deal with citation, we never quite grasp what is at the heart of Godard's work. My chapter on Godard will argue that his oeuvre is deeply logocentric and pictorial while it also entertains abstractions. In order to improve our understanding of Godard, I have decided to do exactly the opposite of Aumont and deal with intertextuality in *Pierrot le Fou*. First of all, my analysis of Godard's sources discloses that even if his cinema is visually stunning, *Pierrot le Fou* is built like a collage of words and images, graphics and colors, lines and volumes. All these oppositions, in turn, signal the director's preoccupation with sexual difference, a barrier he utilizes for his creative purposes but which he would also like to overcome for emotional reasons.

The fantasy at the heart of *Pierrot le Fou*, then, is one of overcoming the boundary between man and woman, the verbal and the visual pole, by depicting something between these poles that is neither but could become both. In particular, Godard's "endless eye" is ongoing to the extent that the dialectic of word and image in collage can reoccur between any two other sets of opposites, yet it seems to me that it is less incomplete than Aumont allows, for it is animated by a logocentric impulse, even if the images of Godard's cinema remain most compelling.

Unlike Aumont's work, which celebrates Godard as painter, my analysis of *Pierrot le Fou* leads me to conclude that Godard's cinema is iconophobic. I see Godard as first setting up an equation between the spectacle of the female body and the allure of the pictorial image, and then seeking to abandon the visual register for the sake of an empty canvas, a blank sky, a colorless sea, or a black screen—voids where the mind, through language, can project all its abstractions. In other words, Godard avails himself of collage rather than painting, because collage's ability to thrive on the boundary between word and image reflects Godard's use of semiotic permutations in the attempt to overcome the pain of sexual difference.

It is possible that Aumont might have missed the collagist-iconophobic thrust of Godard's work because he has been concerned with the late films of Godard such as *Passion* (1982). I have decided not to analyze *Passion* since so much powerful criticism has recently been published on this film. In addition, focusing on *Pierrot le Fou* enabled me to link Godard with collage and to demonstrate his intense antipictorial vocation, even though the appeal of painting constantly resurfaces in his images. Finally, I feel that the splendid canvases brought to life in *Passion,* although they seem to support Aumont's labeling of Godard as painter, do not at all refute my view of Godard as a collagist. In fact, the opening of *Passion*—the image of an airplane whose wake produces a sort of writing or trace across the empty sky—is one more reminder that even this film, a work built around classical painting, is animated by a voiding of visuality in favor of language, writing, abstraction, absence.

It must be clear by now that while I support Aumont's project of thinking in terms of representation and not of art, of considering cultural strategies and not aesthetics, my disagreements with him about specific directors or films are quite substantial. One reason for this is the completely different scale of our approaches: I like working with stylistic detail and the single image; Aumont tackles big issues at a much more abstract level. If Anne Hollander's argument is too narrow because it deals only with the influence of Northern European painting on film, Aumont's view is too broad. My project is to carve out a space of close reading that is centrally located between these two extremes; using the single filmic text as a unit of measure, I hope to use close reading to achieve broad theoretical ends.

My method is somewhat closer to Pascal Bonitzer's *Décadrages* and to Jean-Louis Leutrat's *Kaleidoscope,* in that these studies on cinema and painting capitalize on citation and intertextuality without shying away from such larger issues as realism, referentiality, temporality, framing, construction of space, and spectatorship. Yet I differ from them as well. Like Aumont,

Bonitzer and Leutrat organize the discussion around a series of theoretical issues, whereas I have structured my book around individual films and have surveyed many fewer paintings and films than they. My analysis is clearly more intensive than extensive. No individual analyst, however, can produce a definitive interpretation of a work of art, so my readings neither claim nor wish to exhaust intertextuality.[4]

My discussion of the use of paintings on the screen sets many competing definitions of the cinema against each other. In contrast, Brigitte Peucker contends that the cinema is a machine of dismemberment,[5] an interesting argument but one that cannot account for Rohmer's and Tarkovsky's well-known opposition to the scissors of Eisensteinian montage, Mizoguchi's uneasiness with the cuts of editing, Murnau's fascination with movement in real time, his efforts to preserve the intergrity of real space, and his view of editing as empathy.

The collusion of cinema and painting works more like a subtraction than an addition, for it leads outside vision into feeling, thinking, and abstraction. In *Nosferatu* and in *Andrei Rublev*, Murnau and Tarkovsky respectively tell of longing for something divine or transcendent; Godard and Mizoguchi, uneasy with the female body as an analogue for the image, adopt an antivisual stance; for Rohmer and Godard what is visual should always become something else so that cinema may convey thoughts or transform itself into poetry. Finally, from the encounter of cinema and painting in the films of Antonioni, Minelli, and Cavalier, we learn about psychic change, emotional upheaval, and feminine subtlety. Thus the meeting of screen and canvas makes visible the invisible and favours absence over presence, mind over body.

CHAPTER I

Vincente

Minnelli's

An American

in Paris

~

Painting as

Psychic

Upheaval

*B*etween 1957 and 1962 the critics of *Cahiers du Cinéma* discovered Vincente Minnelli as an "auteur." Jean Domarchi and Jean Douchet argued that Hollywood was made not only of studios and genres but that it was also a cinema of highly original artists. In retrospect, the auteur theory was symptomatic of a desire to grant artistic status to Hollywood cinema, which until then had been considered only as a producer of popular entertainment.[1] The auteur theory argues that, Hollywood notwithstanding, certain directors are capable of leaving the mark of their personal preoccupations in their films. These directors are auteurs rather than "metteurs-en-scène," because they do not just apply studio priorities or rehearse generic conventions but also work through and transform the resources and the constraints of the industry to express their unique vision. According to the critics of *Cahiers,* the auteur's signature can be detected in how traits peculiar to a single director manage to reappear across different genres subject to the formulae of the industry.

More prudently than the French critics, the Italian Roberto Campari and the American Stephen Harvey propose that Minnelli's authorial signature is the product of a dialectic between his collaborators in the studio system and his directorial personality. This combination of efforts produces a signature characterized by "a lush and daring use of color, the seamless fusion of music and camera movement, and a decorative scheme that mates the cast with inanimate objects in voluptuous counterpoint."[2] While Minnelli's style can be seen as an epitome of the Metro-Goldwyn-Mayer (MGM) studio style, it is also unique. James Naremore argues that the fusion of heterogeneous elements is Minnelli's trademark: "Only a few years after Bertolt Brecht had argued for a radical separation of elements in musical theater, the Broadway stage and Minnelli in particular were working in an opposite direction. Minnelli's shows were strongly unified and marked in various ways with his 'touch.' "[3] In short, according to Harvey, it is difficult to distinguish between Minnelli as an artist apparently at home only in Hollywood and Minnelli as one of the most imaginative interpreters of the industry's approach.

Even in the late fifties, when a steady commitment to one studio had become unusual, Minnelli remained a faithful, salaried MGM employee. During this period, Minnelli directed several of his most important musicals and melodramas: *Gigi* (1958), *Some Came Running* (1959), and *Home from the Hill* (1960). Harvey concludes that it would be too simplistic to assume that Minnelli's attachment to the highly professional working methods of MGM guaranteed a perfect fit with his own style: "If the idiosyncratic beauty of Minnelli's style transcended MGM's trademark gloss, the fundamental pessimism of his viewpoint just as surely sabotaged their upbeat ethic."[4] Minnelli's signature carries over from the melodramas to the musicals, so that one genre functions as the foil of the other. Hence Minnelli's pessimism is latent even under the happy surface of *An American in Paris*, a fairytale musical he directed the year of his difficult divorce from Judy Garland.[5]

Many film historians have suggested that Vincente Minnelli's training in the visual arts enabled him to develop a filmic style that would transcend the routine look of an MGM production, without going against the fundamental tenets of the industry. Minnelli's passion for painting was already well under way when, shortly after high school, instead of attending a university he took classes at the Chicago Art Institute. There, not only did he come into contact with a fine collection of Impressionist paintings, but he also immersed himself in the work of Marcel Duchamp, Max Ernst, Salvador Dalí, Jean Cocteau, and Luis Buñuel. Throughout his career as a filmmaker, Minnelli continued to tackle the theme of painting as creativity whether he was directing a melodrama about Vincent van Gogh going mad or a musical about a mediocre painter in love with a French girl. In short, Minnelli is torn between a celebratory view of art in *An American in Paris* (1951) and one that sees art as a terrifying disease in *Lust for Life* (1956).[6] Minnelli's view of art as self-expression and art as madness develops out of an eclectic use of art-historical sources throughout his career: Thomas Eakins in *Meet Me in St. Louis* (1944); the surrealism of Christian Bérard, Yves Tanguy, and Joan Miró in *Yolanda and the Thief* (1945); late nineteenth- and early twentieth-century French art in *An American in Paris;* seventeenth-century Dutch painting in *Brigadoon* (1954); French Impressionism and Art Nouveau in *Gigi;* Amedeo Modigliani and Marc Chagall in *Designing Woman* (1957); and Van Gogh, Camille Pissarro, and Paul Gauguin in *Lust for Life.*

In *An American in Paris* painting has positive and negative connotations. While it can be reconciled with love, painting is caught between art and money, between the flights of the imagination and the laws of the market. Furthermore, although it enables self-expression, painting also brings to the surface conflicts of national and sexual identity. Thus Minnelli's work bears witness to his reputation as a highly visual director in Hollywood, while it also points to the opposition that Hollywood locates between American masculinity and artistic creativity. Minnelli's split attitude toward art reflects the popular discourses enveloping Jackson Pollock's charged artistic persona in the forties and the fifties. This is not to say that Minnelli had Pollock in mind while he was shooting *An American in Paris* but that the positive and negative responses elicited by Jackson Pollock's visceral approach to abstract art match, on the one hand, Minnelli's attraction toward painting as creativity and, on the other, Hollywood's condemnation of abstract art as insanity.

Although no direct evidence of Pollock's influence on Minnelli can be found, both these artists were deeply interested in the way Surrealism linked artistic creativity to the unconscious.[7] They both cherished the well-known American values of youth, energy, and spontaneity, and they both fantasized about a fusion of self and other, of subject and object, that is, becoming one with the image. To convey this desire, they transformed painting into dancing, while subscribing to a primitivist approach that enables the artist to reach back to the roots of his creative impulse. Whereas modernism emphasizes the autonomous and self-reflexive nature of each artistic medium in isolation, primitivism refers, on the one hand, to a subjectivity in which all the senses operate in unison and, on the other, to a prehistoric, mythical realm, one in which the self does not have to measure itself against an ideal image but is totally fused with it. The attainment of a unified, collective unconscious is the ultimate goal of Minnelli's celebration of male creativity in the long, central ballet of *An American in Paris.* These very same themes also inform Jackson Pollock's action painting, in which the painter literally dances on the canvas and the artist's moving body merges with the picture being made.

Hence, in *An American in Paris,* painting is doubly defined as psychological upheaval, which is what Pollock came to embody. For Minnelli the auteur, painting means creativity and art, whereas for Minnelli the MGM employee, painting means neurosis and an unsettling indulgence in the senses, in the image. In order to achieve a compromise between Pollock and Hollywood, Minnelli turns the Paris of nineteenth-century painters into a Disneyland attraction—a Parisland—so that that quintessentially American institution, the theme park, contains the staging of French culture. There, for the span of a dance, painting does disclose the creative potential of a self perfectly integrated with an image of its origins. Yet, the primitivism Minnelli shares with Pollock does not lead to the radical rebirth sought by Abstract Expressionist painters. Instead, Minnelli's primitivism helps to perpetuate a stereotypical American identity.

Art and Love, Love and Money

Andrew Sarris has argued that *An American in Paris* is not a film typical of the Hollywood musical as a genre:

> It always struck me that there was a fatal emotional rupture in the plot
> between the black-and-white Beaux Arts Ball and the climactically
> rainbowish *American in Paris* ballet. Despite the conventionally happy ending
> of romantic reconciliation between Kelly and Caron, the film ends in a
> somber, downbeat mood that I have never been able to explain or evaluate
> or even attribute.[8]

Sarris questions the structural unity of one of the most famous, expensive, and successful musicals MGM ever produced. (It won six Academy awards.) *An American in Paris* is the story of an ex-GI, Jerry Mulligan (Gene Kelly), who paints in Paris and woos Lisa Bouvier (Leslie Caron). The "emotional rupture" Sarris cannot explain occurs when Jerry, after having lost Lisa, finds himself in the middle of a polychromatic feast celebrating images of Paris in painting. In this city of the mind, Jerry dances with Lisa again, while she impersonates the women subjects of famous French paintings. The colorful ballet sequence contrasts with the black-and-white forest built by art students for the New Year's Eve Ball at the Moulin de la Gallette. There, Jerry sees Lisa leaving for America with his rival, a French chansonnier, Henri Borel (Georges Guetary). Eventually, the colors of painting will bring Lisa back to Jerry, yet once the artist's dream is over, the two lovers must reunite in a nonpictorial world.

By arguing that a few loose ends undermine the structural unity of the plot, Joseph Andrew Casper echoes Sarris's doubts about the happiness of Minnelli's happy ending:

> Something must be said about the plotting of *An American in Paris,* however, whose last quarter is uneven and disconcerting. Jerry's artistic life is not resolved. It is presumed. But then, what about Milo? Also, Adam is forgotten about. . . . Finally, there is the problem of the ballet at the end of the film which, as part of a whole, is too ambitious for its own good. It throws the entire film out of kilter.[9]

If we combine Sarris's remarks with Casper's criticisms, we can see how Jerry avoids losing himself in painting thanks to his love of Lisa, while the happy ending with the French girl distracts us from the difficulty of being an American male and a painter in Paris at the same time. From the plot alone it is hard to tell whether Jerry will continue to paint after marrying Lisa. Perhaps the happy ending would have been much stronger if it had made perfectly clear that Jerry, in winning Lisa, gains full access to French art. Furthermore, the reunion of the two lovers ties up only one narrative thread, because, as Casper reminds us, we never learn the fate of Milo (Nina Foch) and of Adam (Oscar Levant). Milo is an American heiress who sponsors Jerry's artistic endeavors, and Adam is a neurotic concert pianist who puts all his energies into making art rather than love. Finally, the ballet of Parisian canvases is so stunning in length and energy released that Minnelli's film, while implying that only Hollywood love can neutralize the unhealthy side of Parisian art, does not completely resolve the rivalry between art and love, between unbound male creativity and the routine to which marriage leads.

"Brother, if you can't paint in Paris, you'd better give up and marry the boss's daughter," Gene Kelly states in voice-over narration as Jerry. Kelly's remark implies that only in Paris, and not in Hollywood, can an American paint. Kelly also declares that only a wealthy American woman can push an unsuccessful artist in France up the ladder of success. An opposition thus emerges between the psychological nourishment an American artist can receive from French culture and the dependency of art made in France on American money.[10] This economic interpretation, however, glosses over the dangerously anticonformist, bohemian side of painting. Kelly's address to a "brother" invites us to speculate whether, for Minnelli, a happy ending with the boss's daughter may function as an antidote to the homoerotic potential stored in the joining of masculinity with art, of Americanness with paintings produced in a country notorious for its refined taste. Minnelli must have half understood the difficulty of equating painting with work, especially since French bohemia strikes a clear note of contrast with the utilitarian approach of American puritanism.[11]

From the standpoint of Hollywood, painting is a sensorially overloaded, time-wasting enterprise that weakens the masculine self and does not fit in with a fast-moving, profit-oriented society. How, then, could Minnelli rely on MGM to celebrate art? The final ballet is an energetic demonstration of the technical and financial resources that MGM could command to conjure cinematic dreams. With Minnelli, however, the self-reflexivity typical of the musical genre escalates into the fantasy of a market-free creativity that soars above the dictates of the industry itself. While the ballet bears witness to the economic power of a Hollywood studio and, in so doing, supports Milo's belief that art is only about marketing and money, Jerry's love of painting is so authentic that it longs to flout both the market pressures and the social conventions that regulate the contradictory facets of his identity: a male painter, an American in Paris. Thus, Jerry's heterosexual, American identity is doubly challenged, by painting and by a foreign soil. Precisely because the facets of Jerry's character do not easily fit together, through a cinematic style that emphasizes the fusion of different art forms, Minnelli must turn to an extreme definition of painting, one that not only includes fame or creativity but that also relies upon a special kind of regression into the most secret and emotional core of one's self. Eventually the weakness of the happy ending indicates that art cannot win over both love and money; rather, it is love that becomes an ambivalent sign of how much Minnelli wants to be for art and how much he has to be for money.

National and Sexual Identity

During the ballet of French paintings Jerry finds his true artistic self; in a nonpictorial Paris, he must confront challenges to his national and sexual identity. Before becoming an expatriate artist in Paris, Jerry was an American GI. Jerry's interaction with the French natives inevitably depends on war memories that ruffle intangible layers of cultural difference and release subtle historical ambiguities. Two episodes in particular illustrate the web of social contradictions pulling apart Jerry's self. While playing the piano Jerry's best friend, Adam, remarks that Henri Borel prefers the Viennese waltz to a jazz rhythm. This juxtaposition of German and American music casts a shadow on the number that follows, "By Strauss," in which echoes of Nazism arise from dance steps reminiscent of military drills and from faked German accents in the spoken parts of the song. Despite its light-hearted surface, this musical interlude associates Henri Borel with the specter of collaboration. Later on, Lisa makes sure to situate Henri in the French Resistance, yet strong doubts remain about the performer's national loyalty. Henri's eagerness to incorporate American steps and words into his song-and-dance routine—a routine surely modeled on the work of Maurice Chevalier, another Frenchman whose reputation was tainted by collaboration[12]—makes us wonder whether Henri had just as easily added the goose-step to his repertoire during the Occupation.

To be sure, the interaction between Jerry and Henri is complicated not only by political overtones but also by sexual ones. At the beginning of the film, the voice-over narrator mistakes Henri for a younger man whose passing reflection appears in a mirror hanging on a wall in the street. Adam is a workaholic, Jerry is trying to find his true artistic self through love, but Henri appears to be very fond of how he looks, and he admires himself in the same mirror that had intercepted the younger man's passing reflection. The homoerotic connotations of Henri's narcissism are echoed by the uneasy fit between Jerry's roles as an American male and as an artist in Paris. Unaware that they are both attracted to the same girl, Henri and Jerry sing together and exchange dance styles, thus forging a pact between males in the name of a love whose object is erroneously defined. As if the association with the vain Henri had not sufficiently destabilized Jerry's masculinity, his heterosexual identity is further threatened by Milo's appropriation of a traditionally male initiative. The American heiress lures the painter into an evening tête-à-tête, after promising Jerry that an "extra girl" will be there.

By virtue of his artistic vocation and his dependency on Milo's money, Jerry himself risks turning into that extra girl.

Minnelli's introduction of Jerry as a character suggests that heterosexual masculinity must conform to one stable identity. At the beginning of the film, Minnelli's camera plays with the possibility that the spectator might mistake each male character for someone else, or that Henri, Jerry, and Adam might have a doppelgänger, or hidden self.[13] The presentation of Jerry, for example, makes it clear that the American painter is caught between art and love, even though he would like to achieve both. Minnelli's camera, by moving upward along a picturesque building in Montmartre, leads us to think that Jerry is the man passionately kissing a girl in front of an open window. Yet the voice-over narrator quickly informs us that we are looking through the wrong window. Jerry, the painter, is the man sleeping in a fetal position in the loft above the couple caught by the gaze of the camera. Instead of making love, Jerry is barely emerging from the world of dreams; he wakes up in front of a self-portrait, not a picture of his beloved. His stern expression in the self-portrait is perhaps an attempt to qualify him as an intellectual artist, but most important, it suggests a link between art and unhappiness. Jerry's fetal position spells out his desire to reach back into a primitive origin. Yet, Jerry's search for his most authentic persona through art and dream is somewhat denied as soon as he wipes the self-portrait smudging it beyond repair.

During the ballet, Lisa's impersonation of Toulouse-Lautrec's Jane Avril, of Renoir's *femme-fleur*, and of Henri Rousseau's gypsy girl reinforces the association of art with femininity. Henri had made this connection much earlier through a fantasy sequence. Lisa is so much the singer's "ideal girl" that she can become all the different kinds of women he might fancy. In Henri's mind, Lisa multiplies herself into a kaleidoscope of art-historical styles. Lisa's joyful Charleston follows the serious mood of a Jacobean set, and a Romantic ballerina turns into the elegant arabesque of a Rococo chamber. Lisa is all the periods of the history of art that popular knowledge associates with an exaggerated stress on ornament at the expense of substance. If Lisa is art, and art is Lisa, as an artist Jerry loves the paintings Lisa can become, while his reunion with her in a nonpictorial world means that a Hollywood happy ending is the closest thing to artistic fulfillment.

For Henri, Lisa's beauty is comparable to different styles of interior decoration, but for Jerry, her charm becomes the crucial source of his creative imagination, the inner motor of his psyche. As a result, Henri's view of Lisa as ornament is meant to suggest the superficiality of the chansonnier's involvement with art. By contrast, Lisa's pivotal role in Jerry's balletic dream spells out the painter's genuine love of painting. Henri's notion that art is nothing but decoration discloses what an Englishman or an American would see as typically French behavior—superficial, volatile, effeminate. By contrast, Jerry's sense that art *is* life in a meaningful way keeps at bay doubts about the American's heterosexual identity.

Two other episodes reassure us about the painter's sexual and national allegiances. When Jerry arrives in Montmartre riding in Milo's big American car, all the children gather around him. The iconography of this scene and its happy atmosphere recall the Allies' arrival in Paris when, as liberators, they were greeted by an enthusiastic French crowd. This episode firmly posits Jerry's American origin. Finally, the magic pas de deux the painter dances with Lisa endows heterosexuality with a dreamlike aura, which prepares us for the collusion of art and love in the ballet and also dispels the implied homoerotic connection between Jerry and Henri.

Cinema and Painting

If Lisa is for Jerry a legitimate, heterosexual substitute for that extreme identification with French painting he would like to achieve but, as an American male, cannot experience, the ballet is all Minnelli has at his disposal to compensate for the impossibility of art in Hollywood. MGM feasts us with an abundance of citations only to mask the absence of the objects cited. Yet the invisibility of painting does not prevent art-historical references from proliferating across the whole film, well outside the boundaries of the ballet.

On his way to a favorite spot for exhibiting his artwork, Jerry walks by an old man who looks just like Toulouse-Lautrec. Milo's hairdo and her evening gown that bares one shoulder are based on the famous Greek statue with only one arm. The black-and-white Beaux-Arts Ball is vaguely reminiscent of Edouard Manet's *Ball at the Opera* (1873), while the shadows surrounding Adam's performance of George Gershwin's Piano Concerto in F Major recall the atmosphere and the lighting of some opera scenes by Edgar Degas.

Although the protagonist of the film is a painter, we never get a sense of Jerry's technique. We see him apply only a few dabs of paint to a couple of portraits, to a still-life with flowers, and to a view of the Opera. Lisa, the source of Jerry's artistic inspiration, can hardly believe that a young, athletic American will paint like a French master. Half joking, Jerry admits that he might remain forever a great but undiscovered painter. Even Jerry's clothing is a denial of painting as high art, for he wears a white cap that makes him look more like an American housepainter or a baseball player than a bohemian Parisian artist. Finally, paintings are strangely absent in Milo's lavishly furnished apartment, despite her role as patroness of the arts.

What is, then, the nature of the relationship of the final long ballet to the rest of the film? To begin to solve this problem we might consider the director's personality and ask the question whose answer the *Cahiers* critics took for granted: to what extent do Minnelli's own preoccupations make their mark in such a cooperative venture as a Hollywood musical? Undoubtedly, George Gershwin's music, Ira Gershwin's lyrics, Preston Ames's art direction, Irene Sharaff's costume design, and Kelly's choreography compete for authorial recognition in this film, and yet it is one of Minnelli's major themes—the dialectic of cinema and painting, Hollywood and art—that underpins the relation between the final ballet and the rest of the film. Still, it remains unclear why, in *An American in Paris*, that dialectic runs so far out of control that it does not resolve the conflicting demands of art, love, and money within the formula of a happy ending.

Perhaps some helpful clues can be found in the critical responses to the concluding ballet sequence. Critics noted that its excessive length (seventeen minutes) and cost ($450,000) appear to be marks of exaggeration. The pace is invariably described as "frantic," and the fireworkslike bursting of colors as "delirious." The intensity of the ballet's emotional and visual impact on the viewer is also remarked upon. All these excessive features point to Minnelli's surrealistic insight that the artist can transfigure what is imaginary into a reality more compelling and more real than the real world itself. Put another way, while Minnelli did attribute a liberating force to art, he also knew that art's transfigurative energy in the end would more likely lead to a predictable escape from a bleak world rather than to a viable utopia or social alternative.[14] What does this unruly festival of French paintings mean? Minnelli and his collaborators did not conceive the ballet as a story with a clear, logical development but as a series of psychic associations. The ballet starts with the halves of a black-and-white sketch coming together. In his despair at losing Lisa to Henri, Jerry had previously torn the sketch, but its seamless reconstitution, followed by the appearance of color, is a breathtaking moment. It lets the audience know that they are entering the world of magic, miracle, fantasy. Now logic and reality do not matter.

The black-and-white sketch is reminiscent of Raoul Dufy's shorthand calligraphy, and it brings to mind several possible references to the artist's work. Minnelli's use of the sketch as a gateway to fantasy can be linked, for example, to Dufy's depiction of a threshold in *The Gate* (1930). In this oil painting, the graceful undulations of the trelliswork allow Dufy to pursue his inclination toward baroque playfulness, executed in nervous but elegant short lines. Instead of walking through a gate, Jerry stands in the entrance of a park, where short columns support statues of rambunctious horses on each side. Like these two horses eager to leap from their marble pedestals, Jerry is about to launch himself into a dream. This particular set was probably based on Dufy's views of Saint-Cloud, a park on the left bank of the Seine, to the northwest of Paris. In *Park of Saint-Cloud* (1924), the gravel path in the foreground leads to a balustrade, below which flows the Seine. Likewise, Jerry's dream begins while he is standing on a balcony, with the whole city of Paris stretched out at his feet.

The arabesque, even oriental sinuousness of Dufy's contours introduces the idea of a lost Paris, namely the Paris of nineteenth-century painters, for this city always looks better in an image, a remembered past. To an American in Hollywood, Paris is a mythical place—exotic and beautiful. Color is indeed an important aspect of the ballet. Dufy's style, in which clouds of color float out of details in the line, facilitates the change Minnelli makes from black and white in the Beaux Arts Ball scene to color in the ballet sequence. This change also posits that the Beaux Arts Ball organized by the art students is closer to the social life of the art market than to the needs of individual creativity. It has the prosaic status of a nonpictorial world. There Milo is with Jerry, Lisa dances with Henri. By contrast, in Jerry's Paris, color means fantasy, emotion, psychological upheaval, and fear, too. Furthermore, Minnelli's use of color reflects the ambivalence toward art that characterizes his cinema. On one hand, by calling attention to the absence of paintings, the variety of colors used in the ballet sequence suggests a longing for the richness of French art. On the other hand, the wide range of colors employed risks overwhelming the viewer with a feast of special effects that turns painting into kitsch.

A free adaptation of Pierre-Auguste Renoir's *Pont-Neuf* (1872) follows Jerry's anxious dance with the white and red female Furies in a Dufy-esque Place de la Concorde (figs. 1 and 5). To be sure, *Pont-Neuf*, with its delicate pastel colors, simply serves as a painterly location and a spatial framework within whose boundaries MGM builds a flower market. Stands of light-blue flowers complement Lisa's metamorphosis into the *femme-fleur* of the Surrealists, for whom woman is always a bridge to the unconscious. The seasonal iconography used for this surrealist revisitation of Renoir's *Pont-Neuf* rehearses the stereotype of "April in Paris," while it connotes an expansiveness and generosity linking love with mild weather and out-of-doors pastimes.[15]

In line with this conventional use of seasons to signify moods, Dufy's black-and-white sketch of Saint-Cloud flies across the ground in a swirl of autumn leaves. Autumn is associated with Jerry's sadness after his separation from Lisa. Spring, by contrast, signals a newly found peace; Jerry's dance slows down to match the pace of Lisa's classical steps in the flower market. Renoir is spring, Dufy is fall, and Rousseau is summer. The Douanier's colorful flags and thin branches surround happy communal dances, outdoor carnivals, and children's entertainments. The use of Rousseau is comparable to the handling of Dufy in the sense that no specific work by the naïf painter is accurately cited in its entirety. Rather, Minnelli appropriates and reconfigures key elements of Rousseau's iconography for successive phases of the ballet (fig. 2).

The Rousseau section of the ballet starts with a brief pan of a few yellow dunes, which have been taken from *The Sleeping Gypsy* (1897). The striped vest of Rousseau's gypsy appears on Minnelli's female dancers, following the lead of Leslie Caron. Finally, the lion of *The Sleeping Gypsy* is a cardboard silhouette standing in the background, next to a tall giraffe, and glimpsed only at the end of the Rousseau ballet. The male tap dancers lined up with Kelly at the center are a variation on Rousseau's *Football Players* (1908). The painter's characters wear outfits with horizontal stripes (fig. 3). Minnelli's tap dancers, however, have borrowed their flashy outfits of white pants and colorful jackets from Eugène Atget's famous photograph of a Parisian shop window, entitled *Men's Fashions* (1925–1927). We encounter Atget's picture later, in a winding alley of Montmartre done up in the somber tones of an eponymous 1912 canvas by Maurice Utrillo (fig. 4). Rousseau's football players are full of movement, about to dance out of the frame. In semicircular formation they chase a football with a suggestion of speed that matches the film's tap dancers', who spin around swinging their canes. From Rousseau's players to Atget's dancers, the ballet links cinema, photography, and painting in a way that produces a brief but perfect cooperation of the arts.

In a festival of painterly sources about Paris, Minnelli could not neglect to include Rousseau. Ronald Alley summarizes the painter's approach to the city:

> Rousseau painted a number of small landscapes, almost all of Paris and the surrounding area. . . . The great boulevards and the scenes of café life were not for him, nor did he paint the artists' quarter of Montmartre, as Utrillo

FIGURE 1. *A set from* An American in Paris *(directed by Vincente Minnelli, 1951) based on the painting* Pont-Neuf *(1872), by Pierre-Auguste Renoir. Film Stills Archive, The Museum of Modern Art, New York.*

FIGURE 2. *A set from* An American in Paris *based on paintings by Henri Rousseau. Film Stills Archive, The Museum of Modern Art, New York.*

FIGURE 3. The Football Players (1908), by Henri Rousseau. Solomon R. Guggenheim Museum, New York. Photograph © The Solomon R. Guggenheim Foundation, New York.

was to do: his motifs were drawn from the unfashionable suburbs of the city, its streets and parks and the banks of its rivers. . . . His landscapes . . . do not have the drama of some of his work, but they are not devoid of poetry and strangeness.[16]

Minnelli combines the exotic animals of Rousseau's jungle scenes with a replica of the kiosk the painter included in his *View of the Parc Montsouris*

(1895). The thick, flat leaves of Rousseau's tropical forests surround Minnelli's version of one of the painter's little white houses on the outskirts of Paris. This disparity in proportions, for which Rousseau's paintings are known, has an uncanny quality. Rousseau no doubt appealed to Minnelli for the surreal potential of his primitive style. Rousseau's antinaturalistic scale, bold areas of color, and use of enchanted objects linger in the viewer's consciousness as if they were the residue of a dream landscape painted by a child.

Minnelli's ballet exudes such energy that art becomes a temporary alternative to love, and male creativity seems to be more enthralling than heterosexual union itself. This interpretation is confirmed by a touch of misogyny in the costuming of the female Furies. Three women in white, along with three women in red, wear wedding gowns, but strangely enough, they seem to chase and threaten Jerry. Since the ballet recasts Jerry's experiences in Paris, the red and white Furies are probably a dream expression of his relationship with Milo. Milo wants Jerry because she is more interested in male artists than in art, while Jerry wants Lisa because she stands for art in Paris (fig. 5).

What is at stake in this love triangle is whether art should be aligned with the docile femininity of Lisa, with the creative masculinity of Jerry, or with the entrepreneurial aggressiveness of Milo. These alternatives narrow themselves down to form the happy ending, which suggests that an American male can be a painter in Paris as long as he marries a French girl. But Lisa is not just any French girl. She is Jerry's model, and in this role, she confirms Hollywood's belief that a woman must always be an image for the man. Yet by marrying his subject matter, Jerry can still become one with painting while avoiding the danger of an overinvolvement with the image. Thus the homoerotic interlocutor of "Brother, if you can't paint in Paris" is elided in the name of true, heterosexual love's triumph over money. Art is as desirable as love, but if art cannot be achieved, love is still a lot better than money. Milo, the daughter of a "boss" in the suntan-lotion industry, loses her battle for Jerry.

Pollock and Minnelli

According to the film critic Diane Waldman, Hollywood's hostility toward the artistic avant-garde found in Jackson Pollock's Abstract Expressionism an ideal scapegoat. Waldman links the rejection of abstract art to a xenophobic anti-intellectualism, which she sees developing during the early years of the Cold War. In those days popular journalism praised the illusionist

FIGURE 4. *A set from* An American in Paris *based on the painting* Montmartre *(1912), by Maurice Utrillo. Film Stills Archive, The Museum of Modern Art, New York.*

codes of painting because Renaissance perspective spelled out "Americanness."[17] Waldman, however, overlooks the similarities between the arguments used by the European totalitarian regimes of the thirties to persecute the artistic avant-garde and the arguments adopted by some American art reviewers. Although Pollock and the Abstract Expressionists received mixed evaluations from *Life* magazine between 1948 and 1951, Waldman forgets that during World War II certain areas of American society took on the responsibility to defend the arts against Fascist obscurantism.[18] Pollock was attacked for his incomprehensible arabesques, which, Waldman reports, were compared to the scribbles of either a childish or a deranged mind. Yet during the Cold War, Abstract Expressionism became the flag of American individualism and freedom of expression.[19] In inspiring the seditious heroes portrayed by actors like Montgomery Clift, Paul Newman, Marlon Brando, and James Dean, Pollock was "a *real* version of the Hollywood and Madison Avenue he-men"[20] offered to audiences craving rebellion and nonconformity in button-down, homogenized postwar America.

That Pollock became both an icon of rebellion and a role model for the American painter was brought about by the contradictory stance of *Life*

FIGURE 5. *A set from* An American in Paris *based on Raoul Dufy's serpentine outlines. Film Stills Archive, The Museum of Modern Art, New York.*

magazine itself, whose main purpose was to reconcile the masses with the art-world elite. Such a goal, indeed, is not incompatible with the celebration of communal values typical of a Hollywood musical. Even though the roundtables on European abstract painting organized by the magazine kept returning over and over again to the values of American realist art, *Life* deserves credit for elevating Pollock to the rank of a pop-culture phenomenon. As a result of all this media attention, anything Pollock did, from buying gas to shopping for groceries, from walking down the street to painting, was a matter of interest among the general public. Thus Pollock "became the leading figure of the era partly because he best embodied the Vie-de-Bohème stereotype."[21] In other words, he was the irascible man, the troubled revolutionary, the romantic artist that Hollywood could appropriate for its construction of new images of masculinity and that anybody in mainstream America could adopt as a secret, hidden self.

As a dandy and a protoimpressionist painter, James McNeill Whistler can be considered Vincente Minnelli's father figure. Caught as he was between painting and commerce, aesthetics and entertainment, the American director was inevitably in touch with Whistler's fin-de-siècle sensibility,

FIGURE 6. *Prehistoric art in* An American in Paris. *Film Stills Archive, The Museum of Modern Art, New York.*

according to which the meaning of art is redefined in the context of mass society and as a result of the advent of mechanical reproduction. In the case of *An American in Paris,* however—a Hollywood musical in which paintings dance and dancing conveys the creative drive—Pollock seems a more appropriate term of reference than Whistler, especially when we remind ourselves that the values of fusion, creativity, and spontaneity were celebrated not only in the context of Minnelli's musical but also across all areas of culture. For instance, Method actors, such as Clift and Brando, were supposed to live the experiences and the emotions of the characters they portrayed.[22] In addition, Martha Graham's choreographies have titles that often evoke Pollock's, while her Jungian approach is compatible with Minnelli's search for a forgotten self to create art. The dance critic Roger Copeland explains, "Pollock painted *She-Wolf, Pasiphäe, Guardians of the Secret,* and *The Totem, Lesson I.* Graham danced works bearing equally incantatory titles: *Cave of the Hearts, Errand into the Maze,* and *Night Journey.*"[23]

Although Jerry Mulligan is a tame, good-hearted, all-American guy, his geographical dislocation and eagerness for psychological fulfillment through artistic creativity suggest that he also might be out of touch with the conservative America of the fifties, where Robert Lindner's best-seller *Must You Conform?* (1956) gave final expression to male anxieties about social integration. The adjectives used for Pollock—violent, savage, undisciplined, and explosive—emphasize a "ravaging aggressive virility."[24] Even one of the artist's most quoted statements about his work ("When I am painting, I am not aware of what I am doing"[25]) underlines that the loss of self into painting plays a key role in strengthening the primitive side of a masculinity that refuses to sell out to middle-class normality. It was therefore expedient for Hollywood to use the Pollock phenomenon to revitalize the cowboy type—marginal and laconic, lonely and intense.

Pollock's method of dripping paint over the canvas to visualize the inner recesses of his psyche can be compared to Minnelli's reliance on dance and color, camera movement and music, to convey the emotional appeal painting holds for Jerry Mulligan during the ballet. By contrast, Jerry's desire to become one with the image—a fusion typical of Pollock's Abstract Expressionist style—is by far more problematic for Hollywood, because it transgresses the sexual subtext that traditionally associates the subject of painting with a male artist and the painted object with a woman. In *Lust for Life*, Vincent van Gogh's gradual descent into the abyss coincides with the fatal pull entire canvases exercise on his psyche.[26] Thus, in *An American in Paris*, painting—whether as madness or as femininity—poses a threat that Minnelli must neutralize while simultaneously celebrating creativity.

The impact of art on the self is the object of a conversation between Jerry and Milo at the Café Flaubert. "Marriage or work keep the personality together," the painter explains to his divorced and idle patroness, thus leaving open the question of where painting might fit. The answer to how painting can keep the personality together does not rest with Jerry's conformist set of options but can instead be found in the primitivist decor used for this scene (fig. 6). This interest in tribal motifs appears not only in *An American in Paris* but also runs across Minnelli's work. As James Naremore explains, Minnelli

> was aware of the European modernists' appropriations of African art (as in postimpressionism, in some aspects of early futurism and cubism), and he also knew that the most sophisticated forms of American vernacular music, including the best songs of Berlin, Gershwin, and Porter, were deeply indebted to Afro-American culture.[27]

FIGURE 7. The She-Wolf (1943), by Jackson Pollock. Collection, The Museum of Modern Art, New York. Photograph © 1992 The Museum of Modern Art.

Were we to pursue further the argument that the values of primitivism such as instinctiveness and authenticity underpin the collusion between Pollock and Minnelli, we cannot help wondering whether, by resembling the Lascaux cave paintings, the artwork on the walls of Café Flaubert might be considered a cultural manifestation parallel to *The She-Wolf* (1943), a canvas Pollock executed shortly before the findings at Lascaux in 1940 but certainly after the landmark exhibit of 1937 at the Museum of Modern Art (MOMA) entitled "Prehistoric Rock Pictures in Europe and in Africa" (fig. 7). It is likely that for *The She-Wolf* Pollock might have also used prehistoric art from the caves of Altamira and Font de Gaume he saw reproduced in the 1931 edition of *Art of the Cave Dweller* by Gerard Baldwin Brown. Minnelli might also have been familiar with the MOMA exhibit on prehistoric art; between 1931 and 1940, when he was a Broadway set and costume designer, he was a regular at the museum. Furthermore, the scene at the Café Flaubert is remarkable for its blend of jazz and beatnik atmosphere, two elements that remind us of America and of an unconventional life style worthy of an "angry young man" like Jackson Pollock.[28]

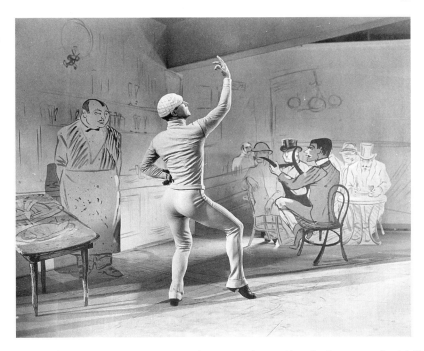

FIGURE 8. *Gene Kelly as the dancer in the Toulouse-Lautrec drawing* Chocolat Dancing at the Achilles Bar *(1896), in* An American in Paris. *Film Stills Archive, The Museum of Modern Art, New York.*

Toulouse-Lautrec Is Happiness

Minnelli's allusion to primitivism in the Café Flaubert prepares us for Jerry's deep psychological transformation during the ballet. Jerry finds his true artistic self through his interpretation of a drawing by Toulouse-Lautrec, *Chocolat Dancing at the Achilles Bar* (1896; fig. 8). Minnelli's musical is made of music, painting, and dancing, but dance wins. Only the energy of Gene Kelly can bring to life European art. In discussing the beginning of the film, Rick Altman observes, "*An American in Paris* shows us no human beings until it has characterized Paris as a city of statues, beautiful, but inanimate, lacking the energy which Kelly and Caron will provide."[29] While valorizing a conventional view of Paris as the city of culture, Minnelli suggests a negative view of high art as something removed and cold, static and linked to the past. This perception of Paris reappears in Milo. In contrast to Lisa, who is a dancer, Milo is as cold as a Greek statue. She embodies all the worst American fears about French art, while the missing arm of the famous Venus of Milo declares the heiress's inability to nurture. Only the filter of popular dance can warm up a museumlike city and make it appealing to an American audience. Thus modern dance is represented as the great American art form, while painting appears to be a desirable but also foreign domain. Jerry may not be a great artist, but he can certainly make all sorts of French people dance with him. Hence the climax of the ballet must coincide with a drawing by Toulouse-Lautrec, the painter who loved popular dances.

In *Chocolat Dancing at the Achilles Bar,* Toulouse-Lautrec depicted a black man from Bilbao who would perform for his own pleasure after his appearances at the Nouveau Cirque. Horst Keller describes the emotional economy of Toulouse-Lautrec's style:

> The scenery is unusually self-sufficient. In a narrow bar, made even narrower by the molelike waiter at the left, a marvelously limber Negro in a tight sporting suit is shown dancing. His cap with its large checks is pulled far down over his bluish face. The chanson, which is still known, is accompanied by a strident lyre plucked by a seated boy with knobby knees. The blackness of the lyre and of a top hat in the background compete with that of Chocolat's raised hand, the most delicate and subtly finished detail of the entire drawing. Here all of Toulouse-Lautrec's fine-nerved abilities can be seen at work. He always knew just when the culminating point in the development of a movement had been reached.[30]

While Minnelli maintains the molelike waiter and the black lyre, the unarrestable beat of jazz music replaces Toulouse-Lautrec's reference to a popular French song. If Jerry reaches down into the core of his personality, Minnelli recovers the black origins of the Hollywood musical by introducing jazz music with Toulouse-Lautrec and tap dancing with Rousseau. While, as we have seen, Minnelli is sensitive to the complex interplay of national and sexual facets in Jerry's character—as an American, he is an athletic, heterosexual dancer; as an artist, he risks drowning in the depths of an unknown, foreign self—the director, however, does not allow blackness to highlight any racial identity. After all, a white dancer takes over the act of a black man, thus performing the same operation of whitewashing carried out by the musical, which appropriated black music and black dance for the entertainment of white audiences. In *An American in Paris,* blackness instead comes to mean foreignness. Thus, blackness only spells out how a white American dancer can draw energy from a Toulouse-Lautrec drawing while paradoxically bringing it to life.

Since so many painters depicted the communal entertainments of Paris, the question arises as to why Toulouse-Lautrec's *Chocolat* became the centerpiece of Minnelli's Parisland. Gene Kelly claims responsibility for the decision: "I was only adamant about one thing: we must not use the paintings of Degas."[31] Kelly's preference for Toulouse-Lautrec over Degas was probably due to Degas's reputation as the painter of classical dancers. To Kelly, Degas's ballerinas at the Opera might have appeared too involved with high art to be compatible with the musical's emphasis on the popular arts. After all, Toulouse-Lautrec was the painter of the cancan. This explanation is confirmed by the association of Degas's ballerinas, glimpsed in the window of a dark shop, with Milo, an upper-class American. Finally, as Horst Keller begins to suggest, Toulouse-Lautrec's sense of movement is more psychological and, I would add, less mechanical than Degas's.[32] To be sure, *Chocolat*'s raised hand poignantly conveys the attainment of that blissful state that the musical's integration of painting, dance, and music always strives for.

The Paris of Painters as Disneyland

Through Jerry's identification with Toulouse-Lautrec, Minnelli indicates that French painting holds an appeal more liberating and utopian than the industrial approach of Hollywood cinema. Yet, before the ballet, Minnelli suggests that an excessive passion for art can produce a dystopia. This is especially true in the case of Adam, whose creative urge swells to the point of madness as he envisions himself performing the multiple roles of orchestra conductor, concert pianist, and wildly applauding spectator while also playing the violin and a huge pair of bongos. Minnelli's dramatic lighting and his extensive use of bronze and black shadows capture the intensity of Gershwin's Piano Concerto in F Major. The method used in this sequence recalls Dufy's experiment with "tonal painting" for his *Red Concert* (1946), in which the painter powerfully conveyed the feeling of music through color.

Adam's dream is a sexual fantasy in which the self frantically multiplies to compensate for the loneliness of his situation. The end of the dream coincides with an image of the musician lying in bed, with his hand in his pocket and a cigarette in his mouth. He goes over to the piano, on whose top an elegant ice bucket stands out. Instead of an expensive champagne, Adam pulls out a bottle of Coke. This is clearly a joke on his poverty and Americanness. Most important, the joke deflates the dream and makes the audience forget its most unsettling aspects.

Indeed something maniacal and dark is in Adam's reverie—something clearly different from the alternation of bright colors and pastel hues or the oscillation between anxiety, repose, lightheartedness, and enthusiasm that shapes Jerry's ballet. Dystopia, then, occurs when art takes over the self and plunges it into extreme forms of egotism. Here Minnelli is rehashing the old equation of art with madness and uses Adam's chain-smoking to enact the artist's pathology of everyday life. The staging of Adam's first appearance in the film offers a clue about the origin of the concert pianist's unhappiness. Casper reports the scene: "The camera frames a man placing a parakeet, after bussing it, into a cage. The image denotes the placid contentment Adam seeks. 'That's not me,' Adam groans, 'he is too happy.'"[33] Clearly Adam's problem rests in his inability to set boundaries to contain his creative drives. Unlike the neighbor who imprisons the bird, the symbol of a formerly uncontrolled imagination, Adam fragments himself into all the roles contributing to the experience of a Gershwin concert.

Unlike Adam, Jerry avoids the cage and steps inside the frame of a work of art. Although Jerry's transformation into Chocolat marks the American's full access to French painting through dance, the ballet of nineteenth-century paintings is hardly French. The world of that ballet is much more like an American theme park, a fantasy space or Parisland, where art history does not hang on the walls in hieratic immobility but dances in a series of intertextual combinations. Except for the episode devoted to Toulouse-Lautrec, Hollywood prevails over Jackson Pollock, in the sense that Disneyland, instead of American Abstract Expressionism, is the model Minnelli follows to stage French painting.

In contrast to Hollywood's Paris before the ballet, Jerry's Parisland of art is a special space where conflicts of national identity are overcome. Gene Kelly explains,

> When we did the Rousseau, the zoo thing, I purposely had the fellows do everything the way George M. Cohan would do it, like an American would do it. In the middle of that Frenchy scene, . . . I wanted to do something immediately identifiable as American. The little girls came out with their hats and had their hands up in little white gloves, which we tried to make look like white doves, Frenchy as could be. But the American men were to be as American as you can get.[34]

Under the auspices of dance, the reconciliation of national differences is easier to achieve in Rousseau's landscape of parks, zoos, and botanical gardens, since all these spaces exist between the city and the countryside, in a

FIGURE 9. Eiffel Tower with Trees *(1910), by Robert Delaunay. Solomon R. Guggenheim Museum, New York. Photograph by Robert E. Mates,* © *The Solomon R. Guggenheim Foundation, New York.*

territory outside the shadow cast by the French flag. By contrast, Dufy's Paris is adorned with the colors the French flag shares with the American.[35] But red, white, and blue, rather than symbolizing the affinities between the two nations, instead stress Jerry's role of American intruder in the world of Parisian art.

At the beginning of the ballet, the American painter's path is repeatedly blocked by French gendarmes, while native passersby reject or ignore Jerry's attempts to communicate. Critics have also remarked that Gershwin's music throughout the film conveys a mood of nostalgia for America.[36] This exploration of the challenges that a foreign place poses to national identity is a reversal of Minnelli's predicament as a Europeanized director in the Hollywood industry. While his interest in art history pulls him toward European culture, the director's work, to some extent, must conform to the all-American system of values that the musical traditionally celebrates.

It would seem, then, that Minnelli is caught between painting and cinema, art and mass culture, Europe and Hollywood. Perhaps this kind of dilemma is responsible for the disjointed structure and the weak ending of *An American in Paris.* By assessing how truly utopian Minnelli's representation of painting is in the ballet, we might better understand where the work of this director stands in relation to Hollywood films of the forties that condemn abstract painters as the deranged authors of childish scribbles.

With his opinions about modern art, Minnelli's Jerry does not seem to differ much from the middle-class characters Diane Waldman discusses in her analysis of *The Two Mrs. Carrolls* (1947), directed by Peter Godfrey. Jerry pokes fun at a canvas reminiscent of Miró by demonstrating that with abstract art, it is difficult to know which end is up. Furthermore, Jerry's paintings rely on traditional rules for figurative art. Jerry may love French art, but he does not seem keen on the recent avant-garde styles. Significantly, the fragmented Paris of Robert Delauney is absent from the ballet (fig. 9).[37]

In the wake of Sir Thomas More's famous island, which resembles the ordinary world but has none of its evils, Disneyland is America's utopia or safe haven: a sanitized place apart, designed for a celebration of childhood. Children suggest a link between Disneyland and Minnelli's ballet. They appear in the sequence devoted to Rousseau as if to remind us that a child-loving American would be happier dancing in the landscapes of a naïf, primitive painter than among the intellectual abstractions of Miró.[38] The presence of children reverberates across the whole film, as if to underscore the freshness and the spontaneity of the American spirit. Children are a conventional ingredient of spectacle and plot in fairy-tale musicals: *South*

Pacific, The Sound of Music, Oliver!, Mary Poppins.[39] Childhood, however, is a theme charged with ambivalent connotations in *An American in Paris.* The figure of the child plays a key role by setting up the contradictory terms of Minnelli's attitude toward art.

Children confine Jerry to a Hollywood fantasy but can also launch him into a utopian space of creativity. Most important, the child participates in Waldman's chain of derogatory metonyms for modernist, abstract art: "the childish, the insane, the ugly." At the beginning of the film, children's voices persuade Jerry to snap out of a reverie in front of his self-portrait as a serious artist. In this case, children bring Jerry back to reality, instead of surrounding him in a Rousseau-esque moment of fantasy. Campari adds that Minnelli often depicts childhood and adolescence as transient states, comparable to a creative trance from which the artist must awaken in order to remain sane.[40]

Despite its reputation as a place for fantasy, fun, and games, Disneyland is only apparently a utopian space where the imagination can run free. In fact its attractions survey different aspects of American history and are planned according to a rigid geographical scheme that parallels Hollywood's assembly-line regimentation, an approach that is stifling and formulaic but that also remains completely hidden behind a facade promising entertainment and escape. In his essay on Disneyland as a degenerate utopia, Louis Marin observes:

> One of the most notable features of the utopian picture is its *limit:* the utopian discourse inscribes the utopian representation in the imaginary space of a map, but at the same time, it makes this inscription in a geographical map impossible. . . . The utopian land belongs to "our world," but there is an insuperable gap between our world and utopia. . . . *it is a semiotic transposition of the frame of a painting.* This gap is a neutral space, the place of the limit between reality and utopia: by this distance which is a zero point, utopia appears to be not a world *beyond,* but the *reverse* side of this world.[41]

Jerry's uneasiness with the "limit" or frame of his painting and Minnelli's difficulty with the boundary between Hollywood and art become most apparent in one specific episode. Jerry is standing in a room full of recently finished canvases for an art show organized by Milo. With a puzzled expression on his face, he holds a frame in one hand, and with the other he tries picture after picture, trying to find one that will fit the frame. The humor, of course, stems from Jerry's failure to understand that the best way to fit a frame to a picture is to try many different frames on one single picture. Yet this painter who cannot paint, who holds a frame he cannot match up with a picture, is not simply comic but also emblematic. Jerry exemplifies Minnelli's peculiar position in Hollywood. Like the protagonist of his film, the director cannot quite set the boundary that an authentic utopian discourse would need to produce a space similar to social reality but also totally beyond it. As a result, in Minnelli's film, Jerry's frame risks ending up on the wrong picture, and the limit, so indispensable to utopian discourse, keeps shifting. Instead of framing Disneyland away from American society as it is, by indicating the radical distance as well as the implicit parallel between the two, it only marks the similarity between Hollywood and Disneyland.

By acritically upholding the values of the American way of life, without calling attention to "the differences between social reality and a projected model of social existence"[42] in the same way a frame marks the distinction between a painting and the world, Disneyland degrades itself from utopia into myth. Utopia, for Marin, is the realm of impossible possibilities, while myth is the realm of possible impossibilities. With its unconscious critical power, utopia is the reverse of myth. Myth does not criticize from beyond the limit but perpetuates what is already in place, inside the limit. By definition, the utopian space is no-where in reality yet now-here in fantasy. On the contrary, a collective fantasy space like Disneyland exploits history and geography to say that the American dream has become real right now, right here, for everybody. In a similar fashion, Minnelli's ballet uses music and dance, song and painting, to stage the possession of Jerry's creative soul, thus perpetuating the myth that in Hollywood's Parisland an artist can find his true self.

Unable to draw the boundary between dream and reality, art and Hollywood, Minnelli cannot fully revel in painting as creativity and thus criticize the collective myths that American cinema, like Disneyland, produces. Thus the director balances himself right on the border between cinema and painting, while holding onto a compromise between these two worlds. This limit-bound placement of Minnelli—neither in Hollywood nor in art, which reflects his need to keep flourishing in the industry while nourishing himself on painting—becomes apparent in Robert Lang's description of Minnelli's protagonists in his melodramas: "To find that space, somewhere between madness and authority, between the Imaginary and the Symbolic, between . . . 'one kind of dream, and another kind of life,' is the central passion of several of Minnelli's protagonists."[43] By standing right on the threshold between cinema and painting, Minnelli assumes a precarious position; and the anxiety that comes along with his tightrope act plays itself out in *An American in Paris*, a film obsessed with finding a temporary space between the demands of the box office and the madness that American culture attributes to art, between the promise of self-realization stored in the ideology of heterosexual love and the boundaries containing the full outburst of masculine creativity.

The intertextuality of cinema and painting in *An American in Paris* is made of broken frames. Yet frames—unbroken frames—can be found throughout the film. At the level of narrative structure, the idea of the frame becomes the limit separating the ballet in color from the Beaux-Arts Ball in black and white. Casper remarks that with Minnelli

> every film . . . portrays two types of festivity. One is formal, organized and imposed from without, an affair that the protagonist must attend, resulting in embarrassment and hurt. The other arises extemporaneously, a creation of the protagonist, a buoyant and lively occasion.[44]

It is as if an invisible barrier were standing between the space of dream and painting and the space of social conformity and marriage. Casper sharpens his insight by observing that Minnelli actualizes the concept of the frame at the level of decor:

> One piece of decor continually crops up in a Minnelli musical—the window frame and its extension, the balcony ledge. Besides providing a frame to the composition, . . . the image crystallizes plot, conflict, and theme. The window frame and balcony ledge, situated yet opening onto a view, prospect or horizon like some wharf on the infinite, contains the dialectic of immanence-transcendence, present-future, reality-fantasy.[45]

The climax of the ballet—when Kelly becomes Chocolat—marks a moment of perfect coincidence between the frame of cinema and the frame of painting. The dissolution of one into the other rhymes with Lisa's disappearance behind Jerry's towering figure during their dance on the fountain. By contrast, the happy ending of *An American in Paris* is weak, because it marks a compromise between art and love set against the beautiful skyline of Paris at night. When they finally reunite, Jerry wears a black-and-white outfit, while Lisa is in virginal white. They stand on the same side of a long rail and meet halfway along a deep flight of stairs. The rail signifies that they can be together because they both stand on the same side of the frame, while the barrier between Hollywood and art is firmly reestablished.

The French critics were the first to detect Minnelli's auteurist signature, yet they did not fully grasp its contradictory components. The happy ending of *An American in Paris* clearly bears the trace of an inner struggle, but it is no unhappy conclusion, for Jerry does avoid the worst, namely, marrying the boss's daughter. Minnelli became an auteur because, while conforming to Hollywood's containment of art in the name of love, deep down he never resigned himself to working in an industry so hostile to painting. Minnelli's resistance to the industry is exemplified in the pictorial nature of the cinematic style that made him famous and that also enhanced MGM's reputation. Pollock's expressionist style comes to fruition when Gene Kelly's dancing meets Toulouse-Lautrec's painting. Both Minnelli and Pollock believe in a renewal of the self through primitive art. Yet the director cannot openly side with Pollock's abstraction, for Hollywood perceives this style to be elitist and foreign and clearly at odds with its mandate to address mass audiences through pleasurable and easy-to-understand images. In *An American in Paris*, the representation of French art is caught between two extreme versions of the American identity: Pollock's rebellious search for origins and Disneyland's return to the happy days of childhood. Thus, in *An American in Paris*, French art goes to America, and it enables Minnelli to interrogate himself about his persona as an artist or auteur in relation to the way his own cultural background defines national and sexual identity.

CHAPTER 2

Michelangelo

Antonioni's

Red Desert

~

Painting as

Ventriloquism

and Color

as Movement

*S*hot during the fall of 1963 in the industrial harbor of Ravenna, Michelangelo Antonioni's first film in color, *Red Desert*, has been repeatedly compared to abstract painting. In 1942 the director drew an equivalence between color and painting: "In the cinema, black and white is to color what drawing is to painting." With another statement made in 1964, Antonioni linked color to the future: "In our contemporary daily life, color has acquired a meaning and a function it did not have before. I am sure that black and white will be stuff for the museum."[1] Although the director's statements associate color with painting and the future, the purpose of this chapter is to expand our thematic understanding of the meaning of color in *Red Desert*, by paying attention to the representation of history, to art-historical allusions, to the dialectic of word and image, and to the sexual politics that characterize Antonioni's direction of his leading actress, Monica Vitti.

As the film's title suggests, red rules over an empty space, but the desert is born again through the most intense of all colors. It is unclear whether the desert of *Red Desert* is the vacuum left behind by an ecological catastrophe or a brand-new space of unexplored possibilities. In either case, Antonioni seems to be fascinated with the imaginative potential of emptiness. This openness toward an uncertain future suggests that Antonioni's project in *Red Desert* is to explore an uncharted territory of creativity. The director, however, shares this penchant for the new with his female protagonist.

In reentering normal life after a stay in the hospital, Giuliana (Monica Vitti) casts a look on the world that ranges from suffering and troubled to inquisitive and exploratory. Giuliana's existential crisis not only echoes the director's willingness to experiment with color but also resonates with radical changes in the landscape around her.

If *Red Desert* is indeed a film about historical transformation and psychological change, it is not surprising that Antonioni uses color to alter the nature of cinematic language, namely to paint the world anew according to an abstract sensibility. Yet, despite his bold statements about color as abstract painting and color as the language of the future, Antonioni is aware that he is first and foremost a filmmaker who relies on direction of actors, framing, and camerawork to tell a story. The director's self-consciousness that painting with color in film implies a statement about his artistic persona transpires from a remark published by *Positif* in 1985: "I am not a painter, but a filmmaker who paints."[2] Because throughout his career Antonioni has never denied his interest in painting, while always reminding his listeners of his identity as a filmmaker, a certain aura of transgression hovers over the images of *Red Desert.* The transgression, however, is double: one from a cinema of architecture to a cinema of painting, and the other from neorealist documentation to pictorial abstraction.

By devoting the first sequence of *Red Desert* to a strike, Antonioni immediately echoes Vittorio de Sica's *Umberto D* (1951), a neorealist film that begins with a public protest by retired government employees to signal how the civic ideals of the Resistance movement have been betrayed. With this kind of opening Antonioni also alludes to the social turmoil that characterized the early sixties in the wake of the so-called economic boom of the previous decade. Factories and refineries have replaced churches and trees, while new financial ventures and cutting-edge technologies have upset traditional relations, not only between workers and management but also between human beings and their environment.[3]

The production history of *Red Desert*—a film shot in real locations that were, however, literally painted over to accommodate the director's experimentation with color, and a film in which professional performers (Monica Vitti, Richard Harris) worked with a newcomer to the set (Carlo Chionetti, a Milanese lawyer in the role of Ugo)—spells out the director's oscillation between a neorealist background and the ambitions of contemporary abstract art. In regard to natural settings and to an art that uses walls (and, in the case of *Red Desert*, swamps, fields, docks, riverbanks, shacks) to liberate textures and surfaces in a painter's canvas, the director declared to *L'Express* in 1960, "They stimulate me more. It is the same as it might be with a painter to whom someone said, 'Here is a wall which is to be covered with frescoes, so many yards long and so many yards high.' These are the kinds of limitations which aid rather than fetter the imagination."[4] To pursue further Antonioni's links to neorealism, his observations here seem to refer back to Leonardo da Vinci, who felt that artists could find creativity by staring at a crumbling wall and letting the mind wander:

> When you look at a wall spotted with stains, or with a mixture of stones, if you have to devise some scene you may discover a resemblance to various landscapes . . . or, again, you may see battles and figures in action, or strange faces and costumes, or an endless variety of objects, which you could reduce to complete and well-drawn forms. These appear on such walls promiscuously, like the sound of bells in whose jangle you may find any name or word you choose to imagine.[5]

During a strange winter party, inside a shack with little heat and wooden walls painted in an aggressive red—Corrado (Richard Harris) tells Giuliana that her question "What should I look at?" echoes his dilemma "How should I live?" This analogy between looking and living suggests that for Antonioni painting in *Red Desert* is no decorative citation; rather, it is the other side of lived experience, for the landscape itself, in true neorealist fashion, furnishes the materials of art.

Antonioni's parallel between looking and living sets up a corollary equivalence between subjectivity and context, perception and placement, which points to André Bazin's insight that the neorealist documentary image can shift its orientation from the outside to the inside and become a private hallucination. In an essay entitled "Reflections 1964," Antonioni explains,

> It's something that all directors have in common, I think: this habit of keeping one eye open inside and another outside. At a certain point, these two visions begin to resemble each other, and like two images coming into focus, they overlap. It is from this agreement between eye and brain, eye and instinct, eye and consciousness, that the desire to speak or to show comes.[6]

Thus, in *Red Desert*, the dialectic of an inward-bound eye and an outward-bound one parallels the mirroring between internal psychological development and external, historical transformation.

Finally, that natural settings are the other side of art, and vice versa, is confirmed by the following statement from Antonioni, published in 1958 by *Bianco e Nero:* "I cannot understand how they manage to shoot from little designs and plans they have drawn on paper ahead of time. I feel that the composition is a plastic, figurative element which ought to be seen in its exact dimensions."[7]

Here Antonioni rejects drawings on paper and seems to describe himself standing outdoors and arranging actors and objects, colors and shots, in relation to real buildings. Indirectly the filmmaker's words set up an opposition between creating indoors and directing outdoors. While it is well known that Hitchcock planned all his films shot by shot on little scraps of paper, it is also true that the painter as well as the architect works indoors. Yet by virtue of its final execution in public outdoor spaces, architecture has historically addressed the social sphere more forcefully than traditional painting, for the latter is an art form that usually travels from the walls of the studio to the safe enclosure of the museum.

From whose standpoint is Antonioni, therefore, speaking? When the director offers these statements, does he define himself as a filmmaker, or as a painter, or as an architect? I feel that Antonioni purposefully speaks in an ambiguous manner that interlaces architecture with painting, thus inadvertently evoking a comparable overlap at the heart of the International Style, an experience marked by Le Corbusier (who worked both as a painter and as an architect) and by Ludwig Mies van der Rohe (who, as an architect, was especially sensitive to modern abstract painting).

Nevertheless, as I readjust this key feature of the International Style to

Red Desert, I propose that Antonioni's statement—"I feel that the composition is a plastic, figurative element which ought to be seen in its exact dimensions"—has an especially powerful, active ring, in which making, arranging, directing, and moving around prevail over seeing, responding, reacting. This is why I would argue that here Antonioni talks more like a filmmaker and an architect than like a painter, as if he had unconsciously aligned architecture with his power to control performers and spaces as a male director, whereas painting comes to fall under the rubric of femininity, or at least to that artistic side of himself he is exploring in innovative ways through color and his direction of Monica Vitti.

Antonioni's most incisive self-description and most famous statement about the roots of his inspiration sounds closer to architecture than to painting: "When I shoot a film, that is all I am doing. I arrange things and people the way they ought to be."[8] It is as if Antonioni were trying to mask his transgression from a cinema of architecture to one of painting by allowing the male characters in *Red Desert*—as well as the critics of the film—to frame Giuliana, the director's female alter-ego, in the role of a neurotic who primarily reacts to circumstances instead of reorganizing the world or ruthlessly carrying out an action.

Despite his attachment to real locations and natural landscapes, Antonioni's painting in *Red Desert* is more abstract than figurative, more avant-garde than traditional. Precisely because this was a project born under the auspices of artistic creativity rather than of documentary accuracy, the director finds in the female protagonist's malaise an expedient set of eyes through which to unleash freely (but also conveniently to justify) his most daring images and delirious metamorphoses.

Much more than all the other characters, Giuliana senses the prodigious and unsettling quality of historical change—a situation she recasts in the solipsistic effort to recuperate from a suicide attempt after a car accident. Early on in the film, Antonioni establishes a clear contrast between Giuliana's uneasiness with the industrial world and her husband Ugo's unquestioning faith in scientific and rational values. Ugo's identification with the factory, however, accounts for his one-dimensional personality, whereas Giuliana's crisis heightens her desire for change—an orientation that a brief affair with Corrado, one of Ugo's colleagues, hardly fulfills. In the narrative universe of *Red Desert,* therefore, oppositional elements such as old and new, technology and the past, a masculine penchant for science and a woman's attachment to memories, are not stable categories; rather they often exchange positions in an eerie circularity. For instance, Giuliana's child, Valerio, paints with vivid colors while his art hangs on the wall of his mother's bedroom. Just like Valerio, Antonioni wants to paint a picture of the future, even though he cannot forget that his origin lies in a woman's womb.

During her wanderings across the industrial wasteland of Ravenna, on one hand Giuliana aspires to a new sense of self as a woman, while on the other she regrets the permanent loss of a former way of being. Giuliana's oscillation between old and new resurfaces in a statement made by the director in 1961: "While we are eager to get rid of old scientific notions, we wallow in the close analysis, the dissection of . . . outdated feelings. Unable to find new attitudes, we fail to bridge the gap between moral man and scientific man."[9] Were we to rethink Antonioni's opposition of scientific man and moral man in the light of the tensions that upset Giuliana and Ugo's marriage, we can guess that the contrast is not so much between science and morality as it is between the traditional association of masculinity with technology and the future and of femininity with nature and the past.

Inasmuch as *Red Desert* is "an account of individuation,"[10] the story of a woman searching for her own individuality at a time when gendered power relations are changing, the film also tells us about Antonioni's struggle as a filmmaker who wants to become a painter engaged in the depiction of vanishing objects with unstable contours and of industrial products glowing with the harshness of alien creatures. More specifically, in order to paint with colors, Antonioni relies on Giuliana, whose illness has exasperated her perceptual abilities to such an extent that moments of unexpected clarity alternate with instances of blurred vision.

In his astute commentary on *Red Desert*, Pier Paolo Pasolini has summarized Antonioni's subterfuge of using a woman to paint in film as a "soggettiva libera indiretta," or "free indirect subjective," approach. Antonioni's strategy of giving prominence to a feminine vision or a special kind of hypersensitivity is well known all across his films, from *Le Amiche* (1955) to *La Notte* (1961). Yet in the case of *Red Desert*, stepping into a woman's shoes, so to speak, is a measure of his will to change and experiment, while it also conveys a certain uneasiness with painting, an art form he has cultivated with the same intensity he has always shown toward architecture.[11]

Although Antonioni sees through Vitti's eyes, and he does not really speak through her body, he establishes a visual ventriloquism with her. In a way my comparison of Antonioni to a ventriloquist makes more precise the sexual politics underpinning Pasolini's insight that a "free indirect subjective" approach is at work in *Red Desert*. Although *ventriloquism* means to speak through someone else's belly—or better, to make it seem that a silent dummy is speaking, when it is really the person who holds the dummy who does all the talking from behind—Antonioni does not quite endow Vitti with the power of winning words but only lets her have visions so pictorial and so abstract that they push outward the boundaries of what until now we have considered acceptable for the visual track of a European art film.

Thus, the metaphor of ventriloquism specializes Pasolini's insight to the extent that through Vitti, Antonioni gains representational freedom, even though the images he assigns to his actress are subjective in an unsettling way, if not visceral, to return to the corporeal etymology of ventriloquism.

In short, ventriloquism is only another way of saying "free indirect subjective" approach, by throwing together the belly with the word, the body with the mind; it is this odd combination of elements that discloses how Antonioni, in *Red Desert*, strikes a very precarious balance, for his allegiances are deeply split between the past and the future, a masculine and a feminine position, innovation and tradition.

Ventriloquism implies a transfer of authorship from director to actress, an operation that emerges between the lines in this remark by Antonioni: "Of all my films *Red Desert* is the least autobiographical. In this film I kept looking at the world outside. I tell the story as if the plot were unfolding right in front of my eyes."[12] By combining a denial of autobiographical elements with a self-portrait of visual apprehension, Antonioni offers us a contradictory model of detachment and involvement, removal and observation.

As a directorial stand-in—who sees in ways that Antonioni does not extend to other characters' points of view but reserves only for himself as the filmmaker—Giuliana might more appropriately be called, instead of a neurotic, a convalescent. Indeed there is a long tradition in European culture (Baudelaire, D'Annunzio) that equates convalescence with creativity and artistic expression with pathology. William Arrowsmith reminds us that the neurotic patient is a born artist: "In Jung's judgement, the courageous neurotic is the patient who copes creatively with his own life, who comes to terms with himself by confronting the reality of his own nature and his responsibility for his illness or health. The neurotic in this sense is of course only the classical hero in disguise."[13] Giorgio De Chirico, a painter beloved by Antonioni, understood that convalescence, even in the form of a lingering sickness, is "the ground of a new consciousness":[14]

> Let me recount how I had a revelation of a picture that I will show this year at the Salon d'Automne, entitled "Enigma of a Summer Afternoon." One clear autumnal afternoon I was sitting on a bench in the middle of the Piazza Santa Croce in Florence. It was of course not the first time I had seen this square. I had just come out of a long and painful intestinal illness, and I was in a nearly morbid state of sensitivity. The whole world, down to the marble of the buildings and the fountains, seemed to me to be convalescent. In the middle of the square rises a statue of Dante draped in a long cloak, holding his works, clasped against his body, his laurel-crowned head bent thoughtfully earthward. The statue is in white marble, but time has given it a gray cast, very agreeable to the eye. The autumn sun, warm and unloving, lit the statue and the church facade. Then I had the strange impression that I was looking at all these things for the first time, and the composition of my picture came to the mind's eye.[15]

In short, the scenario of convalescence at the heart of *Red Desert* not only fits the theme of artistic creativity for the director and of attainment of a new sense of self for the female protagonist, but it also intertwines with the need to clear the ground, to start with a tabula rasa, to produce a temporary void, which is typical of traumatic historical change and melodrama.

By melodrama I mean, in Peter Brooks's footsteps, a mode intended to acknowledge that something sacred or original or ideal has been forever lost. Melodrama, therefore, cherishes impossible values to compensate for this trauma, while it is capable of meditating on public experience only in personal terms.[16] In other words, *Red Desert* is an existential melodrama that suggests an evaluation of how far Italian society has come since the end of World War II in its pursuit of modernity and technology.[17]

To someone familiar with Antonioni's rejection of facile plot lines, with one coup de théâtre leading into the next, or to someone aware of the director's tendency to undo narrative development into *temps morts*, waiting and duration, the label "melodrama" may seem wholly inappropriate for *Red Desert*. Furthermore, the allusion to the legacy of postwar neorealist cinema at the beginning of the film may also discourage the association of *Red Desert* with a melodramatic mode. Yet neorealist cinema, just like melodrama, is characterized by a certain muteness, since for its construction of character it relies more on gesture and mimicry, on landscape and architecture, than it does on dialogue and introspection.

The painful clash of old and new that Antonioni analyzes in *Red Desert*, using Ravenna's periphery as an allegory for Italian society, finds an appropriate channel of expression in the director's use of color. As a nonverbal element of the mise-en-scène invested with a poignancy that well fits the radicalized polarities of an old order dying and a new system about to be born, color in *Red Desert* makes up the "text of muteness" that Peter Brooks finds to be typical of melodrama, a mode concerned with those "extreme moral and emotional conditions"[18] that, I would add, always characterize historical change.

To sum up, besides making a case for *Red Desert* as a melodrama concerned with historical change and psychological transformation, the purpose of this chapter is twofold: to explain that Antonioni's allegiance to both painting and architecture in his cinema is predicated on the battle of the sexes; and to argue that Antonioni's visual ventriloquism through Monica Vitti in *Red Desert* is both experimental and exploitative, for while he uses his actress's eyes to work innovatively with color in film, her power resides more in the muteness of the images she shares with the director than in the dialogue. Put another way, from an artistic point of view the word is less daring than the image, yet Giuliana's impact on the world is limited by the alignment of the dialogue with a masculine perspective.

Although other critics before me have argued how Antonioni's cinema is torn between a fear of the future and a dissatisfaction with the past, my discussion strives to show how in *Red Desert* Antonioni on one hand needs a woman's vision to experiment with painting and abstraction, while on the other, by linking color to muteness and femininity, he pushes his female protagonist away from technology and verbal assertion into a primitive and speechless realm. It is precisely because the director's project is so contradictory and multilayered that *Red Desert* is not only a melodrama but also a film tinged with a baroque sensibility.

Giuliana's and Ugo's antithetical personalities, besides reiterating the struggle between art and technology, can also be said to repeat the well-known opposition between modernism, with its penchant for ordered rationalism, and the baroque, with its rejection of closure and fixity. By honoring a certain madness of vision, and by celebrating the dazzling, disorienting, ecstatic surplus of images, and by expressing intense emotion through coloristic impressions, the baroque in *Red Desert* underpins all the pieces of

FIGURE 10. *A street from* Red Desert *(directed by Michelangelo Antonioni, 1964) with an atmosphere reminiscent of Giorgio De Chirico's paintings. Film Stills Archive, The Museum of Modern Art, New York.*

the puzzle: Giuliana's illness, Antonioni's striving for creativity, and the stereotypical association of femininity with excess.[19]

By decrying the loss of pure values, melodrama is a modern form that idealizes the past or an ahistorical realm of unattainable ideals, such as the defeat of evil and death by innocence and love, whereas the baroque, although invented to promote the status quo and seduce with a plethora of discontinuous and curvilinear effects, has an open-ended quality that points toward the future. One may wonder, however, how these two modes can coexist in the same film. As we learn from Brooks, melodrama originates from the ashes of the French Revolution. By contrast, the baroque is a program of restoration to prevent a revolution rather than a post-revolutionary response to a traumatic experience. It is because melodrama and the baroque offer an oppositional but complementary orientation to the historical process that Antonioni can interlace the battle of the sexes in *Red Desert* with the tension between old and new, by situating color right in the middle, ranging from melodramatic muteness to baroque sinuosity, so that color is the element that marks the strange circularity of futurism and primitivism.

The Challenge of Historical Change

In *Red Desert* Antonioni stages the clash of old and new, especially through the interplay of history and geography and through his use of objects and decors. One could argue that Antonioni has found the iconography of this staging in the paintings of Giorgio De Chirico. One sequence in particular (fig. 10) looks like a whole canvas by De Chirico: The deserted, gray street where Giuliana plans to open a store winds up into a claustrophobic rather than empowering vanishing point. Meanwhile an abandoned sheet of newspaper is blown along the pavement, bearing witness to the banality of time. Nearby a self-absorbed old vendor stands next to a cart covered with whitish fruits that loom like someone's mementos.

In De Chirico's paintings, the train of technology is allowed to run only on the borders of piazze punctuated by monuments and arcades, which transform a very theatrical space into a site of archeological investigation. In *Red Desert*, as the credits roll on the screen, a thick fog envelops the industrial skyline of Ravenna, where high-rises recall the elongated shape of medieval towers. Likewise, the workers on strike wear transparent raincoats, which make them resemble Hieronymus Bosch's frantic but also fragile figures in an allegory about damnation. Thus images of contemporary social turmoil slip back into ancient icons of mankind's plight between heaven and hell, the skies above and the abysses of the earth. In a sense Ravenna's modern look is only one side of an environment slipping back into the past, much in the same manner that Giuliana dreams of herself sinking into quicksand during a restless night. In a similar fashion, De Chirico's iconography oscillates between the tall, dark chimneys of factories and the equestrian statues of innumerable ancient Italian towns.

Such a precarious placement between old and new also characterizes the parallel Antonioni establishes between Italy and Patagonia, a virgin land at the end of the globe where Corrado wants to start a cutting-edge industrial enterprise. As he stands in front of a blue, green, and yellow map whose color scheme meaningfully repeats the juxtaposition of natural and artificial waste in Giuliana's neighborhood, Corrado coolly explains to the workers what their work in Patagonia will entail. Antonioni's camera slowly surveys these nameless men's weathered faces, which silently remind us of the scorching sun in southern Italy, of painful immigration stories, and of neorealist cinema's reliance on physiognomy. Finally, the workers' questions about details of daily life in the new land reveal that even the most radical geographical displacement can hardly lighten their baggage of memories, attitudes, and habits concerning women, leisure time, and family.

Antonioni's ambivalent stance between technological rebirth and nostalgia for a natural past plays itself out in geographical terms through one more episode—a fairy tale Giuliana tells her son, Valerio, one morning when the child says he cannot move his legs. Valerio's paralysis can be read as a psychosomatic response to an excess of technology. Just like the child who is not in control of his legs and freezes into a sort of inorganic immobility, the adults are so out of touch with their emotions that during the party in the red shack they engage in futile gossip until the arrival of an ominous ship releases a chain of repressed emotions ranging from fear to loneliness, from desperation to rejection.

The setting of Giuliana's fairy tale is a deserted island, off the coast of Sardinia in the Mediterranean, the same sea that witnessed De Chirico's childhood in Greece and nourished his eerily sunlit museological settings. In this enchanted place, a girl happily swims, plays with the birds, and explores the huge anthropomorphic rocks of the beach. In contrast to the foggy opening sequence in Ravenna, on the fantasy island the horizon is open, the air is filled with light, each shade of color breathes along with the reverberations of the sea. Even if it stems from Giuliana's imagination, this virgin landscape is far less hallucinatory than the documentary images of Ravenna's industrial area that Antonioni offers us at the beginning of the film.

In comparison with the red desert of postwar Italy, the pink beach appears to be the perfect site for a recovery of humanity according to natural laws. The innocence of the girl suggests a perfect unity between body and landscape, even though the huge rocks, with curvilinear, gigantic contours, stand like arcane presences. Their prodigious size implies that the price for this organic fusion might be, after all, a certain loss of humanity, or at least a regression into the darkest times, when only gods and giants and not human beings ruled. Furthermore, Antonioni's island, as beautiful as it may be, is somewhat conventional. The pink sand and the blue-green sea recall the perfect pictures advertising a hidden paradise for a vacation in a travel brochure. Since the island cannot quite belong to the mediocre present, but only to a mythical past, it can only deceive humans, soothing them with a certain longing for a primitive origin that was never entirely their own.

A song without words performed by a female voice floats over the industrial landscape of the credit sequence and the beautiful beach of Giuliana's fairy tale. In the island scenes the voice grows out of the rocks; it is full of desire, as if it belonged to an ancient soul forever imprisoned in the stone but still striving to reach out. In the credit sequence, the voice is so melodious that it seems full of corporeal abandon. This half-human, half-divine voice follows a mixture of industrial noises, whose calculated dissonance is reminiscent of Futurist concerts where traditional instruments are replaced or accompanied by the sounds of technology. Needless to say, Antonioni's combination of melodic singing and the jazzlike, discontinuous music of Giovanni Fusco points not only to the melodramatic nature of *Red Desert* but also to its baroque integration of emptiness and fullness, of jagged outlines and round volumes. And the baroque sensibility is involved with the effort of transition, with the painful breaking through of new forms out of old molds.

By setting references to De Chirico's art next to Futurist music, Antonioni reminds us that these two branches of the Italian avant-garde at the beginning of the twentieth century became a foil, one for the other, in that they explored the painful but also exhilarating impact of technology in a society that lagged behind other European countries in its progress toward modernity.

After all, De Chirico's puppetlike intruders in his airless piazze are nothing but the other side of F. T. Marinetti's mechanical man, whose direct descendant we encounter in the toy robot moving up and down Valerio's room and interrupting Giuliana's natural sleep. Through allusions to the Futurists and De Chirico, Antonioni sets up a middle ground of art and industry, nature and technology, which allows him to associate the objects and the decors of *Red Desert* with the great tradition of industrial design in Italy—a practice which, just like this director's cinema, combines an ancient aesthetic sensibility with a daring penchant for innovation.

According to Andrea Branzi in *Learning from Milan*, industrial design is a tradition especially intertwined with the contradictions of delayed industrialization in Italy. In Fortunato Depero's and Giacomo Balla's workshops of applied art, "it was more a question of applying the Futurist code to reality than genuine design activities. In short, the idea of producing on an industrial scale was totally absent."[20]

How do we explain, then, the flourishing of design during the postwar economic boom that surrounds the making of *Red Desert*? As the historian Fernand Braudel would say, Milanese stylists have capitalized on "the advantage of delay."[21] It is appropriate, therefore, for Antonioni to mix a high-tech look with antique pieces of furniture in Giuliana's apartment, since *Red Desert* is a film about the impact of technology upon a society not quite accustomed to it. Likewise, natural plants sit on the old-fashioned table of a worker's apartment. This domestic space, in turn, is situated in a building whose street entrance spells out high-tech, rationalist values. This mixing of old and new characterizes Giuliana's taste in clothes as well. As she speaks to Corrado in her newly painted store, she wears a formless, handmade country shawl on top of a svelte urban outfit.

While Valerio's bedroom is cluttered with mechanical toys and the den where the child plays with his father resembles a scientific lab for experiments in physics and chemistry, Giuliana and Ugo's bedroom includes a rococo chest and some upholstered mahogany chairs. Thus the aseptic, nearly chilling atmosphere of the upper-floor landing where Giuliana seeks refuge during a sleepless night—with metallic, tubular railings and long, rectangular windows—blends in with a few collector's items that spell out the economic power of a social class used to purchases from antique dealers. In contrast to Giuliana and Ugo's taste for a few precious, old pieces set amid rather barren, pristine white walls, within an infrastructure of opaque glass doors, the apartment of the worker whom Corrado would like to recruit for Patagonia is a darker but also much warmer space.

The building where the worker lives with his family is so modern that its blue, green, and yellow walls in the internal courtyard preceding the silvery and Plexiglas lobby seem to defy our expectations for solid volumes, with an orchestration of flat panels veering toward a traditional Japanese architectural taste. This modern beginning, however, is quickly superseded as soon as Giuliana and Corrado stand in front of a thick wooden door, from behind which the worker's wife emerges wearing a traditional black dress underneath a bright red apron, which she embarrassedly takes off. The comfortable but outmoded furniture of the worker's apartment well fits the wife's opposition to the possibility that her husband will leave his family to pursue profit and a career in Patagonia.

On one hand, the wife's apron signals the worker's dependence on the factory, where red, yellow, and dark blue, as primary colors, announce the birth of a new epoch. On the other hand, the worker and the woman who show up at the red shack during the party wear black and brown, the muted colors of the dying landscape. Even if Max, one of Ugo's colleagues, crassly questions his employee on sexual technique, the episode's conclusion—

with the working-class couple walking in the winter fog with nowhere to go on a Sunday afternoon—suggests that a sense of desolation and emotional disorientation pervades everybody's life, regardless of level of income.

The Battle of the Sexes

That heavy industrialization has had a deeply psychological impact on sexual roles, well beyond superficial class adjustments, becomes especially clear as soon as we compare two episodes of *Red Desert* that raise once again the question of how much interior design mirrors a changing sense of self.

In Giuliana's newly painted store, where she hopes to start a career as an independent businesswoman, the ceiling is green and the walls are light blue. Through color she has inverted the predictable scheme of sky and earth, of mind and body, and thus, thanks to her willingness to experiment, she has distanced herself from that stereotypical association of the ground with the womb, of femininity with nature, which always seems to place her in opposition to the world of science, factories, and cerebral coolness.

Giuliana's unconventional placement of colors, however, is not enough to dispel the aura of helplessness that surrounds her. She wavers in deciding on the type of merchandise she should sell, and neither does she seem capable of using the telephone to organize her business. By contrast, at the beginning of *Red Desert*, to help his colleague Corrado, Ugo relies heavily on a series of quick phone calls to gather the names of workers to be sent to Patagonia.

Giuliana is so afraid of crossing the line between old and new, of transgressing, that Antonioni repeatedly shows characters standing behind grids, which either enclose them in their obsessions or isolate them from each other. One element of the mise-en-scène especially captures Giuliana's endless wavering between liberation and resignation. A mysterious vessel that the girl in the fantasy island sees from afar promises adventure, whereas the cargo ship that stops by the red shack, flying a yellow flag to signal an epidemic on board, stands out as the symbol of a society plagued by unknown diseases.

Giuliana's constant touching of objects and fabrics, her testing of the solidity of the ground on which she walks, and her lingering footsteps on the newspaper that lands between her and the enigmatic street vendor suggest a tactile, regressive orientation, an instinctive probing for what is visceral, arcane, and below. Significantly, for Pier Paolo Pasolini, *Red Desert* was an excellent example of the "cinema of poetry," because Antonioni's stylistic liberty with the medium signaled that underneath the film there was another irrational film, one "that springs from cinema's deepest, and most essential, poetic sub-stratum."[22]

This drive toward hidden, unconscious forces, however, is not antithetical to her interest in a group of huge radio towers, which like magic antennas stretch across the sky, listening to the voice of the stars. These towers signify escape, perhaps through voyages into the unknown reaches of outer space, but however futuristic they may seem, they look like skeletons of prehistoric monsters (fig. 11).

In contrast to Ugo and Corrado, Giuliana truly inhabits a no-man's-land, an in-between region where the garbage of civilization mingles with the earth and propels its cycles forward; at the same time, the landscape exercises a strange pull on her, to the point of inhibiting her progress. In the red shack, she cannot take her eyes off the movement of the waves in the sea, as if their constant reconfiguring were symptomatic of her flexibility and openness toward the future but also of her inability to hold on to a well-defined identity.

This is perhaps why Antonioni insists on framing Giuliana in compositions that are highly self-conscious about the dialectic of figure and ground. Such an approach harks back to the tradition of Renaissance painting in which the body is a unit of measure of the architectural surroundings, and in Arrowsmith's words, it also conveys "her fear of separation—of being cut away from a landscape, from the past, from the 'ground' of her own being."[23]

Unlike Giuliana, who is caught between the sky and the ground, Corrado has once and for all abandoned his work in geology, and in the aftermath of his father's death, he is much keener on building tall silos in Patagonia. This drastic change in career calls attention to Corrado's desire to pass on a masculine legacy under the auspices of science between himself and Valerio. It also marks the triumphs of the superego and of paternal authority at the expense of more libidinal energies, which the frequent outpourings of smoke from the factory's boilers barely manage to discharge. Despite all his vertical yearnings, Corrado can engage only in a directionless survey of the Italian territory, as he keeps changing city, from Trieste to Bologna, from Milan to Ravenna.[24]

Although Ugo, as a male, lives much more in the public sphere than his wife, he is hardly aware of the historical transformations—big and small—

FIGURE 11. *The industrial landscape of Michelangelo Antonioni in* Red Desert, *between prehistory and the cosmos. Film Stills Archive, The Museum of Modern Art, New York.*

occurring around him. When Giuliana has her car accident, he ignores the event and chooses not to return from London to Ravenna. Unlike his wife, who declares to Corrado that were she obliged to leave, she would take everything and everybody with her, Ugo is inclined to dismiss the past with indifference. He despises Giuliana because she keeps wearing the same old pair of shoes, while he allows an old hut on the riverbank to go to ruin, with little regard for a vivid picture of wild zebras on one of the walls.

In contrast to that form of mural art, which is reminiscent of the pre-historic cave graffiti discovered at Lascaux, Ugo is far removed from the deep, primitive, emotional core of his being. This is certainly not the case with Giuliana, who is the only one to experience the aphrodisiac effect of the quail eggs eaten during the party in the red shack. Ugo's metaphors about Giuliana's difficult recovery after the accident all depend on his tech-nological training, as if his wife were a machine incapable of functioning despite several attempts at repair. Regardless of all his futuristic ideas, Ugo clings to old-fashioned views about the role of women in society and finds distasteful his wife's intention of starting her own business.

It is also true, however, that Ugo has an exploratory, creative side, even if his curiosity is strictly limited to science. With the help of a yellow toy, Ugo introduces Valerio to the gyroscope, a mechanism that allows ships to keep their balance during storms. Were we to compare the effects of heavy industrialization to a sea storm, we would conclude that to resist the waves, holding onto a reflective stance, is Antonioni's intellectual ambition. This is why at the end of *Red Desert*, when Giuliana is dressed very much as she was at the beginning of the film, as if hardly anything had really changed, she delivers a statement of acceptance from the standpoint of Antonioni's alliance with Ugo in the name of technology. In answering Valerio's question about the danger a poisonous yellow flame represents for birds, she simply concludes that natural life has to adjust to technological conditions. Somehow her words stressing compromise are at odds with the radical nature of her vision, one that suggests no mediation, but traumatic change.

Precisely because the director seals his story as a true ventriloquist by speaking through the body of his main actress, *Red Desert* is punctuated by many confrontations between the sexes. When Ugo tries to soothe Giuliana during a nocturnal crisis, they are both wearing white pajamas. While their similar outfits contribute to a desexualization of the couple, as spectators we cannot help wondering whether this visual echo between male and female at the level of clothing is nothing but Antonioni's projection of a utopian time of togetherness beyond sexual difference. Still, Ugo looks helpless in front of Giuliana's desperation, and his words make him sound more like a reassuring father than a companion on an equal footing.

Despite its obvious transgressive nature, even Giuliana's affair with Corrado ends with a disappointing return to the status quo, namely a lack of productive communication between men and women, one so extreme that Giuliana's attempt to talk with a Turkish sailor who cannot understand her is paradoxically more satisfying. To this foreign listener she can fully express her evaluation of how far she has come in the struggle to change her life. This is not to say that at least for a while she does not view Corrado as a catalyst for transformation. In fact, when the two embrace in his hotel room, Vitti's acting reaches a peak of protean effort, an extreme of discontinuities at the level of posture and gesture, to the point that her erratic, curvilinear, ever-shifting silhouette reminds us of the contortions performed by the divas of silent melodramas (fig. 12). In a sense, Vitti is Antonioni's diva, for *Red Desert* is a historical melodrama about

FIGURE 12. *Monica Vitti as diva, in* Red Desert. *Film Stills Archive, The Museum of Modern Art, New York.*

the female condition, which captures a woman's ambition and ends with her containment.

Finally, this aura of ambiguity hovering over Giuliana's progress is echoed on the fantasy island, where the young girl, cut away as she is from the world of adults and the company of people her own age, seems to enjoy an unparalleled degree of freedom. Her life truly unfolds outside the demands of sexual awakening. This interpretation stems from the girl's decision to remove the top of her bathing suit, thus staging a self-image of androgyny.[25] When the mysterious vessel appears, an icon of civilization disturbing a perfectly uncontaminated landscape, it overlays the theme of impurity onto a female sexuality still in search of self-expression. Thus, after the failure of Giuliana's affair with Corrado and the limitations of her marriage with Ugo, Antonioni's film ends by asking the viewer to contemplate only one possible strong couple: that of mother and child. If this pairing, by definition, suggests the beginning of a new world, the future of life out of the death in the present, nevertheless Giuliana's character hardly develops itself in a brand-new direction and remains pigeonholed in the two extremes of girlish innocence and maternal duty.

Architecture and Painting

The metaphor of ventriloquism describes the replacement of a man's camera with a woman's eyes; it finds an echo in Gilles Deleuze's insight that Antonioni's cinema is characterized by a dualism of mind and body:

> His work . . . passes through a dualism which corresponds to the two aspects of the time-image: a cinema of the body, which puts all the weight of the past into the body, all the tiredness of the world and modern neurosis; but also a cinema of the brain, which reveals the creativity of the world, its colors aroused by a new space-time, its powers multiplied by artificial brains. If Antonioni is a great colorist, it is because he has always believed in the colors of the world, in the possibility of creating them, and of renewing all our cerebral knowledge. . . . The world is painted in splendid colors, while the bodies which people it are still insipid and colorless. The world awaits its inhabitants, who are still lost in neurosis.[26]

Deleuze's association of mind with creativity and the future, and of body with neurosis and the past, discloses that Antonioni's use of an actress's eyes to paint serves to increase his freedom as a director who wants to insert abstract images into the cinema, a medium so implicated in a commercial circuit that it is primarily devoted to figurative representation.

In addition Deleuze's distinction between a cinema of the mind and a cinema of the body illuminates Antonioni's fear that Monica Vitti (although useful), as a woman, by virtue of her proximity to nature and the earth, might pull him down and away from his fascination with artificiality and the sky. In one of his short stories, the director writes, "The sky is transparent and it gives the impression that at any moment it might be possible to see through it, all the way to the infinite. The sky is a color. The infinite is another color, which we do not know."[27] In a sense, by removing the sky away from nature into a sheer mental space, Antonioni relates to it the way the Italian artist Piero Manzoni seeks a glimpse of the infinite in his perfectly empty and colorless canvases.[28]

Most important, as a canvas of the mind, Antonioni's sky calls attention to the director's project to empty the shot. In Pascal Bonitzer's words, "Antonioni looks for the desert. . . . The object of Antonioni's cinema is to reach the non-figurative through an adventure whose end is the eclipse of the face, the obliteration of characters."[29] In agreement with Bonitzer, Roland Barthes has also dwelt on how Antonioni's fascination with the void echoes the aesthetics of oriental art.[30] This is why as she walks up and down a small stairway in her apartment, Giuliana seems either to congeal into a presence or to vanish into the snail-like twist of the steps. This character's vanishing is charged with ambiguity, just as the desert of *Red Desert* exists between life and death. This fading of the character also stands for a drowning in the mindless realm of the body, whose reward, however, is a discarding of one's own historical baggage. Vitti's disappearance into the decor reaches a climax when we see her hands and nape merge with the oriental pattern of a sofa in the worker's living room. This piece of furniture instantly evokes Henri Matisse's use of fabrics in his paintings. Here the actress seems to surrender her outline to the labyrinthine, impenetrable configuration of her own womb.[31] Although Vitti's loss of self into a regressive realm may suggest a negative stereotype of femininity, it is also true that Antonioni's images, here, revel in the contradictions between surface and depth, thus exhibiting an open-ended and unstable baroque quality.

To be sure, Deleuze's dualism of mind and body is not a stable system of oppositions. It is based on the transformation of architecture into painting that occurs at the beginning of *Red Desert*. The film's first sequence is characterized by a series of highly self-conscious compositions that map over and over different sections of the gray terrain surrounding the factories. With an infrastructure of horizontal passageways and vertical chimneys providing a network of internal framelines, these shots spell out Ugo's and the director's controlling rationalistic outlook on life.

Despite their strong kinship with architectural illustrations, these industrial sites preserve a pictorial quality to the extent that they stem from a pattern of seeing, a diagram of sight. In Dudley Andrew's words, "Antonioni's world is . . . a program of vision which removes itself from simple recording in order to see *how* people see."[32] Besides Andrew, other critics have commented on the self-conscious pictorialism of Antonioni's images. According to Roberto Campari, for instance, "The images of *Red Desert* are insisted upon, poignant in their duration just like painterly images, whereas the framings of *Blow-Up* [a film about photography] are a lot shorter."[33] For Richard Roud, instead, it is Antonioni's extensive use of a telephoto lens that accounts for a mediation between the past and the future, between "Byzantine two-dimensionality" without the depth of focus typical of a realist approach and a lack of perspective that well fits Antonioni's intention to indulge in purely pictorial effects the way an abstract, modernist artist wants to paint about painting itself.[34]

Just as architectural measuring paves the way for pictorial seeing, the opening shots of well-established volumes, distances, and heights gradually unravel into an ill-defined conglomeration of moving elements (the workers on strike) and uncertain apparitions (the figures of Giuliana and Valerio slowly progressing from the background to the foreground). Put another way, the geometric rigor of these views is so extreme that despite their purpose to document a technological landscape, their figurative content seems to recede in favor of the mental effort to frame carefully and to quantify plastic and logical relationships over psychological and narrative ones.

In his commentary on Antonioni, Barthes has cited Georges Braque's statement: "The painting is finished as soon as it has erased the idea."[35] In light of Deleuze's definition of Antonioni's cinema as a cinema of the mind, it would be more appropriate to reverse Braque's comment and say that a framing by Antonioni reaches perfection when it erases the image, when it controls so completely that it delivers only the coordinates of the director's gaze. This approach becomes especially apparent in the decor of the worker's living room, where several folding chairs of different colors are set against the wall, with their closed frames producing geometric patterns reminiscent of Piet Mondrian's orderly intersections of lines charting an empty field of mental activity rather than a full object independent of someone's vision. Antonioni's emphasis on the axes of looking, to define the object seen as being subjectively perceived, reappears in the director's habit of shooting Monica Vitti from behind, lingering over the nape of the neck.[36]

This is why outside the factory, first during the strike and later during a conversation with Corrado, Antonioni's and Ugo's self-confident visions begin to lose their hold on concrete objects, which in turn undo themselves into fog and rain, smoke and mud. By contrast, the introduction of mother and child in the narrative suggests that brand-new generations of images, which are at first blurry or at best a murky field of points in motion, can be born from underneath a surface clarity that is not meant to last.

The replacement of an orderly shot with a confused one whose gradual sharpening of detail matches the dissolution of the previous one conveys a cyclical view of the historical process and also an oscillation between a masculine and a feminine sensibility. In 1964 the director declared,

We know that underneath the displayed image there is another one more faithful to reality, and underneath this second there is a third one, and a fourth under the previous one. All the way to the true image of that reality, absolute, mysterious, that nobody will ever see. Or all the way to the dissolution of any reality. Abstract cinema, therefore, would make sense.[37]

Here Antonioni clearly reveals his split allegiance to two different yet complementary kinds of images. The first is an ancient and mysterious origin that no geological excavation will ever be able to reach once and for all; in contrast to this foundational image, which in a sense has generated all the subsequent ones, the second is by definition a nonimage, for it occupies the opposite extreme, where visual representation has exhausted itself, lost its object, and come to coincide with a subjective projection forever in search of a referent.

As if Giuliana's walking with Valerio signaled the origin of a new chain of beings, the emergence of the female character into the shot announces the unraveling of the director's style from architecture into painting. This process complicates itself in the sequence in which Corrado and Giuliana discuss traveling and loss, mobility and memory, on the cluttered deck of a cargo ship floating out on the open sea. There, the rusty cables of the ship and its round boilers, its colored pipes and metallic loopholes, repeat the internal decor of the factory. While all these elements could function as practical objects, with their outlines and bulky shapes repeating the themes of measurement and sturdiness already encountered in the opening architectural outdoor shots, the components of the ship, to our surprise, transfigure themselves into elegant design. It is as if heavy, mundane technology had become subordinate to a light aesthetic exercise.

More specifically, this metamorphosis from industrial ugliness to beautiful design hides a fear. Perhaps, as a result of the shift from masculine architecture to feminine painting, from an aggressive form of industrial art to a private kind of reverie, one might slip into a pleasurable numbness, as soothing as a regression into the maternal womb, leveling all differences into quick gratification, much in the same manner that the massive production of consumer items in the fifties fostered the illusion of a happy, classless Italian society.[38]

The glossing over of class differences echoes the primitivist fantasy of Giuliana's tale, in which the self exists in harmony with the rest of the world. In Ravenna, however, objects have dissociated themselves from the humans who produce them. When we first see Ugo and Corrado inside the factory, for instance, all the shelves are empty, as if all these machines were perfectly sterile. By contrast, immediately after Corrado's speech to the workers on their way to Patagonia, the camera surveys a large quantity of blue glass globes and yellow straw containers—an innumerable series of mute demijohns whose proliferation diminishes the size of Corrado's figure timidly crossing the storehouse in the background of the shot.[39] While the oversized containers seem to take over the space surrounding Corrado as if they were threatening, artificial creatures at the beginning of a new age, these demijohns are also relics from the past. In fact, the huge shed where Corrado speaks is a glass-blowing factory that has stopped producing demijohns—an important means of transporting and storing wine in Italy for centuries—because everybody now buys or sells wine in expensive liter bottles.

By making Corrado disappear in front of the objects, Antonioni indicates that the self has drowned in a sea of desirable commodities. Thus the director echoes Andy Warhol's famous insight into how the daily items used in American Pop Art are meant to explore the meaning of social sameness and the collusion of what is human with what is inorganic: "I paint cans of soup because I want to be a machine. . . . It doesn't matter who did it. Everybody thinks the same, and every year that goes by we resemble each other more and more."[40] In a sense Valerio's paralysis marks the final stage of this fading of the subject into an undifferentiated objecthood.

In *Red Desert* if architecture applies to masculinity, painting leans toward femininity. The question therefore arises: what kind of painting does Vitti allow Antonioni to perform? Except for the well-known encounter of Claes Oldenburg with the director and for Antonioni's declaration that just like Mark Rothko, he paints "nothing," no extensive record exists of Antonioni's habits as an art collector or as a regular visitor of museums, galleries, vernissages, and studios.

We do have, however, several statements made by the director on the issue of pictorial influence. In a contribution made in 1961 at the Centro Sperimentale di Cinematografia, Antonioni acknowledged his love for painting by saying that it ranked second, along with architecture, in his interests, with the cinema above everything else, of course. Most significant, Antonioni added, "I do not think that by putting together certain compositions I was trying to draw parallels with a specific painter. . . . It is a shared experience

FIGURE 13. Periferia Industriale *(Industrial Landscape) (1927)*, *by Mario Sironi. Staatliche Museen zu Berlin, Preussicher Kulturbesitz, Nationalgalerie, Berlin.*

that spontaneously stems from the fact that *I have been following developments in contemporary art,* and that obviously I have oriented myself toward a certain taste, a certain tendency."[41]

Antonioni's repeated denials of pictorial influence, however, do not discourage us from comparing specific shots in *Red Desert*—namely the factories at the beginning and the view from the window of the worker's living room—with the gloomy industrial landscape of Mario Sironi (1885–1961) in *Paesaggio urbano* (1930) and with the provincial, pastel-colored streets and houses of Ottone Rosai in *Case di Borgo Stella* (1952). The sites chosen by Sironi and Rosai are meant to comment on the national condition, and Antonioni is using Ravenna as an allegory for Italy. Sironi seems an especially appropriate term of reference for *Red Desert,* for his view of industrialization is less optimistic than the Futurists'. In particular Sironi's *Periferia industriale* (Industrial Landscape) of 1933, in which a mother with her child stands in front of a beggar crouching down in the middle of a bleak industrial landscape (fig. 13), anticipates Antonioni's strategy for

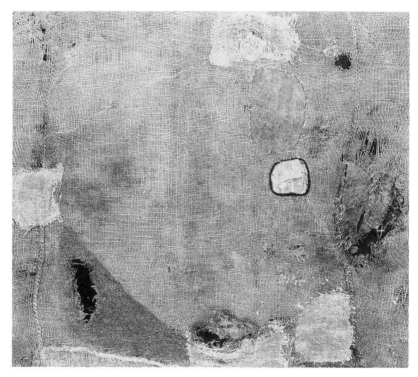

FIGURE 14. Sackcloth 1953, *by Alberto Burri. The Museum of Modern Art, New York. Mr. and Mrs. David M. Solinger Fund. Photograph © 1994 The Museum of Modern Art, New York.*

signaling that all couples—except Giuliana and Valerio—are on the way to dissolution.

Film historian Mira Liehm has tried to explain the red of *Red Desert* by turning to the paintings of Alberto Burri (1915–). In fact, this artist juxtaposes patches of chemical, violent red against the natural browns of old wood and cloth. In showing the disintegration of red, Burri's work can be seen as illustrative of what will happen to the industrial objects of *Red Desert* once their cycle is over.[42] Burri's colors—black, white, brown, red, gold— are not Antonioni's colors, yet the humbleness of his materials along with his intense chromatic expressivity reappear in the red wooden boards Corrado breaks apart to light a fire during the party in the shack (fig. 14).

In destroying sections of the shack Corrado cooperates with industrial technology by clearing away the old before a rebirth into the future. This theme of bringing civilization down to a tabula rasa is typical of many avant-garde artists, but especially of Kurt Schwitters (1887–1948), a Dada artist who made collages out of scraps of rubbish from the city. Just like Schwitters, Antonioni in *Red Desert* shows that art can be born out of waste. This is why the huge radio antennas that fascinate Giuliana during her wanderings with Corrado are reminiscent of Simon Rodia's towers in Watts, a work of art that began to be discussed in the middle of 1959. It took Rodia, an unschooled man, thirty-three years to create his stunning architectural complex, using discarded materials such as broken tiles, dishes, bottles, and seashells.

By changing the amount of red included in the shot, Corrado's destruction of the decor makes us aware that our perception of chromatic relations between characters and costumes, characters and objects, is subject to variations at the level of framing and composition. With its downplaying of narrative development for the sake of a free interaction of people and things, of red and other colors, this episode resembles a happening (a typical activity among the theatrical avant-garde of the sixties) while teaching us that color for Antonioni, inasmuch as it signals a pictorial sensibility linked to static images, is first and foremost an aspect of cinematic movement linked to minute historical transformations and to shifts in personal experience.

In short, color in film is not still painting but, as the abstract language of the future, conveys movements or changes at a psychological level.[43] While citing Matisse's use of color to chart subjective responses,[44] Antonioni has always advocated a nonnaturalist approach. This is the case in *Red Desert* because Antonioni wishes to convey how a newly painted environment can externalize inner psychic mobility. Most important, Antonioni regards the industrial pollution of Ravenna as a positive experiment rather than just as a negative catastrophe, for the odd alterations of water and grass at the level of color produce a whole new set of emotional and artistic possibilities. As sheer cinematic movement and psychological history, color can only veer away from realism toward abstraction.

In attempting to establish which kind of taste or pictorial orientation Antonioni might have been identifying with for *Red Desert*, Robert Benayoun and Roger Tailleur propose a long list of artists—Jean Dubuffet, Wols, Nicholas de Staël, Pierre Soulages, and Jean Fautrier, among others—all of them associated with the so-called Art Informel of the fifties, a European response to American Abstract Expressionism, which in Italy found with Burri's lacerated and tortured materials an adequate voice. As different as all these artists may be from each other, through a variety of techniques

FIGURE 15. Painting *(1944–1945)*, *by Wols. The Museum of Modern Art, New York.*
Gift of D. and J. de Menil. Photograph © 1994 The Museum of Modern Art, New York.

such as tachism, action painting, dripping, and perforation, they all share
an interest in primal matter undergoing decay and regenerating itself into a
new kind of image or object.[45]

In this regard, vital (although subterranean) are the connections between Art Informel and a baroque penchant for open-ended, unthreaded,
irregular forms charged with expressionist color whose intensity disrupts
all shapes, exasperates all meanings. It is possible that this aspect of *Red
Desert* might have escaped the critics' attention so far because of Antonioni's
reputation for a minimalist, understated style. However, Antonioni's method
of undoing dramatic plot and of lengthening uneventful moments is based
on a microscopic analysis of historical change, which is also central to the
agendas of melodrama, Art Informel, and the baroque.

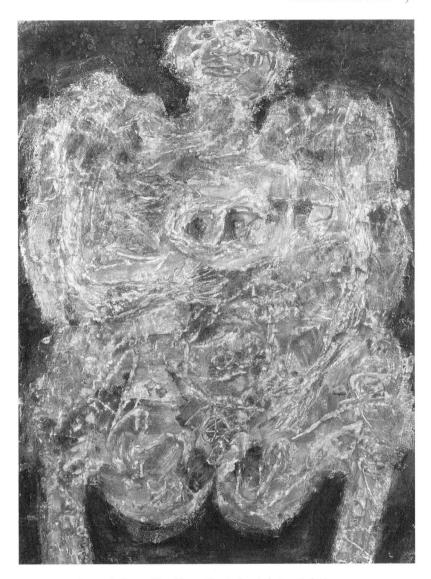

FIGURE 16. Corps de Dame: Blue Short Circuit (1951), *by Jean Dubuffet.*
The Museum of Modern Art, New York. The Sidney and Harriet Janis Collection.
Photograph © 1994 The Museum of Modern Art, New York.

Although Antonioni's horizon of art-historical references in *Red Desert* is quite international, it is important to remember that European Art Informel in Italy is bound up with a contradictory evaluation of the post-war period as a phase during which a yearning for renewal had sunk into a feeling of frustration, while a certain amount of hope for the future was still alive in the wake of the excitement caused by the economic boom of the fifties. As the label "informel" itself suggests, in *Red Desert* Antonioni, along with the artists listed by Benayoun and Tailleur, sets out to explore what is formless and open to the future but also potentially unstable and regressive.[46]

Were we to adopt Benayoun and Tailleur's insights on the pictorial sources of *Red Desert*, we would also have to add that Art Informel had been widely exhibited and discussed by the time Antonioni started working on his film. Wols, for instance, whose artworks strongly resemble the thin threads of muted colors scattered on the wooden walls of the red shack, had his first exhibit in Milan at the Galleria del Milione in 1949, and the Venice Biennale of 1958 dedicated at least two rooms to his canvases in which abstraction mimics the trail left behind by fireworks in the sky or by semi-transparent creatures with long tentacles at the bottom of the sea (fig. 15). In 1962, less than two years before the making of *Red Desert*, art critic Franco Arcangeli curated a major exhibit in Bologna entitled "Nuove prospettive della pittura italiana" (New tendencies in Italian painting). Following an interdisciplinary debate on Art Informel published in *Il Verri* in 1961, Arcangeli's show reasserted the links between Italian abstract painting and the biomorphic, fossil-like images of Dubuffet and Fautrier, whose pictorial pigments seem to be animated from the inside by an unsuspected level of productivity, leading, especially in Dubuffet's case, to the origination of a tentative figure out of chaos, of individuality out of an undifferentiated mass.[47]

In a sense Dubuffet's work ("Hautes pâtes"), with its oscillation between low materials with the look of excrement, mud, or decomposing bones and childlike outlines of highly simplified characters (fig. 16), parallels the struggle for self-assertion experienced by Giuliana in *Red Desert*. Dubuffet's materials are so close to the origins of our human birth, made of blood and feces, that death blends with life in those works in the same disturbing way that Giuliana's femininity threatens the director with a fall back into something liminal and unnameable.

Unlike Dubuffet's dark but also mesmerizing canvases where the left-

FIGURE 17. Hostages Black Background *(1944–1947; printed c. 1962), by Jean Fautrier.*
The Museum of Modern Art, New York. Arthur B. Stanton Fund. Photograph © 1994
The Museum of Modern Art, New York.

overs of civilizations sparkle like mysterious fragments of jewels or mosaics, Fautrier's work, earthy as it may be, has a lighter quality (fig. 17). Instances of this French artist's influence on Antonioni can be found in the pastel shots of swamps and canals near the factory. There, formless masses of chemical waste take on the strangest densities with pink or azure colorations reminiscent of Fautrier's delicate impastos ("Otages"). Indeed, Fautrier's pictures seem to have been born out of crushed flowers, leaves, and rocks, as if inorganic materials had the strange ability to ferment into new life.

The patches of red, blue, yellow, and green applied to the side of an old hut Ugo lets go to ruin are reminiscent not only of the tassels in Ravenna's Byzantine mosaics but also of the thick dabs of contrasting colors that Staël, another proponent of Art Informel, specialized in (fig. 18). At the beginning of the film, while Giuliana is furtively eating a sandwich, her eyes dwell on black shapes on the ground whose broken outlines and corporeal densities echo the black blotches Soulages is most famous for (fig. 19). The mélanges of art and industry, science and nature, reappear on the rusty,

FIGURE 18. Painting *(1947), by Nicholas de Staël.*
The Museum of Modern Art, New York. Gift of Mr. and Mrs. Lee A. Ault.
Photograph © 1994 The Museum of Modern Art, New York.

FIGURE 19. Abstraction *(1953), by Pierre Soulages. The Museum of Modern Art, New York. Larry Aldrich Fund. Photograph © 1994 The Museum of Modern Art, New York.*

FIGURE 20. *Monica Vitti as Giuliana in* Red Desert. *Film Stills Archive,*
The Museum of Modern Art, New York.

metallic side of the cargo ship, an area seemingly set on fire with an internal,
hellish neon-lighting effect.

Allusions to Art Informel coexist with a reference to the collage aesthetics of Nouveau Realism. In the footsteps of Giuliana leaving Corrado's
hotel, Antonioni's camera intercepts layers of torn posters on a street corner that immediately bring to mind Mimmo Rotella's commentary on city
life and mass media.

Besides painting, sculpture is another art-historical term of reference in
Red Desert, for through a thin metallic structure, a half-toy, half-decorative
object in Valerio's room, Antonioni seems to refer to the machines of Jean
Tingueley, which by dismantling themselves criticize the striving for efficiency
of high-tech culture. In addition, Mathias Goerits's snakelike, black, ominous
industrial sculpture seems to punctuate the dock Giuliana crosses on her way
to the ship, before her verbal exchange with the Turkish sailor (fig. 20). To
sum up, through Giuliana's agency and through color, Antonioni explores the
tensions inherent in sexual difference, by setting up a series of contrasts between biology and public history, private psychic experience and the transformation of the landscape, and painting and architecture.

Word and Image

By using Giuliana to authorize unconventional images, Antonioni comes to resemble a ventriloquist who speaks through someone else's body. The fact remains, however, that in a ventriloquial relationship, someone is inevitably silenced or condemned to muteness, which, as we have seen, is intertwined with neurosis and melodrama, creativity and historical change. With Giuliana as the source of visual inventiveness and pictorial energy in the film, it is not surprising if several episodes suggest how the struggle between word and image stems from her difficult communication with men. Outside the factory, at the beginning of the film, even though the noise of the machinery is deafening, Ugo and Corrado continue talking. All their verbal activity, however, has a touch of impotence, for it does not propel the narrative forward in any way. By contrast, even if Giuliana's remarks about the ship with the yellow flag are not taken seriously by her husband, she quickly characterizes Corrado's eloquence about politics and personal morality by pointing out to him that he speaks in an empty language. In other words, although language belongs more to men than to women, Ugo and Corrado are unable to use it to say something interesting or new. This is perhaps why the magazine illustrating the effects of polio that Giuliana consults during Valerio's temporary paralysis contains only large photographs with a minimal amount of text.

In contrast to Ugo and Corrado, however, Giuliana does use speech to disclose powerful insights, even if they are underrated by those around her. She is the only one who understands that the ship with the yellow flag of illness is an allegory of their unhappy lives. After her brief affair with Corrado, meeting him again in the shop meant to fashion a professional identity for her, Giuliana does not hesitate to tell her lover that she is disappointed.

Although she is unable to answer Ugo's and Valerio's scientific questions as they play together, Giuliana's statements throughout the film are the only ones that take on issues instead of circling around them. Thus, her moments of muteness during her long walks with Valerio or her reluctance to assert herself whenever her husband frames her into the role of neurotic can be seen not as a negative and definitive condition, but rather, in Dubuffet's words on the prelinguistic dimension of matter, "There is a primal moment of creativity at which we still cannot quite speak through it."[48] In short, Giuliana's linguistic inarticulateness is a positive zero, a silence open to the production of new images.

The metaphor of ventriloquism fits Antonioni's well-known statement about the kinds of actors he likes to work with:

> I want them passive . . . to have acting come not from reason, but from instinct. An actor's brain is not his most useful instrument, and although he is an element of a shot, he is not always the most important element. Many times the suggestions given an actor—how to make a gesture, speak a line—are intuitive and are of the same nature as those which make me include, or leave out, a tree.[49]

This ventriloquism, of course, is more advantageous for the director than for the actress. As the conclusion of *Red Desert* demonstrates, a man's artistic experimentation wins over a woman's yearning for a new sense of self. As they were at the beginning of the film, Giuliana and her son, Valerio, are walking in the poisonous air and littered fields near the industrial complex. They respectively wear green and brown coats, while a bright yellow flame intermittently pushes its way out of a factory's chimney set against a light blue sky. The colors of nature—brown, green, and blue—coexist with a chemical substance so powerful that it seems to have replaced the yellow of the sun. Likewise, Giuliana explains to her child, the birds have learned to fly away from the yellow flame and content themselves with a smaller space.

It is exactly at this point that Antonioni, after painting like a woman, speaks like a man through the actress. Even though the director has the last word, *Red Desert* is an important film not by virtue of its dialogues but thanks to its images.[50] This prevalence of the visual over the verbal stems from melodrama's tendency to encapsulate powerful emotions in tableaux vivants, whose visual effect is more memorable than a hundred words of explanation. The tableaux vivants of melodrama, however, are also moments of crystallization and temporary fixity, which make even more painful the characters' struggle to overcome their fate, to win over the past. In this respect Antonioni's images exist precisely between movement and pause, experience and inertia, cinema and painting. In a sense, at the level of language alone, because the film is so involved with a circumscribed and long-gone historical context, *Red Desert* today feels inevitably dated. The film therefore is comparable to the daily newspaper, with a lot of print and hardly any image, that Giuliana tramples over in Via Alighieri. Unlike that ephemeral token of the nature of time, the yellow flame at the end of the film, burning up the sky and rerouting the birds, will remain indelible in our eyes forever.

In contrast to the conclusion, which stresses compromise and adjustment, Giuliana's behavior at the beginning of the film had been much more adventurous. As she goes by the factory during the strike, she sees a worker standing away from the faceless crowd as he eats a sandwich. Desperately eager to get some nourishment, she buys the half-eaten sandwich from him and temporarily gives up her traditional motherly role. In fact she leaves her child behind to seek some privacy while she voraciously consumes her food amid industrial waste. William Arrowsmith has perceptively remarked that it is "the individual workman—that isolated but healthy young man, seen in clear focus," rather than the strikers, who feel stronger by virtue of their number and anonymity, "who interests Giuliana because she unknowingly desires what [he has]—the courage to be [himself], to accept separation, against the coercion or comfort of the crowd."[51] Giuliana's hunger suggests a set of unfulfilled needs that no peaceful coexistence of birds and factories can resolve. Significantly, eating (just like lovemaking) is difficult in *Red Desert.* During the party in the red shack, we see only Giuliana consume some quail eggs with an aphrodisiac effect while her friends superficially gossip about sexual liaisons. In a way, Monica Vitti's last line in *Red Desert*, about learning to survive in a hostile environment, describes her position as an actress in relation to Antonioni, to the extent that she is never allowed to overcome the role of neurotic, whereas the director, thanks to her, can be both filmmaker and painter, and experiment freely. Indeed he does succeed in expanding our understanding of color, for he uses it not only in a pictorial and abstract way, but he also links it to cinematic movement. Somehow, the capture of Antonioni's color between painting and cinema—another way of saying stillness and movement—reproposes the coexistence of melodrama with the baroque, for the first one is made up of spectacular moments that arrest the narrative flow, while the second thrives on rhythm, peaks, vertigoes, and interruptions.

At first it may seem that *Red Desert* is primarily a film about the clash of nature and culture, with the industries eating the landscape away, yet it might be more accurate to say that the narrative stems from a central issue, that of the power relations between male and female, director and actress. Antonioni's ventriloquist approach not only enables the crossover from a cinema of architecture to a cinema of painting but also sustains a mysterious osmotic activity between natural landscape and industrial technology, one merging into the other, and finally, this strategy of vicarious storytelling promotes an ongoing exchange between what is abstract and what is figurative, what is organic and what is lifeless, as if one pattern could slowly emerge out of its opposite. While this circularity of permutations suggests a cyclical view of the historical process,[52] a turning over of a primitivist realm into a futurist milieu, it does not compensate, however, for the director's double standard, since Antonioni's commitment to change is based on the assumption that although it is a woman who enables him to envision what is to come, in the end femininity must be aligned with the past.

CHAPTER 3

Eric Rohmer's

The Marquise

of O

~

Painting

Thoughts,

Listening

to Images

*T*he confrontation of word and image is so central in Eric Rohmer's cinema and writings that in *The Marquise of O* (1975), a film based on Heinrich von Kleist's eponymous novella (1811) with a neoclassical setting, the director inevitably summons a tradition dating back to the eighteenth century and carrying over into the nineteenth. In *Laocoön* (1766), Gottfried Lessing argued that literature is an art of time, while painting should primarily deal with space. Later, the poet and British aesthetician Matthew Arnold (1822–1888) stated that "poetry thinks and the arts do not."[1] Were we to consider jointly Lessing's and Arnold's views on the verbal and visual poles, we would conclude that as an art of time, literature is for the mind, while as an art of space, painting is for the senses.

It is these oppositional terms that Rohmer sets out to rearrange in *The Marquise of O* by attributing a plastic edge to words and by endowing the images with an introspective aura. Thus, in *The Marquise of O*, painting is linked to thought. It is neither a mask nor a camouflage flattening the cinematic image, but it refers instead to the characters' mental activity, namely a convoluted path of ideas, emotions, misunderstandings, and expectations. By virtue of its association with thought, therefore, painting lends depth to an otherwise one-dimensional surface and makes the cinematic image multifaceted, if not architectural.

To be sure, in *The Marquise of O*, Rohmer transcends the opposition of word and image, even though the dialectic of literature and painting remains the founding problem of his creative and critical work. While Rohmer's statements may seem contradictory, in this film the polarities of word and image, literature and painting, undergo a reversal as powerful as the joining of opposites in an oxymoron. By painting thoughts and making images out of words, Rohmer demonstrates that both his preparatory approach to and his cinematic execution of Kleist's text thrive on the oscillation between *ut pictura poesis* and *ut poesis pictura;* that is, as mute poetry, painting opens to abstraction, whereas as a speaking picture, poetry absorbs the senses. In the end Rohmer's approach defies Lessing's and Arnold's attribution of separate areas of competence to each art form.

During an interview published in 1988 Rohmer stated that he thinks of himself not as a director-painter but as a director-architect for whom the cinema is the art of organizing a staging in order to make visible a spatial organization already latent in the world.[2] Through his self-description as an architect, Rohmer is still echoing his admiration as a young critic for F. W. Murnau's *Faust* (1926), in which the subordination of painting to the brute photographic power of the cinema releases the inherent beauty or pictorialism of reality.[3]

Rohmer's thinking is thus in line with Blaise Pascal's famous aphorism, "How vain an art is painting, which attracts our admiration for representations of objects which we do not admire in the original."[4] Excessive aestheticism occurs when painting is not subordinated to the staging of the world, and therefore, for Rohmer, cinema can benefit from painting as long as they meet in a shared sense of theatrical space—one not based on artificial display but linked to the world through the living presence of the actors.[5] Within this scheme where painting becomes invisible or transparent, either as a form of introspection or as the soul of the world, language does not simply allow the cultivation of ideas, but by virtue of its enormous power over the mise-en-scène, it becomes a tangible object, if not a sensuous element of quasivisual impact. Word and image exist between theater and architecture because literature, the art of time, stages itself and becomes a spatial object, while painting, the art of space, lends a temporal accent to labyrinthine psychological developments. Put another way, the dialectic of word and image in *The Marquise of O* is predicated on the conflict between the mind and senses, reason and emotion.

Word and Image in Rohmer's Theory of the Cinema

It is not difficult to find statements made by Rohmer in favor of painting and against the word, but it is just as easy to find him speaking in defense of literature at the expense of the image. For example, in 1971, after the international success of a brilliantly verbal film like *Ma nuit chez Maud* (1969), the director declared that a cinema reduced to the image

> hasn't anywhere much to go. In the realm of pure plastic expression, the portrayal of action, and even the presentation of life, the cinema has done wonders; but it has proved pretty restricting when it comes to portraying reflection, a character's developing awareness of himself, which is the subject not only of most French but also of most Anglo-Saxon literature, which is as moralizing as ours. Purely visual cinema was incapable of exploring this realm.[6]

Such a statement in favor of the word and the suggestion of an incompatibility between the visual and the reflective dimensions may lead one to assume that with *Ma nuit chez Maud* Rohmer is rehashing Alexandre Astruc's call for a literary cinema and subscribing to Astruc's denunciation of the "tyranny of the visual." In 1949, in a seminal essay for *Ecran Français* entitled "Naissance d'une nouvelle avant-garde: Le caméra-stylo," Astruc formally declared that the seventh art had come of age. The critic stated that the cinema could aspire to the rank enjoyed by painting and the novel, yet the visual arts quickly disappeared from his discussion. Without the beneficial intervention of the word or of a literary orientation, the cinematic image by itself, for Astruc, was thick, heavy, and reducible to a single meaning: that of the object shown. Astruc's ideal filmmaker would use the camera with the same liberty and subtlety with which a writer uses the pen.

Clearly for Astruc "literature" meant any kind of writing devoted to the exploration of the mind or to the psychology of reason. In this regard, still provocative is Astruc's claim that René Descartes, were he alive today, would use a sixteen-millimeter camera to "write" his *Discourse on Method*. Astruc's invitation to take full advantage of the literary and philosophical potential of cinema found an excellent interpreter in Eric Rohmer, who even defined his artistic identity in the light of a literary tradition:

> In French there is a word *moraliste* that I don't think has any equivalent in English. It doesn't really have much connection with the word "moral." A *moraliste* is someone who is interested in the description of what goes on inside man. He's concerned with states of mind and feelings. For example, in the eighteenth [*sic*] century Pascal was a *moraliste*, and a *moraliste* is a particularly French kind of writer like Bruyère or La Rochefoucauld.[7]

While the director's *moraliste* side and verbal wit in *Ma nuit chez Maud* are undeniable, it would be a mistake to think that Astruc's Cartesian logos can neutralize the profound visual vocation of Rohmer's cinema.

The links between Astruc's principle of the "caméra-stylo" and the literary flavor of Rohmer's cinema may be apparent to the critics but not always to Rohmer himself. In an interview published in 1982, he stated,

> I don't believe in "direct writing" in the cinema. There are not so many examples of that, and in general the films that have been made like that are not among the most successful. There is no such thing as what Alexandre Astruc has called the "camera-pen," that is anyone who makes a film the way he writes a book. The work in film is always a job of staging, and staging begins by adaptation of a work which exists by itself in a literary way. There is no film which can exist literarily in one way or another.[8]

Rohmer's rejection of literature reminds us that his interest in painting dates back to his essays on film and the other arts in "Le celluloid et le marbre," published by *Cahiers du Cinéma* in 1955. In this context Rohmer's recuperation of painting, by definition a spatial art in contrast to the temporal orientation of literature, was most compatible with André Bazin's cinema of realism, which opposed what Rohmer called "the weakening of space" brought about by Soviet montage, a technique based on "leaping" from one viewpoint to another, with little regard for "the expressive value of relationships of size and mass, of the movement of lines within the limits of the screen."[9]

While condemning the impulse behind montage to reshape the world and express the vision of a revolutionary age, Rohmer deeply admired the films of Murnau and Roberto Rossellini, where the world is not fragmented for the sake of a thesis but is gradually revealed as a complex and resonant whole. For Rohmer, the cinema of montage, or of stylistic manipulation, can never improve on reality, because beauty is a quality not of art but of the world.[10] Through his realist stance, the director embraced the Pascalian theme of the hidden God. As Roger Hazelton explains, for the Jansenist philosopher: "All things cover up some mystery; all things are the veils that cover God. Christians ought to recognize him in everything."[11] Because God's hand is present in the world, stylistic changes or technical transformations are a form of arrogance or self-love. As a corollary to the presence of God in the world, Pascal argued that visible things represent the invisible, "being the sensible image of what is spiritual, so that nature becomes an image of grace."[12] While rejecting literature because, like montage, it distorts reality with metaphors, Rohmer argued that cinema as painting and as space was "more suited than . . . marble in capturing the eternal essence of things."[13] The emphasis on exteriority and appearance, which is typical of the screen and of the canvas, was neither a limit nor a hindrance to the exploration of an intangible, invisible dimension; on the contrary, it was a vantage point from which to depict the life of the soul in all its movements, thus turning literal portrayal into spiritual figuration.

Rohmer's Approach to Kleist's Text

In the shift from Rohmer's theoretical statements to his adaptation of the novella, the interaction of word and image settles into a system of oxymorons as tight as the extreme dualities and unexpected reversals in Kleist's plot: the Marquise of O is Giulietta, a young widow living with her family in a northern Italian town, a citadel besieged by a Russian army during the Napoleonic wars. After being assaulted by a group of ferocious soldiers, the Marquise is rescued by a handsome Russian count, who later rapes her while she is asleep under the effects of a potion. The child Giulietta bears as a result of her unconscious encounter with the Count is as inexplicable as a divine gift or a sudden manifestation of the grace of God: it cannot be earned, only received, and it is hard for her and her parents to accept. After much personal anguish, Giulietta decides to place an announcement in the local newspaper stating that she will marry the father of her child if he comes forward by a certain date. The tale does not quite end with the reunification of the Count and Giulietta; it really concludes with her recognition that human nature is double-sided.

In Rohmer's *Marquise of O*, the word calls attention to itself, instead of simply functioning as a source or goal for the image. One factor in this exhibition of the word was the director's decision to shoot the film in German, which made Rohmer especially sensitive to the sound, shape, and rhythm of a foreign language. Furthermore, he cast professional German theater actors, who could most skillfully carry the weight of a literary text and gratify Rohmer's taste for an ethnography of conversation and a cinema through which "to explore how we live in relation to how we speak, who we are in relation to what we say."[14]

Rejecting Astruc's one-way association of the cinematic image with the literary word, Rohmer turned to Kleist's novella for the visual nature of this literary text, which the director approached as a ready-made script that needed little alteration to adapt it for the screen. Kleist's text, despite its archaic-sounding German (which the producers of the film at first opposed), is for Rohmer an objet trouvé: what strikes him is its cinematic qualities. First of all, the length of Kleist's novella does not clash with the approximate duration of an art film available for wide, commercial distribution—in this case, one hour and thirty-five minutes. By not having to cut anything out, Rohmer conveys how underneath the relentless sequence of Kleist's short sentences lurks a taste for the paradoxical, the supernatural, and even the bizarre. More specifically, Rohmer's adaptation is so literal that he reproduces even minor syntactic patterns in Kleist's text. The film's spoken dialogues have the crispness of written speech, yet the spectators are made to feel that the situations they see are intarsia of word and image. The director's obsession with the word never degenerates into verbosity. Instead, it binds the viewer even more tightly to the film's images, since what the characters think is not always expressed in what they say, but the contents of their minds hover in the visual spaces—gestures, poses, objects, expressions—that exist between the ordinary and polite sentences they offer to each other.

Second, the novella takes place in 1799, in the midst of the Age of Sentimentality when the external devices of pose and gesture signified internal states of mind, approximately one century before Sigmund Freud's discovery of the unconscious. Therefore, Kleist's narrator describes everything from the outside, thus paralleling the situation of Rohmer's camera, which can record only what goes on externally. In the film, Rohmer turns action into introspection in order to deal with the problems of self-image and self-knowledge. As a result of his emphasis on exteriority, Kleist has to detail with amazing precision the movements and the attitudes of his characters, while also mentioning the objects that surround them, as if he had in mind a list of all the props necessary to Rohmer's staging of the text. In short, the intense visual nature of Kleist's very literary text allows Rohmer to carry out an adaptation that is not a translation of one medium into another but a refraction of word into image and vice versa. "Refraction" here means a mirroring or a duplication that also contains a reversal across different signs and that never collapses into a perfect identity but instead thrives on the very otherness of word and image.[15]

The productive discrepancy between these two media of expression reappears in the way gender invests with different connotations the plight of the Count and that of Giulietta. As the critic Edith Borchardt remarks, "Whereas the Count has to reconcile the disparity between what he is and what he seems to society and particularly to the Marquise, the story of the Marquise herself is clearly connected with the discovery of ultimate things."[16] In other words, the Count's struggle is social before it is individual, whereas the Marquise's is primarily individual. He worries about the social impact of his tarnished reputation, whereas she is concerned with her inability to rationalize the pregnancy, an unforeseen aspect of herself. Of course, she is conditioned by the norms of the community in which she lives, and he feels guilty for what he has done. Yet marriage is sufficient for him to achieve a reconciliation with himself and the rest of the world. By contrast, the wedding ceremony is not enough for her to come to terms with the coexistence of good and evil. Her discovery of "ultimate things" does not consist in finding out the identity of the father of her child; rather, it coincides with accepting that the Count is both angel and devil. For this dualistic view of human nature Rohmer is indebted to Pascal's "ni ange ni bête." Only months after the wedding, she accepts that we all are both pure and tainted—and in this we are like the beautiful swan Tinka, whose image the Count fancied as a child. A beautiful sight self-assured of its own purity, the swan was swimming when the young count threw mud at it. After diving beneath the surface of the waves, the swan reemerged, immaculate as ever.

Alan Spiegel explains that the tale is "a Black Forest variant of the orthodox Christian 'fortunate fall' that conceives sin as a prelude to grace and wounding as necessary to healing."[17] The fall and rise of the swan reappear in the emotional ups and downs experienced by the characters, who sink into brutal violence, deception, and arrogance, but also rise to forgiveness, self-discovery, and acceptance. By recognizing in the Count's story of the swan an image of her own inner divisions between reason and emotion, purity and desire, the Marquise can at last transcend all the dichotomies he can only mechanically reconcile through a public ritual. Hence Giulietta's discovery of "ultimate things" coincides with the acquisition of a knowledge that has, in testing the limits of rational thinking, a spiritual value well beyond the constraints of social rules.

The Meanings of Adaptation

Despite Rohmer's duplication in reverse of words into sensuous objects and of images into thoughts, in the novella and on the screen the characters hardly ever look at themselves in the mirrors that hang on the walls. Unable to engage their own self-images, they acquire very little knowledge of themselves. During the scenes of family debates about the Count's plea for the Marquise's hand, or in the course of quiet meals, or in the midst of highly controlled rituals of arriving and departing or sitting and standing, the characters' figures reappear only in small, marginal portions of the house mirrors. Only once do we see Giulietta looking at herself in a mirror, and this rare instance of self-reflection occurs just before her reconciliation with her father. Although she has not come to terms with the dual nature of the Count, she has begun to find a new strength in herself despite her father's indictment. By contrast, when we see Giulietta painting in her room, standing in front of the canvas—probably a neoclassical landscape with picturesque ruins—she is totally indifferent to the huge mirror decorating the wall beside her.

While pointing to the characters' struggle between rigid social norms and self-evaluation, the mirror is not a mere decorative element of the mise-en-scène but a clue, instead, to the director's special chemistry of reversals between word and image for his work of adaptation. This metanarrative function of the mirror becomes clear in two instances. First, Giulietta's painting is interrupted by the arrival of her daughter, who wants to show her progress in calligraphy. Beautifully designed letters of the alphabet—a, k, l, f—find a place on the painter's canvas before the reflections of Giulietta, the daughter, and a servant unwind on the silent surface of the mirror as they leave the room. The alphabet as a special kind of image, the painting as the space of writing, the specularity of the screen in relation to the spectator, the movements of the figures resembling the modulations of a chain of thoughts—these are the ingredients of Rohmer's cinema in one of its most intimate settings: the study of an early nineteenth-century woman painter.[18]

Second, Rohmer's formula for adaptation is spelled out in the first scene of *The Marquise of O,* which takes place inside an inn. Rohmer's camera intercepts the figure of a waiter moving away from its reflection in the mirror over the bar. He is serving drinks to a few male customers, who mock the Marquise's decision to publicize her pregnancy in the local newspaper. As they gossip, the Gothic letters of the announcement's German text take over the whole screen. This opening sequence anticipates the end of the narrative, which is marked by a comparable dialectic of word and image. The final words of Kleist's text occupy a title card: "A whole line of Russians now followed the first," and this folk-tale ending replaces the image of Giulietta and the Count at last embracing. The mirror housing a series of reversals is, then, the appropriate figure for a cinematic adaptation that begins and ends with a written text reproducing the role of the image.

Adaptation may be seen not only in terms of the metaphor of refraction or of duplication as reversal but also as a form of intellectual rape or textual alteration. At first sight, rape may seem too violent a metaphor, given the intense compatibility between Kleist's pictorialism and Rohmer's literariness. To be sure, the director had declared that he was attracted to the novella because he did not have to "touch" it. Rohmer, however, changed Kleist's text in three small but highly significant ways.

To begin with, in the novella, the rape of the Marquise is suggested by an ellipsis in the narrative. A dash stands out against the white of Kleist's page, at once an unassuming and haunting marker: "where she sank down completely unconscious. Here—he made arrangements, since soon after her frightened women appeared to call a doctor."[19] But in the film, this empty, or at least graphically impoverished, place is filled with an explicit reference to a painting, *The Nightmare* (1781) by Henry Fuseli (fig. 21).[20] In this famous gothic fantasy, a beautiful young woman, aroused by some powerful dream, has thrown herself partly from the couch. Her attitude of extreme abandon shows that she is prey to an incubus, or an ugly little demon that squats just below her chest; meanwhile, a horse with staring, gleaming eyes transfixes her voluptuous body from beyond the curtain. Likewise, Giulietta, who has drunk a sleeping potion to calm her nerves after the attempted rape, appears in a seductive pose to the Russian count (fig. 22). With a lamp in his hand, he discovers her during his nightly tour of the conquered outpost. Her shimmering, white nightgown blinds the Count, whose intense gaze replaces the staring eyes of Fuseli's horse. His transgressive behavior is signified, first, by the frontality of the camera on his face in close-up and, second, by the darkness that engulfs him and us, as if Fuseli's incubus had traveled into his mind and our eyes. As Pascal Bonitzer remarks, the invisibility of Fuseli's incubus in Rohmer's film rhymes with the ellipsis of violence in Kleist's text.[21] Thus Rohmer reorients the violence of the Count's action, turning it away from the Marquise, an outside object, to the recesses of the Count's subjectivity. In the same way, Fuseli's painting is not so much a spectacle of female eroticism as the mirror of a dark, male desire that the spectator is inevitably made to share. In other words, the image displayed turns into private thought.

The addition of Fuseli's *Nightmare* to Kleist's novella is an example of visual insertion. Rohmer, however, also makes one minor but meaningful verbal addition to the text. The director assigns a brand-new line to a female servant who orders the handsome coachman Leopardo to fetch a sleeping potion for the Marquise, who is shaken by the danger she has just lived through. Critics have remarked that the introduction of this device in the narrative is meant to free Giulietta of any suspicion of "cognitive duplicity"[22] in regard to her pregnancy. By entrusting the Marquise to the embrace of Morpheus, Rohmer can push her state of inner division to an extreme: the erotic swoon she experiences while asleep remains totally unknown to her, even though the drives of the id pierce the surface of her very proper behavior. It remains unclear, for example, why she is so eager to thank the Count the morning after her rescue, or why she feels her father should have stopped the Count from leaving again after his sudden reappearance. Second thoughts and psychic evasion, hidden feelings and half-understood motives, clearly inhabit her attitude of restraint and submission. Still, the device of the sleeping potion allows Rohmer to displace the question of the Marquise's subconscious motivation, the more to emphasize the challenge of taking responsibility for her own predicament in full consciousness. In a sense, the Marquise's announcement in the newspaper, which follows her admirable decision to devote herself totally to the care of her children, is an extreme act of courage, even of arrogance. By confronting the disapproval of others, Giulietta can be even more like the swan Tinka sailing on the waves, all puffed up in glory. Thus, with his attention equally divided between the conflicting levels of consciousness and the unconscious, between reason and emotion, Rohmer balances the insights of the *moraliste* with those of the *psychanalyste.*

Another interpretation of the sleeping potion is also possible. As she requests some opium tea, the female servant speaks her lines in voice-off. Thus her absence from the visual field makes it even more apparent that these words are external to the literary source. In a sense, the auxiliary but also quite marginal role of the female servant is comparable to the peculiar position of the director. While Kleist delights in the absurd flavor of his tale because it exposes the hypocrisy of social norms and the contradictions of individual actions, Rohmer concentrates on the strength of character it

FIGURE 21. The Nightmare *(1781), by Henry Fuseli. The Detroit Institute of Arts, Detroit. Photograph © The Detroit Institute of Arts 1991.*

FIGURE 22. *Edith Borckhardt as Giulietta, in* The Marquise of O *(directed by Eric Rohmer, 1975). Film Stills Archive, The Museum of Modern Art, New York.*

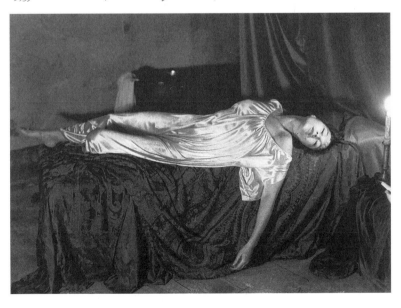

takes to accept the irrational. With the introduction of the voice-off and the sleeping potion, which frees the Marquise of any taint of complicity, Rohmer fully dramatizes the clash between ineffective explanations based on reason and conduct moved by faith toward the gift of divine grace.

Beyond the boundaries of this episode, the equivalence between directing a film and supplying others' wants continues to define the unobtrusive yet daring nature of Rohmer's adaptation. Again Rohmer's approach to Kleist's novella is comparable to the Count's rape of Giulietta. His contact with her is as invisible as the director's intervention on Kleist's text, because the Marquise is asleep. Yet the violence of the rape is as extreme a gesture as Rohmer's decision to shift words into images and images into thought. Anonymous servants take care of the major characters by handing them letters and newspapers, lighting candles, announcing guests, guarding gates. These nameless figures are stand-ins for Rohmer, who never fails to stage Kleist's short, quick sentences about the flow of minute, apparently insignificant events. The metaphor of adaptation as rape is further confirmed by how Rohmer steps into the shoes, so to speak, of Leopardo, the servant whom the mother temporarily blames for her daughter's pregnancy. Indeed, Leopardo's tall, wide-brimmed hat does resemble the Count's, and as if this detail were not enough, Rohmer adds a third, microscopic change to Kleist's text: a shot of Leopardo staring at Giulietta in the cellar, right after her rescue.

In short, as Leopardo enables Rohmer to bring the sleeping potion to the Marquise and as the suspicion of the rape hangs over him, the analogy between adaptation and rape comes full circle. Finally, the association between Rohmer and the servants reverberates in the director's cameo appearance as a Russian military officer who stands by a huge map spread on a table, while the Count answers questions about his soldiers' assault on Giulietta. For Rohmer, Kleist's text is a map of actions, which he understands as intimately as the servants know each corner of the house where they quietly work.

Pictorial, Architectural, and Filmic Space

In discussing Murnau's *Faust*, Rohmer distinguished among pictorial, architectural, and filmic spaces. The adoption of these levels of organization in *The Marquise of O* confirms that for Rohmer the cinema is an art of space. This is not to say that the director ignores the temporal markers of Kleist's novella, which he faithfully visualizes through a series of title cards. Furthermore, Rohmer's adaptation respects Kleist's split temporal structure: an explanatory flashback leading up to Giulietta's decision to search for her child's father, and the family's anxious wait for the solution to a mystery that has been all along an open secret for the audience. Finally, the emotional pace of the film is based on the progression of Giulietta's pregnancy. Yet, unlike Alain Resnais's *Last Year at Marienbad* (1961), *The Marquise of O* is not a story about the power of memory but one about the meaning of locations. Having been raped while asleep, the Marquise has nothing to remember but everything to decide in regard to the Count's entrance into her family space.

Rohmer's interest in space over time fits within his project to create a cinema whose painterly approach can achieve the conceptual refinements of the verbal arts. It is also true, however, that Rohmer's sparing use of camera movements and his preference for static shots have earned him the label "theatrical." Yet it is the theatricality, or the dramatic compositions, of classic figurative painting and not of the theater that Rohmer adopts to stage Kleist's text. This is the case because Rohmer's project in *The Marquise of O* is primarily to achieve a reversal of image into word or of painting into thought, whereas the director's interest in the theater and, more specifically, in working with stage actors is subordinate to his sense that a film should not be made of beautiful paintings but should call attention to its origins in the world through the performers' bodies.

Rohmer's paradigm of cinema-space-painting-introspection emerges from some observations about the theater that the director published in *La Revue du Cinéma* in 1948:

> The very nature of the screen—a completely filled rectangular space occupying a relatively small portion of one's visual field—encourages a plasticity of gesture very different from what we are used to seeing on stage. For example, the arm movement common to an opera singer . . . is more easily justified in theatrical space, which is at once *fixed* and *undefined*, than inside a rectangle whose edges are *clearly indicated* and that *only provisionally circumscribes a variably wide portion* of the surface where the action takes place.[23]

By concluding that "compared with the theatrical space, cinematic space would thus be defined by the narrowness of its visual surface and by the breadth of its place of action,"[24] Rohmer suggests that in film, much more than in theater, painting can interact with the plasticity of the screen to make actions breathe along with the rhythm of the actors' thoughts.

Rohmer's inclination toward painting is not symptomatic of a museological obsession. Without ever falling into the cliché of the tableau vivant, which would reinforce Pascal's equivalence between painting and vanity or painting and artificiality, Rohmer in *The Marquise of O* relies on the visual register to fulfill Bazin's definition of adaptation as a "window onto the world of a space oriented toward an interior dimension only."[25] In mirroring Kleist's word, Rohmer's pictorial screen is indeed the Bazinian window—an idea the director evokes again in one of his most telling statements on space in painting, from "La Celluloid et le marbre": "The frame of a painting constitutes an area of disorientation in space. A frame juxtaposes a space oriented inward, a field of reflection open only inside the painting, to the space of nature and our active experience which sets the marks of its external limits."[26] Painting for Bazin is a landscape of the mind; likewise, Rohmer's choice of pictorial sources for *The Marquise of O* is meant to reproduce the period's conception of itself,[27] its inner image, and thus reflect the issues of self-discovery, self-knowledge, and self-acceptance confronted by the characters.

In keeping with the temporal framework of the novella, Rohmer's art-historical allusions tap the hybrid territory between the postrevolutionary neoclassical style and the protoromantic sensibility of the late Enlightenment. The measured actions of the characters, their unspoken belief in civic virtues, and their simple way of life produce a stoic aura that is reminiscent of Jacques-Louis David's appreciation of the lessons of antiquity for the ethics of newly born republican France. Yet, in David's *Oath of the Horatii* (1786; fig. 23), male camaraderie and courage are juxtaposed with female piety and suffering. Using a similar contrast of reason and emotion, the pure lines of Rohmer's mise-en-scène vibrate with emotional pressure, as if the smoothness of their surfaces were nothing but a social convention challenged by the same intensity we sense underneath David's classical forms. Furthermore, just as the pictorial space of the *Oath* is divided according to gender, so it is in the household of the Marquise; mother always sits with daughter, and father with son. Only at the very end of the film will the Count and Giulietta share the same seat and, with it, an understanding of the mistakes they made about themselves and each other.

As a result of Rohmer's belief that painting in film must surface through acting (which is to say, through the overlapping of the world with the theater, of staging with reality), David's portraits provide the poses and objects Rohmer needs for the depiction of Giulietta and her mother. For instance, the Marquise's headband and the furniture in her room during the doctor's

FIGURE 23. The Oath of the Horatii (1786), by Jacques-Louis David. The Toledo Museum of Art, Toledo, Ohio.

FIGURE 24. Madame Récamier (1800), by Jacques-Louis David. Louvre, Paris. © Photo R.M.N.

FIGURE 25. *Young Woman Sewing by Lamplight (1828),*
by Georg Friedrich Kersting. Neue Pinakothek, Munich.

visit recall David's *Madame Récamier* (1800; fig. 24). For a touch of color,
emotion, or desire, Giulietta and her mother punctuate their simple clothing with a shawl, a long scarf, or a corset with a few, loose straps. Here
Rohmer's actresses bring to life David's *Elisabeth Bonaparte* and his *Madame de
Servan.*

Still, Rohmer is a French filmmaker directing German actors, so the
Napoleonic exuberance of David's portraiture is toned down by some ref-
erences to an early nineteenth-century Flemish Romantic, Georg Friedrich
Kersting, whose domestic scenes with women working in silence by them-
selves (*Young Woman Sewing by Lamplight*, 1828; fig. 25) or with whispering couples
(*Couple at the Window*, 1817) remind us that the politics of adaptation in *The
Marquise of O* are bound to overlay French with German sources.

In addition to David's celebration of ancient history, Jean-Baptiste

Greuze's scenes of domestic conflict, such as *The Paternal Curse* (1777–1778; fig. 26) and *The Punished Son* (1778), inspire Rohmer's rendering of the conflict between father and daughter and of Giulietta's impulsive rejection of the Count after his admission of guilt. Stretching arms up into the air, fainting, pleading, delivering ultimatums, and slamming doors lean dangerously toward either the tragic or the comic pole. Despite these excessive gestures and behaviors, which risk degenerating into sheer performance, a certain seriousness and genuine concern characterize the countenance of Rohmer's characters. They do not quite slide into irony or parody because they are sincere in what they feel or believe, even though social rules prevent them from revealing their darkest emotions and expressing their most secret doubts. Despite their overcivilized, stiff manner, they never completely identify with their public roles the way the family members do in Goya's *Family of Charles IV* (1800), with their extreme shrinking into an empty facade. The lives of Rohmer's characters, in fact, are punctuated by neoclassical busts, columns, statuettes, pilasters. These decorative objects are there to remind them of how they are supposed to behave, while making even wider the gap between ideals and realities, duty and impulse.

Greuze's blend of tones earned the approval of Denis Diderot, who found the painter's view of bourgeois life most sentimental, to be sure, but also pedagogically useful, especially after the immoralities and frivolities of François Boucher's mythological allegories and Jean-Honoré Fragonard's rococo seductions. For Diderot, Greuze's display of emotion was at the service of a neoclassical program of moral edification, since the painter's yes-and-no gestures were performed by characters modeled on classical statuary and on Hellenistic examples of lucid action and ennobling pathos worthy of a canvas by David.[28]

The extensive use of David's and Greuze's paintings calls attention to the moral norms by which Giulietta and her relatives live. On the other hand, a couple of references to Fragonard point to the passions that also exist under the innocent surface of family mores. Right before the rape, thanks to Nestor Almendros's skillful lighting, the accent of Fuseli's painting is on Giulietta's dazzling white gown, but next morning, when the Marquise and her father reunite, Giulietta's white figure seems to sink into an intense red curtain whose prominence recalls a similar bit of set design from Fragonard's *The Bolt* (1780; fig. 27). By embracing his daughter and saying, "I had to surrender, but my honor is safe," the father initiates the parallel between war and love that is also at the heart of Fragonard's *Storming the Citadel* (1771; fig. 28). In this painting a gallant suitor climbs over a wall to

FIGURE 26. The Paternal Curse (1777–1778), by Jean-Baptiste Greuze. Louvre, Paris. © Photo R.M.N.

FIGURE 27. The Bolt (1780), by Jean-Honoré Fragonard. Louvre, Paris. © Photo R.M.N.

FIGURE 28.
Storming the
Citadel (1771), by
Jean-Honoré Fragonard.
Frick Collection,
New York.

FIGURE 29.
The Count pursuing
the Marquise, in
The Marquise of O.
Film Stills Archive, The
Museum of Modern Art,
New York.

FIGURE 30. Garden Terrace *(1811–1812), by Caspar David Friedrich.*
Staatliche Schlösser und Gärten, Potsdam.

reach his beloved in the privacy of a garden, thus echoing the Count's viola-
tion of the boundaries of the Marquise's estate (fig. 29).

While Fragonard provides the iconography for Rohmer's depiction of
the Count pursuing the Marquise in her villa, the airy lighting and the open
space that envelop Giulietta are reminiscent of Caspar David Friedrich's
Garden Terrace (1811–1812), in which a woman reads alone under a tree in a
property surrounded by a wall (figs. 30 and 31). Once again, in a French film
based on a German novella, French sources coexist next to German ones.

Unlike in Rohmer's film, where the rape is eclipsed by the sleeping
potion, in *The Bolt* the disorder of the bed, a general atmosphere of negli-
gence and secrecy, and the voluptuousness of the folds in the red curtain
suggest what is about to happen between man and woman after the locking
of the door. Thus Rohmer's allusion to Fragonard's set design endows the
embrace between father and daughter with incestuous connotations. This
interpretation finds support in the father's unreasonable opposition to the
Count's proposal of marriage. Yet Rohmer avoids too mechanical a rendi-
tion of an Electra complex, preferring to measure the father's and the
daughter's incestuous behavior against the viewer's right to sit in judgment.
Through the mother's nightly tour of the house, Rohmer establishes a contrast between a rape that is not seen and an embrace between father and

FIGURE 31. *The Marquise reflecting on her pregnancy in the peacefulness of the park,* in The Marquise of O. *Film Stills Archive, The Museum of Modern Art, New York.*

daughter that is shown in all its affection. Like the Count checking on the welfare of his soldiers, the mother wanders from room to room with a candle, making sure that the beds are warm and the food is ready. The warm glow of faces and objects emerging from the dark, cozy domestic setting reminds us of Georges de la Tour's lighting method, while it prepares us for the erotic overtones surrounding the reconciliation of father with daughter. The Count's open, frontal gaze is replaced by the mother's peeping through a keyhole. As she watches her husband and daughter embrace, is she just another voyeur? The viewers (and the critics as well) must confront their own impurity of thought and feel slightly inadequate before such an unrestrained expression of family affection.

The pictorial allusions in the film reinforce the polarities of classical control and melodramatic expression, polite manners and illicit love. This dualistic approach also justifies Rohmer's use of Fuseli's *Nightmare,* for this is the painting that any standard survey of the history of art will cite to call attention to the founding dichotomy of the Napoleonic era—namely, an obscure feeling of unrest growing underneath the call to public morality. While Fuseli serves as lustful foil to postrevolutionary austerity, Eugène Delacroix, one of the most Byronic of Romantic painters, is the unexpected source of a neoclassical outline. In fact, Rohmer refashions the sensuous

FIGURE 32. The Death of Sardanapalus (1826), by Eugène Delacroix. Louvre, Paris. © Photo R.M.N.

profile of a female slave in *The Death of Sardanapalus* (1826; fig. 32) into a tense, curved pose that conveys the desperation of Giulietta's struggle against the Russian soldiers while also echoing the defiant pose of the swan.[29]

The effects of Fuseli's restless sleep reappear in the characters' anxious wanderings from location to location: the daughter and the mother travel to and fro between the father's house and the country estate; the son shuttles between his parents' quarters and his sister's rooms, and toward the end of the film, he returns to the inn where we had first encountered him; and most of all the Count—a Russian who speaks in German, fights in Italy, and looks like David's portrait of Napoleon—travels between Constantinople and Naples, between Naples and Saint Petersburg. All these journeys are movements of the soul. The psychological meaning of so many changes in location, however, acquires relief thanks to Rohmer's downplaying of the outside. We never see aspects of the town surrounding the Marquise's family. By contrast, inside Giulietta's house, the "carefully groomed and quarantined suburban spaces (gardens, parlors, vestibules, bedchambers, and dining rooms)"[30] hide a storm of feelings whose power can be seen in the overturned furniture we glimpse at a moment of crisis: the father resents the Count's conquest of the citadel and of his daughter; the mother is torn between condemning a pregnancy out of wedlock and hoping that her widowed daughter will remarry anyway; the Marquise herself is attracted to the Count but does not want to admit it.

Seeing Fuseli's *Nightmare* as the dark side of David's neoclassical style also explains Rohmer's allusions to Goya's war scenes at the beginning of a film about a pregnancy induced by Morpheus, the god of sleep. In depicting the conquest of the citadel, Rohmer, like Goya, avoids a grandiose scale, uses muted colors, includes plenty of smoke, prefers an eye-level view to a glorifying low angle, and, instead of equestrian groupings, shows tangles of bodies on the ground. Notorious for his realistic portrayal of suffering and death, the Spanish painter is most famous for an engraving entitled *The Sleep of Reason Produces Monsters* (1794–1799). Like Fuseli's *Nightmare*, this work was symptomatic of an increasing interest in the supernatural, the unconscious, and the horrific at the end of the Age of Reason. Rohmer, however, never refers directly to this specific engraving by Goya, perhaps because its oneiric theme could potentially break the film's subtle balance between a moralistic and a psychoanalytic pole and thus risk affirming the primacy of irrational instincts over conscious choices. Yet Rohmer's allusions to Goya's war scenes, memorable for their denunciation of the horrors of war, heighten the aura of absurdity and hallucination surrounding the most natural of phenomena: a pregnancy. In other words, the potential for Goya's inclusion among Rohmer's pictorial sources brings to fruition Kleist's biting social criticism by making us wonder about the logic of a society where giving birth is monstrous and making war is normal.

Rohmer's images make visible the invisible. In comparison with the rest of her family, the Marquise, who undergoes the most intense degree of stress, speaks very little. Despite her silence, we feel that we can nearly grasp the Marquise's thoughts, especially when we see her holding a paintbrush in midair, pacing her room with a small book in her hand, doing a little embroidery, or sitting in her garden in a halo of light. These moments of silent reflection and psychological intimacy are made most eloquent by the absence of music—an art form that for Rohmer combines the abstractions of literature and the sensuousness of the visual arts and that he consistently leaves out of his films in order to push to an extreme the dialectic of word and image, his use of painting as inner speech and of the word as theatrical prop. In *The Marquise of O*, the absence of music, besides facilitating the linking of the word to the eye and of the image to the ear, also produces an especially active role for the spectator, who is asked to fill in what is open or empty. In Giulietta's house, a huge but always silent harp tunes us to the sounds of the characters' thoughts.

Rohmer's emphasis on space makes the story seem to grow out of the architecture and decor of the house. Different kinds of seats—bergère, dagobert, recamier—record subtle changes in atmosphere. Frequent, box-like shots of corridors, doors, gates, windows, and walls set in motion a dynamic of open and closed, stable and fluid spaces, thus leading the viewer to wonder whether situations are about to resolve themselves or to become more complicated. In particular, the viewer's expectations or doubts are channeled across corridors or echoed by glimpses of larger rooms behind alcoves, door frames, and curtains. The mother has to go through a gate to reach Giulietta in the estate, and Giulietta is always separated from the Count and from her father by walls and doors.

Rohmer's architectural space is an abstract region where decorative elements do not seem to have much weight, while surfaces of pure colors—white, light blue, dark reds and dark greens, black and some gold—produce a pattern reminiscent of a canvas by Mondrian.[31] The characters' indecisions and changes of mind ring against a grid of colors that is as rational and clear as a theorem, while the partitions of space turn into overlapping lines of thought and dialogue. By avoiding the subjective point-of-view shot, Rohmer shoots entire conversations from the outside. His refusal to step into the mental space of a character is intended to show how external changes in space mark meaningful shifts in relationships that occur inside the actors, behind their surface behavior. Rohmer's geometry of the word makes us aware, for example, that the Count's first visit to his family is characterized by an alternation between at least three spaces: the conversation he conducts with his father, the exchange of looks he initiates with the rest of the family, and the family members' reactions to each other as they listen to the Count and his father speak.

The filmic space of *The Marquise of O* is characterized by such austerity that the few movements the camera makes acquire undeniable significance, if not deep emotional resonance. Rohmer mostly remains on the edges of the action; the nuances of the word orient and design the image from within. Yet two camera movements, in particular, achieve a mixed effect of visual and mental expansion. Horizontal pans and tracking shots are usually linked to the surface of family routines and societal norms, while vertical movements stand out for their intensity. The camera, for example, follows the Count and Giulietta down a narrow staircase into the cellar shortly after the soldiers' attempted rape. This downward motion haunts the rest of the film: it accompanies the Count to Giulietta's bed during his nocturnal visit, thus measuring the abyss of his violence. It follows Giulietta down the stairs in her home as she begins to entertain the first suspicions that she is pregnant. The vertical movement of the camera also outlines the handsome back of Leopardo, the coachman, to whom Giulietta and her mother, in a moment of lightheartedness, are attracted. Finally, during the wedding ceremony, Giulietta's gaze scans the vertical composition of a huge, baroque canvas depicting Lucifer's fall from Heaven. The most beautiful of angels turns into the most terrible of devils. But human beings, she has come to realize, have a nature in which good and evil are mixed; she begins to understand the limits of one-sided self-righteousness.

The dualistic nature of the Count may be seen as a metaphor for Rohmer's artful naturalness in his cinema. More than once Rohmer has defined himself as an "auteur-in-absentia" or a director whose signature springs from the effort to erase style as embellishment, vanity, and self-love. Rohmer's commitment to humility also explains his rejection of modernist abstract art, in which the subject is not the world seen but the artist's performance. This view of nonrepresentational, modern painting takes us back to the Count's lustful thoughts as he watches the Marquise sleep. In fact, an equally sinful moment seems to emerge from Rohmer's own words when he describes his response to Henri Matisse:

> Through the channel of the eyes, a drug was getting inside of me; a charm as irresistible as that of a musical phrase was taking me over; I was moving toward the highest, most violent pleasure which could be offered to sight; I was understanding, approving the uncontrolled pride of the modern painter, our religion of the trait, the touch, the signature. . . . But already, during the most intense stage of contemplation, a doubt was rising in my mind, not of the quality of this pleasure, but of the purity of my gaze: Was it innocently looking at the naked work? Wasn't it dwelling rather on the thick web which links this painting to a hundred thousand others by the same painter, by his contemporaries and predecessors? I thought I was appreciating as a connoisseur, yet I was admiring as a scholar. In fact, how could an innocent eye have been able to evaluate that painting? Probably it would have only seen in it infantilism and savagery.[32]

Here the impure primitivism of Matisse becomes the other side of the lustful thinking linked to Fuseli, and thus also points to the duality at the heart of Rohmer's method: painting as tableau with a classic conception, and painting as the cinematic "plan-tableau" built around Fuseli, where the spatial coincidence of painterly frame and cinematic framing guarantees the seamless conjunction of two distinct objects, screen and canvas, into an image as double-sided as the Count.

Put another way, as a director Rohmer, who practices adaptation as a form of unobtrusive intervention or quiet violence, oscillates between two extreme positions: the first one fits the Count as rapist and Matisse as self-absorbed performer of his own signature regardless of the world, whereas the second fits the role played by the silent servant who controls the household's space but also remains unnoticed in the background. Yet in a film where adaptation is comparable to a rape and the literary source is equivalent to a female body, Rohmer's struggle between mastery of the means at his disposal and humbleness in front of the world is never fully resolved, so the reconciliation of Giulietta with the Count never acquires the flavor of too easy a happy ending.

As we have seen *The Marquise of O* is a remarkable film not only because it expands our views on adaptation but also because it establishes that the dialectic of word and image is central to an understanding of the encounter between cinema and painting. Pictorial allusions proliferate in *The Marquise of O,* but instead of thickening the image, they make it lighter and simultaneously enrich it with the subtlest psychological nuances. Thus Rohmer, who condemns the arrogance of the nonrepresentational modernist art of Matisse, paradoxically works like an abstract painter: he achieves pictorialism by transforming painting into what cannot be seen, although it is spatially experienced or felt in the acting style, the use of colors, the architectural detail. On the other hand, it is as if the attributes of painting—shade, shape, size, and coloring—had been transferred to language. This displacement echoes the repression of painting as emotion and as a sensual sight, while painting itself reappears in the form of a pulsing logos, in clear contrast with the cool rationality of verbal wit. Rohmer relies on architecture to transform the screen into a mental space and on the theater to link it to the world outside through the mediation of the actors, living reminders of the profilmic event. Between these two extreme polarities of the world seen and of the thinking mind, Rohmer's cinematic style becomes as transparent as unstaged reality, the screen fades away, and the director disappears, leaving us, the viewers, with this reward for encountering painting in Rohmer's cinema: the pleasure of feeling through thought and a renewed level of visual attention to what surrounds us.

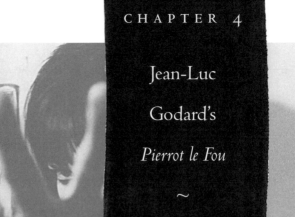

CHAPTER 4

Jean-Luc
Godard's
Pierrot le Fou

~

Cinema as

Collage

against

Painting

*S*hot in two months, during the summer of 1965, with hardly a script but two big stars (Jean-Paul Belmondo and Anna Karina), with only a few key locations in mind (Paris, southern France) and at a fast pace to make possible its premiere on August 29 at the Venice Film Festival, Jean-Luc Godard's *Pierrot le Fou* is truly a breathless film characterized by a pictorial use of color and a disjunctive montage. It coincides with the disintegration of the director's relationship with his wife, Anna Karina, while it marks the end of Godard's so-called existential phase, before the political upheavals of May 1968.

Godard's dialectical method and his taste for heterogeneity are well known. Alan Williams, for example, describes Godard as an "omnivorous" collector of literary and visual sources,[1] which in *Pierrot* range from high art to comic strips, from Pop Art to television broadcasts, and include all manner of written texts and book covers, anagrams and record jackets, neon signs and advertisements. Echoing Williams, Pierre Sorlin underlines Godard's delight in playing with the high and low registers of culture: "*Pierrot le Fou* was studded with elements such as colours, drawings or paintings, which were not related to the plot but which could be linked together because they shared some similarities. Godard used them to suggest that many combinations, many texts dealing with various aspects of art, were to be found in a film."[2]

Just as the cinema produces new combinations by reconfiguring opposite levels of culture, collage replaces the distinction between high and low with a structure in which each element is as important as the others. The advent of collage shattered into pieces a traditional view of art as something separate from life. In collage the frame does not regulate any longer what gets into the composition; life seems to hit the canvas and leave its traces in defiance of aesthetic norms and standards of good taste. Cultural historian Marjorie Perloff's description of collage fits well the narrative structure of Godard's film: "In collage, hierarchy gives way to parataxis— 'one corner is as important as another corner.' Which is to say that there is no longer a central ordering system."[3]

That *Pierrot* equates cinema with collage is confirmed by the advertisement used for the film, a paragraph structured like an inventory, or "parataxis," of references to the rest of the director's work: "*Pierrot le Fou* is: a little soldier (petit soldat) who finds out with contempt (mépris) that you have to live your life (vivre sa vie), that a woman is a woman (une femme est une femme), and that in a new world, you have to keep to yourself (faire bande à part) to not find yourself out of breath (à bout de souffle)."[4]

It is not surprising that Godard welcomes the iconography of Pop Art within the collage aesthetics of *Pierrot le Fou*, which in turn includes an array of industrial objects beloved by Pop Artists: cars, walkie-talkies, T-shirts, lipsticks, jukeboxes, and pinball machines. Although collage dates back to the various modernisms flourishing at the beginning of the twentieth century—Cubism, Dada, Surrealism—it is the world of Pop Art, with its mixing of high and low, reality and abstraction, that in the mid-sixties provided the stimulus for a renewal of interest in the meanings and effects of collage.

As a text *Pierrot le Fou* is thin, because its storyline develops in a chaotic manner, and thick, because it is crowded with allusions, and Godard's oscillations between these two extremes of all or nothing are in line with the workings of collage. There, many fragments accumulate, create density, while any sense of centering is lost. Yet the possibility of superintegration coexists with what Jean-Louis Leutrat calls "excentration." With objects from the world piercing the fabric of the fiction like meteorites, the narrative itself is about to unravel into many other potential stories and characters lurking at its borders. This inclination of *Pierrot le Fou* to develop into many different genres, ranging from love story to adventure tale to gangster film to comedy, resurfaces in the restless list that Marianne (Anna Karina) makes of possible places where she and Ferdinand (Jean-Paul Belmondo) could run to: Nice, Florence, Athens. The threat of disintegration, however, is kept in check because in collage, even though "the center has disappeared," there are still "series which state their differences all by themselves."[5] Leutrat's "series" apply well to the structure of the collage and to Godard's construction of the image, for in both cases, word, image, color, and line challenge each other over and over again without ever coalescing into a unified whole. Most important, the two series of Godard's collage in *Pierrot le Fou* underpinning the interaction of all the other elements are the polarities of sexual difference, the well-known scenario of the battle of the sexes, a theme the director uses for the title of the film he directed immediately after *Pierrot, Masculin/Féminin* (1966).

As a collage shuttling between high art and popular culture, *Pierrot le Fou* includes direct references to Diego Velázquez, a seventeenth-century Spanish painter, and to Samuel Fuller, a Hollywood director, because Godard must have felt that these two artists were interested, just as he was, in middle grounds and transitions, in what happens in the space between conflicting elements.

Right after the credits, we hear Ferdinand's voice offscreen, reading about Velázquez from Elie Faure's *History of Art*, a text that despite its lofty subject invokes popular culture right away. In fact, shortly before the shooting of *Pierrot*, Faure's work became a best-seller, or a "livre de poche," easily found in small-town bookstores all over France.[6]

While the combination of Faure with Velázquez functions as a reminder of high and low, the mention of a Spanish painter in a French film brings to mind Georges Bizet's opera *Carmen*, which, as Laura Mulvey explains, will become a source for Godard's 1982 film, *Prénom Carmen:*

> *Pierrot le Fou* was already a version of the *Carmen* story. That is, a story of *amour fou*, in which an essentially respectable and law-abiding hero is

seduced by an irresistible, unfaithful woman into a descent into an under-
world and a life of crime, on the run from the police. . . . In both cases,
amour fou leads to violence and a journey of crime, pursuit, and death
("Une saison en enfer").[7]

In *Pierrot*, as in the opera *Carmen*, a woman leads her lover to suicide, even
though Godard's Marianne and Ferdinand play out their destructive romance not in Spain but in the secluded and beautiful island of Porquerolles,
a resort not far from the city of Toulon.

Besides issues of high and low and geographical echoes of the famous
opera, Godard's choice of Faure's text on Velázquez throws light on how the
director, in the painter's footsteps, strives to depict what can be felt at an
emotional level but cannot quite be seen: a character's thoughts, the chemistry of a relationship, the flavor of a landscape, the atmosphere of a room,
the feeling of death creeping over objects and colors, and the ominous
weight of cars.

Sitting in a bathtub, surrounded by white blank walls, with a cigarette
arrogantly dangling from his lips, Ferdinand reads,

> After he reached the age of fifty, Velázquez no longer painted anything
> concrete and precise. He drifted through the material world, penetrating it,
> as the air and the dusk. In the shimmering of shadows, he caught unawares
> the nuances of colour which he transformed into the invisible heart of his
> symphony of silence. . . . His only experience of the world was those
> mysterious copulations which united the forms and tones with a secret, but
> inevitable movement, which no convulsion or cataclysm could ever interrupt
> or impede. Space reigned supreme. . . . It was as if some tenuous radiation
> gliding over the surfaces, imbued itself of their visible emanations, model-
> ling them and endowing them with form, carrying elsewhere a perfume, like
> an echo, which would thus be dispersed like an imponderable dusk, over all
> surrounding planes.[8]

The painter's emphasis on space between forms sets the stakes for the director who in 1965 stated, "It seems to me the greatest problem in filming is
to decide where and why to begin a shot and where and why to end it."[9] Just
as Velázquez at the end of his career moved away from classical, representational painting toward a more abstract depiction of colors, forms, tones,
spatial nuances, surfaces, and echoes, Godard's ambition is to film what

separates high and low, a man from a woman, through the dialectic of word and image, of onscreen and offscreen space, of loud noises and musical voices, of jump cuts and long takes. Put another way, "Godard's aim is to see the boundaries, . . . to make the imperceptible visible."[10] Godard is interested in images that disclose feelings, and collage, by virtue of its accumulation of fragments and lack of hierarchy, generates a dynamic that emphasizes contrasts in textures, tones, and shapes and thus evokes what is not there, or what simply exists in an intangible, unrepresentable manner.

If *Pierrot* is instructive about collage, collage itself tells us a great deal about the nature of the image for Godard, who in turn finds a definition of his cinema in a statement delivered by Sam Fuller, playing himself as an American director who is in Paris to film *The Flowers of Evil.* Asked by Ferdinand to explain what cinema is all about, Fuller replies by using a metaphor that captures the dynamics of collage: "Film is like a battleground." He then goes on to list the contenders in this battle: "Love. Hate. Action. Violence. Death. In one word, Emotion." Fuller's statement immediately brings to mind his *Pick-Up on South Street* (1953), in which the battle of the sexes not only looks like a boxing match but also sets in motion and charges emotionally all the rest of the mise-en-scène.

Fuller's view of the cinema is delivered through the agency of a young woman. She translates from English into French for Ferdinand, who stands between her and the American director. Ferdinand's rhythmic turning of the head between the two guests and the two languages recalls the back-and-forth trajectory of a ball during the tennis game seen immediately after the credits. This understanding of translation as tennis across different languages or artistic media clarifies Godard's own definition of the cinema as a transforming mirror where shapes become letters, letters become words, words become objects, objects in turn become shapes again.[11]

Since cinema is a collage in which a battle between man and woman and among various elements or competing registers unfolds, the question arises as to who is the winner. For Godard, indeed, the best image is one that does not remain limited to the visual register but can always undo itself by turning into something else. In Velázquez's wake, Godard too strives to move beyond the corporeal materiality of the image for the sake of an interest in echoes and nuances. Thus, the fantasy at the heart of *Pierrot* is the possibility of overcoming sexual difference as well as the boundary between the verbal and the visual poles.

Paradoxically, it is as if the motto of *Pierrot,* a film replete with art-historical allusions, were in Godard's own words utterly antivisual: "The urgency to describe it with language!" In a sense, just as collage (with its mixing of daily debris and aesthetic elements) exists in opposition to painting (high art framed away from life), Godard's cinema, despite its visual energy and the brilliant colors of Pop Art, is driven by a logocentric vocation, or a love for language in all its manifestations: alphabetical and literary, graphic and acoustic.[12]

Most important, the victory of the word over the image stems from what Richard Roud calls Godard's "puritanical"[13] sensibility, an attitude possibly linked to the Swiss Calvinist background of the director's family. This is perhaps why *Pierrot le Fou* is marked by an unusual sense (for a film) of physical chastity: when Ferdinand wakes up in Marianne's apartment after spending the night there, we sense that something about the sexual body has been elided from our vision. Likewise, when Ferdinand walks by a woman with bare breasts at a party, the camera records the situation with complete indifference. Somehow in *Pierrot* Godard tries hard to dissociate the cinematic image from the spectacle of the female body. Godard's project to bypass the body erotic as woman and as image points back to his struggle in *Vivre sa vie* (1962), in which he tried to achieve a cinematic portrait of the loved woman, Anna Karina, by using verbal interviews, philosophical conversations, chapter headings, letter writing, and reading of literary texts aloud. Yet portraits in film or films conceived as portraits—precisely because this genre of painting exists in opposition to collage and is associated with the ideal values of art and beauty—always signify a loss: "A painted portrait in a film reminds us that love results from framing, from a flashing fetishization, without duration."[14]

Significantly, by allowing the debris of daily life to deposit itself onto its surface composition and by preferring an abstract arrangement over a figurative one, collage blows to pieces the portrait's ambition to idealize the sitter without giving up resemblance.[15] As a filmmaker Godard seems to have understood the lesson taught by collage on the limitations of painting. He knows that portraiture of man and woman together in film is doomed to failure. Even if woman is the most sought image, cinema can never quite grasp her. Thus Godard's awareness of sexual difference as something unrepresentable in visual terms alone finds an adequate outlet of expression only in his use of the screen as a battleground between word and image, line and color. By spelling out the crisis of traditional art, collage enables Godard to stage the confrontation of man and woman until heterogeneous combinations of signs break through their boundaries and become poetry, and maybe even love. In other words, collage is Godard's method, but emotion is his goal, for by pushing to the limit of signification all the components of his cinema—image, sound, movement, line, color, editing, scale—the director does not simply strive for a specific style based on discontinuity and transformations, plastic details and glimpses of abstraction, but he also wants to show how the effect of a poem cannot be reduced to any one of its components.

Narrative Structure

Just as the organization of collage is based on parataxis rather than hierarchy, the narrative structure of *Pierrot* does not depend on a causal chain but rather amounts to a series of tableaux that rhyme with one another. The ending of the film, for instance, takes us full circle to the opening credits. After a long shot of Ferdinand alone on a cliff, the camera pans slowly toward the calm open sea. He has killed Marianne, and now he blows himself up with dynamite. As a result of the explosion, the luscious landscape of southern France seems to deny itself in favor of an abstract, newly found space made only of water and clouds. Now that image, colors, and shapes are all gone, we can hear at last Marianne and Ferdinand whispering together across the horizon a few lines from Arthur Rimbaud's poetry:

> MARIANNE OFF: She's found again . . .
> FERDINAND OFF: What?
> MARIANNE OFF: Eternity.
> FERDINAND OFF: It is the sea . . . run away . . .
> MARIANNE OFF: With the sun . . .

Perhaps she has become the sea, he is now the sun, and they have run away together to the end of time. A sense of organic fusion between heaven and earth marks this reunification of the couple in a place we cannot see but only imagine through the agency of the two voices, without bodies, speaking from beyond the screen.

At the end of a film about miscommunication between man and woman, it is possible to use language again. Yet this was not the case at the beginning of *Pierrot*, when instead of hearing sentences of love spoken against the sunlight, we would only see a black screen with a scattering of red and blue letters in isolation. Rimbaud's poetry about eternity at the end strikes a note of contrast with an initial image of the alphabet in a state of disarray.

To be sure, Godard refers to Rimbaud not only at the conclusion of *Pierrot* but also earlier on, when a portrait of the *poète maudit* provides one more example of the tension between speaking and picturing, the sounds of language and the muteness of colors. In the opening credits the letters of the alphabet are isolated units with only graphic or chromatic values rather than linguistic or phonetic ones, since only music and no dialogue accompanies this tableau. Later we are reminded of how the film started as soon as we spot colored vowels marking Rimbaud's face—as if he had a disease some might call aphasia, a speaking block based on the inability to organize the linguistic chain. Thus the draining of sound out of language through the silence of the colors escalates into a scattering of the alphabet across a portrait. Collage has already begun to rearrange an image that by definition claims to capture someone's personality as a coherent whole.

More specifically, the design of the credits and the poet's portrait produce an eloquent summary of the director's method, which is based on bold redistribution and irreverent conjugation of competing sign systems. Thus Godard disassembles language into images and makes language out of images. This is why the camera fawns over the body of letters composing wall graffiti and neon signs like OASIS and RIVIERA. Even though Marianne and Ferdinand encounter death on the Riviera, its sign becomes VIE, while the first sign, by breaking down into red OAS and blue IS, uses the contrast in color to signal the dissolution of the couple.

At first sight it may seem that the beginning and the ending of *Pierrot* are meant only to establish the difficulties or the boundaries of communication. Yet a more optimistic reading is also possible. Both the credits and the final sequence are empty spaces out of which something new and unregimented is struggling to be born. In a sense the black screen and the wide open sea are echoed in the blank white walls of Marianne's apartment and of Ferdinand's bathroom. The bedroom Ferdinand shares with his wife has wallpaper and velvet upholstery, gilded frames and thick draperies. By contrast, Marianne's living space resembles a campsite, with pots and pans, suitcases, and guns thrown around as if she had just moved in or was about to move out.

Ferdinand's departure with Marianne for the South is an attempt to

FIGURE 33. *Anna Karina and Jean-Paul Belmondo as fugitive lovers, in* Pierrot le Fou *(directed by Jean-Luc Godard, 1965). Film Stills Archive, The Museum of Modern Art, New York.*

leave traditions and conventions behind (fig. 33). Their hope is to find happiness by reinventing love, but this requires a break with a personal past as well as with the history of the cinema. Significantly, the darkness of the night, with red, yellow, white, and blue reflections of neon lights gliding across the car's glass, witnesses the couple's first amorous dialogue. Indeed we understand that Marianne and Ferdinand, who had been previously involved with each other, are falling in love again as soon as they begin to play with language in talking to each other—not after they have spent the night together in Marianne's apartment. Somehow language is a better carrier of love than the body, whose appearance cannot change, rooted as it is in the difference between the sexes. During the reunited couple's nocturnal drive, the reappearance of the iconography and the atmosphere of the credits underscores their decision to start a new chapter together. Their reunification thrives with all the energy of a clean start, an empty space, despite the romantic failures of the past. "Centuries after centuries plunged into the distance like tempests," says Marianne's voice offscreen, over an empty sky with a few clouds. This blank, immaterial landscape, however, easily fills up with all the accoutrements of civilization: telephone poles, road signs, and the ever-present car that the couple tries repeatedly to get rid of, as if it were a bad habit, while constantly resorting to its use once again.

This sense of rupture or starting over explains why Godard has always discussed *Pierrot* as the antithesis of Luchino Visconti's *Senso* (1954).[16] In his film Visconti repeatedly emphasizes the need to establish a relation between figure and ground. Thus characters are unable to break away from the past because their bodies cannot be severed from their contexts. In *Pierrot* Godard borrows Visconti's feeling of being trapped in the decor only to comment on Ferdinand's stifling relationship with his Italian wife. Their marriage is as airless and as stagnant as the atmosphere of their bedroom, where the walls are overwrought with tapestries and stuccos, velvets and paintings. By contrast, in Marianne's apartment, the art posters glued to the walls are either too small to be easily compared with the characters' postures or, through the use of flash shots, they take over the whole screen, thus exploding any sense of hierarchy between what is decorative commentary and what is a fundamental element of the mise-en-scène. When a wide-angle, distorted close-up of a murderous midget pointing a pistol at the camera is followed by an exterior long shot of a skyscraper, the foreground becomes disproportionately huge in relation to the background. It is as if in *Pierrot* the relation between figure and ground has gone out of control, in order to underline how Marianne and Ferdinand do not fit the world they live in.

Besides this existential argument, there are other ways of explaining why Godard upsets the relation between figure and ground by using montage to paste together macroscopic with microscopic images. First of all, these abrupt switches in scale remind us of the decoupage of comic strips. Second, changing proportions is a typical tactic of Pop Art, in which, according to Roland Barthes, objects are neither metaphoric nor metonymic; rather, they present themselves as if they were cut off from sources and surroundings.[17] Outside any context, they simply are archetypes of banality endowed with the implacable strength of routine. Set against white walls or blank surfaces, the art-historical citations on Marianne's walls are not only posters but also Pop Art objects. Finally, besides recalling comic strips and Pop Art, disruptions at the level of size take on a surrealistic flavor, for the dislocation of objects and their erratic positioning in collage are meant to release the mysterious core of daily debris. A child's red go-cart, for instance, threateningly blocks the foyer of Ferdinand's elegant apartment. Another example of surrealistic displacement occurs when a huge black car looms in the middle of a bar where the protagonist meets a nameless individual who reminds him of an affair Ferdinand must have had with the man's wife the year before.

The aura of uncertainty released by the empty spaces between the letters of the credits, and the promise of the sea to host a rebirth from beyond the line of the horizon, can be juxtaposed with Godard's insistent use of empty, open frames to signify the negative dissolution or the positive merging of the self into water, sand, and nature. For instance, Ferdinand drives a stolen car into the deep water of a river; he and Marianne become microscopic dots amid expanding cornfields. Their feet and hands emerge one by one out of a thick blanket of sand that covers their entire bodies. For a moment they resemble fantastic creatures exploring the surface of the world with their extremities. The landscape seems to swallow the couple in a protective embrace, which in turn could easily become a form of drowning or suffocation. From time to time Marianne and Ferdinand disappear into the thick vegetation of the island where they finally settle down.

Color and Line, Word and Image, Male and Female

In his essay on collage, the art historian Donald Kuspit argues that this artistic form hardly ever congeals into a synthesis, while patterns of line or color dabs help to establish tentative relations among incoherent fragments from the world.[18] Furthermore, on the relation between verbal and visual elements in collage, Perloff writes, "In Picasso's collage, the image is constantly being read as something else: the "URNAL" of "(J)OURNAL" suggests "URINAL," the violin shape looks like a female torso, the wine glass embedded in the newsprint is also a man reading a newspaper. Transformation is central to the process."[19] The transformative orientation that Perloff attributes to words and images in collage also applies to Godard's handling of line and color in *Pierrot le Fou*, in which the connotations of these two elements often shift to underscore the tension between the sexes.

As the equivalent of line in collage, screen movements are an important aspect of Godard's construction of character in *Pierrot le Fou*. Film critic José-Luis Guarner comments on the anarchic quality of Belmondo's pattern of movement: "He seeks liberty through illogicality: . . . leaving the straight line and taking the curve to drive his car into the sea, walking along the middle of a river instead of along the bank, entering a dancing club through the window."[20] Guarner, however, forgets to mention that when

Marianne and Ferdinand are in the woods, he walks in a straight line while she dances around him. The last time he sees her, Ferdinand tries to understand what has happened to them through counting.[21] By contrast, when she exercises on the beach with a group of dancers who are dressed like mercenaries, she seems to generate the curvilinear trajectory of Henri Matisse's *Dance* (1909). By taking advantage of the tendency in collage to read the image of a word "as something else," Godard here reverses one character's pattern of behavior into another's, as if these exchanges were meant to contain the miscommunication between man and woman.

To be precise, Belmondo's character is torn between linearity and incoherence. An avid reader of novels, he thrives on the ordered development of events typical of realist fiction. Through an allusion to *César Birotteau,* a tale of financial ups and downs, Honoré de Balzac's legacy lives on during a party where Ferdinand observes guests speaking to each other in the language of advertising. While Ferdinand wants life to achieve the well-balanced architecture of a nineteenth-century novel, Marianne is much more in tune with the ever-changing configurations of modern life. Ferdinand's commitment to classical literary models, however, is not rigid. In Ferdinand's literary pantheon—as well as in Godard's catalogue of citations—there is room for Louis-Ferdinand Céline, who challenged the coherence of the traditional novel in *Voyage au bout de la nuit* and in *Guignol's Band.* In particular Godard's sound track imitates Céline's mixing of verbal idioms, speech patterns, and linguistic styles, for the director creates a patchwork of intermittent music, monologues, repetition of lines, and poignant silence. Needless to say, the acoustic collages of *Pierrot le Fou* want to become poetry as well, by capitalizing on the evocative power of different textures in collision with each other.

In Ferdinand's diary, the red lettering of Marianne's name undergoes a series of permutations that match the linguistic creativity at the heart of James Joyce's *Finnegans Wake:* Arianne, Mer, Ame, Amer, and Arme. Somehow this anagrammatic treatment of the word "Marianne" takes us back to the aestheticizing function of the line in collage. For if Ferdinand oscillates between a clear sense of direction and total disorientation, language stops referring to the people and objects in the world in order to function, instead, like a red thread woven across Godard's film, linking the sea, the guns, the soul, the labyrinth where Theseus follows Arianne, American imperialism, and a feeling of bitterness, which anticipates the price one must pay to find eternity.

Ferdinand's nostalgia for the days when the linearities of literature seemed capable of guaranteeing a certain order in life is counterbalanced by Godard's preference for arbitrary sequences and abrupt interruptions. Although *Pierrot le Fou* is divided into chapters, just like a traditional novel, chapter 7 follows chapter 8. As Robert Stam remarks, "The chapter titles . . . have neither parallelism nor coherence. They mix numbers (Chapter 12) with general rubrics ('Désespoir') and plot résumés ('Nous traversons la France'). . . . The gratuitous consecution of 'chapitre suivant' is followed by the even more gratuitous 'chapitre suivant sans titre.'"[22] Godard himself has pointed out that the rhythm of *Pierrot le Fou* is meant to mimic American television: "There one doesn't just watch a film from beginning to end; one sees fifteen shows at the same time while doing something else, not to mention the commercials."[23]

In addition to line, color is another element of collage that invites the viewer's eye to establish tentative connections across disjointed parts. In particular, Marianne's constant use of different clothes—sometimes red, sometimes white, sometimes the two colors combined—heightens our sense that a collage can become a kaleidoscope of chromatic effects. In addition, these unmotivated and sudden changes of costume replace the alternation of smooth and rough surfaces in collage, in which changes in materials all by themselves can add a new spin to the whole ensemble.

To be sure, *Pierrot le Fou* derives its aura of mystery from the fact that colors tell a story the characters are never aware of or quite in control of. This is especially true of the use of blue as a shifting marker of approaching death, male identity, and national origin. During the party sequence Ferdinand, standing inside a blue monochrome frame, describes his splintered self in a way that underlines how the series of word, image, color, and line has become hopelessly autonomous in the collage of contemporary life: "I have a mechanism for seeing, called eyes, for listening, called ears, for speaking, called mouth. I've got a feeling they are all going their separate ways." Here Ferdinand echoes Rimbaud's "dérèglement de tous les sens," an experience of perceptual dispersal that well conveys the intricate, unstable nature of intertextuality in *Pierrot le Fou.*

Ferdinand's little daughter wears a white dress with a blue border on the collar. Perhaps the child's colors speak of the future her father will find after painting his face blue and blowing himself up on the white sea. Blue also participates in a larger chain of colors: red, yellow, and blue in the towel Ferdinand uses after taking a bath, and in the sticks of dynamite he ties around his face. Red, yellow, and blue are primary colors, which by existing outside any combination and on a comparable footing with primary surfaces, such as the white sea or the black screen, underscore the characters' journey toward a liminal space, where they can be either swallowed by the past or propelled into the future.

While belonging to a discursive chain about history, blue is also one of the colors shared by the American and the French flags, along with red and white. Of course, the confusion at the level of color between France and America takes us back to Godard's *Breathless* (1960). There an American girl (Jean Seberg) looks like the young woman in Pierre-Auguste Renoir's *Mlle Irène Cahen d'Anvers* (1880), and Renoir's portraiture reappears in *Pierrot* as a term of comparison for the French actress Anna Karina when she becomes the girl in *La petite fille à la gerbe* (1888). If colors destabilize national identity by virtue of their easy transfer from one metonymic chain to the next, Godard's female protagonists are also difficult to pin down as soon as the different nationalities of Seberg and Karina are reduced to the common denominator of Renoir's paintings depicting other women we hardly know and that forever escape our grasp into other images of femininity, which in turn tell us little about the sitters themselves but much more about men's anxiety to fix their ideal woman by making her an icon of high art.

Most important, red, white, and blue—as well as red, yellow, and blue—link *Pierrot le Fou* to a painterly tradition with a Fauve taste shared by Pierre-Albert Marquet, Raoul Dufy, and Henri-Charles Manguin, all of them specializing in village life, national holidays, and coastal scenes comparable to the small towns and the island exoticism that we glimpse in Godard's film.[24] With the Fauvists, colors are flat and hard, simple and primitive. In a sense these painters establish a precedent for the highly saturated and artificial palette of Pop Art. As Roland Barthes explains, Pop Art's plastics and acrylics, lacquers and metals, "seek to cut short desire, emotion: we might say, at the limit, that they have a moral meaning, or at least they systematically rely on a certain frustration"[25] (fig. 34). Put another way, color in *Pierrot*'s Pop Art is both aggressive with its demands and helpless in its results to the extent that it communicates without success an endless need for love, while the exchange between man and woman remains static and frozen inside well-defined activities conducted in isolation. Ferdinand writes his diary, while Marianne walks alone on the beach.

Thus, were we to graft color onto sexual identity, blue belongs to Ferdinand in the sense that it defines him as separate from his wife in red,

FIGURE 34. Drowning Girl *(1963)*, by *Roy Lichtenstein. The Museum of Modern Art, New York. Philip Johnson Fund and gift of Mr. and Mrs. Bagley Wright. Photograph © 1994 The Museum of Modern Art, New York.*

or from another woman also in red, out of a Za La Mort comic strip, which in turn echoes Roy Lichtenstein's adoption of a popular-culture style in his painting. Marianne, who represents both freedom and destruction, puts on a white dress, behind a red folding screen. She will take Ferdinand to the white sea, but just like his wife, she will be obsessed with money and will hate Ferdinand for having burned a suitcase full of bank notes. Their two colors, blue for Ferdinand and red for Marianne, are ironically reversed during their last encounter as a couple, when he sits in a red car and she occupies a blue one.

Indeed, the red of blood haunts the film in positive and negative ways. Red brings out the passionately desperate core of Godard's tale. According to the surrealist Louis Aragon, writing on *Pierrot le Fou*, red looks back at Eugène Delacroix's Romantic painting. Aragon's insight finds a certain resonance in the very romantic ingredients of Godard's narrative—love, death, and betrayal—and also in the film's setting, southern France, which summons the tradition of medieval romances: "the blood of the *Massacres de Scio*, the blood of *La Mort de Sardanapale*, the blood of July 1830, their children's blood that will be shed in the three *Médée furieuse* paintings (the one from 1838 and the ones from 1859 and 1862), all the blood that covers the lions and tigers in their battle with horses."[26] Red as blood also painfully confirms Faure's remark on Velázquez that "space reigns supreme" to the point of degenerating into emptiness. Hence the color red widens the gap between man and woman. Meanwhile an allusion to Pablo Picasso's *Lovers* (1923) and the techniscope image of *Pierrot le Fou*, two 1:1 squares, assert that the film is about being one on one; that is, Godard's story deals with the painful formation of the couple. The theme of red as distance, however, is counterbalanced by a white boat with a red rim that leads to the blood on Marianne's pallid face. Furthermore, on his way to the party in monochrome tableaux, Ferdinand wears a red tie, whereas Marianne, in her role of baby-sitter, has put on a dark blue jacket.

Color separates but also ties together the two protagonists, thus echoing a similar economy of juxtaposition and exchange across male and female at work in Godard's dialectic use of word and image. Godard's grafting of color onto sexual difference recalls how in collage the commutation of word into image and vice versa may suggest the possibility of communication between two elements without ever achieving it. Feminist theorist Janet Bergstrom eloquently summarizes this dialectic: "Godard's heroes want to identify with the woman, or with the feminine. And the woman, insofar as she is desirable, is by definition in his films unknowable; the omnipresent theme of communication, much less commutation, is not possible between masculine/feminine."[27] Language between Godard's two characters repeatedly fails to take the shape of a conversation. In the car, on the night when they declare their love for one another, they do not quite communicate but rather use words in a creative fashion as if they were thinking out loud by themselves. Needless to say, they also misunderstand each other. Among the trees Marianne sings, "Ma ligne de chance," but Ferdinand answers, "Ta ligne de hanche." Besides soliloquy prevailing over genuine verbal exchange, small narratives embedded in the larger narrative raise questions about the nature of the space or the gap between Marianne and Ferdinand.

Marianne, for instance, tells Ferdinand a story about her parents, who could not bear the thought of separating from each other.

Kuspit proposes that collage is "a mockery of conventional conceptions of art-making."[28] If it is hard to take collage seriously as high art, collage in turn calls into question the whole idea of art as imitation of nature. This attack against mimesis leads to Godard's self-conscious use of language and distancing techniques. Ferdinand and Marianne either look at or speak to the camera, while new individuals walk into the film in the wake of an interview. We temporarily meet a Lebanese princess who raves about her past vicissitudes on a dock by the sea, a student who is also a political refugee, an extra in the film industry, a young woman who sells perfumes in a department store. In particular, these last three characters reinforce the interview framework by declaring their anagraphic generalities. Thus they make us wonder, how much or how little do we really know about Marianne and Ferdinand as individuals, and how did they ever come into a position of prominence in the film? Godard knows all too well how the fragmentation of modern life undermines our belief in persons as cohesive entities. His cinema, therefore, highlights the discrepancies or the interstices between body and costuming, language and behavior. As we learn from a cameo appearance by Jean Seberg, who points a movie camera at Ferdinand as he sits in the darkness of a movie theater, "We are carefully looking for . . . that moment when one abandons the fictional character in order to discover the true one . . . if such a thing exists."

Even though great distance seems to accumulate between Marianne and Ferdinand, Godard's montage and camera movement never cease to establish analogies among disparate elements. The director's method bears witness to what F. T. Marinetti has described as the power of collage to assemble "distant, seemingly diverse and hostile things" in the name of a "deep love."[29] Most important, the two themes—of potentially hostile components thrown together and of a sudden attraction between elements that according to the rules of society and art should not blend—are at the heart of the etymology of collage, since the verb *coller* means not only "to glue together" but is also a colloquialism for "to have an illicit love affair." Inasmuch as the couple threatens to disintegrate, collage as romance, or to use Fuller's word, cinema as "emotion," keeps alive a flicker of hope in harmony and integration. This striving toward unity through a series of alternations and repetitions becomes particularly clear in the scene when Marianne and Ferdinand leave the apartment. T. Jefferson Kline comments,

FIGURE 35. Girl before a Mirror *(1932)*, *by Pablo Picasso. The Museum of Modern Art, New York. Gift of Mrs. Simon Guggenheim. Photograph © 1994 The Museum of Modern Art, New York.*

Godard has Belmondo and Karina articulate the voice-over narration, alternating every other word. Then images begin to be repeated, but not quite, suggesting not only that visual linearity has been forsaken but also that visual reliability has been compromised. It is as if the camera is trying to "get it right" by repeating their flight from this apartment in a variety of slightly different takes.[30]

FIGURE 36. The Roumanian Blouse *(1940), by Henri Matisse. Centre Georges Pompidou, Paris.*

Even if Marianne and Ferdinand are unable to produce a conversation, to master a dialogue, their respective means of expression, ranging from word to image, from dance to writing, seem to chase one another relentlessly, as if each medium were aware of its incompleteness and needed to gain from the encounter with a different form. This is why the film ends with a broken sentence, while the camera continues to pan on the sea, asking us to decide whether for Godard a collage should end with an image taking over life or with an unfinished sentence pointing to life out there.

Subjectivity: Collage as the Anti-Portrait

Kline has observed that most of the paintings cited by Godard in *Pierrot le Fou* are portraits by Renoir, Picasso (fig. 35), Modigliani, Matisse (fig. 36), and Georges Rouault. Such an emphasis on portraiture provides an ironic counterpoint to Godard's depiction of subjectivity in crisis. As soon as we see Ferdinand shopping for paperbacks at a bookstore called Le Meilleur des Mondes, we understand through this allusion to Voltaire's *Candide* that the portrait, as a statement on the representability of the self, does not hold any longer in the modern world. As Kline explains, Voltaire produced "one of the first works of the French Enlightenment to challenge the predominant Anglo-Saxon view of the world as a coherent system, made in the image of God."[31] It is as if the colorful fireworks punctuating the black Parisian sky of *Pierrot le Fou* had blown up the whole genre of the portrait and replaced it with the incoherent fragments of collage. That the portrait has reached the end of its life span is also suggested by a reference to Van Gogh's *Café by Night*, which depicts the last place visited by the painter before his self-inflicted mutilation and painful disfigurement.

Instead of reminding us of the image of God, a portrait by Picasso, *Jacqueline aux fleurs* (1954), appears upside down as if, on its way to disintegration, it had absorbed all the violence of the comic strips Ferdinand constantly reads and of the gangsters who chase him relentlessly. During an interview, Godard himself comments on how portraiture is exactly what all representation would like to become, while the portrait itself confirms that the self is unrepresentable: "I read something by Borges where he spoke of a man who wanted to create a world. So he created houses, provinces, valleys, rivers, tools, fish, lovers, and then at the end of his life he notices that this 'patient labyrinth is none other than his own portrait.'"[32] Borges's man plays at being God, but unlike God he cannot produce a clear image.

The view of the portrait as a labyrinth also applies to the contradictory identity of most of the characters: Marianne could be either a baby-sitter or a call-girl. Fred, whom Marianne claims as her brother, is really her lover; although he works for TV Montecarlo, he is also involved in smuggling weapons to African countries. Ferdinand used to teach Spanish and could get a job in the corporate world, but he really would like to become a writer. Most important, he does not even have a stable name, for Marianne starts calling him Pierrot as soon as she finds out that he would like life to match art. Interestingly, "Pierrot le Fou" was the nickname of a famous French gangster,[33] whereas "Ferdinand" was the name of the king of Spain in the days of Velázquez. Needless to say, "Ferdinand" is not a name but a crossroad of literary, art-historical, and cinematic allusions:[34] when we see Belmondo in *Pierrot* wearing a gangster's suit, we compare him to Marianne's brother, Fred, to Michel Poiccard as Humphrey Bogart in *Breathless,* and to Julien Duvivier's *Pépé le Moko* (a 1937 film about an outcast played by Jean Gabin, which Godard takes pains to refer to). If names do not stabilize characters, their choices lead to unpredictable outcomes so that life appears to be a web out of control. To avoid self-destruction, Ferdinand leaves his wife for another woman, who, however, leads him toward death. This tragic development of events justifies one more reference to Jean Renoir's *La Chienne* (1931), the story of an affair in which both mistress and wife take advantage of the male protagonist.

Ferdinand/Pierrot is a residue of the theme of the doppelgänger. The theme of the double seduces us, at least for a moment, with the ambition of the portrait to function like a mirror. In a world dominated by mass media, however, all differences between the original and copy have disappeared. The last flicker of individuality applies not even to characters, but only to cars, which Marianne avidly distinguishes by brand name: Alfa-Romeo, Sedan, Ford Galaxie, Lincoln, Bentley. In recounting a short story by Edgar Allan Poe, Ferdinand explains that William Wilson ended up killing himself by mistake, for he was unable to distinguish his own Self from his Other. The desperation of this situation, in which the image is the stereotype and the stereotype is the image, emerges from a monologue delivered by Belmondo, when, standing in the middle of a cornfield, he declares, "We live in the Age of the Double-Man."

The serialization of the self has become so extreme that mirrors reflect nothing but only look like obsolete objects as soon as their power is tested against Andy Warhol's hyperaccurate reproductions of popular-culture icons, ranging from Campbell's soup to Marilyn Monroe. Indeed, Ferdinand's awareness that everything has its haunting replica fits Pop Art's obsessive practice of multiplying the same image until, as Roland Barthes remarks, "the Double is harmless, has lost all maleficent or moral power, neither threatens nor haunts: the Double is a Copy, not a Shadow: *beside,* not *behind:* a flat, insignificant, hence irreligious Double."[35] Thus, Pierrot is not even the true yet hidden Ferdinand, but only an additional, banal version, one circulating as sheer surface with neither substance nor "behind," one just like other innumerable, disposable objects in a world of restless stimuli paradoxically inducing a sense of numbness.

Precisely because the portrait has become a collage, characters long for the steady identities enjoyed by the heroes of classic American cinema. Marianne borrows a trick from Laurel and Hardy to knock out a gas station attendant, and Ferdinand flings cream pies in the guests' faces at the monochrome party. When Ferdinand and Marianne steal a big American car, their choreographed energy and playful circumspection bring to mind the mathematical precision of the actors' movements in a Mack Sennett comedy. Yet it never becomes clear whether these references to Hollywood are meant to show how creative the characters can be with popular culture or how unimaginative they have become as a result of their enslavement to mass media. For instance, when Ferdinand says to the attendant of a gas station, "Put a tiger in the tank," he parodies but also perpetuates a well-known television commercial. This dilemma of originality and repetition is also at work in Picasso's collages, which suggest how the highly clichéd language of the mass media is the only language available for a renewal of expression.[36]

That Godard's characters are split becomes apparent when Marianne tries to bring some cohesiveness to her own self-image and to Ferdinand through language. While they are both staring into the car mirror, she does offer him a definition of who she is in relation to him, yet her words evoke James Dean, one of the most troubled stars of American cinema: "Well, I can see the face of a woman who is in love with a man who is just about to throw himself over a precipice at a hundred miles an hour." Thus, instead of producing coherence and unity, language in the end only makes apparent the gap between speaking and acting, thought and gesture, intention and action. Although Marianne says, "I'll put my hand on your knee," she remains immobile. Caught as they are between taking an initiative and a tragic sense of impotence, Godard's characters seem to rehearse the Sartrean notion that free choice is always mingled with an inevitable destiny. After choosing suicide, Ferdinand/Pierrot tries to put out the fire that he has lit and that is now moving toward the dynamite, but, of course, it is too late.

At first sight it may seem that when the portrait is disassembled into a collage, Godard's balance sheet will inevitably yield a note of pessimism, the sense of a breakdown. According to this reading, then, *Pierrot le Fou* is an art film about an existential crisis, sealed with suicide. Yet another interpretation is also possible. In fact, the transformation of the portrait into collage can also pave the way for a new level of energy, while disclosing the possibility of an unexpected rebirth. According to Kuspit, as soon as fragments from the debris of daily life enter a collage, they overcome their banality and numbness, while their gain in expressive intensity is due to their participation in a brand-new artistic effort: "The fragments that find their way into the field are only superficially found by chance. Chance is a disguise for the uncertain yet highly personal significance they are felt to have. . . . Freedom and chance, the determinate fragments and the indeterminate sense of their relation, become confused, making the fragments even more stimulating than expected."[37]

That randomness and a restless will, arbitrariness and spontaneity, characterize the structure of collage becomes clear when Ferdinand/Pierrot fails to congeal into a new self right before his suicide. As Peter Lehman explains, "He calls his home desperately attempting to make contact with his literate past, with what he once was. (The number he is calling is Balzac 75-02.) Although he has destroyed the identity of that past, associated with the name Ferdinand, he has failed to achieve a new identity—he responds to a question over the phone by answering, 'It [the call] is not on anyone's behalf.'"[38] While for Lehman this episode anticipates the negative dissolution of the self into the incoherent fragments of the explosion, for Kuspit Belmondo's statement would be likely to underline the productive openness of fragments in collage, oscillating as they are between being and becoming, a narrow sense of self-determination and a blind momentum open to all possible outcomes. Put another way, collage depends on an equivalence between uncertainty and the processes of its own making, between creativity and incoherence.

A final shot of Ferdinand's diary with the pages all stained in red follows the phone call, and again, according to Lehman, this image of writing is an icon of failure sanctioned by the protagonist's composition of the word "mort" with the "m" from "Marianne," while the alphabetical compatibility of her name with death spells out the woman's role of femme fatale in Godard's narrative. In contrast to Lehman's pessimistic interpretation, were we to look at the diary as an expanded signature to the film, or as a manifestation of the author in the text, we would agree even more with Kuspit's view of collage as an artistic exploration of what it takes to generate oneself anew. Yet Godard's handwriting on the screen is a distinctive, unique way not only of claiming his work but also of declaring the writerly nature of his images.

Writing the Image

To end *Pierrot le Fou* with an image of writing suggests that Godard's primary source of creativity stems from his efforts to write the image or, better, to translate the image into writing, which also means to reinvent vision through language. The director's logocentric orientation is fulfilled by Anna Karina, who, standing between two paintings by Picasso (*Jacqueline aux fleurs* and *Portrait de Sylvette au fauteuil vert*, 1954), with the help of an exaggerated close-up, thrusts against us spectators a pair of scissors, as if she were about to slice the image away from our eyes (fig. 37). A certain fantasy of blindness or iconoclasm underpins Ferdinand's decision to burn his car, while a flame puts an end to his life. In the movie theater, he watches a newsreel about the Vietnam War full of bombs and explosions. The motif of fire suggests that Godard's secret ambition is to have language burn the cinematic image from within, as if to purify it before giving it a whole new life in a different form.

Language prevails whenever Belmondo devotes his performance to reading out loud all sorts of literary passages. Language wins again when Godard introduces the character of Marianne Renoir. First, Ferdinand's voice offscreen pronounces her full name against a dark night punctuated by fireworks. By contrast, the second time we hear her full name, the flash shot of Renoir's painting *La petite fille à la gerbe* intervenes. In short, Marianne Renoir's name is grafted onto the two competing visual registers that in the course of this analysis we have respectively assigned to *Pierrot* and to *Senso*. The first one is empty and abstract; the second is crowded with detail and figurative. Whenever she is a disembodied entity, one to be spoken about rather than to be looked at, Marianne Renoir stands for romance and freedom. But as soon as Marianne Renoir becomes a painting by Renoir or an image with an erotic appeal, she leads Ferdinand to death. Finally, the rejection of woman as painting and as body echoes the danger that an excess of red holds for Ferdinand. As the color of blood and the body, red used in isolation inhibits the translation, or the tennis game, across different signs, while it signals that the gap between man and woman is about to become murder. With a feeling of helplessness, he cries out, "I can't stand blood."

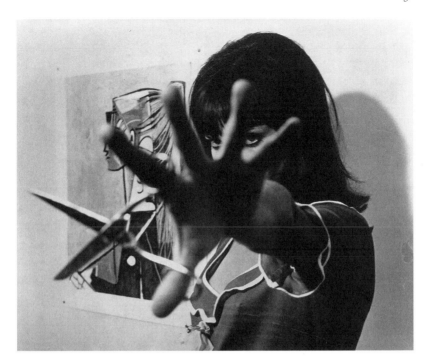

FIGURE 37. *Anna Karina pushing a pair of scissors toward the camera, making explicit Jean-Luc Godard's iconophobic vocation, in* Pierrot le Fou. *Film Stills Archive, The Museum of Modern Art, New York.*

Red, however, is not the only color to mark a dead-end situation. Before committing suicide Ferdinand/Pierrot paints his own face blue. This gesture is terminal not because of the color blue but because of the conjunction of painting, color, and body. In other words, Ferdinand becomes a pictorial surface that cannot reverse itself into anything else except death. Such a liminal situation discloses that for Godard whenever the cinematic image, the actor's body, and painting implement each other the way they do in Visconti's *Senso,* no translation can occur, no tennis game across word and image, color and line, beginning and ending, full and empty frames, can take place. Sitting in the bedroom with his wife, Ferdinand breaks the claustrophobia produced by the collusion of image, body, and painting—or better, decor, class, and history—by mocking an advertisement for women's lingerie through a playful montage of pictures and graphic elements, spoken and printed words. All these elements play off each other without ever coalescing into a unified whole. We are still at the beginning of *Pierrot* and collage can function as a breath of fresh air or an antidote to the burden of tradition. At the end of Ferdinand's journey in search of a new self, no spoof on popular culture would be enough to jolt him out of his extreme state of alienation. Painting the body means that his image has reached a point of no return, hence only a violent bursting onto the sea, a radical leap into an empty screen, can reestablish the possibility of moving across media of expression and of experiencing, once again, the emotion of creativity as translation, the power of poetry and love as breaking through boundaries.

The power of collage to transform one element into something else is reminiscent of dream work, in which one image displaces itself into the condensation of something else. This oneiric view finds support in Kuspit's insight that "collage . . . is very much about these dark fringes, these absences, as well as about the positive presence of positively apprehended fragments."[39] In Kuspit's footsteps, we may begin to think of painting as the "dark fringe" or the repressed side of collage. One episode of *Pierrot le Fou* is especially characterized by a dream aura, or by the surfacing of untapped emotions that in turn invest the citation of paintings with all the energy of collage, until a new set of combinatorial possibilities launches the mind beyond the constraints of vision.

When they reach a small town in central France, Marianne and Ferdinand reveal their talents as storytellers by relying on two utterly different styles of narration. Concrete, linear, classical, she tells a story with blood, battle, an abandoned damsel, and a heroic knight. By contrast, Ferdinand is elusive, evocative, and abstract. It is only when he begins to talk about the seasons, of unexpected encounters, of lovers breathing the cool evening air, that his audience is truly interested. During Marianne's narration, the camera stays on her and her listeners, whose span of attention she secures with bold, dramatic gestures. As soon as Ferdinand finds his own storytelling style, Godard moves away from him and his public by inserting two long shots of glistening waves in bright sunlight, with a close-up of a sensuous female nude by Renoir (*Baigneuse*, 1880) between them.

Because in Ferdinand's case the camera abandons the circumstances of storytelling in favor of an uncontrolled string of images that amount to a stream of consciousness, Ferdinand's narrative is the most oneiric, while its poetical flavor is further reinforced by Marianne's quasihypnotic voice-over. But if Marianne is the one speaking Ferdinand's images, the question arises, whose dream is this? This section of the episode is clearly about Ferdinand's and Godard's dream to transcend a definition of the image as something sensuous and corporeal, which can only be looked at but not thought of, anchoring us to the earth and the past. In other words, Godard's project is to transfer the erotic charge released by Renoir's female nude onto an empty canvas or sky, a colorless sea or screen, where the mind can project all its abstractions.

Even if Godard wants to replace the corporeal vibrancy of Renoir's painting with an eclectic montage of fragments, the contrast between the female nude and the two shots of the open space is so powerful that this sequence stands out as one of the most romantic moments in the film. It is as if Godard had succeeded in utilizing Fuller's battleground to the utmost by setting the body against the mind for the sake of an unrepeatable poetic moment. A comparable effect occurs in the second most romantic sequence of the film when Ferdinand and Marianne lie on the beach under a full, white moon. After telling Marianne a story about two astronauts, the American White and the Russian Leonov, trying to exchange Coca-Cola and Leninism, Ferdinand uses the distancing approach of the third-person singular to transfigure Marianne's body into language: "Because he thinks you are very beautiful. He admires you . . . your arms . . . your breasts . . . are very moving." Inasmuch as these words are charged with desire, they seem to melt in a long shot of the sea, while the camera pans up to the sky accompanied by grandiose music, building up to a huge climax. Ferdinand's verbalization of Marianne's body anticipates her disappearance into the sea by the end of the film. The abandonment of the image is the necessary premise for the reinvention of love sought by this complicated couple.

Even if the promise of romance is attached to the loss of the image, body and painting return relentlessly to the surface of the narrative with all the power of something repressed. Belmondo's and Karina's acting styles, for instance, are remarkable for "the spontaneous splendour, the almost animal grace" of their movements.[40] On the other hand, the body as image can strike a note of sheer vulgarity. This is why a picture of a half-naked woman (probably ripped from a pornographic magazine) is glued to the wall in Marianne's apartment.

Godard's ambivalence toward the body and painting, as something to be rejected in favor of abstraction but also to long for through language, reemerges in his attitude toward vision in general. Before dying in front of the white sea, Ferdinand makes himself blind by wrapping a bunch of dynamite sticks around his face painted in blue. Thus, the loss of sight is the last necessary step before finding eternity. Blindness, however, becomes a form of torture in Marianne's apartment, where the gangsters wrap a red dress around Ferdinand's face and nearly suffocate him with splashes of water from the shower head.

As *Pierrot le Fou* ends with a feeling of suspension about the future of the couple in modern life, it also raises a question about the cinema itself: would moments of blindness help this medium negotiate between the pleasures of vision and art and the demands of thought and life? What Ferdinand and Marianne find beyond the line of the horizon is perhaps the possibility of tying together, as in a collage, the two separate poles of this director's cinema: in Godard's own words, "To see clearly . . . to reason with life."

CHAPTER 5

Andrei

Tarkovsky's

Andrei Rublev

~

Cinema

as the

Restoration of

Icon Painting

*I*n his book on filmmaking, *Sculpting in Time,* Andrei Tarkovsky states that cinema cannot be simply an amalgam of contiguous art forms.[1] Film critics nevertheless associate Tarkovsky's visual style with an eclectic and unpredictable list of painters (Fra Angelico, Duccio di Buoninsegna, Vittore Carpaccio, Eugène Delacroix, Hieronymus Bosch, Rembrandt, Théodore Géricault, Peter Paul Rubens, M. C. Escher, to name a few). But no matter how many art-historical allusions can be found in a film by Tarkovsky, the two issues that really count are the director's belief in the unique qualities of cinema and his sense that art-making is a way of praying. For Tarkovsky, therefore, film is the one and only contemporary art form suited to a revival of religious feeling in our contemporary world plagued by materialistic values and cold cerebralism. As film historian Anna Lawton explains, "The

main theme that runs through all of his films is the disruption of harmony—the separation of the spiritual from the material—and the
protagonist's quest for its recovery."[2]

Instead of doctoring or improving the world about to be filmed with
art-historical references, Tarkovsky prefers to show the paintings he has in
mind as plain objects hanging on the wall. In this respect, his friend Mikhail
Romadin, a painter, offers a telling anecdote from his recollections of the
production of *Solaris* (1972): "But realizing that here he couldn't get away
without painting, he shot the episode in the library with a picture by Pieter
Brueghel, the Elder, *Hunters in the Snow*, as something actually in the space
station. This beautiful scene, full of longing for the earth, is contained
within the framework of his aesthetics."[3]

While echoing Romadin on Tarkovsky's lack of interest in imitating
painting, the Finnish architectural critic Juhani Pallasmaa points out that
the director "utilized . . . pictorial means of rendering space in order to
achieve . . . emotional impact."[4] In *Andrei Rublev* (1966), for instance, the
sequence devoted to Christ's Passion in a wintry Russian landscape clearly
follows Brueghel the Elder's habit of setting a timeless religious subject in a
contemporary Northern European environment (*Census-Taking in Bethlehem*,
1566). Close-ups of feet dragging step by step and long shots of a small
procession accompanying Christ to his death, on one hand, evoke Brueghel's
taste for ever-shifting series of smaller fields of action involving people and
animals and, on the other, convey an escalation of feeling. Were we to combine Romadin's insight into Tarkovsky's dislike of a cinema made of "living
pictures," or tableaux vivants, and Pallasmaa's sense that the director uses
art to charge his images, we would conclude that while the Russian filmmaker does not reject citations of Brueghel and others, his goal is really to
use painting to activate a movement in our souls as we respond to images
that are ancient, but also very alive, and that are borrowed from a visual
tradition, but also deeply rooted in the way the world is.

While Tarkovsky does not hesitate to dissociate painting as artifice
from the cinematic screen, he thinks of his medium as something consubstantial with the four natural elements. Water especially is important for
the director, because in its ever-changing reflections the moving image finds
a perfect mirroring as well as an equivalent of time passing: "Water is a
substance that is very much alive, that changes all the time, that moves. It is
a very cinematic element, and through it, I have tried to express the idea of
passing time. Water conveys depth, a sense of transformation and reflection. It is one of the most beautiful things in the world, and I cannot imag-

ine a film without water."[5] At first sight the director's sense that the most cinematic image is one made of movement, water, and time brings to mind André Bazin's contention that the psychological appeal of cinema originates in this medium's power to defy time and, through movement as an expression of life, in this medium's ability to create an illusion of immortality. Yet, in contrast to Bazin's view of cinema as an embalming force, for Tarkovsky the movement of water not only conveys the passing of time but also mirrors inner changes. This is to say that for the Russian filmmaker the image is cinematic when it becomes a vessel of transformations, not only from water to fire, from fire to air, or from water to earth, but also from life to death and from death to life; whereas for Bazin the vocation of the cinema is to circumvent death once and for all, by conveying an image of things in time, "change mummified as it were."[6]

Tarkovsky's fascination with water and fire, air and earth, coexists with his interest in the visual arts, which he studied in conjunction with music and cultivated as a young man, sketching landscapes during a geological expedition in Siberia. Hostile as he was to painting's eclipsing nature, Tarkovsky argued that his intent had always been to avoid symbolic or metaphorical images in his films.[7] More specifically, whenever he was asked about the meaning of the four elements in the mise-en-scène of his films, he firmly replied that "water is simply water and rain is intended to convey the experience of rain."[8] Thus water, fire, earth, and air are not intended as symbols but as primal images, so natural and therefore so inexhaustible in their signifying power that they are capable of reorienting our imagination away from a rational, technocratic worldview toward something infinite and unspeakable, endless and mysterious.

It is as if for Tarkovsky the four natural elements through the cinema had the power to release the magic, esoteric side of life, while the Russian director's conceptualization of the medium echoes Bazin's sense that film, in comparison with other art forms, gets "closer to reality,"[9] with all its rough edges and loose ends. Yet Tarkovsky goes a step farther. Like Bazin, he rejects pictorialism, theatricality, artifice, and manipulation, but while he lets the world play itself out on the screen through all the different manifestations of air, fire, earth, and water, his project is to release the mystical core stored in the Bazinian realist approach.

Tarkovsky thinks of himself as a sculptor who endows something as intangible as time with a substance of its own. To be precise, instead of using a scalpel to chip away the marble from a block until a form emerges, Tarkovsky handles the filmic image in such a way that it looks as if it were constantly accreting onto its outside surface the shaping rhythms of internal forces: "Rhythm in cinema is conceived by the life of the object visibly recorded in the frame. Just as from the quivering of a reed you can tell what sort of current, what pressure there is in a river, in the same way we know the movement of time from the flow of life process reproduced in the shot."[10] Tarkovsky's understanding of cinema as making time visible—namely the movement and the rhythm of matter, whether it be fire or water, earth or air—explains his rejection of Sergey Mikhaylovich Eisenstein's montage, which he considers an external intervention on images that stifle their autonomous inner life, their emotional or spiritual growth, their ability to yield a glimpse of God.

Precisely because the filmic image is meant to make visible something invisible, to release from the inside out a shape that is made of emotional nuances, or otherworldy energy, cinema cannot resemble any other art form. Like poetry, in which language plays itself out to the limit, cinema is untranslatable. For Tarkovsky, the more the filmic image is enmeshed in the world—limited and fragile, without technical manipulations or decorative improvements—the more it can disclose a glimpse of the eternal. The director writes, "Through the image is sustained an awareness of the infinite: the eternal within the finite, the spiritual within matter, the limitless given form."[11] Although he is deeply aware of how the photographic origins of cinema tie his medium to mechanical reproduction, a practice linked to science, the director cannot consider the filmic image to be a mere index or extension of the referent the way Bazin would, but he senses, instead, its potential to reach out for an irrational and a supernatural dimension.

Put another way, for Tarkovsky, the filmic image is not a sign standing for something else but a site where something other or divine, lost or repressed, manifests itself directly, in first person, for our eyes. In this respect, Tarkovsky's filmic image is meant to function much like an ancient religious icon (fig. 38). According to the Russian Orthodox dogma concerning the incarnation of Christ, the divinity exists in human form through the presence of the icon itself, a special kind of image system, since the boundary between signifier and signified is so elastic that the beholder can relate to the representation as if it were the represented itself, to the image of God *as* to God.

In agreement with Bazin, Tarkovsky feels that his task is to work only with what is already there in the world. Thus his approach stands in contrast to that of Eisenstein, the filmmaker-engineer of constructivist background, who combined pieces of the world—faces of nonprofessional ac-

FIGURE 38. Saint George, *icon (tempera on wood, Russian, sixteenth century).*
The Metropolitan Museum of Art (Gift of Humanities Fund, Inc., 1972), New York.

tors and close-ups of objects, monuments and stairways, rivers and crowds—
to produce a narrative universe that could not have existed on its own otherwise, while using montage to endow it with a thesis about power and
history. After arguing that Eisenstein prevents his spectators from discovering the meaning of a scene for themselves, Bazin rejects Eisenstein's mon-

tage on moral grounds for the sake of a style more conducive to freedom of choice. By contrast, in making tangible the emotional and spiritual dimensions of ordinary things, Tarkovsky's project stems from an ancient religious practice, one that believes that God inhabits the humblest images.

Even if Bazin condemns Eisenstein's manipulative montage because it imposes an imaginary scheme on the world instead of re-presenting it the way it would appear to us, the French theorist does know that realism as a style comprises a subjective side and an objective side, so that cinema, born out of photography, produces a hallucination that is also a document. Although Tarkovsky is likely to be sympathetic to Bazin's philosophy of the image, he differs from the French theorist to the extent that, because he has aligned his filmmaking with the religious practice of Russian icon painting, realism for him cannot be just a style or an aesthetic mediation between the imaginary and the documentary, a hallucination and a referent. As soon as we agree that realism is a style, we imply a suspicion of what we see. This means that a certain iconophobia is still at work, even if Bazin's approach is marked by a humility or acceptance of the world as it is, at least in comparison to Eisenstein's interventionist attitude. It is this distrust of the image that Tarkovsky wants to defy by developing a cinema that will function like a religious icon, with the power to bring God back among us and restore our faith in the inexplicable and the supernatural.

Despite Tarkovsky's rejection of painting as artifice, his cinema respects the long-standing Russian artistic tradition of icon painting. The director's allegiance to this heritage is nowhere more self-conscious than in *Andrei Rublev*, a film, set in medieval times, about an icon painter who travels with two fellow monks, Kyrill and Danyl, from the monastery of Andronikov to the city of Vladimir. In *Andrei Rublev*, Tarkovsky describes a transitional period when icons have ceased to occupy "a very special position, somewhere between art and religion," and when "no inner thread of continuity" between art and life could be easily found.[12] In the words of Theophanes (Rublev's master from Greece), the icon, instead of being a devotional aid, has replaced the most menial of tools: an instrument to press cabbage.

Although many scenes are devoted to discussions on art and religion between the Greek and the Russian painter, Tarkovsky centers his film on Rublev because Theophanes' disciple replaced his master's terrifying God with a much more merciful, loving figure. In fact, Rublev's work, after becoming a standard of artistic production in 1551 thanks to a church council decree, contributed to the building of Russia's national identity as a Christian society.

Tarkovsky's narrative is a *via crucis*. The episodic development of the film is comparable to a series of separate panels, just like the sections of an ancient icon or the stations of the cross. Ten episodes pace the spiritual progress of the protagonist. They are usually listed with the following titles: The Prologue or The Balloon, The Jester (1400), Theophanes the Greek (1405), The Passion According to Andrei (1406), The Holiday or The Pagan Rite, The Last Judgment (1408), The Raid (1408), The Silence (1412), The Bell (1423), The Epilogue. Andrei's journey is, of course, a quest of the heart, in which his private dilemmas about the meaning of his art overlap with the vicissitudes of the Russian people.

By developing a filmmaking style that is entrancing and mobilizing, oneiric and ethnographic, Tarkovsky succeeds in drawing a parallel between cinema and icon painting as two practices whose aim is to invest simple materials with a transcendental quality. More specifically in *Andrei Rublev*, Tarkovsky is concerned with the renewal of artistic inspiration in a world full of famines, suffering, and wars. It is well known that icon painting was a religious cult, so much so that it had nothing to do with exhibitions and markets. This explains why none of Andrei's fellow artists ever mentions money in conjunction with this art form. Rather the crisis of creativity affecting Rublev is predicated on a sense of social impotence and a loss of religious meaning. Artistic paralysis means that Rublev cannot find God within himself any longer, and it is precisely this recovery of the divine in the ordinary that the icon enables by fostering an intuitive inspiration or, in Tarkovsky's case, a reawakening to the prodigious aura released by the four natural elements.

Making Visible the Invisible: Face and History

The face of Christ was thought to be the most fundamental of icons (fig. 39), meant not as a portrait likeness but as a conduit between the worshipper's soul and the Divine. In Tarkovsky's cinema, too, the face acquires unusual prominence. Memorable in *Andrei Rublev* are the moments when the camera dwells on the expression of an old woman lulling herself into a trance as she stands in front of a miserable dwelling. Her immobile expression, petrified by age, is enough to set in motion the possibility of a whole personal story within an otherwise modest and transitional sequence.

The notion of the icon as an image of pure "fixation,"[13] incompatible with anything ephemeral or transient, also applies to the face of a young apprentice who sits by a lake with the rest of Rublev's group. He looks

FIGURE 39. The Face of Christ Not Made by Human Hands, *icon (tempera on wood, Russian, sixteenth–seventeenth century). The Metropolitan Museum of Art (Rogers Fund, 1975), New York.*

suspended in a half-conscious meditation, so much so that the viewer is willing to pay more attention to the landscape of his features than to narrative development. Finally, Tarkovsky's camera interrogates the face of a young woman with an enigmatic, Mona Lisa smile, who rests her cheek against her arm while her mind pursues the unfathomable thread of her imagination. Somehow the mystery of her expression defeats the exploratory power of Tarkovsky's medium, for the camera can only dwell on the very edge of her psychology.

Tarkovsky's refusal to attach these faces to a situation, to a decision, or to an exchange of looks with another character makes these anonymous and minor figures especially elusive. Yet their impact is undeniably strong. It is as if the viewer's mind, unable to read the characters' eyes, turns away from the distractions of the world toward deeper and unspeakable regions, thus reacting in a way comparable to the beholder of a holy face in an icon. Art historian John Baggley explains how this contemplative mood was achieved according to a rigid set of rules: "The face and head may be disproportionately large in relation to the rest of the body; eyes and ears are enlarged, while the mouth may be very small and the lips tightly closed, thus conveying a sense of inner watchfulness and attention; eyes often seem to be inward looking, turned away from the external world of the senses."[14] In order to avoid the naturalism of the traditional portrait, in which the emphasis is on exteriority as a mirror of individuality rather than on inner spiritual alertness, Tarkovsky handles the face with cinematic techniques that differ greatly from the rules listed by Baggley (except for his reliance on frontality): he positions his characters far away from each other in order to stress their speechlessness and privacy, or he sets his figures against natural landscapes that are barren and simple to the point of veering toward abstraction as they lose their immediate organic character.[15]

In icon painting the objective was not to make a portrait that resembled the sitter as closely as possible but rather to depict something according to the representational codes prescribed by the Church. Tatiana Vladyshevskaia makes this point especially clear: "The task of the . . . painter was not self-expression, not creation, not the embodiment of individual, personal principles, but the comprehension and reproduction of . . . divine images that were transmitted by means of ancient religious archetypes."[16] In the case of portraiture, the face of Saint Nicholas was instantly recognizable not because it looked like the saint but because it had all the attributes that the Church traditionally associated with this figure.

Because the artist's purity is a prerequisite of good painting,[17] Andrei's costume matches the clothing of saints in icons, whose long drapings serve to conceal the tempting forms of the flesh. During the pagan rite in the woods at the beginning of spring, Andrei, the monk, shies away from the sight of naked youths running toward the water. Like a priest, the iconographer was supposed to lead a life based on renunciation. Significantly, this dictum of simplicity reappears in the materials used for icon painting:

> Until the eighteenth century, oil paints were not acceptable on icons, but were eschewed as a worldly, sensuous medium suited only for secular art.

The ascetic choice of materials was a firm tradition in iconography. Icon panels were carefully selected from well-seasoned woods, without knots: lime, alder, birch, cypress, pine and oak. Generally a square of woven linen was glued to the wood and coated with three to eight layers of gesso, preferably made from ground alabaster.[18]

That the icon originated from the trees of Russia becomes apparent in *Andrei Rublev* when, after the Tartars' attack against the city of Vladimir, Tarkovsky shows the altarpiece of the cathedral in flames. Each panel of the iconostasis seems to regress into the thin, wavering outline of a birch tree. Gaston Bachelard described a similar transformation, saying that Claude Monet wanted his cathedral to be airy and "took from the blue-colored mist all the blue matter that the mist itself had taken from the sky."[19] With Tarkovsky, in a cinema in which movement coincides with water, it is not surprising if the icon returns to the forest.

Tarkovsky's lack of interest in portraiture goes hand in hand with his refusal to construct Andrei Rublev as a bigger-than-life character in control of the historical process. At first sight, the high production values of *Andrei Rublev* in wide-screen and its monumental length (three and a half hours) would lead one to believe that Tarkovsky has attempted an epic of Hollywood proportions. Yet this is not a conventional historical film, for the focus is really on the intimate thoughts of a monk. Andrei's stance of peripheral spectator rather than central actor in relation to public events is intertwined with the icon painting's placement of people and objects outside historical time so that they could function as signs of the divinity:

> Events as manifestations of reality and their representation in historical "images" are unknown to the icon painter: his task is to express facts through allusions, through "signs," but in such a way not to distract the faithful from moral elevation, from concentration in prayer, from an escape—once the earthly concerns have been given up—in harmonic solitude with the hypostasis released by the image, from a magical identification with it.[20]

Put another way, communion with the transcendental realm presupposes giving up action in favor of reaction, so that Andrei's passivity cannot be entirely reduced to inertia or cowardice or hesitation, even if these states of mind may play a part in his long artistic crisis. Rather, Rublev's holding back is a necessary stage of inactivity preceding illumination.

By emphasizing reaction over action in the depiction of his protagonist, Tarkovsky seems to invite his spectators to take on a similar attitude.
Thus the director's construction of spectatorship is indebted neither to
Bazin, who celebrates a viewer actively and independently involved in the
interpretation of the image, nor to Eisenstein, who shot by shot would like
to predict and control everything the audience should think or feel. In
contrast to Eisenstein's montage and Bazin's realism, Tarkovsky's model of
spectatorship is based on the director's familiarity with Eastern philosophies and art. Rublev's preference for contemplation over intervention resembles the surrender of an active self at the heart of Zen. The artist's
marginalized stance in relation to the historical process allows for a stasis,
which in turn promotes "discipline of mind" and "nobility of imagination."[21] These two goals, "discipline of mind" and "nobility of imagination," are relevant not only to Russian icon painting but also to Japanese
haiku, an art form cherished by the director, and not surprisingly so, since
Russian culture did develop between the East and the West, and Tarkovsky
himself studied Asian languages.

Unlike Eisenstein's interest in the Japanese ideogram as a montage of
word and image,[22] Tarkovsky's fascination with haiku, a composition made
of ideograms, has to do with its dependence on common images of nature
that "mean nothing beyond themselves, and at the same time express so
much that it is not possible to catch their final meaning."[23]

An image in *Andrei Rublev* whose ascetic composition comes close to the
simple but inexhaustible structure of haiku occurs when Rublev dreams of
himself alone in the wind and in the rain, near a tree that stands alone in a
large field. This configuration echoes a previous low-angle shot of a majestic tree set against the skyline of Vladimir, practically emerging out of the
camera's gaze searching for a web of strong and far-reaching roots. While
the combination of tree and city suggests something defying death, well
beyond the turmoils of history, Tarkovsky's reduction of the frame during
Rublev's dream to an absolute minimum of signifying elements endows the
whole sequence with an oneiric edge. Field and tree, rain and wind, have
replaced all other images in Rublev's mind, while their calm and definitive
exclusion of everything else in the world, ranging from history to architecture, spells out that feeling of inner centeredness that always precedes a
renewal of the self.

In keeping with Tarkovsky's construction of a central but passive character, Andrei Rublev can only witness the horrors of torture, during the
battle of Vladimir, or the triumph of betrayal, when his fellow monk Kyrill

denounces to the authorities the irreverent routine of a jester performing for a group of peasants. At times Andrei avoids involvement altogether. For instance, he sits still in his boat without showing much interest in the escape of a peasant girl who swims away from a group of soldiers chasing the participants in a pagan rite. On the other hand, when Andrei kills a Tartar during the battle of Vladimir to defend a dumb girl he has befriended, this violence leads him to embrace a long period of silence in the attempt to seek atonement.

Andrei's marginal position in regard to the action is confirmed when another icon painter, Theophanes, confuses Kyrill with the famous Rublev. This misunderstanding also indirectly establishes how difficult it will be for us viewers to count on the catalyzing energy of an easily recognizable protagonist. Furthermore, during the making of an iron bell in honor of the local grand duke, Andrei remains outside the casting pit, looking down on it from above. A young peasant, Boriska, who has claimed his father's expertise in casting metal, supervises the entire operation all the way to the point of physical exhaustion.

Although Andrei befriends Boriska, in whom he sees a fellow artist, the iconographer is never shown painting with bold strokes or at ease with the creative process. We see him painting only once, as he sits on the threshold of a door in the palace of the Grand Prince, while touching up a small wooden icon. Boriska, whose effort over a large crowd of assistants makes him resemble a film director, is not in control of art-making either. He literally stumbles on his material by accident. While he is reveling in a patch of earth under the rain, he discovers the perfect clay for the mold.

Doors and Windows

The prominence of the face in Tarkovsky's mise-en-scène accounts for a downplaying of the word. Dialogues between characters are not always even exchanges but often tend toward soliloquy. This speaking to oneself while talking to another person is most apparent when Andrei takes leave of Danyl, whom he has always considered a mentor. Language is also depicted as inconclusive. While standing in a huge field crossed by one thin road stretching toward the vanishing point, Andrei explains to Danyl why he does not want to paint the fresco commissioned by the Grand Prince. The depiction of the Last Judgment would require one more representation of punishment in a world already devastated by suffering.

Set against a strongly perspectival composition, the dialogue between Andrei and Danyl seems all the more inadequate in envisioning a new role for the artist in society. In a similar fashion, the dialogues on art and life between Kyrill and Theophanes or between Theophanes and Andrei are lengthy and heavy to the point of discrediting the value of the script, in contrast to the power of images, which by themselves can convey new ways of being or externalize complex states of mind.[24]

During the battle of Vladimir, for instance, Tarkovsky's camera captures the feeling of emptiness experienced by a Russian prince who has betrayed his twin brother and led the ferocious Tartars against his own countrymen. The prince's face occupies the center of the screen, while pillaging unfolds in slow motion in the background. By "making the viewers aware of the passage of time" and "of its rhythmic pressures,"[25] Tarkovsky visualizes, without the help of any speech, the core of the prince's alienation during the conquest of the city.

To be sure, Tarkovsky's filmic image is conceived more as a door leading to the soul and less as a window open onto the world, reversing the well-known metaphor associated with Albertian perspective and Renaissance painting. In fact, the Albertian window, which channels an omnipotent view out of an enclosed space toward the external world, contrasts with the organization of space in the Russian home, where the point of visionary energy is not the windowsill but the upper corner of the room, the site traditionally reserved for the placement of religious icons.

Put another way, the Albertian window is plainly antithetical to the functioning of religious icons, which are characterized by the use of "inverse perspective." More specifically, inverse perspective in icon painting prevents the beholder "from entering the holy image or from imagining its space as a continuation of its own."[26] As Baggley explains, the evocative power of the icon originates in the inversion of the perspectival system, as if an emotional bond inside the viewer has replaced the unreachable aura surrounding the vanishing point:

> When this technique is used, the lines of perspective are reversed, to converge not at some distant point in the scene, but in front of the icon in the eyes of the beholder; one is left feeling that the beholder is essential to the completion of the icon. The essence of the exercise has been to establish a *communion* between the event or persons represented in the icon and those who stand before it, to "make present" to another person what is presented in the icon.[27]

By exchanging physical distance for psychological mastery, Renaissance perspective fosters in the viewer the illusion that looking leads to corporeal penetration and economic acquisition. By contrast, in the tradition of Russian icon painting, as we learn from Baggley, once the perspectival lines are reversed, they converge right in front of the viewer. Instead of possessing the space lying outside an image structured like a window, the beholder *communes* with the religious scene or figures in the icon, while the icon in turn is one of the ways in which God exists in the world.

This combination of psychological resonance and physical separation between viewer and image characterizes the behavior of Tarkovsky's camera during the final exhibition of Rublev's icons. As Italian art historian Nicoletta Misler remarks,

> The final reading of Rublev's icons does not emerge from a fixed image, "the immobile eye" of Renaissance perspective, . . . but rather from fades, superimpositions, and camera movements that imply a fragmented but real perception, comparable to the so-called inverse perspective of the icons, which by virtue of having a vanishing point outside the picture, oblige the viewer to scan the pictorial surface with a moving eye.[28]

In contrast to the Albertian model, in which the vanishing point is distant and stable while catering to a sense of mastery, the inverse perspective of icon painting lends itself to unexpected and unsettling apparitions. By avoiding windows as openings onto narrative developments and using doors instead to frame the arrival of new characters, Tarkovsky conveys this sense that the filmic image, just like the religious icon, summons otherworldly presences. A riderless horse, for instance, wanders in through the doorway of the cathedral of Vladimir. While the animal's unexpected entrance into the church is a measure of the disarray left behind by the Tartars after raiding the city, the majestic and peaceful advance of this horse with no master, no harness, and no duty seems to mark the beginning of a new life of freedom along an uncertain path of development.

There is further confirmation that the Albertian metaphor of the window does not apply here: Russian icons never take on a frame, a device that traditionally emphasizes the illusionistic nature of images. By contrast, the borders of the icon are usually flat or slightly raised. In a way, Tarkovsky captures the anti-illusionistic economy of religious icons by accentuating the ghostlike quality of characters suddenly appearing in the frame or disappearing behind a tree in the middle of a philosophical dialogue, as if their status were as evanescent as the natural divinities peasant folklore associates with seasonal changes and lakes.

The activity of looking through windows—which is embedded in images based on Renaissance perspective—implies a viewer in a situation of safety, who can dominate the world outside, without giving up control of private space. By contrast, in *Andrei Rublev* the lives of individuals are not only at the mercy of violent events but also in the proximity of wondrous and half-witted creatures, of which the orderly panoramas of Renaissance perspective cannot quite make sense. Hence it is appropriate that a doorway, instead of a window, in the palace of the Grand Prince—where Andrei is hesitating to paint a huge fresco of the Last Judgment—marks the entrance of a dumb girl, an echo of the Holy Fool, a saint and a rebel touched by both insanity and wisdom.

Doors do not protect individuals in the safety of their homes. Put another way, the absence of a boundary between public and private space indicates that Rublev's world is still medieval rather than Renaissance. The absence of the door as barrier leads to a sense of imminent danger from all sides, while it also discloses a set of unknown, exciting possibilities. In the episode of The Balloon, for instance, Tarkovsky's camera follows Efim, a peasant, as he dizzily moves inside the base of a church belfry, whose round plan is punctuated by several arched thresholds leading to the outside. The aura of disorientation and excitement enveloping the peasant's trajectory is enhanced by the camera's shuttling from door to door, unable to choose a path and yet eager to find one. In a sense the multiple exits pave the way for the ambivalent ending of the episode: after an amazing flight over the countryside, Efim crashes to the ground, but his final fall strangely rhymes with the sensuous movements of a beautiful horse on the bank of the river.

If doors do not hold threat at bay, individuals are also not in control of their fate. In contrast to the emphasis on mastery and personhood typical of the Renaissance, in Rublev's medieval world the designs of God are inscrutable. This is perhaps why Tarkovsky uses high-angle shots with exhilarating vertigoes or bird's-eye overviews of endless plains to show us that the people below, like a crowd of damned souls in a large canvas by Bosch, are desperate, microscopic participants, agitating in vain against incommensurable events like the taking of the cathedral of Vladimir.

Instead of relying on special effects to convey the presence of the supernatural, Tarkovsky uses framing to suggest a realm beyond the borders of the screen, while avoiding well-balanced and artful compositions. A case in point is when the soldiers, sent by the prince who wants a new bell, interrogate Boriska on the whereabouts of the village's craftsmen. Tarkovsky squashes the image into an odd combination of elements: Boriska's resigned expression as he lists all the deaths around him, the rough tail of a horse, and a niche in a wooden wall, or perhaps a small window open onto a pitch-black night, whose bottom frame supports a small hen. The soldiers' questions are in voice-over, while the lack of an establishing shot underlines the suffocation of daily life and also stimulates the viewer to imagine everything that is not shown and literally exceeds the frame. As Maurizio Grande observes, "There is . . . something that remains outside the borders of the screen . . . and which Tarkovsky's cinema does not want to pick up, does not want to exhaust in a totalizing rewriting, rather he prefers to maintain it as a dialectical opening toward what cannot be said."[29] It is as if by blocking a full view of objects and people Tarkovsky were better able to charge the image with the unknown and make its incomplete edges and asymmetrical space resonate well beyond the sheer documentation of an environment into the disjointed details of a hallucination. This approach clearly privileges affective impact over informational value. The flatness of Tarkovsky's composition and its decontextualization of disparate elements brings to mind icon painting's habitual rejection of depth.

Architecture, Objects, and Animals

The rejection of history typical of icon painting accounts for the iconographer's use of unrealistic architecture—edifices smaller than the figures depicted (fig. 40), churches in the middle of the desert. The icons' fantastic settings explain why in *Andrei Rublev* Tarkovsky reduces the number of buildings to a minimum in favor of natural landscapes such as thick forests and vast plains, where it is easy to become disoriented and envision inexplicable happenings. In the episodes shot outdoors, away from the artificiality of the studio, Tarkovsky feels freer to underline the surreal edge of natural phenomena, which someone might expect to be closer to the document than to the dream. Hence the sudden apparition of Theophanes in the woods, with his body covered by crawling ants, does not startle Andrei or his assistant, Foma.

Most of the action occurs *en plein air*, except for two important and long sequences: Andrei's artistic paralysis in the palace of the Grand Prince, and the ransacking of the cathedral of Vladimir. Although these two spaces are characterized by a strong architectural style that links them to a specific historical period, Tarkovsky manages to downplay the solidity of the walls

FIGURE 40. The Annunciation, *icon (tempera on wood, Russian, second half of sixteenth century).*
The Metropolitan Museum of Art (Gift of Humanities Fund, Inc., 1972), New York.

by staging a dreamlike snowfall, first inside the palace, then in the cathedral.
More specifically, the space of the palace unravels into a different mental
landscape for each character. As Philip Strick observes,

> Posing the cast with evident satisfaction against the white walls and the
> sparse, angular scaffolding . . . Tarkovsky develops the setting as confronta-
> tion, each occupant seeing in it what he wants. Amid its indecipherable

maze, unknown men appear as if imagined and make their claims, the reality of the building slowly decaying. . . . The Grand Prince . . . sees political achievement. . . . His children, giggling through the arches, see it as a playground. . . . The stone masons see it as something they could improve on, given better materials. . . . Foma decides its sterility is a good reason to accept an invitation to set up as a painter on his own, and leaves.[30]

This unraveling of architecture into a subjective spectrum that includes play, hostility, ambition, and imagination confirms that for Tarkovsky the inner self is more important than the outside world, even though these two spheres are always interrelated. Thus, shots frequently include unfinished structures, scaffoldings, precarious arrangements of people and objects, because Rublev's difficult task is to reinvent himself as a believer and as an artist. In this respect, horrifying as the Tartars' pillaging of Vladimir may appear to be, the transformation of the cathedral into a ruin, or "skeleton of memory, a sheer melancholic presence,"[31] releases the protagonist from the patterns of the past.

Finally, the frequency of outdoor scenes establishes the Russian land-scape as a character in Tarkovsky's film, while it reminds us of the popular roots of icon painting. In contrast to sculpture (which was forbidden by the Church), frescoes (which were limited to stone buildings), illuminated manu-scripts (which never spread from Western to Eastern Europe), and mosaics (which flourished mostly in the Byzantine world), this art form was widely spread among the peasantry. To be sure, according to Nicoletta Misler, Tarkovsky's staging of the pagan rite—with candles in the night, rustling of leaves, and a silvery moon—captures the folkloric, fairy-tale dimension of a comparable scene painted by Kazimir Malevich, in *The Female Bathers* (1908): "Looking at these corporeal, although evanescent forms, opaque and solid against the background of the lake, one is reminded of the naked female peasants in the fog during the pagan rite of *Andrei Rublev;* these images, in other words, refer to the Russian tradition of the rusalki, of the sirens in the swamps of Russian folklore and fairy tales."[32]

The links between religious icon painting and the peasant world are also relevant to Tarkovsky's use of animals throughout *Andrei Rublev.* Just as iconographers often place sheep and cattle next to saints and angels with the intention to address more effectively a peasant audience, the director turns to domestic or local animals. Although one may speculate on Tarkovsky's populist inclinations as the director of a large-scale film about a major national figure, I would contend that here his intent is mostly iconographic, to remind us that the cinema has replaced icon painting and it is in the cinema where we find nourishment for our souls. In the film, after denouncing the jester's irreverent routine to the Boyars, Kyrill returns to the hut with a small black bird perched on his arm. Later on, this same character, torn as he is by rivalry with Andrei, will abandon his community after violently beating a dog. Besides including animals in the mise-en-scène, Tarkovsky reveals ties between icon painting and rural life in his mixing of farm, artistic, and military utensils: buckets, ropes, rags, chopped wood, chains, spades, shields, paint brushes, hammers. All these objects enhance the tactile quality of Tarkovsky's images, since it is through them that the viewer can "feel . . . the ever-changing texture of daily routines."[33]

This broad overview of material culture, however, does not result in a merely faithful, archeological reconstruction. Objects instead seem to draw life from their context to the point of acquiring a kinesthetic intensity of their own: the balloon made of rags and ropes Efim uses to fly over the countryside like a Russian Icarus or a creature painted by Chagall, and the bell whose sound mesmerizes a whole community, for example, are not abstract symbols of creativity but physical entities with a tangible texture and an imaginable weight, whose intense physicality transmits all the more convincingly the peasants' stubborn belief that the icon (along with other sacred objects, such as holy relics and liturgical props) was actually the divinity made human in the world.

For Tarkovsky the filmic image is something that creates, by virtue of its ontogenetic relationship to reality, the possibility of listening to "something deep which blossoms out," and "whose meaning resonates in increasingly distant echoes."[34] This theory finds its example in the episode of the casting of the bell, which begins with so much emphasis on its material features—the search for the right clay, the intervention of fire, and the suspenseful interrogation of its surface right before the outside crust is removed—and ends on an invisible, acoustic note.

This awareness that earthbound objects contain spiritual beings also justifies Tarkovsky's insistent use of a camera looking down to the ground during Efim's "brief, uncontrolled" flight.[35] The peasant avoids all sorts of violent struggles on the land underneath and, after climbing a belfry, launches himself into the open sky. His flight, however, is no escape toward a higher realm but rather an opportunity to absorb the rivers and the plains below in all their immensity. Put another way, the more Efim gets away from the earth, the more he can experience its total embrace. Paradoxically, physical distance feeds psychological closeness. Such an experience of an earthbound communion also characterizes two poignant gestures: Foma in the forest covers his face with mud, and Christ during the Passion covers his face with snow.

While Efim's leap into the unknown is comparable to the beholder's willingness to open up to the irrational call of the icon, Tarkovsky's high angle from Efim's balloon is never answered by any low angle of peasants or animals, for a look from below toward what is above would only bring to mind the well-known stereotypes of sociorealist cinema. In this tradition images of rural life stand in statuesque fashion against the horizon of endless fields and a blank sky. Although critics constantly compare Tarkovsky to Alexander Dovzshenko by stressing that these two filmmakers privilege the earth over the sky, the episode of the balloon remains a rejection of the populist collective values of Soviet silent cinema. Even if Efim abandons the life on the land to explore the sky all by himself, his adventure spells out a creative yearning of choral proportions. In contrast to the frozen and monumental depiction of an earthbound existence typical of sociorealist cinema, Tarkovsky's camera right before Efim's flight relentlessly moves from door to door at the bottom of the belfry, while it acquires the fluidity of water running through a maze of interconnecting channels.

To be sure, Misler observes that the theme of flight spells out Tarkovsky's cultural identity. In other words, even if Tarkovsky's cinema exists in opposition to Eisenstein's, it is possible to attempt a comparison between the director and Malevich, since flying brings Tarkovsky close to the artist-scientist and to the artist-craftsman of the Soviet avant-garde:

> In regard to the theme of flight in *Andrei Rublev*, I feel that a reference to Letatlin, a flying apparatus of Leonardesque memory planned by Vladimir Tatlin (1895–1953), is appropriate. But also we should associate the theme of flight with the ascetic Pavel Filonov (1883–1941) or, most of all, with Kazimir Malevich (1878–1935), who conceived of Suprematism as a contemplation of the world in its totality, beyond ordinary sense perception.[36]

What Misler really means in defining Suprematism as "contemplation of the world in its totality, beyond ordinary sense perception," is that

> Malevich refused any and all allusion to reality, to the café or the still life of Picasso and Braque, to the sensation of nature that lurks behind even the most extreme statements of Mondrian and Kandinsky. What he accepted, however, was another concept—of infinity—and it is this sensation that dominates Suprematist paintings.[37]

FIGURE 41. Suprematist Composition: Red Square and Black Square *(1915)*, *by Kazimir Malevich. The Museum of Modern Art, New York. Photograph © 1994 The Museum of Modern Art, New York.*

Both Malevich and Tarkovsky strive to make visible the invisible. Yet Malevich goes a few steps farther without renouncing altogether the legacy of icon painting, but rather taking it to the extreme of an avant-garde sensibility. Unlike other modernist artists, he does not paint about painting and does not paint about the end of painting in a world of mechanical reproduction, where random fragments of lived experience end up in a collage, but he seems to represent the unrepresentable through the effacement or the reduction of painting to a few hieratic signs: squares, lines, and circles (fig. 41).

Despite his total abandonment to risk, Efim's exhilaration in the sky is short-lived. After his collapse to the ground, it remains unclear whether the peasant is alive or dead. We see only an awesome mist rising from a pile of rags. Yet his sacrifice is not in vain, for by cutting from the freeze-frame impact to the slow-motion shot of a black horse frolicking in the grass to the soothing notes of a harp, Tarkovsky seems to suggest that the soul of someone else will soar high again over the infinite expanse of the land. When the young Foma stumbles upon a dead bird in the middle of the forest, it is as if Efim's legacy has been passed on to the apprentice painter.

As the last extension of Efim's breath turns into the soft focus enveloping the luscious image of the lonely but contented horse, it points to the fragility of the filmic image, which, soaked as it is with the proximity of invisible things, will transform itself, later on, into the fog surrounding the evanescent silhouettes of Andrei, Kyrill, and Danyl crossing a field of solitary haystacks. In particular this vanishing of the image into fog reminds us that Tarkovsky appreciated Chinese painting, as well as the asceticism of Japanese haiku. In this tradition the artist is skillful only when, by painting the minimum, he enables empty space to structure detail-filled areas. Likewise with Tarkovsky, the fog makes sense of the figures moving in the sequence.

Just as Tarkovsky portrays the movements of a wild animal in a decelerated fashion after Efim's flight in The Prologue, at the end of the film a group of black horses slowly soothe themselves by rolling in the moist earth. The slow movements of the animals convey a sense of discovery and pleasure, comparable to Boriska's happiness when he accidentally discovers the right clay for the casting of the bell. The transition from icon painting to a natural landscape reaffirms that for Tarkovsky cinematic creativity derives more from the natural landscape than from the museum. The depiction of the horses in slow motion suggests that the experience of time pulsating through the filmic image is the best modern equivalent for the transfiguring force icons were supposed to possess in ancient times. Somehow slow motion releases a maximum of affect, for the sinuous contours of the horses impregnate the frame.[38]

The theme of flight in *Andrei Rublev* does not stem from a desire for superhuman mastery or disembodied omnipotence, but in the wake of icon painting as a religious tradition, it is really a search for spiritual elevation. The balloon episode is characterized by a double, crosslike emphasis on the horizontal plane of the land and the vertical ascension to the sky. These two axes reappear in Tarkovsky's camera movement and depiction of water. Spectacular dollies and fluid tracking shots, for instance, characterize the battle of Vladimir, in which the Tartars' desire to conquer space contrasts with the Russian prince's vertigo of loneliness when, from the top of a wall, we see a swan precipitating toward the bottom.

According to a similar combination of horizontal and vertical axes, water in *Andrei Rublev* is either mixed with the earth or it falls from the sky as a sign of renewal.[39] For instance, two drunken peasants brawl in the mud of the riverbank shortly before the jester's arrest. Their heavy and slippery movements endow the scene with an uncanny rhythm, which calls attention to the centrality of violence and dream, to the heaviness of the body, and to a loss of control at the heart of peasant life. In contrast to dirty water, the clean rain beating on the leaves during the dream in flashback, in which Andrei reenvisions himself as a young man, anticipates the positive outcome of the molding of the bell. Mark Le Fanu observes, "The bell begins to be built as the snows are clearing, and is completed a year later as they melt again. Thus it is as if the whole film is conceived of within the compass of the natural cycle."[40] The congruence between the passage of the seasons and a collective effort of artistic production, or the rain falling on Rublev's icons at the end of the film, suggests that natural matter is the unconscious of creativity, while an imaginative dialectic exists between the four elements of nature—air, water, earth, fire—and the stuff of our dreaming.

Restoring Tradition, Reawakening Emotion

Tarkovsky's refusal to anchor authorship in a web of social and historical factors suggests that for him, since modern rationalism cannot fully explain the creative process, art in turn cannot quite teach a lesson. This is perhaps why, instead of learning the secret of casting bells from his father, Boriska relies on a visceral intuition. In depicting the devils of hell or the merciless features of Christ Pantocrator, Theophanes' icons are clearly out of touch with the peasants' imaginative yearnings. By contrast, in the director's words art should give "a jolt" and provoke a "psychical experience."[41] This sense of emotional expansion resides in the materiality of painting itself. In a moment of frustration, Andrei splashes some dark paint on a white wall. The stained wall elicits the empathy of the dumb girl, who cries after touching the paint. Through her response Tarkovsky suggests a parallel between open, bleeding wounds and angry brush strokes. In a cinema in which movement coincides with water, it is not surprising if paint is replaced by blood or milk. This parallel culminates in the mixing of blood and paint in a rivulet running through the forest when, during the episode entitled The Raid, soldiers blind a group of artists.

In addition to a view of art as "psychic jolt," Tarkovsky associates the creative process with a series of intuitive flashes or instances of illumination, which artists and children, thanks to their openness to the imaginary realm, are more apt to experience than pragmatic adults. In the palace of the Grand Prince, a little girl splashes Rublev with milk. Based as it is on a carefree sense of play, her gesture strikes a note of contrast with Andrei's frustrated throwing of dark paint against a white wall. Milk, in this episode, does function as a reminder that the creative process feeds off natural substances. Needless to say, egg tempera was used in icon painting.

Tarkovsky's epiphanic moments stem from milk, fire, rain, and, generally speaking, from the emotional resonance of the earth with its secret cycles of growth and decay. In the forest, when Andrei's eyes turn to a pool of water crowded with dead leaves and broken twigs and teeming with insects, we tend to associate this iconography with a process of inner awakening. The proliferation of elements in the water evokes the mysterious, overlapping marks of a secret code or the lines of a miniature riddle whose solution is possible only for those who have been initiated into a special cult. In a similar fashion, the pagans' candles wavering in the darkness and the flames attacking Rublev's robe during the rite, the ambers burning near the casting pit and the dirty chunk of snow Rublev carries out to the fire during his period of silence, suggest an interest in mixing the elements, as if he were looking for a new kind of spiritual alchemy.

Just as the icon is a combination of opposites, in the sense that a spiritual power resides in a concrete object, Tarkovsky's weaving of images of water with fire, earth, and air recharges the viewer's imagination by tapping contradictions that exceed or precede culture, as they reach back into the core of life itself. This strategy of switching across oppositions reaches its climax at the end of the long film, heretofore entirely in black and white, when, all of a sudden the director adopts color to survey Rublev's icons in all their splendor.

The same strategy is especially apparent in the episode of the Jester, which casts the performer's convulsive rhythm against a stableful of peasants of all ages, some of them absorbed by drinking, some immersed in daydreaming. In particular, a young girl has the all-knowing look of an adolescent painted by Balthus, whose innocence goes hand in hand with a touch of perversity. Like the four elements of nature, which for the director have both destructive and regenerative powers, here "hideousness and beauty are contained within each other,"[42] so much so that our emotional channels are kept in a state of suspense between two possible, conflicting outcomes.

Despite its visual and psychological power, *Andrei Rublev* was equally misunderstood at home and abroad. Persecuted by the Soviet censors, it was officially released in 1972, thus confirming Tarkovsky's unique political predicament in his own country: on one hand, he was able to secure the financing from the ruling establishment for the production of *Andrei Rublev;* on the other, through this film he was celebrating the worst enemy of the state, a religious worldview.

Awarded the International Critics Prize at the 1969 Cannes Film Festival, *Andrei Rublev* elicited a great deal of admiration and much criticism, especially from Italian critics, who in the wake of 1968 were sensitive to Tarkovsky's search for freedom of expression but also unsympathetic toward a director who seemed more interested in the life of the soul than in sociohistorical analysis.

Today, after the fall of Communism and the disintegration of the Soviet Union, and in conjunction with a resurgence of interest in the religious past of the Russian people, Pan-Slavic traditions, and icon painting, *Andrei Rublev* has aroused a new wave of interest. Should we admire Tarkovsky for maintaining a lonely stance in the Soviet state, an isolated artist making important films about values that the authorities could only condemn? Or should we see in him only a deeply nostalgic temperament? Although Tarkovsky's work with the four elements of nature is meant to bring about a radical change in his viewer, his cinema remains a project of restoration for the sake of icon painting. One may wonder whether this orientation strikes a note of contrast with the socialist utopias envisioned by the modernist avant-garde of the early twentieth century.

These questions are not easy to answer, especially after reading Margaret Betz's remarks on how icon painting subtends the image of the Tsar as well as that of Lenin:

> While the rest of Europe developed the theory of the divine right of kings, political thought in Russia tended to focus on the Tsar as "the living icon of God, just as the whole Orthodox Empire is the icon of the heavenly world." Even today [1977], pictures of Russia's political leaders serve a function similar to that of the icon. Isaak Brodsky's *Lenin in the Smolnyi Institute*, 1935, though it eschews all the formal characteristics of icon painting, is clearly the image of Russian Communism's patron saint.[43]

Perhaps Tarkovsky himself, were he alive today, would be hard put to answer these questions, but my guess is that he would still cling to his beliefs in the filmic image as a vehicle that moves toward something limitless and invisible and in art as an instinctive and intuitive experience.

Although the theological underpinnings of icon painting may account for the omnipotence of the Tsar and the centralization of the state around Lenin, Tarkovsky was not interested in an overpowering, disembodied, God-like mastery but in illumination, elevation, inner awakening. Many sequences in *Andrei Rublev* never achieve stability or settle into a single meaning. For instance, from Efim's flying point of view, we see a herd of wild horses running as freely as the wind across the countryside. While this image powerfully conveys the exhilaration of creative expression, it also announces the beginning of the attack against Vladimir, when the Tartars launch their horses at great speed toward the walls of the city. The question of whether the ideology of icon painting leads to freedom or to oppression remains open for us to ponder, while we become aware of how the same kind of image system can be put to use in entirely different ways, according to competing ideological agendas.

CHAPTER 6

F. W. Murnau's

Nosferatu

~

Romantic

Painting as

Horror and

Desire in

Expressionist

Cinema

F. W. Murnau's *Nosferatu: A Symphony of Horror* (1922) was one of the earliest films about vampires. Most of the plot elements of Bram Stoker's *Dracula* (1897) may be found in *Nosferatu*, as in many other twentieth-century treatments of the vampire legend. No other film about vampires, however, has received such weighty critical attention. In Murnau's version, a young businessman, Hutter, leaves his wife, Ellen, and travels to the castle of Count Orlock in order to complete the sale of a house in Germany to the aristocrat. The Count is really a vampire, or a "Nosferatu," one of the undead. After buying the house, the legendary creature leaves the wild forests and mountains of Transylvania and travels by sea to his new home in Wisborg, bringing the plague with him. He drains Ellen of blood throughout a night of terrifying shadows and dies, struck by the first ray of sun, at daybreak.

There are two widely known critical claims about *Nosferatu*. In his famous psychological history, *From Caligari to Hitler* (1947),[1] Siegfried Kracauer maintains that the vampire Nosferatu is a foreshadowing of Nazi tyranny; in *The Haunted Screen* (1952),[2] Lotte Eisner argues that Murnau's visual style in *Nosferatu* reaches back to Romantic painting, especially the work of Caspar David Friedrich (1774–1840). Eisner's insightful observation calls for further inquiries into Murnau's art-historical training and into his taste outside the academy, but Kracauer's interpretation is so powerful that it has discouraged alternative readings of the film.[3]

The purpose of this essay is to attempt to weave together Eisner's and Kracauer's lines of thought and move beyond them. In particular it will discuss the visual sources deployed in the film in order to explore whether the character of Nosferatu may indeed stand for something larger than an anticipation of Hitler. In the course of my discussion, the reassessment of Nosferatu as a character outgrowing Nazism, the psychohistorical framework most familiar to Kracauer, will go hand in hand with a sense that Expressionist cinema looks back at Romantic landscape painting as something forever lost but also constantly longed for.

While Murnau's film mediates between the national legacy of the Romantic past and the more internationally minded avant-garde at the beginning of the century, the director also uses the character of Nosferatu to convey his ambivalent position between cinema as art and cinema as technology. As the undead—or a creature between life and death, stillness and motion, film and painting—the character of Nosferatu combines love and tyranny; he is both helpless and terrifying, striving for harmony and completion beyond the divisions of the modern self, while bringing destruction to everyone who comes in contact with him. Nosferatu's two sides—one inspiring desire, the other eliciting fear—replay Murnau's double-edged view of the cinema as a machine made of painting and mechanical reproduction, of auratic pleasure and deathlike serialization. In light of Murnau's definition of his own medium, the character of Nosferatu can be seen as an embodiment of Romantic painting, of the supernatural in daily life, of an unfulfilled yearning toward the divine, which, as Thomas Elsaesser might put it,[4] returns as technology or as the horror of cinema.

Murnau's inclination to assign positive and negative sides to art as well as to technology mirrors the Expressionist double rhetoric of regression and rebirth, of a return to the past and a liberating drive toward the future. The shift from Romantic mysticism to Expressionist despair at the heart of the encounter between cinema and painting is really grafted on a cyclical view of the historical process, in which the modern returns as the primitive, and the primitive paves the way for tomorrow.[5] Franz Marc, Murnau's friend since their student days in Berlin, eloquently describes this sense of being torn between what lies behind and what is ahead: "What can we do to be happy but give up everything and run away, draw a line between yesterday and today?"[6]

Murnau's Education in Berlin and Heidelberg

It is nearly impossible to know exactly why and how every art-historical allusion made its way into this film, which was the result of a cooperative effort on the part of the director, Murnau; the scriptwriter, Henrik Galeen; and the set designer, Albin Grau. Yet an awareness of the intellectual climate surrounding Murnau during his formative years may disclose the debates, the trends and schools of thought which are likely to have had an impact on the director.

Murnau was born into the upper-middle-class family of a textile manufacturer in 1888. As an adolescent, he made several visits to the art capital of the world, Paris, and learned to speak French quite well.[7] He also began to cultivate an interest in the arts through his half sister, who was a painter and loved to stage plays. After passing his baccalaureate exams, the young Murnau arrived in Berlin in 1905. In those days Berlin was a tumultuous city: it competed with Paris for leadership in the arts,[8] it polarized a whole nation in a search for political unity and identity, and it was undergoing a traumatic increase in population and industrialization.[9] As Murnau began to settle in, Georg Simmel, who taught in Berlin between 1900 and 1914, was already mesmerizing various intellectual circles with his double-edged view of modernity as that which liberates but also enslaves. A year after Murnau's arrival, the National Gallery hosted a huge retrospective devoted to the last one hundred years of German painting. It was in this context that Caspar David Friedrich began to emerge as the key painter of the early nineteenth century. The art historian Joseph Leo Koerner reports,

> Rediscovered, he [Friedrich] was at once hailed as uncannily modern for his time. Reviewers of the 1906 exhibition, in which Friedrich was represented by thirty-six oils and over twenty drawings and watercolors, saw in his treatment of light and color an anticipation of Impressionism, while

Friedrich's distinctly German sensibility and subject matter were celebrated as prophetic of an authentic national tradition whose triumph, these reviewers predicted, was still to come.[10]

Murnau could hardly have missed the debate surrounding Friedrich's work that was spurred by the exhibit. In addition, he was at the University of Berlin between 1905 and 1910 as a student of philology—namely, the study of historical sources for the comprehension of texts—and must have heard echoes of the great rivalry between two prominent lecturers: Heinrich Wölfflin (1864–1945), who was chair of art history between 1901 and 1912, and Julius Meier-Graefe (1867–1935), a former student of Wölfflin's and a Francophile art critic who had just published the controversial *Evolution of Modern Art* in 1904. In the wake of Alois Riegl's (1858–1905) notion of *Kunstwollen*—a pervasive spirit or impulse motivating and shaping the art of a certain period or ethnic group[11]—Wölfflin launched art history as an academic discipline with his *Fundamental Principles* (1915), in which he moved beyond an anecdotal and hagiographic approach toward a history of vision and formal comparative analysis. Yet Wölfflin's views were far more nationalistic than those of Meier-Graefe, who was a great supporter of Gauguin, Van Gogh and Toulouse-Lautrec.[12] Instead of paying attention to the Expressionists or to recent French art, Wölfflin admired Chancellor Bismarck and loved the neoclassical style and the mythological scenes of his personal friend Arnold Böcklin (1827–1901), a painter of Swiss origin who embodied the bourgeois ideals of Wilhelmine Germany, who was hated by the avant-garde, and who was defended by prominent figures like Thomas Mann and Hugo von Hofmannsthal.[13]

The dispute between Wölfflin and Meier-Graefe over the so-called Böcklin case is important to an understanding of Murnau's art-historical training, for after leaving Berlin (probably without completing his degree in philology), Murnau studied the work of Albrecht Dürer, Matthias Grünewald, and Hans Holbein; German Romantic literature and Shakespeare; and Latin, English, and French at the University of Heidelberg. Murnau's mentor in art history at Heidelberg was Carl Neumann, a follower of Wölfflin.[14] As a student in Berlin, Murnau became a good friend of the Expressionist painter Franz Marc, the theater director Max Reinhardt, and two remarkable women, the sculptor Renée Sinténis, and the poet Else Lasker-Schüler. He also spent all his father's money traveling abroad, learning about recent French art, and assembling a small, eclectic collection of contemporary artworks. Despite Murnau's interest in the recent international art scene, it is likely that in Heidelberg the history of art department exposed him to a strictly Wölfflinian approach, in the sense that his teacher, Neumann, was concerned with what makes German art German and how German artists over the centuries had renewed themselves by engaging in dialogue with the masters of the Italian Renaissance. Wölfflin reached a definition of German art by setting up contrasting visual polarities, which allowed him to argue that Northern art, compared with Italian art, was more pictorial and dark rather than linear and clear. In any event, as was the case in Berlin, Murnau did not graduate from Heidelberg. Along with his best friend (and perhaps his lover), Hans Ehrenbaum Degele, an art collector and the son of a Jewish banker, he dabbled in music, theater, and literature; he was learning about contemporary art through his friends and not in school.

While he was spending time with the avant-garde outside the university, Murnau was probably exposed to Wilhelm Wörringer's books *Abstraction and Empathy* (1907) and *Form in Gothic* (1912), which had great influence among the Expressionists. Wörringer (1881–1965) had studied in Berlin before coming to the University of Bern, where he was a lecturer between 1909 and 1913. Like Wölfflin, Wörringer was influenced by Riegl's concept of *Kunstwollen*, inasmuch as he argued that stylistic peculiarities stem from an artistic volition that directs itself toward the satisfaction of fundamental psychic needs.[15]

Against the background of a traditional education with a strong philological-historicist flavor, Murnau's intellectual oscillation between Romantic painting and Expressionist art explains the rich range of *Nosferatu*'s actual visual sources and potential intertextual references—which, as we shall see, range from Friedrich to Edvard Munch, from Böcklin to Marc. The allusions to Friedrich's landscapes and Biedermeier decor must have been consciously planned by Murnau and his collaborators, who traveled to specific sites before shooting and worked from a script that included sketches of furniture. However, the links between *Nosferatu*'s apocalyptic view of the historical process and Marc's animal paintings or Munch's anguished vision of modernity may stem from the film itself, from its power to convey the climate of an age well beyond the immediate intentions of the director and his team. With *Nosferatu*—the first successful film of a little-known director who was surrounded by individuals (Albin Grau, Henrik Galeen, Fritz Arno Wagner) already at home in their crafts—Murnau negotiated between the old and the new in an aggressive, national film industry. In the midst of what was called the *kino-debatte*, the cinema in Germany competed against more-established art forms, such as literature and the theater, by marketing its products as art and by training its audiences to appreciate abstraction and ambiguity.

Romanticism and Expressionism

Lotte Eisner has contended that *Nosferatu* makes apparent the continuity between a Romantic sensibility and the Expressionist project. That contention finds support among art historians who have argued that the German avant-garde, although constantly in touch with other artistic movements abroad (such as Cubism, Futurism, Fauvism, and Post-Impressionism), was characterized not only by a sense of national identity[16] but also by a self-descriptive rhetoric and iconographic vocabulary that latches onto the Romantics' interest in subjectivity and the unconscious, in mystery and the imagination, in a revival of Gothic taste and a sense of communion between artist and nature.

Even if art historians agree on the connection between Romanticism and Expressionism, Jacques Aumont and Thomas Elsaesser have questioned the usefulness of the category "Expressionist" film altogether, by arguing that Weimar cinema is too diversified and contradictory to fit under a single label:

> But first it is worth clarifying a common assumption: that Murnau was an Expressionist director. Most so-called Expressionist films (but especially Murnau's) properly belong to the stylistic heritage of German Romantic painting . . . rather than to the bold colors, the shifting perspectives and the jagged lines of the artists associated with Die Brücke or Der Blaue Reiter.[17]

Although I agree with Aumont and Elsaesser that stylistic labels tend to simplify cultural production, the fact remains that German silent films looked different from their French or Italian counterparts. Despite the limitations of "Expressionist" as a deceiving umbrella term, in this essay I am holding onto the term not to indicate a clear-cut, stable set of features or a specific group of films but to refer generally to the multifaceted development of a national style, one that drew its visual energy from the Romantic movement. It is not the term "Expressionist" in and of itself that interests me. Rather I want to set into relief how the origins of *Nosferatu* reach back to the previous century. Lotte Eisner deserves to be credited for being the first film historian to mention these Romantic roots, yet her discussion in *The*

Haunted Screen is so brief that we must, before we side with Aumont and Elsaesser and get rid of the label "Expressionist," explore at least for a moment what the word "Romantic" means in *Nosferatu*.

The terms of analysis applicable to *Nosferatu* have been much complicated. As a result of its naturalism, Murnau's film has been considered an anomaly of studio-bound German Expressionist cinema, whose most representative text (before Elsaesser's denunciation of the label) was Robert Wiene's *Cabinet of Doctor Caligari* (1920). While *Caligari* relies heavily on painted sets built in the studio, *Nosferatu* uses real locations.[18] Whereas in *Caligari*, the distorted quality of the sets makes apparent the internal workings of an anguished self, and the Expressionist image is static and artificial, in *Nosferatu* the forces of evil may be intangible, but they constantly move and lurk beneath the surface of ordinary life.

Were we to turn to Expressionism in painting, we would quickly discover that the extremes of Caligarism and Murnau's more subtle way of rendering the dark side of quotidian life are not at all irreconcilable. Instead, these two approaches roughly correspond to two different yet complementary methods used in Expressionist painting for externalizing states of mind, for investing the objective with a subjective gaze—a gaze ranging from fear to pleasure, from torment to contemplation. The two methods were espoused by two groups. The painters of Die Brücke (founded in Dresden and active between 1905 and 1913) emphasized distortion, restlessness, quick discharge of emotion, discontinuity, and demonic elements; the painters of Der Blaue Reiter (founded in Munich in 1912 and active until 1914), on the other hand, were interested in imaginative content, depth of expression, spiritual meanings, and inner poetic reality.

The Janus-like quality of the Expressionist movement reenacts the oscillation between the macabre and the lyrical that is typical of the Romantic experience. It also reappears in the character of Nosferatu, for the vampire is made of harsh, inorganic discontinuities and jagged, forced contrasts.[19] Murnau's mise-en-scène, in Charles Jameux's words, "is based on an imprint of life: it is ephemeral, mobile, unstable, a series of reflections, luminosities, nuances, clouds, vapors, and shadows."[20] Thus, in *Nosferatu*, we reencounter the horror about the modern condition that the members of Die Brücke expressed through their tortured canvases as well as the longing for something impossible or forever lost conveyed by the painters of Der Blaue Reiter.

In contrast to Elsaesser, who locates an antithesis between Murnau's naturalistic orientation and the self-consciously abstract style of Die Brücke and Der Blaue Reiter, I see these two groups as the two sides of a shared Romantic legacy. I locate Murnau's oscillation between nineteenth-century and twentieth-century art in the character of the vampire itself, who is a creature of horror and desire—two psychological states well suited to the emphasis on subjectivity that links Romantic to Expressionist painting and flourishes in Weimar cinema.

The Romantic Aspect and German Identity

Even though Murnau was involved in acting through Max Reinhardt (who became the director of the Deutsches Theater of Berlin in 1905), and his film develops the Romantic literary theme of the double, in *Nosferatu, art* is primarily *landscape painting.* In fact, this genre best satisfies Romanticism's tenet that the imagination cannot be limited by a concrete object, as in a sculpture with precise contours, but should float freely on the wings of interiority. In other words, in the wake of Romantic painting, in which landscape becomes a mental projection, Murnau learns to use the cinema to make visible the invisible, while imbuing objects and decor with intangible states of mind.

In contrast to history painting, which is firmly built around the human figure, landscape painting, with its emphasis on atmosphere, fulfilled this ideal of ambiguity. As we learn from Koerner, sculpture rather than music is the primary point of reference in history painting: "All painterly means (composition, light, color, etc.) must function to valorize, which is to say, to *isolate* and *distinguish,* the upright figure over against its ground."[21] By contrast, Koerner continues, "In place of figure painting's unity of the body, landscape substitutes the constructed coherence of the viewer's visual field."[22] Just as the project of Romantic landscape painting is an exploration of subjectivity, Murnau's images in *Nosferatu* suggest the inscription of the spectator's gaze, in the sense that daily objects and natural landscape grow beyond their harmless appearance as if they had absorbed hidden fears and desires.

The dependence of cinema, as the art of representing dark and occult forces, on Romantic landscape painting in *Nosferatu* does not mean that Murnau avoids citing other genres and traditions. Murnau's pictorial allusions reinforce the aura of cultural prestige cherished by the Weimar film industry. In addition, they either invoke a German national identity or reinforce the fantastic orientation of his tale. Considering the stir caused by the rivalry between Wölfflin and Meier-Graefe during Murnau's studies in Ber-

FIGURE 42. The Isle of the Dead *(1880)*, by Arnold Böcklin. *The Metropolitan Museum of Art (Reisinger Fund, 1926), New York.*

lin, it is significant that the director alludes to *The Isle of the Dead* (1880), by Böcklin (fig. 42), in the scene in which the vampire crosses a canal in a small boat to reach the entrance of the dilapidated, abandoned house he has purchased from Hutter. The spectral quality of Böcklin's nocturnal scene is visually manifested in the supernatural motion of the boat, which glides across the water by itself, with Nosferatu standing still in the darkness.

The facade of Nosferatu's new house in Wisborg is punctuated by a series of dark windows whose impenetrable and yet empty surfaces recall the surreal, stagy atmosphere of Giorgio De Chirico's paintings of alluring arcades, in which the suspicious regularity of the design can only release something dark hidden behind it.

Although film historians (Eisner, Elsaesser) tend to refer to Carl Spitzweg's (1808–1885) town scenes to account for Murnau's use of houses with steep gables typical of Baltic architecture, I feel that the lighting employed for the streets of Wisborg makes the buildings look more mysterious than picturesque, and in this respect, the atmosphere fits De Chirico's haunting depiction of public space rather than Spitzweg's charming view of life in a small town with cheerful civil servants and lovely girls. Whether or not Murnau encountered De Chirico's art during one of his trips abroad or in the context of conversations with Franz Marc (who went to Paris at least five times) remains to be proven. We know only that the Italian painter studied in Munich, lived in Paris between 1911 and 1915, and must have dabbled in German circles, for he had a fascination for things German to the point that Nietzsche, Friedrich, and Böcklin became strong influences on his work.

A haunting sense of perspective, reminiscent of De Chirico's tendency to push this convention to the edge of rationality, inhabits the narrow streets of Wisborg. They stretch all the way to the vanishing point, denying the citizens any escape from provincial narrowness, contagion, and eventually the disciplined rituals of death: processions of coffins and doors marked with crosses.

The De Chirico flavor of Murnau's images helps to explain the Surrealists' admiration of *Nosferatu*. For example, the bridge Hutter crosses into the land of phantoms is compatible with Surrealist iconography and also provides a possible reference to Alfred Kubin's fantastic pictures of coaches traveling through the forest and bad dreams assailing harmless sleepers.[23]

Besides using De Chirico and Kubin, Murnau plays up the fantastic register by transforming Ellen into a white-clothed creature out of a Moritz von Schwind painting. In her long, billowing nightgown, Ellen sleepwalks while calling out for her love. Likewise, in Schwind's *Apparition in the Forest* (1858), a woman walks under the moon; she is barely touching the ground and her back is turned toward the viewer. As a Romantic artist specializing in Nordic folktales, Schwind helps the director call attention to the popular and ancient origins of his story—a tale in which the main interest does not lie in the utilization of a well-known plot but in the mastery of atmosphere.

In addition to German sources, Murnau also turns to Dutch painting as a way to signal his intellectual citizenship in the centuries-old tradition of Northern art, rather than in the Romantic period only. For instance, Rembrandt's *Anatomy Lesson* subtends the sequence in the town hall in which Hutter's friend, the wealthy shipbuilder Harding (who takes care of Ellen during Hutter's absence), Dr. Sievers, and other town dignitaries gather to analyze the body of one of Nosferatu's victims: the captain of the vessel in which the vampire hid in order to reach Wisborg from his mountains in Transylvania. As they alternate between the examination of the ship's log and the wounds on the throat, medical expertise, economic power, and civic authority do not reach any concrete conclusions, except to confirm what is already more or less known: the plague is in town. In the wake of the Expressionist rejection of the rational, prosaic, and philistine outlook of Wilhelmine bourgeois society, Murnau seems to suggest that technology, science, and trade are false deities. These modern forms of knowledge do not defeat the vampire, but they produce the machines, commercial interests, and new discoveries that bring the devastation of World War I—a conflict whose horror Murnau experienced directly as a pilot in the German military.[24]

Despite his extensive art-historical knowledge, which he will fully display in *Faust* (1926), Murnau does resist the temptation to include too many eclectic allusions to other works of art, perhaps because the director's project in *Nosferatu* was primarily Wölfflinian: to make a German film using German sources. The director must have known that the landscape paintings of the German Romantic artist Caspar David Friedrich were the closest to his own intensely abstract and subjective stylistic orientation in *Nosferatu*. Friedrich distinguished himself by his gradual abandonment of the traditional iconography of either elegiac or sublime[25] painting—ruins and churchyards, avalanches and erupting volcanoes. Instead he concentrated on the quiet, personal evocation of infinities in forests and seascapes, "not as attributes of setting or event, but as simply the transformation through painting of how we see."[26] A century later, Friedrich's clouds and mists, which appeared to float out of the viewer's mind rather than out of the painted sky, were still informing the seascapes of Emil Nolde, a representative of the Blaue Reiter's orientation toward lyrical mysticism.

Murnau and Friedrich: Painting as Desire

A certain self-reflexive edge characterizes Friedrich's canvases of unfathomable expanses, in which landscape becomes a meditation on vision itself, and Murnau's use of landscape as an analogy for the desiring self. Heinrich von Kleist's observations on Friedrich's *Monk by the Sea* (1809–1810; fig. 43) are particularly applicable to the mood hovering over Ellen as she waits on the beach for Hutter's return—a situation charged with erotic ambiguity since it is Nosferatu who travels by ship, while her husband moves across the land. Appropriately, Kleist reports his response to Friedrich's canvas in subjective terms: "that one has wandered out there, that one must return, that one wants to cross over, that one cannot, that one lacks here all life and yet perceives the voices of life in the rushing tide, in the blowing wind, in the passage of clouds, in the solitary birds."[27] Like the nameless subject of Kleist's commentary, Ellen, too, wants to reach out for something infinite, supernatural, and eternal, although her sitting by the sea recalls a situation of confinement comparable to the one she experiences as she looks at the

FIGURE 43. The Monk by the Sea *(1809–1810)*, by *Caspar David Friedrich. Staatliche Museen zu Berlin, Preussicher Kulturbesitz, Nationalgalerie, Berlin.*

world through a window, day after day. Only men can be seen on the streets of Wisborg.

Just as Friedrich inserts an anonymous figure with a hidden gaze, turned away from the viewer and toward an open vista, to suggest the visionary nature of his landscapes, so Murnau places Ellen in the shot as a "Rückenfigur"[28] (fig. 44). In this way, the sea becomes not just the sea but something viewed, a mirror of interiority. Clearly, Murnau's adoption of Friedrich's device is very self-conscious, for Hutter, too, is positioned as a Rückenfigur, standing in front of a thick forest with a narrow path leading into it, out of which Nosferatu's coach emerges. Although Murnau places Hutter at the lower right corner of the frame, the director must have had in mind Friedrich's *Hunter in the Forest* (1813–1814), in which the hunter is placed firmly at the center of the composition. In both cases, the use of the Rückenfigur spells out the ambivalent connotations of the landscape—a site of fears and expectations that overwhelm the viewer in the picture, while making the filmic spectators aware of their own projections onto the image.

Contrast in scale is another device that Friedrich and Murnau share. Hutter's silhouette and the anonymous figure of *Hunter in the Forest* appear terribly small against the huge, tall trees. As markers of a human presence

FIGURE 44. *Ellen as a Rückenfigur, in* Nosferatu *(directed by F. W. Murnau, 1922). Author's Collection.*

FIGURE 45. *The shrine in the forest, in* Nosferatu. *Author's Collection.*

FIGURE 46. The Cross in the Mountains (1807–1808), by Caspar David Friedrich. Staatliche Kunstsammlungen, Gemäldegalrie, Dresden.

set against something out of reach, they bear witness to a higher, divine order, which contains them but which they would like to appropriate in the privacy of their solitary journeys. This is why, as Hutter proceeds deeper and deeper into Nosferatu's mountainous region, he seems to lose himself in the massiveness of the landscape, while a little roadside shrine on a rocky

elevation nearby (fig. 45) reminds the spectator that during the Romantic
period "the mysteries of religion" have "left the rituals of the church" and
have "been relocated in the natural world."[29] Murnau's insertion of a Christian element in the wilderness echoes, of course, Friedrich's famous *Cross in
the Mountains* (1807–1808; fig. 46), a controversial work in its own day, since
it incorporated landscape scenery into the form of an altarpiece.

In a similar vein, the crosses planted in the sand dunes next to Ellen
suggest that Murnau has emptied his filmic canvas by stretching the sea to
the horizon and minimizing Ellen's size, "to imagine, through an invoca-
tion of the void, an infinite, unrepresentable God."[30] It is also significant
that Wisborg is devoid of explicitly religious signs. In a sense, the crosses
can only be near Ellen, for she is ill, she is an outcast, and she longs for
something the rest of the town is not interested in.

Such a yearning for the divine also explains why Murnau begins the
film with a high-angle shot of the town square. This privileged but also
ominous view, stemming from a disembodied and perhaps unforgiving gaze,
is centered around a Gothic turret, which by the end of the film will echo a
low-angle shot of Nosferatu's castle, half ruined and half reabsorbed into
the mountain out of which it sprang. Interestingly, the taste for Gothic
architecture as a "God-made object, its forms almost identical with the
growth of leaves and branches, its cathedral naves a metamorphosis of a
forest of trees,"[31] travels from the Romantic period to the Expressionist
avant-garde, so Murnau's opening of *Nosferatu* (fig. 47) is clearly reminiscent
of *The Red Tower in Halle* (1915), by Ludwig Kirchner (fig. 48). More specifically, Expressionist artists shared with Wilhelm Wörringer an understanding of Gothic art as an art of inner feeling, leading in turn to the yearning
for the infinite in nature typical of German Romanticism. The art historian
linked not only medievalism but also orientalism and primitivism with spiritual renewal.[32] Thus Nosferatu's long nails bring together the notion that
the vampire is a creature born out of the darkness of nature, the image of
the oriental despot, and the elongated lines of Gothic architecture.

Murnau alternates shots of Ellen sitting by the sea with shots of silver
waves rushing in toward the shore and glistening under the pale northern
sun. As soon as the director drops the human figure from the image, an
invisible barrier between a perceiving subject and its desired object becomes
all the more palpable. For both Friedrich and Murnau, liminality is figured
in the guise of the mind longing for something powerful out there, but also
turning back to what is close and familiar. This is why the heavy door of
Nosferatu's castle (fig. 49) functions both as a threshold and as an obstacle,

FIGURE 47.
*The opening view
in* Nosferatu.
Author's Collection.

FIGURE 48.
The Red Tower in Halle
*(1915), by Ernst Ludwig Kirchner.
Museum Folkwang, Essen.*

FIGURE 49.
*The heavy door of the
vampire's castle, in*
Nosferatu.
Author's Collection.

FIGURE 50.
The Churchyard
*(1825–1830), by
Caspar David Friedrich.
Kunsthalle, Bremen.*

much as a wooden gate slightly ajar does in *The Churchyard* (1825–1830), by Friedrich (fig. 50). If the Romantic painter is interested in blurring the limit between the natural and the supernatural, the director, on the other hand, underlines the entrance into a forest, or the meeting of land and water at the shoreline, precisely because his fantastic tale is about the unstable boundaries between what is real and what is imaginary, what is normal and what is monstrous.

Liminality also means passage. Murnau tends to use either chiaroscuro or the dancing of light on bodies and objects to dematerialize solid things into "impalpable, translucent rays that evoke unworldly, spiritual realms."[33] The morning sun, for instance, lightens up the heavy decor in Hutter's bedroom at the country inn, and the reverberations of twilight make Nosferatu look even more impalpable during his walk across the city.

In a similar fashion, the theme of passage from the world below to the heavens above, from life to death, reappears in Murnau's low-angle shot of a ship's prow proudly pointing toward the vast sea. In contrast to Friedrich's similar composition in *On the Sailing Boat* (1818–1819), in which a couple drives the vessel toward a foggy skyline punctuated by minuscule Gothic cathedrals, in Murnau's shot no person or human creation is in sight, so the spectators have plenty of mental space to feel the presence of the vampire aboard. Nosferatu's energy, his power to propel the ship forward, seems to inhabit the ship's ropes, sails, and masts. It is as if the rigging of the ship were meant to map vectors of ominous forces. Just like the painter, the director is a master "of all transitions between the visible and the invisible."[34]

Finally, the stillness of Friedrich's Rückenfigur enhances the introspective quality of his paintings. Murnau transfers Friedrich's emphasis on attentive immobility to the intense looks repeatedly exchanged between Hutter and Nosferatu, Hutter and Ellen, Hutter and his boss, Knock, the real estate agent who sends him to Transylvania. Although this kind of emphatic looking is certainly a code in the acting style of silent, Expressionist cinema, the fact remains that it enhances Murnau's exploration of interiority. This is also why the black, gaping windows of Nosferatu's abandoned house in Wisborg look like a series of staring, bottomless eyes that look into the darkness of our hidden selves.

Painting as Horror

Friedrich's use of the Rückenfigur calls attention to subjectivity in his paintings. Likewise, the decor of Murnau's *Nosferatu* continually reminds the viewers that even when the vampire is not visible, we bring the monster to life: *our* imagination gives him the power to exist. It is in fact the viewer's gaze that, by sensing Nosferatu everywhere in the mise-en-scène and therefore by feeling beyond seeing—or by "seeing too much," according to the etymology of the Greek word "horror"—moves beyond the boundaries of the tangible objects in the world and summons, with their help, the dark forces of evil.[35] For instance, Nosferatu's arrival in Ellen's bedroom is preceded by a flattening frontal shot of the vampire standing at his window, his eyes never losing sight of Ellen's gaze directly across from his building, as if he were a puppet who has to stay in touch with his master's desires.

The film critic Roger Dadoun dwells on how the vampire's power is visualized in the decor. The vampire's absent presence allows our minds to summon something that is not in the shot. In moving from the intangible to the plastic, Murnau performs a significant reversal of Friedrich's method, for the painter undoes landscape into an intangible state of mind. Dadoun writes, "But the fantasy also needs its anchorage points, just as the story needs action. The . . . structure of the global form . . . has to find an echo in other forms. It has to be embodied or reproduced in miniature. It requires precise details and markers around which psychic crystallisation can take place."[36] Dadoun's insight finds confirmation in several significant visual details. For example, Nosferatu's bald and pointed head is echoed by the Gothic arches that punctuate Murnau's mise-en-scène: the outline of the door of Hutter's room in the castle exactly repeats the narrow shape of Nosferatu's skull; a severe arch with its vertex aiming at the sky marks the vampire's entrance into Wisborg. The tiled floor in Nosferatu's castle reappears on Ellen's balcony, and the vampire's ability to communicate his presence across distances and barriers is suggested by the wind, which repeatedly fills the long, white curtains in the bedrooms of helpless women. In addition to decorative detail, Murnau's use of spatial depth suggests that the monster is as invisible as the horror we cultivate inside our heads. Inasmuch as we would like to deny our ability to guess, we cannot help but anticipate the vampire's arrival. The camerawork lengthens corridors and stretches rooms in the castle, while the huge fireplace and the exaggerated height of the chairs point to a feudal past.

To signal that what we see is a figment of our imagination rather than a concrete object, Murnau depicts the human figure with varying degrees of density and substance. In an extreme dematerialization of the body, Murnau shows us Nosferatu's encroaching shadow on the staircase leading to Ellen's bedroom, reducing the physicality of the vampire to a helpless

reverberation of something eager to possess a woman's body. The demateri-
alized body also reappears in the form of black silhouettes contained in the
small, oval frames of the Biedermeier decor; a skeleton stands on top of an
old clock in the castle; and after destroying a scarecrow during a moment of
collective rage, a crowd leaves behind only sticks and rags. Finally, in the
country inn, Hutter's young, half-naked body welcomes fresh water and the
morning sun with a nearly feminine complacency, which leads us to wonder
about the orientation of our own sexual desire invested in the image.

Clearly, the emotional resonance of German Romantic landscape painting lives on in our relationship with Nosferatu the vampire. Rather than
standing for the distant yet benevolent God of Friedrich's world, the supernatural returns in the guise of a haunting curse, as though, with the advent
of mechanical reproduction, the shift from the Romantic to the Expressionist sensibility had caused a split between the human and the divine that
no historical cycle will ever be able to heal. Whereas Friedrich's Rückenfigur,
although lonely, still participated in the world of nature, Murnau's individual, caught in the aftermath of World War I, finds himself abandoned by
God and by civil society. As a result of this painful transformation, the
interdiction against speaking Nosferatu's name (explained in an intertitle)
makes even more audible the primordial anguish of the desperate cry of
Munch's passerby in The Scream (1893).

A major source of inspiration for the Expressionist avant-garde, Munch's
work was at the center of attention in a Berlin café called Zum Schwarzen
Ferkel (At the Black Piglet), where Meier-Graefe engaged in debates not
only on the Norwegian painter's notorious antibourgeois, solipsistic stance
but also on August Strindberg, Henrik Ibsen, and Fyodor Mikhaylovich
Dostoyevsky. Although the exhibitions devoted to Munch in 1893, 1902,
and 1903 preceded Murnau's arrival in Berlin, in 1906 the painter executed a
mural for the hall of the Kammerspiele (theater). This local event must
have been discussed enough to reinforce Murnau's sense that avant-garde
art was both outside and against academia; it may also have rekindled his
uneasiness with the stale conventions of Wilhelmine society.

The Expressionist Aspect: Nosferatu as Cinema

Nosferatu's existence as a projection or manifestation of our subjective horror derives from the interiorized mode of address of Friedrich's landscapes.
After an exile in a prehistorical realm—the Carpathian forests—the vampire returns into history not only as painting but also as cinema. Yet for

Murnau, cinema is a double-edged creature with positive as well as negative connotations. Nosferatu as cinema is, first of all, an image marked by absence and death; the vampire is figured as a phantasmal entity so insubstantial that once he arrives in Wisborg, he literally disappears for a good stretch of the narrative to merge with its deserted, dreamlike streets. In a sense, Nosferatu's bloodsucking, which drains the world of its vital forces, plays on the notion that cinema, the art of movement as life, may also be a form of death at work, with one image exhausting itself into the next.

This sense of a death drive stored inside the celluloid of the film itself reemerges in the highly unstable quality of Murnau's shots, including his infrequent close-ups. It is as though something in the world outside the borders of the frame were eroding all its details from behind, thus weakening their informational value. This quality is particularly evident at the beginning of the film, when a medium close-up of Hutter fixing his collar in front of a mirror catches us by surprise; the spectral vision of Hutter's face that appears reflected in the mirror lacks a broader context within which to situate the details of the neck, throat, smile. Our disorientation is intensified as Hutter looks out the window and sees Ellen playing with a kitten, while leaning from another windowsill with an indeterminate location. This pattern of linking window to window without an establishing shot continues as Hutter and Ellen run through doors toward each other, inside their home. Ironically, their interaction as husband and wife occurs within the isolated contexts of individual shots, which in turn seem to gravitate toward a vertigo of displacement onto an unknown realm.

The idea of cinema as death replays itself in the equivalence Murnau sets up between plague and trade. Nosferatu's ship sails into Wisborg, a harbor town whose skyline resembles a seventeenth-century Dutch map. The notion of commerce as an expression of the ephemeral nature of life also lies at the heart of opulent Dutch still lifes, which in fact are called, not coincidentally, "vanitas." Murnau clearly alludes to this pictorial tradition in his lingering shots of the food on the vampire's table and the drinking vessels in the country inn. Even if Nosferatu's castle is in the wilderness and his long nails suggest that he is more a primitive, exotic monster than a civilized Western capitalist, he is nevertheless a man of wealth who does not hesitate to buy a building in Wisborg, just because he wants to be near Ellen. As the owner of the castle and the client of a real estate agency, the vampire is a sort of vanitas, and at the end of the film, when the sun rises, he will vanish into a puff of smoke, which reminds us as well of the perceptual richness and fragility of the filmic image.

Murnau's ability to capture on celluloid the turmoil of his times is as unstable and poignant as the Expressionist experience, which art historians usually date from 1880 to 1916. Thus, in keeping with an allegorical understanding of *Nosferatu* as a narrative about revisiting a national past that has failed to live up to its promise of communion between man and nature, and man and God, the death of the vampire as cinema in 1922 is not only a delayed obituary for Expressionism but also a commentary on the end of the Romantic movement and its fascination with obscurity, which occurred shortly after the invention of electric light in 1879. In a brief sequence, Murnau shows us an old man turning on an oil lamp on a dark street corner, providing a lethal light that kills the cinematic vampire, who, like the filmic image, can exist only in darkness.

This figuration of Nosferatu as cinema points to a self-reflexive awareness running throughout Murnau's tale, which, were it to become too explicit, would upset the already precarious balance between the film's fantastic and its documentary poles. This may partly explain Murnau's decision not to adopt Bram Stoker's setting for *Dracula* (1897), the film's literary source. Instead of setting his vampire film in England, at the end of the century, close to the birth of the cinema, Murnau moves the action to Germany and backward in time to 1838—which is to say, during the Biedermeier period, one year before the official birth of photography (1839) and two years after Caspar David Friedrich's death. Even though the credits of the film cite the literary source, perhaps with the intent of establishing an authoritative precedent and artistic quality, Murnau and his collaborators became involved in a lawsuit over plagiarism, which obliged them to change all the names of the characters. Whether Murnau had to or wanted to, he avoided Stoker's use of traditional elements of vampire lore—such as religious and secular objects (crosses, garlic) to defy the monster, the rebirth of the victims into vampires, the transformation of the undead into a bat or a wolf—in the process slimming his protagonist down to an evanescent, flickering figment of the German nocturnal imagination, thus establishing a more subtle analogy between his character and the cinematic medium.

Biedermeier art was rediscovered in 1906 at the Centennial Exhibition of the National Gallery of Berlin (the same event that gave Friedrich fame); by then the term "Biedermeier" had come to stand for such middle-class virtues as the values of home and family and the celebration of a clean and peaceful existence. In order to emphasize the Biedermeier look of his film, Murnau cast a nonprofessional actress in the role of Harding's sister just

FIGURE 51. *Biedermeier decor, in* Nosferatu. *Author's Collection.*

because she resembled a portrait by Kaulbach, a minor artist who specialized in domestic interiors and family scenes. It is in this spirit that Albin
Grau, Murnau's set designer, adopts a well-kept garden, family portraits,
and flowery wallpaper to depict the Hutter household (fig. 51). Yet Grau's
explicitly theatrical Biedermeier decor includes so many doors, windows,
and mirrors in the domestic scenes that it becomes highly unsettling. Grau's
sets imply that the ideal, happy home celebrated by the Biedermeier style
does not really exist; instead, this impossible ideal is replaced by the coffin
filled with native earth that Nosferatu carries with him from Transylvania
to Germany and through the streets and canals of Wisborg.

Most significantly, however, Murnau's unsettling allusions to the
Biedermeier style spell out the director's dissatisfaction with bourgeois conventions and sentimentality. At first sight Ellen and Hutter may seem happily married, but he does not hesitate to leave his wife for a financial reward,
whereas she does not quite appreciate his gift of freshly cut flowers. When
Ellen is most terrified by Nosferatu's presence, Hutter does not comfort
her by sharing her bed but sleeps alone on a chair nearby. Nosferatu's arrival
in Wisborg further disturbs this already questionable surface of routine
gestures of affection. After destroying the crew and taking over the ship,

Nosferatu looms large on the screen—in a close-up shot from an extreme low angle—before disappearing again. In a sense, the vampire embodies the sweeping rhythm and fast movement of the ship, which in turn serves as a figure for the cinema as a machine capable of mastering endless spaces. Although the cinema's associations with modernity are generally coded as movement, Murnau also associates modernization with stillness and isolation. For instance, with the spread of the plague, the inhabitants of Wisborg adopt a more modern way of living to the extent that they become more and more isolated from each other: they close their windows and a new law prohibits them from moving their sick relatives through the streets.

Murnau's filming of the sea sequence also alludes to the Northern European genre of marine painting. Artists working in this genre often depict vessels caught in the middle of a tempest, since rough waves and stormy winds allow for more daring compositional schemes. Significantly, a painting of this sort decorates the back wall of the room in which the town experts examine the captain's body. Yet when Nosferatu is in charge of the ship, the sea is eerily calm; this deviation from the conventions of marine painting makes the vampire's invisible presence appear all the more powerful. Indeed, the invisible force propelling Nosferatu's ship and the film named for him is the wind of freedom, which blows away all the stale manners of the Biedermeier world. Here Murnau seems to adopt an Expressionist fantasy of purifying cataclysm, of apocalyptic cleansing, "ridding the world of all those institutions and traditions that had hitherto restricted the free play of 'animal' instincts."[37]

In the transition from the nineteenth to the twentieth century, however, the pull of the infinite in Romantic painting loses the warm, all-engulfing glow of Friedrich's *Woman before the Setting Sun* (1818; fig. 52). Here, Friedrich's Rückenfigur seems to welcome the landscape into her womb while simultaneously generating its vibrance. As if Murnau were perversely adapting the painting to the film, the director replaces Friedrich's woman with Knock, whom the crowd subsequently turns into a scapegoat for the plague (fig. 53). Murnau shows us a countryside crossed by a string of black, frantic figures; the real estate agent is no more than a dark speck set against a huge sky. On the one hand, the citizens of Wisborg resemble the dark silhouettes decorating the walls of Hutter's house; on the other hand, the crowd also resembles a moving strip of photographic negatives, a grotesque form of early cinema (fig. 54). As a result of their aggression, they renounce their individual physiognomies, as they feast over the disheveled

FIGURE 52. Woman before the Setting Sun *(1818)*, by *Caspar David Friedrich. Museum Folkwang, Essen.*

FIGURE 53. *The real estate agent Knock as a scarecrow, after turning into a scapegoat, in* Nosferatu. *Author's Collection.*

FIGURE 54. *The crowd as a moving strip of photographic negatives, in* Nosferatu. *Author's Collection.*

carcass of a scarecrow. It is an anticipation of the savage punishment reserved for Knock.

Just as Nosferatu merges into space to the point of vanishing into the
architecture of Wisborg, he is also consubstantial with the photographic
process at the heart of the cinema. This is why Murnau treats us to a series
of special effects that do not occur "amidst hazy shadows, but against a
real, three-dimensional world brought into clear focus."[38] In other words,
Nosferatu as cinema can allow himself to disappear inside a documentary
image, while his hidden presence exposes the hallucinatory quality of daily
life and real locations. John Barlow eloquently describes Murnau's indulgence in technological virtuosity:

> Stop action is used . . . to show Nosferatu piling the coffins on the wagon,
> getting into one of them, and then being driven off at breakneck speed by a
> driverless wagon. Later, the Count materializes in a double exposure sitting
> on a pile of coffins in the ship's hold, while a sick man lies in the hammock
> in the foreground. When the ship's mate smashes his axe into the coffin
> later on, Nosferatu rises up in front of him, stiff as a board and pivoting up
> from the feet. . . . Most of these tricks are unobtrusive. The stop action is a

blunder, as it was in depicting the ghostly speed of the coach earlier. Nosferatu's popping up from the coffin as if on a spring has a fascinating grotesqueness about it, while the double-exposure appearance and disappearance are stock-in-trade representations of ghostliness.[39]

After adding to Barlow's list the doors in Nosferatu's castle that open by themselves, we can conclude that while these examples depend upon specifically cinematic techniques, they also associate the vampire with magic. As a fantastic creature, Nosferatu is the bad conscience of nineteenth-century German mercantilism and materialism, the underside of its celebration of science and technology—two domains that the Weimar film industry, according to Elsaesser, appropriated in order to improve the technical quality of its "art" cinema.[40]

Yet if Nosferatu is an anticipation of cinema as a technology of the imaginary, he is also a creature of nature, a primitive entity related to or in touch with the various animals Murnau includes in his mise-en-scène: horses, rats, spiders. This specifically Romantic iconography of animals in the open wilderness also appears in the horse paintings of Franz Marc. For the Expressionist artist, the animal was a symbol or a vehicle "through which man might once again recapture his lost contact with the forces of a God-given nature, almost reversing the direction of Darwin's theory of evolution."[41] Yet Murnau's bestiary and Marc's animals do not quite tell us whether the return to nature is a search for a primitive authority, invested with the tyrannical features Kracauer sees in Nosferatu as a forerunner of Hitler, or by contrast, an attempt to create an art that would circumvent the bourgeois conventions of Biedermeier, Wilhelmine, and Weimar Germany, thus putting men and women back in touch with their instinctive and forgotten selves along the circular pattern outlined by the organic death-bound drive that Sigmund Freud discusses in *Beyond the Pleasure Principle* (1920).

A Symphony of Horror: Gender and Spectatorship

As suggested by the word "symphony" in the film's title, Murnau holds to a Romantic ideal of the recovery of a lost unity between self and other, a merging or reconciliation of man and nature, of man and society. The musical metaphor in the title is consistent with Friedrich's penchant for vagueness, yet it also reminds us that the Romantics considered music, like dreams, a form of liberation from the restrictions of individuality: "Far more than any other art, music causes the minor ego (the empirical subject, in Kantian terms) to fade at the showing of art's power and give way to the sense of emerging into the All."[42] Stepping back from Romantic music into the terrain of Expressionist cinema, Jameux delineates this striving toward a higher fusion as he eloquently describes Murnau's approach to editing:

> His montage lends a frantic and desperate rhythm to the fantastic race toward death in the second half of the film. It is both linear as well as parallel, both anticipatory and intellectual; it creates effects of collage, it makes actions simultaneous, it confronts time with space. . . . In *Nosferatu*, . . . the montage is fundamentally poetic and visionary: it brings together the most distant realities, it defeats the illusion of time and it makes us get inside the interior duration of mental landscapes.[43]

Despite its faith in the interrelatedness of all things—a faith Jameux calls "poetic and visionary"—Murnau's montage, by linking situations and characters so far away from each other, also undermines the borders of each element, as if the search for unity were only the other side of disturbing exchanges, unthinkable translations. When Ellen, for example, stretches out her arms, calling for her husband across the night, her gesture is rhymed by Nosferatu in the castle, as he turns his head toward her.

This strange form of telepathy between woman and vampire subtends the linking of many other shots that seem, at first sight, to have no immediate reason to be brought together. The elongated shape of Nosferatu's coffin as it appears during the vampire's walk across the city echoes the wooden plank used by inspectors to board the ship, and the kiss between Ellen and Hutter upon their reunification triggers an expression of longing on Nosferatu's face as he stands outside the couple's home.

By privileging an atmosphere of strange correspondences or secret affinities over well-established causal links in the narrative, Murnau's editing is clearly indebted to the principle of empathy, or "Einfühlung," which means literally a "feeling into" another. The cultural historian Donald Gordon summarizes the psychological and aesthetic implications of this concept:

> Crucial in Theodor Lipps's definition of 1903 is the fact of identity loss: "In empathy I am not the real I, but am inwardly liberated from the latter, i.e., I am liberated from everything that I am apart from the contemplation of [artistic] form." Although Wilhelm Wörringer in 1908 was more interested

in "abstraction" than in "empathy" he, too, confirmed that empathy is dualist: it involves not only "self-affirmation" but also "self-alienation." Because "we are absorbed into an external object, an external form," in his words, there is the risk of "losing oneself" in the artwork.[44]

As a "feeling into" another and as a "'losing oneself' in the art work," empathy is not only reworked into Murnau's editing, but it also applies to the theme of the double and to his reliance on pictorial allusions. The process of "feeling into" another is both a threatening and a liberating experience for characters and spectators alike, who translate the discovery of a hidden side of themselves into the aesthetic experience of an art film.

While the spectators discover something about their identity they did not know before, the characters, in their turn, become reflections of other characters. After Nosferatu has drunk Hutter's blood, for instance, Hutter becomes his double. Like the invisible but omnipresent vampire gazing down at the city at the beginning of the film, Hutter dominates the valley below by standing on a hilltop inside an arched pavilion. Nosferatu himself is doubled both by Ellen and by Knock; confined to an asylum in Wisborg, Knock can sense the master's imminent arrival. Like Ellen, Knock longs for a view of the outside world, which he can see only through the window of his cell—an opening he can barely reach by climbing the wall as if he were a spider.

Murnau's handling of the theme of the double is grafted onto an exploration of sexual rather than class identity. Although Hutter leaves Wisborg for Transylvania with the hope of becoming rich, his encounter with Nosferatu has more homoerotic than commercial import. Inside Hutter's house, the castle, and the country inn, we repeatedly see Hutter and Nosferatu framed by round, relatively low arches. This decorative detail strikingly contrasts with the Gothic references in the architecture of the town that are repeated, as we have seen, in the elongated shape of the vampire's body and in his pointed skull. The round arches suggest instead the curving line of the female womb and convey a longing for the mother's body, or for a lost feminine origin. These two contrasting architectural styles, the pointed and the rounded, indicate an oscillation between a male and a female identity, a dilemma confirmed by Hutter's frantic running up and down steep staircases in the castle; penetrating beneath one's own surface behavior is necessary in order to cross over to a new self.

It is well known that Murnau had homosexual tendencies. Lotte Eisner reminds us that the director lived under the ominous shadow of the inhuman Paragraph 175 of the pre-1918 German Penal Code, which criminalized homosexual activity and, therefore, lent itself to all the horrors of blackmail.[45] Interestingly, Murnau's transcripts from the University of Heidelberg include a notation about the student's "good" behavior. This detail leads us to wonder how much, in those days, one's private life was subject to scrutiny. This repressive cultural climate explains why the homoerotic metaphor at the heart of vampirism between Hutter and Nosferatu had to be displaced onto Ellen on the one hand and onto landscape painting on the other.

The theme of the double, then, turns into a triangular configuration, particularly when the Count decides to sign Hutter's contract for the purchase of the house after seeing a medallion with Ellen's portrait. This image of woman thus displaces the money that traditionally marks the mercantile bonding of two men. At the end of his journey, Hutter is a troubled, helpless male and not the rich man he hoped to become in Transylvania. He takes Ellen back to their modest home, whose decor cannot compete with the luxurious house of the Hardings, which is supported by the profits of a shipbuilding business.

While Hutter's gain in self-knowledge remains limited, Ellen and Nosferatu thrive on their mutual fatal attraction, conveyed through speechless exchanges across the night and the wind, deserted streets and empty windows. By obscuring a real estate transaction with this dark love, Murnau seems to suggest that there is more to be gained through the dangers of unconventional sexual exploration than through the benefits of commerce and the advances of science. Like so many Expressionist painters, the director embraces the Nietzschean conviction that the Dionysian side of human nature is more rewarding than the call to rationality and order.

While the emphasis on sexual desire at the expense of class identity questions the bourgeois conventions of Biedermeier life and Weimar Germany, Murnau invites the spectator to indulge in pictorial images in which Hutter's body becomes an object of spectacle rather than a subject of action. This shift is noticeable in the scenes at Nosferatu's castle. The image of Hutter falling asleep near the fireplace has a tinge of debauchery and a sensuous aura that encourage the spectator to relax rigid gender stereotypes. Indeed, it is Murnau's use of paintings rather than his appropriation of a literary source that charges the film with unspeakable meanings. In this regard, the feminist theorist Janet Bergstrom argues that while Murnau hides his homosexual perception of masculinity in art-historical citations, he simultaneously recuperates the dimension of sexual desire by asking his viewer to engage in a slower, "contemplative" mode of looking usually associated with painting rather than cinema.[46]

Instead of using the adjective "contemplative" to describe the kind of looking Murnau solicits from his viewer, it might be more accurate to say that German Romantic painting in *Nosferatu* presupposes an extremely active mode of looking, precisely because for Murnau "horror" means feeling beyond seeing, reaching out beyond the self-image that society allows one to have. Furthermore, this mode of looking is not peaceful or unbiased, the way the word "contemplative" would seem to suggest, but deeply unresolved. As we shall see shortly, what remains ambiguous for male viewers is the object of sexual desire itself, whereas for female viewers what is in question is the entitlement to desire that precedes the choice of object, or what Mary Ann Doane calls "the desire to desire."[47] For instance, in the Hutter household, Ellen is surrounded by thresholds and reflecting surfaces. This space of facades and boundaries closely resembles that depicted by Georg Friedrich Kersting in *Before the Mirror* (1827), an intimate genre scene with a Biedermeier flavor. Unlike Kersting's woman, who stands in front of a mirror placed between two windows, Ellen never contemplates her own image (fig. 55). Although her behavior indirectly reflects Nosferatu's invisible presence, she never acknowledges herself as a sexual being. In this way, Ellen resembles the nun who nurses Hutter back to health after his escape from the castle.

Bergstrom raises the interesting question of what might be at stake for Murnau's female spectator, since Ellen, dressed in black and confined in the home, is presented as a highly desexualized creature, while her secret desire for Nosferatu as the embodiment of a freer sexuality can be read as a mere device used to deflect attention away from the homoerotic subplot. By turning to Freud's definition of sexual choice, Bergstrom not only sheds light on the function of ambiguity in Murnau's visual style but also inadvertently points to the Romantics' preparation for Expressionist abstraction, through their taste for vaguely defined and limitless objects:

> Freud essentially redefines the meaning of "choice" by maintaining that sexual desire is characteristically unstable, both in object and in aim. Most fundamentally because Freud argues for a predisposition to bisexuality, the field of choice of both sexual object and sexual aim is defined as a continuum where the end points (male/female and active/passive) are ideal, or theoretical. Freud's theory of bisexuality means neither "either/or" (heterosexual or homosexual) nor "both" (if that means two fixed choices).[48]

FIGURE 55. Before the Mirror *(1827), by Georg Friedrich Kersting. Kunsthalle zu Kiel.*

Freud's model, in which sexual desire (both object and aim) is a fluid "continuum" rather than a stable entity, allows Bergstrom to suggest that although Ellen finally dies to save Wisborg from the plague, her sacrifice does
not neutralize the liberating and unsettling potential that art-historical
allusions hold for male and female spectators alike. In a sense, then, Ellen
is desexualized, but by using art history for the sake of an active and
unresolved way of looking, Murnau succeeds at least in undermining rigid

gender lines that are oppressive for men loving men and for women removed from the world and eager to latch on to desire even before choosing a sexual object.

The film offers two more examples of Ellen's inclination to transgress. First, of all the characters, Ellen is the most comfortable standing on the edge separating opposite domains. Her sleepwalking, for instance, is a mixture of two states of consciousness; it also occurs on a balcony, at a liminal point between the safety of the bedroom and the darkness of the night, the home and the void. Unlike Hutter, who can hardly endure looking out of windows, opening doors, or discovering the vampire's coffin in the crypt of the castle, Ellen is constantly experiencing more because she disobeys her husband and opens *The Book of Vampires*—and she does have the courage to stand in front of the window.

Second, in the film science and money fail to master the mysterious signs of vampirism. Only Ellen is a good reader, yet her use of *The Book of Vampires* marks a transgression across traditional gender lines. Throughout the film, men read and write, whereas Ellen can write "I love you" only in the form of embroidery. This feminine craft functions as a secret code, for Murnau's editing never makes clear whether the object of Ellen's love is Hutter or the vampire. Indeed, it seems easier to recognize that deep down, Hutter (who does not hesitate to leave his wife alone to go on a business trip) has chosen the vampire, even though he does not have the courage to admit his choice to himself.

The ineffectuality of reading and writing, combined with long shots whose fluid imprecision veers toward abstraction, offers a clear invitation to the viewer to feel beyond seeing. Somehow Ellen's heightened sensitivity is not far from that "inner music," which Franz Marc wanted to make visible in his Expressionist paintings and which Murnau evokes in the second half of the film's title: *A Symphony of Horror.* Ellen reads well because she senses, more than anyone else, the presence of an alien force. While asking his male and female spectators to step into Ellen's position and, consequently, to feminize themselves, Murnau redefines the cinema as a machine of the eye devoted to the painting of the mind.

Thus relying again on an active and unresolved looking (unresolved for men and women both, but for different reasons and at different levels) in *Nosferatu,* we may conclude that Romantic painting returns in Murnau's Expressionist cinema not only as horror but also as desire. This placement of the director between horror and desire, and of male and female spectators between male homoeroticism and female heterosexuality, is confirmed by Murnau's narrative, most of which is about traveling, moving across land and sea, covering the distance between self and other.[49] This is also why, at times, we may feel that little is achieved in terms of storytelling, except for the endless movement of the characters, pacing, running across the space of a room, a garden, a street, a beach, a forest, toward each other, without ever really coming together. Only Ellen seems to get somewhere, shortly before Nosferatu's arrival in her bedroom. By staring intently at the house across the street, she turns the window into a mirror of her own desire; it is her crossing of this threshold between self and other, social duty and private fantasy, that allows Nosferatu to have his image born anew in the reflecting surface of a mirror significantly placed next to the window near Ellen's bed. According to the popular tradition, a vampire's image will not appear in a looking glass; yet Nosferatu, just before his death, comes into his own and takes on life for the very first time, for he ceases to be either invisible or a formless conglomeration of points in the decor that surrounds and supports our own horrified projection of his being (fig. 56). It is important, however, that Nosferatu's reflection is seen only by the film viewer; the vampire does not look at himself.

The question of whether Murnau's ending to the film is primarily optimistic or pessimistic still remains. On one hand, the presence of the light, which models objects in all their singularity, marks the end of a Romantic sense of nocturnal empathy, linked to a conception of the night as the only time individual entities can slip into an ocean of universals. On the other hand, Nosferatu's death also signals the end of the Expressionist faith in the future and the beginning of the so-called Era of Sobriety, or Neue Sachlichkeit, after the currency reform in the winter of 1923–1924. This climate of disillusionment surrounding the production of *Nosferatu* in 1922 was both preceded and followed by a series of traumatic political events that tipped the Expressionist dialectic of gloom and hope, vitalism and desperation, in the direction of an unrelieved pessimism. In particular, it is worth mentioning the Spartacist revolt in the winter of 1918–1919, during which the Marxists Karl Liebknecht and Rosa Luxemburg were killed, the Kapp Putsch in 1920, and the occupation of the Ruhr in 1923 by French and Belgian troops. Aware that the fate of Expressionism was doomed as the Weimar Republic stabilized itself and became a conservative bourgeois state, even Wilhelm Wörringer declared in November 1920 that the dreams of the avant-garde were now history.

Murnau's images in *Nosferatu* eloquently convey this sense of desperation and imprisonment. An intertitle sanctioning the vampire's death is

FIGURE 56. *The vampire at sunrise, in* Nosferatu. *Film Stills Archive, The Museum of Modern Art, New York.*

followed by a shot of Knock in prison, with a rope tied around his short and deformed body. A second intertitle declares that, thanks to Ellen's sacrifice, "there were no more deaths from the plague and that happiness was regained." Yet film critic Bert Cardullo astutely points out that "the camera does not return to the streets."⁵⁰ Finally, even though the Neue Sachlichkeit in Weimar Germany was characterized by great technological progress, Murnau does not hesitate to seal his film with a statement about the impotence of science. Dr. Bulwer stands outside the couple's bedroom looking on, while Hutter, with a leg dangling on the floor, once again does not share the bed with his agonized wife. The shot is constructed across multiple framing devices: the outline of the door is echoed by the curve of the canopy surrounding Ellen's bed, which in turn is reflected in the mirror next to the window, with these two elements linked to vision functioning as the two most distant and inner frames, respectively. This *mise-en-abîme* of frames suggests that in contrast to Nosferatu's brief moment of vitality inside the mirror right before daybreak, Ellen's inclination toward the discovery of her own emotions has been replaced by an interior architecture of seclusion. A final, remote view of Nosferatu's castle growing out of the rock in the mountain seems to compensate for Hutter's helpless posture.

To return to Wölfflin's categories of German art, *Nosferatu* is certainly dark and pictorial, and despite its pessimistic flavor, its ending is more open than closed. To convey the vampire's double-sided nature, Murnau lends both a positive and a negative valence to his use of art in film. Romantic painting returns to the cinema as a force of horror and a figuration of desire, and simultaneously, the director explores the destructive as well as the liberating possibilities of technology. It remains hard to guess, however, how Murnau must have really felt about his own historicist education, his Wölfflinian training, his involvement in Expressionist circles, once the shooting of the film was over. Clearly the director's exposure to philology, art history, and the avant-garde are put to use in *Nosferatu* to raise questions about national origins and sexual desire, class boundaries and the historical process. Perhaps Murnau's film remains incredibly powerful and inexhaustible because it is such an accurate product of its times and, at the same time, an elusive statement about a whole epoch. This is exactly why, as an Expressionist work of art, *Nosferatu* stands up to the comparison with Friedrich's Romantic canvases.

CHAPTER 7

Kenji
Mizoguchi's
Five Women
around Utamaro
~
Film between
Woodblock
Printing and
Tattooing

K enji Mizoguchi's *Five Women around Utamaro* is a melodrama about
the life of a famous Japanese woodblock-print artist set at the beginning of
the nineteenth century. Mizoguchi shot this film in 1946, an eventful year in
Japanese political history. A new set of laws to replace the Meiji Constitu-
tion of 1889 was promulgated in November and took effect on May 3, 1947.
This was only the first step toward the democratization of Japan supervised
by General Douglas MacArthur during the U.S. Occupation, which ended
on April 28, 1952, with a peace treaty signed in San Francisco, while the
Korean War was already in progress. After surrendering to the Americans
on August 14, 1945, Japan was in desperate economic condition and willing
to cooperate with the former enemy to overcome the disasters of war and
the pain of defeat. In the new order, although the emperor continued to
symbolize Japan as a whole in the eyes of the world, paternal rule did not

apply to adult family members any longer. This shift of authority reappeared in the transfer of actual political power to representatives elected by the people. The new emphasis on civil liberties enabled women to vote for the first time and permitted labor unions to organize.

The end of the war and the establishment of Western-style democracy in Japan made even more apparent Mizoguchi's contradictory stance between the past and the future: "I want to continue to express the new, but I cannot abandon altogether the old. I retain a great attachment for the past, although I have only little hope for the future."[1] The director's mixed feelings toward historical change characterized his leadership of the first labor union in the Japanese film industry, organized through the Shochiku Ofuna Studio. In contrast to what is expected of a left-wing militant, Mizoguchi was notoriously shy about talking in public and disliked strikes; and in previous years, his political affiliations had been as ever-shifting as his constant oscillation between period films (jidai-geki) and contemporary subjects (gendai-geki), both genres focusing on the burden of society and tradition and on the struggle of women for a better life.

In this postwar climate of widespread poverty and social upheaval, Japanese audiences looking for easy entertainment and intrigued with the American way of life "streamed into the theaters that had survived the bombings."[2] Even though filmmaking entailed great difficulties due to increasing inflation and shortages of every kind, the film industry hastened to build more theaters and pushed for new productions. The American censors, however, did not support mere entertainment at the movies. As Kyoko Hirano explains in her book on Japanese cinema under the American occupation, *Mr. Smith Goes to Tokyo,* "The 'democratization films' were also called 'idea pictures.'. . . Officials pressured the film industry to emphasize this type of film, at the expense of 'escapist films,' which it considered purely entertainment-oriented and therefore devoid of 'reorientation value.'"[3]

Although it was executed in a rush, Mizoguchi's *Five Women around Utamaro* is no simple escapist tale. In depicting the romantic vicissitudes of five women—Okita, Tagasode, Oran, Yukie, and Oshin—all of them linked in different ways to Utamaro and his circle of disciples, merchants, publishers, and teahouse owners in Yoshiwara, the pleasure district of Edo (ancient Tokyo), Mizoguchi analyzes the clash of rigid social rules and mercantile demands against the workings of male creativity and the transgressive nature of female desire. More specifically, the representation of different art forms in *Utamaro* enables the director to express ambivalence toward the cinema while also giving him the opportunity to spell out his own theory of what the filmic image should be like.

By situating the cinema between tattooing and woodblock printing in *Utamaro,* Mizoguchi interrogates the double-sided nature of his own artistic medium. For the director tattooing oscillates between phallocratic violence and the transformation of the body into art against conventions of markets and prices. This split between rebellion and social conformity is also true of the other art form explored by Mizoguchi in *Utamaro,* woodblock printing. In late eighteenth-century Edo, woodblock printing challenged the Kano school of painting, but it was also a form of commerce instrumental to a mercantile class aspiring to a higher social status. Woodblock printing and tattooing stretch across the opposite poles of mass consumption and unsettling liminality. With a comparable split vocation for Mizoguchi, the cinema either perpetuates social oppression while empowering vision through the cuts of editing and the penetration of space, or it can disclose a realm of freedom through the deployment of all sorts of distancing techniques and a penchant for abstraction and the void.

Just as Utamaro had to struggle against the shogun, who in 1804 arrested him for his irreverent depiction of a political figure,[4] during the making of this film Mizoguchi was obliged to consult with the occupation authorities repeatedly. The Americans feared that a story set in the feudal past of Japan by a director who had previously dealt with hara-kiri and the tea ceremony[5] would inhibit the transition to Western democracy. As a historical film in which the female protagonist murders her former lover and his mistress out of jealousy, thus bringing capital punishment upon herself, *Utamaro* came up against the American ban on productions approving suicide, directly or indirectly, or portraying life as not worth living.[6] It was only after great effort that Mizoguchi sold to the censors the argument that *Utamaro* would be nothing else but a statement in favor of popular art and bourgeois life, rather than a nostalgic recollection of bygone days with samurai and geisha.

Still the Americans became the new oppressors Mizoguchi had to wrestle with, scene after scene, to the point that production was marred by constant arguments, interruptions, and compromises. After the release of the film—perhaps because *Utamaro* was meant to be a metacinematic statement in an autobiographical key of how Mizoguchi perceived his own creative predicament, his loyalty to the arts of the past in postwar Japan, and his relationship to women—the director declared that even though he would have liked to have more time to develop his project, he was standing by the final result.[7]

In a polemic against Mizoguchi's mixed feelings, the critic Kaneto Shindo argued that *Utamaro* was dry and lacking in sensuality. Likewise Kanji Kunieda (1893–1956), the author of the original novel (published in 1942), expressed his disappointment that the film did not sufficiently emphasize how eroticism paves the way for personal freedom. Even Yoshikata Yoda, Mizoguchi's faithful scriptwriter who adapted the novel for the screen, admitted that although he wanted to portray Utamaro as Mizoguchi's alter ego, his handling of the project did not overcome a series of "complex" and "muddled" ideas, which in turn contributed to the "dispersion" and "confusion" of the overall theme.[8]

These shortcomings may be attributed to the limited resources of the film industry in the immediate postwar period. Perhaps, despite the director's reputation for accurate historical detail and pictorial tableaux, Mizoguchi's studio could not afford high production values and expensive decorative touches. Nevertheless, when we consider Mizoguchi's training in the visual arts as a young man at the Aohashi Western Painting Research Institute, it is surprising that he did not use *Utamaro* as an opportunity to indulge much more in the fabrics of courtesans' kimonos and in the secrecy of folding screens.

Thus Mizoguchi did not take full advantage of the pleasurable component of Utamaro's art, which endlessly celebrated female seduction in the context of gardens and carnivals, boating parties and waterfronts, while his courtesans gather shells along the shore and catch fireflies under the moon, or in the privacy of their chambers engage in domestic chores and in the ritual of blackening their teeth for embellishment. In a sense Mizoguchi's reliance on claustrophobic framing, multilayered compositions, and an intricate plot hints at self-censorship, or at a desire to drain visual pleasure out of the image, with characters, clothing, and domestic paneling amounting to a complex intersection of shadowy surfaces.

Put another way, Mizoguchi's visual style in *Utamaro*, a film about an artist and his work, is characterized by an elision of art-historical citations. Only a few iconographic details emerge from a comparison of Utamaro's prints with Mizoguchi's film. Oshin smoking a long pipe, for instance, recalls the carefree attitude of several courtesans depicted by Utamaro. The soft, black cloth draped around Tagasode's face during her elopement with Shozaburo recalls the Madonna-like typical female attire used in a whole string of prints about lovers in flight.

Even though *Utamaro* is about the life of a major figure in woodblock printing, the director's visual style is characterized by a consistent repression of pictorial sources, as if he wanted to empty the filmic image from within of the sensual appeal of Utamaro's work. By withholding the allure of art history, Mizoguchi makes sure his filmic image will veer toward emptiness or absence. Mizoguchi's rejection of art history as sensuality suggests an uneasiness with the female body, whose power to evoke castration the director must have half-consciously compared to the cuts of woodblock printing, filmmaking, and tattooing.

Self-censorship, however, or at least a tendency to frustrate the viewer's visual pleasure by producing a filmic image in which anthropomorphic elements become static shapes and the decorative component veers toward lifeless intarsia, was a stylistic strategy Mizoguchi consistently practiced well before the Occupation. As film historian David Bordwell remarks,

> During the nineteen-twenties and the nineteen-thirties Japan had one of the most stringent censorship codes in the world, and Mizoguchi's films challenge a censorship that banned depiction of adultery, nudity, "glaring eroticism of any kind," and "scenes of the interior of brothels, whether licensed or not." One historical effect of Mizoguchi's long shots and reversals of frontality may have been the downplaying of the immediately sensational aspects of his subjects. (Hence the frequent conflict between a highly melodramatic script situation and a detached staging of the action.) It is also possible that Mizoguchi's long take was employed to create a durational continuum which was difficult for a censor to tamper with.[9]

On the other hand, it is also possible that the reticent, dry mise-en-scène of *Utamaro,* a film set in brothels where the marketing of art runs parallel to the commerce of the female body, might be an attempt to get along with the democratizing mind-set of the American censors, which in turn was compatible with a climate of opinion encouraging the emancipation of Japanese women and condemning prostitution.[10] Even if the American occupation made fashionable kissing in public and the three S's—screen, sports, and sex—an excess of directorial nostalgia for the highly erotic and precious settings of Utamaro's age might have triggered the censors' dislike of brothels.

The question remains, however, why Mizoguchi downplays to such an extent not only the sensual side of Utamaro's art but even the visibility itself of the filmic image. It is as if the director had come to equate a proliferation of art-historical allusions and an excess of pleasurable images with the voyeuristic practices and the obscenities of Western modernity.

The best art for Mizoguchi neither celebrates the singularity of the self nor depends on appropriation or mastery. Rather, it presents a long, passive, distant look. Film critics (Dudley Andrew, Donald Kirihara) agree that *Utamaro's* contemplative camera recalls the attitude of a viewer trained in meditation who bears witness to the exhausting, destructive effects of human passion, one who stubbornly holds on to the role of detached spectator while human life performs the undoing of itself. Mizoguchi's awareness that staring at the world may not change *its* madness, but it can help *us* to get beyond its constraints, finds support in the staging of internal audiences in *Utamaro*, namely disciples witnessing the master's display of artistic skills. The turning of duration into a form of strength not only accounts for Mizoguchi's commitment to the long take at the expense of cutting but also explains the frequent moments of inaction in *Utamaro*. In Donald Kirihara's words, "We wait for figures to move to fill an empty space within the composition; we endure long pauses while characters catch their breath or sip a drink; we linger for an unusually long time on a vacated set before cutting to the next shot."[11] It is this emphasis on holding on to one's own burden to the limit that accounts for Mizoguchi's use of professional actors who can handle the sustained gaze of the camera and function well in single setups deployed for an unusually long time, until decor gradually evolves into intangible atmosphere.

Needless to say, this discipline of patience and sacrifice, of suffering and dying, explains Mizoguchi's obsession with women and melodrama in his cinema, and precedents for the formalization of oppression into art may also be found in the theatrical and narrative traditions of Noh and Naniwa Bushi.[12] Likewise the taste for absence and emptiness spans religion and Asian art, which for centuries has attempted to paint the ephemeral and the insubstantial, such as atmospheres, silences, shadows, and the void. This aesthetic orientation accounts for Utamaro's fascination with the white, smooth back of his models Tagasode, Oran, and Okita, for it is the part of the female body that most resembles a painter's canvas at the stage either before or beyond painting.

The death of Utamaro's women in the name of love can be seen as a projection of the director's notorious ambivalence about femininity, for it is well known that Mizoguchi depended on the other sex for his inspiration, but he also felt threatened by it.[13] This is why, for instance, he thrived working with actress Kinuyo Tanaka, who plays Okita, the female protagonist in *Utamaro*, but he also tried to quash her ambition to become a director. Despite his reputation as a womanizer and as a regular visitor of brothels, Mizoguchi was obsessed with the liberation of women, as if only their emancipation could generate a way out of his own haunting family history. Not only did he grow up with a harsh father and a victimized mother, but he also repeated this abusive pattern, because he relied economically on his sister to launch his career, and his wife ended up in an asylum.[14] Hence, in *Utamaro*, Okita's fate oscillates between jealousy pushed to the extreme of self-destruction—or so it seems from a strictly Western point of view—and a statement of uncompromising desire, which uses death as the void to perform a radical passage into an inscrutable chain of beings, a new form of life, thus defying all social constraints and the limits of the commercial screen. In contrast to Christianity, in which time is linear and has an end, for Mahayana Buddhists like Mizoguchi,[15] dying is a transitory threshold rather than an abrupt stop, for time is cyclical.

In addition, as soon as we consider that the making of *Utamaro* occurs right after the sacrifice of innumerable kamikaze pilots, we have to remind ourselves that death has had a special flavor for the Japanese throughout the centuries. In fact, kamikaze (meaning divine wind) pilots took on suicide missions because for Buddhists death paves the way to spiritual enlightenment and it enables the transformation of an average individual into something eternal.

According to a Buddhist view, Okita's death may be the end of Okita, yet it is not an absolute ending, since life is like a wheel. The idea of death as positive, sliding into the wider cycle of nature, reoccurs in the journeys undertaken by Mizoguchi's characters. As Linda Ehrlich explains, "The journey, with its pattern of embarkation, return, and renewal, is associated in Mizoguchi's films with the working through of a metaphysical or psychological problem concerning the nature of desire."[16] Interestingly enough, in *Utamaro* the artist's journey to the palace of the shogun who persecutes him is never shown. By contrast, Okita's wandering through a beautiful countryside, sparkling with light and water, is reminiscent of the French Impressionist landscapes Mizoguchi studied and loved at the Aohashi Western Painting Institute. Furthermore, Yukie's walk through an awesome forest, in the footsteps of her lost lover, Seinosuke, suggests that women, more frequently than men, have the courage to undertake journeys of danger in the name of an unfulfilled love.

In particular, the ties between Mizoguchi's cinema of desire and emptiness, women and death, become evident as we dwell on one sequence involving a procession of female beauty in *Utamaro*. At the beginning of the film, Mizoguchi's camera tracks against the fluid unfolding of a majestic line of courtesans walking down the main street of Yoshiwara (Nakanocho), under vaporous clouds of cherry blossoms, whose delicate petals announce the arrival of springtime and remind us of the ephemeral nature of all things. The sequence gains a hypnotic edge from the opposition of the camera's speed to the courtesans' slow gait, for they wear tall and heavy shoes, which, step after step, they have to drag across the ground sideways, thus appearing to fall on their own movement forward. Put another way, spiritual enlightenment requires a letting go, which death, as a surrender to absence, encapsulates.

This liquid change of posture well fits the so-called "floating world" of ukiyo-e, or woodblock printing, in Yoshiwara, the region of fleeting pleasures, while it presents us "with the process of coming to a peak of meaning, only to slip off in search of something further."[17] In other words, the courtesans' drooping advance marks a journey downward, which for Buddhism (since it has no equivalent to sin, Christ's passion, or the lost Garden of Eden) can only initiate a resurgence, without marking a stop or a punishment. At the same time, these women's expressionless, hieratic faces under heavy makeup, their enveloping kimonos shimmering in the sun, and stately progress to the rhythm of traditional Japanese music spell out the burden of social conventions.

Okita, Utamaro's most attractive model and the most famous waitress in the Naniwaya teahouse, kills her lover Shozaburo and his mistress Tagasode, thus committing a violent crime for the sake of a radical passion. Okita's gesture comes close to a suicide, but this for the Japanese is not an act of despair. Rather it is a positive statement, especially if it entails dying for a romance. This is so because, in Japanese culture, the legacy of Confucian morality permits casual sex but regards romantic love as a major threat to the social order. The status quo is so strongly grafted onto relations between parents and children that male lovers are inevitably weakened and their women doomed to suffer.[18]

As a form of social rebellion, Okita's violence is a potentially positive measure of her desire, but it condemns her to death while liberating her into an absolute and privileged form of existence, since, by virtue of her extreme action, she will continue to live on in Utamaro's rebellious art. It is therefore her gesture of erasing life from the social frame she inhabits that rekindles the artist's creative impulse, for her exit from the narrative precedes a cascade of splendid woodblock prints. Significantly, it is only right before the screen becomes dark and empty that Mizoguchi feels at ease about citing Utamaro's work directly, for the death of the film releases the artist's work for our view.

By withholding the allure of art history all the way to the end of the film, Mizoguchi practices a form of anticinema, since Western cinema and in particular films about famous artists are based on the spectacle of the female body, the sensuality of the visual sources cited, commerce, and individual mastery. Thus, by withholding direct allusions to Utamaro's erotic prints and in choosing absence, the director comes to occupy a position closer to Okita's gesture of voiding than to Utamaro's productive drive. One could argue that Mizoguchi's two alter egos in the film, Okita and Utamaro, disclose his state of indecision between seeking freedom from the West through Japan's religious philosophy and striving for liberation from oppressive Japanese social customs through Utamaro's popular, commercial art. In fact, just as in Hollywood, Utamaro's art can be only a feminine object serialized with endless variations for male voyeurism.

The impact of Okita's action on Utamaro's creativity clearly surpasses the stimulation provided by the merchants who surround the artist. As soon as Utamaro's output declines in quantity and quality to the point of endangering their hefty profits, the merchants take him to a spectacle of young women undressing on a beach and diving for fish under the vicious gaze of a wealthy lord. With emphatic camerawork that recalls the shooting of the courtesans' procession at the beginning of the film, Mizoguchi tracks along two lines of swimmers who, one after another, take their clothes off with the coordination of dancers in a parody halfway between a multiple striptease and a French cancan.[19] Instead of conveying the transitory nature of life, this procession of female bodies is a triumph of male lust, whose climax is marked by a close-up of Oran from behind, as she enters the water.

The excitement of the scene stems from the way in which the eye of the camera chases the women under the water, pursuing them as eagerly as they swim after the fish. Here the cinema does not bear witness to the ancient traditions of Japan but thrives on an orgy of Western values such as possession and presence, proximity and speed, leading to the transformation of Utamaro's face into a distorted mask of relentless appetite for female beauty.

As Noel Burch explains, Mizoguchi's first postwar films were inflected by a fascination with the "efficiency" and "effectiveness" of Hollywood codes. Yet, just as it is very difficult to catch a fish with bare hands in the water, the cinema cannot capture these women's souls, even though it displays their bodies. In short, Mizoguchi's underwater shot and close-up can hardly bear the comparison with the film's opening scene, when his camera experiences the seduction of its own power to move, as the courtesans periodically fall to rise to a higher spiritual level, in a sequence truly charged with "nostalgia for an exemplary past of personal and national rigour." [20]

Cinema as a Popular Medium against Traditional Art: Freedom or Constraint?

The analogy between cinema as a popular art and woodblock prints is so easy to establish that Mizoguchi's *Utamaro* quickly acquires a self-reflexive edge. The director, however, was much more socially conscious than his famous predecessor. Utamaro's work, by emphasizing hairstyle and dress in a way similar to fashion plates, was meant to keep the morale of the populace high. His depictions of Yoshiwara courtesans and actors, teahouses and brothels, hardly documented life as a whole in ancient Edo. There the rise of the mercantile class occurred amid social strife and within the oppressive grip of the shogun.[21] Utamaro's art was as escapist as the whole district of Yoshiwara, an area of relative freedom, controlled by the authorities but separate enough from the rest of the city so that individuals could temporarily circumvent rigid rules of behavior.

Just as woodblock printing had emerged in conjunction with other popular arts linked to spectacle, prostitution, literature, and entertainment, Mizoguchi came to the cinema after taking on a variety of odd jobs as textile designer, newspaper illustrator, and porcelain decorator. But the links between cinema and woodblock prints are perhaps most apparent in their reliance on the appeal of female stars and on a cooperative form of authorship,[22] which in Utamaro's case included a crucial partnership with Tsutaya Juzaburo (1750–1797), the son of a brothelkeeper in Yoshiwara and a man of astute business sense. The commercial film industry Mizoguchi worked in was as profit-seeking as the entrepreneurs (publishers, booksellers, theater owners) who promoted Utamaro's art; woodblock prints, like films made sure that images of beloved courtesans, famous actors, and all sorts of entertainments would be inexpensive and endlessly available for public consumption.

Although Utamaro's art did not deal with the famines devastating the countryside and the gradual impoverishment of the samurai class, his work maintained a revolutionary edge to the extent that he went against the Kano school of traditional painting. Instead of depicting only religious or natural subjects, Utamaro turned his attention to real people in Japanese daily life, thus rebelling against the authority of high art with the same vengeance that Mizoguchi always showed toward paternal figures in his films. In *Utamaro*, therefore, the system of the arts is grafted onto a family melodrama of sons in revolt and daughters in chains. In addition, just as the cinema for Mizoguchi exhibits a split allegiance toward social constraint and personal freedom, Utamaro's persona oscillates between the roles of oppressive father and helpful negotiator.

At the beginning of the film, Seinosuke, an academic painter, decides to buy a print by Utamaro to amuse Kano, the father of his fiancée, Yukie. As soon as he reads an irreverent inscription by Utamaro against his mentor, Seinosuke decides to challenge the rival to a duel. Not only does Utamaro respond by proposing a contest in artistic skills, but also the image of the sword cuts across, so to speak, Mizoguchi's rejection of phallocratic authority, American censorship, and even questions of historical accuracy.

During the Occupation, swords were prohibited in Yoshiwara, certainly to avert bloodshed between drunken patrons but also to prevent the inmates of the quarters from turning the swords against themselves. While love suicides were a successful and bohemian theme in plays, in real life a courtesan who committed suicide was buried in the position of a dog, because that animal was thought to have no ghost that could return to haunt the brothel.[23] By killing Tagasode, a woman of much higher rank in comparison with a simple teahouse entertainer, Okita, in keeping with Utamaro's populist appeal, establishes that social change as well as personal assertion can come only from the lower, newly emerging classes.

The question of social class reapppears again in conjunction with Utamaro's decision to use Oran as a model. The beautiful diver he has spotted on the beach among many other women is in the service of a high-ranking lord, yet unlike other concubines, she is the daughter of a commoner rather than a samurai. If Utamaro's artistic interest in Oran defines her as a woman of the future, of the new art, it is also true, however, that she justifies her submission to Utamaro by equating the artist's creative urge with her lord's voyeuristic demands. Thus, it seems that although women's behavior points to the dissolution of an ancient social system, without their rebellion in private life, Utamaro's art alone is not enough to upset class boundaries.

In compliance with the American ban on swords, Mizoguchi stages a duel of brushes between the two artists, setting up an opposition between

Utamaro and Seinosuke, a member of an ancient samurai family, who paints according to rules as fixed as the steps of a tea ceremony.[24] The woodblock print artist, however, answers the challenge by improving the image of Kannon, a Buddhist goddess of forgiveness, which Seinosuke outlines with all the respect the Kano school feels toward religious and legendary topics. Despite his rebellious stance, Utamaro works from the tradition and, from time to time, finds himself in the position of loving father.[25] Utamaro's fatherly stance becomes especially clear when Yukie visits him while looking for Seinosuke, who has abandoned her to spend his nights with Okita.

Throughout the narrative Utamaro tries to reconcile Kano's daughter with Seinosuke, his newly acquired disciple. Unfortunately, after seeing the famous master at work, Seinosuke worships his talent and abandons his former school, showing indifference toward Yukie's desperation. In the role of paternal mediator, Utamaro congratulates his assistant, Take, for his decision to marry Oshin, the only woman in the artist's circle who is not feminine and whom he does not seem eager to paint. Unable to appear in any print by Utamaro—at least according to the film—Oshin, in contrast to Okita, Oran, and Tagasode, does not get involved in a web of female rivalries for the same man. Like Oshin, Yukie does not pose for Utamaro. Yet, her newfound role of worker in a woodblock printing shop parallels her unwilling involvement in a contest with Okita first, and Oran later, for Seinosuke's love.[26]

Utamaro's efforts to bring Seinosuke back to Yukie, as well as his delight in Take and Oshin as a newly formed couple, are only one side of the artist's impact on the community in which he lives, for his art either divides people or transforms them so radically that previous relationships based on family or social class do not hold up any longer. This is especially evident when Seinosuke watches Utamaro draw two legendary figures on the beautiful, perfect back of Tagasode, or when Oran, after posing for the artist, abandons her timid behavior to the point of running away with Seinosuke. Likewise, Yukie's social allegiances change as a result of her contact with Utamaro's circle. Even though Seinosuke describes Kano's daughter as a woman forever steeped in the old tradition of birds and flowers painted on silk screens, we shall find her walking alone in the night and earning a living without falling into prostitution.[27] Utamaro's destructive effects on his community also emerge from Mizoguchi's refusal to link the upper level of a building with its lower section. The woodblock printing shop, for instance, is upstairs, but it is not clear what happens downstairs. Likewise, when

Yukie visits Utamaro at night during her search for Seinosuke, the upstairs level appears to be isolated from the rest of the house.

Utamaro's efforts to maintain the status quo within his small social world are the flip side of a force as destructive as Kano's silent rejection of his daughter Yukie. It is as if Mizoguchi were in awe of his own art, while feeling both helpless in front of and attracted to Okita's refusal to compromise. After following with a lateral track Seinosuke and Kano's daughter walking across the room, the camera reorients its position to intercept the ominous figure of the father suddenly emerging in the background of the shot. Kano's arrival and his expulsion of Seinosuke from his house disclose a long, deep corridor stretching into an obscure distance. The evil father summons a vertigo of anxiety, while he stands for a potential gesture of penetration into space.

Although Mizoguchi is notorious for his tendency to keep the editing down to a minimum in favor of the long take, long shots, and extended camerawork, the director's use of characters and objects in the background of the shot is not comparable in any way to the sharp, highly informative, deep focus practiced by Jean Renoir, Orson Welles, and William Wyler. It is also true, however, that *Utamaro* has an unusually high number of medium shots, close-ups, and cuts compared with other films by Mizoguchi, such as *Life of Oharu* (1952), *Ugetsu monogatari* (1953), and *Sansho the Bailiff* (1954), in which the long take leads to an unparalleled suggestion of the ephemeral, to a sense of fluidity, and to an elegiac tone.

Instead of enhancing his viewer's ability to see deeper in space, Mizoguchi distributes the elements of his compositions in ways that obscure their features and how they might relate to each other. On the contrary, by channeling the spectator's attention through a system of looks latching onto the most important objects or through meaningful contrasts between background and foreground, Renoir, Welles, and Wyler establish dialectical nuances and hierarchical values without cutting from one element to another. The responsibility of editing from one shot to the next has shifted from the film's editor to the viewers, who, unable to count on the cuts, are on their own in sorting out all the visual and narrative cues contained within one single, long take.

By contrast, Mizoguchi does not compensate for his dislike of external cutting by encouraging the viewers to do their own editing into the depth of one, single long take punctuated by several reframings and choreographic rearrangements of the actors' positions. His backgrounds remain difficult to see, while characters and objects are often distributed as obstacles to one another. Compared with the deep-focus filming of Renoir, Wyler, and Welles (despite their shared rejection of the Hollywood classical decoupage, in which the establishing shot is followed by a cut to a medium shot and then a cut to a close-up), Mizoguchi's method signals an unparalleled uneasiness with cutting as editing and with penetration of space through camera movement.

The only approach the Japanese director seems truly at ease with is one underlining the horizontality of the image, especially through camerawork that takes advantage of the width of the frame. In addition to this preference for a horizontal rather than a vertical trajectory of the camera, Mizoguchi (just like Yasujiro Ozu), in defiance of Hollywood's rule that the fourth wall of any locale should always remain invisible, will show the same room from four different sides, cutting from setup to setup, without ever getting inside the room's space or to the center of it. This approach is most evident in the section where Utamaro and Take, unaware of Seinosuke's threat, wait for Okita's return in her private quarters, at the teahouse.

According to Pascal Bonitzer, Mizoguchi's cinema is based on a longing for quiet contemplation and stoic endurance, for female passivity and tranquil landscapes, for deathlike stillness and flat waters, because traveling into space and seeing in depth summon a sense of masculine mastery and phallocratic violence: "It is precisely perforation, penetration, that the mise-en-scène keeps at bay, offscreen. Mizoguchi's cinema is based, thematically and formally, on the horror of the father. . . . The horror of the father and that of perforation are the same thing."[28] In contrast to this fear of penetration, in which the risk of seeing too much goes hand in hand with a need to keep violence offscreen and with an anxiety about the sexual act, the camera movement usually associated with Utamaro whenever he steps into the role of benevolent father is a lateral track, which follows him and Seinosuke walking across his living quarters from one side of the frame to the opposite.

Besides the American censors' dislike of violent scenes,[29] Mizoguchi's rejection of deep space also explains why we never see Okita's dagger penetrating Shozaburo's and Tagasode's bodies. Likewise we do not witness the tattooing of Tagasode's back. We only observe Utamaro painting on her skin. After taking over the samurai's sword, the painter's brush replaces the tattooist's needle. Mizoguchi alludes to this troublesome object through a medium close-up of Seinosuke's dangling sword as he storms into the deep corridor leading into the room where the tattooist is waiting for the end of Utamaro's preparatory work.

Okita's weapon, however, appears as a dark silhouette behind a white, paper-thin screen, as if it were a prop in a show of Chinese shadows, an archetypal form of cinema whose potential to show too much violence Mizoguchi chastises in the final murder scene. Mizoguchi's ellipsis of Okita's dagger penetrating Shozaburo's and Tagasode's skin echoes his avoidance of precious art-historical citations. This means that there is a double bind between art and death, in the sense that whether the subject is art history or Okita's violence, the film creates an absence in the narrative with a positive, liberating quality.

Chinese shadows—or the play of light and darkness as the stuff of Mizoguchi's and Utamaro's art—are alluded to twice: first, when in the midst of a creative block Utamaro asks Take to close all the windows and bring in a candlelight; second, when in depicting Oran, Utamaro sees her undressing behind a fragile, transparent screen that does not quite block the dim lighting used for the room. These repeated efforts to adjust the light in order to create, or to paint by seeing the object in a special kind of light that nearly transfigures it into a phantom of desire or an evanescent shadow, suggest that Mizoguchi in *Utamaro* is fine-tuning his definition of the cinema in relation to woodblock printing and tattooing.[30]

By downplaying the clarity of backgrounds through complex camera setups, Mizoguchi exorcises his fear of becoming the evil father or the institutional authority who painfully splits communities, conquers space, dips the tattooist's tool into the skin, and markets the bodies of women. This uneasiness with depth is also why Utamaro, by the end of the film, is no longer a positive paternal figure who negotiates between men and women but is instead an outcast, like Yukie. After Seinosuke's departure, she finds herself lingering alone on the edge of the shot, while her father turns his back to her by occupying the center of the image as he sits in front of a traditional painting. In a similar fashion, at the end of his punishment by the shogun—who has obliged him to spend fifty days with his hands tied, unable to work—Utamaro does not join his friends for a celebration with sake but returns to the marginal position in which we first encountered him, sitting on the border of the image, at the very limit between society and self.

Mizoguchi's contradictory portrait of Utamaro as mediator and divider indicates not only an ambivalent perception of the cinema as an appa-

ratus of ideological control and of psychological rebellion, but it also applies to Okita's unshaken determination and embrace of death as desire in
contrast to the other characters' narrower options. On one hand Mizoguchi's
tendency in *Utamaro* to keep the camera glued to his actors in a steady
medium shot contributes to the creation of a tight environment. On the
other, the unconventional nature of Utamaro's art reverberates in Okita's
decision to control one form of serialized mechanical reproduction, the
press, for she buys all the newspapers reporting that her lover, Shozaburo,
has eloped with Tagasode.

In contrast to individuals who become accessories to the settings, anonymous silhouettes slightly protruding in the background, Okita manages to
personalize her environment when she puts on makeup in front of a small
mirror, shortly before disagreeing with Utamaro about her affair with
Seinosuke. This scene establishes an intriguing parallel between feminine
cosmetics and artistic creativity. Their dualistic natures, sharing beauty and
death, liberation and repression, are conveyed by Okita's and Utamaro's
position in the shot, when they sit leaning against each other, facing nearly
opposite directions.

Besides rejecting the cuts of editing and impeding vision in depth,
Mizoguchi challenges the centrality of the actors as carriers of meaning in
the narrative. In this respect the director's style did not satisfy the American
censors' interest in films that would assert personal values. Mizoguchi's
downplaying of individual psychology reminds us that the genre of the
portrait is for the most part absent from the Japanese art-historical tradition.[31] Even though Utamaro was often praised for his *okubi-e*, or closer
views of courtesans, hairstyle and dress are far more charged with meaningful information than the faces of his sitters (fig. 57). To be sure, the identity
of his female subjects was often indicated, if not in a cartouche then by
means of a family crest on the kimono or by objects held in the hands. In
addition, physical differences were limited to such minor details as the shapes
of the noses.[32] In a sense Mizoguchi's lack of interest in the faces of his
main characters emphasizes their status as agents of a wider social organization, which contains them in much the same manner as his backgrounds
drain all physiognomy out of the nameless figurines who either stand idle
or sit and wait in the remotest corners of the shot.

While Mizoguchi's sacrifice of individual traits to decor suggests a
sense of constraint, it also echoes Utamaro's attempt to create a society
around himself in order to function better as an artist. In fact, as soon as
Okita and Utamaro argue about her liaison with Seinosuke, the artist's

FIGURE 57. An Oiran (A Courtesan), *by Kitagawa Utamaro. The Metropolitan Museum of Art (Bequest of Mrs. H. O. Havemeyer, 1929, The H. O. Havemeyer Collection), New York.*

creative drive withers. Even though he is a rebel, Utamaro's desire to live in a world where individuals fit in with each other parallels a basic conformist drive in Japanese society.

According to Linda Ehrlich, in Japan, it is important to remain part of a larger whole, "reflected not only in Nature, but also in ties to other persons."[33] This sense of needing each other reappears in Mizoguchi's domestic settings, where small indoor gardens or painted screens or kakemonos of landscapes blur the distinction between inside and outside, conveying a longing for a natural harmony and for a return to a motherly embrace. It is well known that the human figurines often found standing at the very bottom of Japanese landscape paintings are summoned by the natural world in front of them, while the depiction of mountains and rivers is usually played out along a vertical axis, with no depth whatsoever, as if the landscape and its inhabitants existed on exactly the same coordinates. This is perhaps why, in preparation for the painful marks of a tattoo artist, Utamaro graces the back of Tagasode with an image of Kintoki, a Japanese equivalent of young Hercules, who happily rests in the arms of his mother, Yama Uba. This legendary couple of woman and child clearly exists beyond the tensions produced by sexual difference that fuel the intricacies of *Utamaro's* plot. It is important to remember, however, that Yama Uba is both a witch and a seductress. Thus, in contrast to Kunieda's use of a different character, Kikujido, for this same episode in the novel, Mizoguchi might have chosen Yama Uba to remind the viewer that his film was meant to work through his attachment to and fear of women, a split stance grafted onto the scenario of castration.[34]

Painting the Body, Emptying the Filmic Image

Just as the cinema can lead to freedom or constraint, tattooing in *Utamaro* is a double-edged medium. In marking the body, it is a form of violence, penetration, and possession. Mizoguchi seems to signal the links between tattooing, cutting, and the patriarchal order he rejects, by having the tattoo bleed, so to speak, across the narrative, which develops along a chain of deadly betrayals. While tattooing can be seen as one of the ways in which phallocracy leaves its mark on the individual's psyche, this controversial aesthetic practice may also exalt the body as art in order to make a highly personal statement of fantasy and desire. Utamaro's decision to paint the body of Tagasode is not only a radical gesture against the Kano school, which often worked on silk, but is also antithetical to the reduction of art to commerce. Unlike any other image, which can be serialized and sold again and again since the advent of mechanical reproduction, the tattoo cannot be separated from the body, and for this reason, it asserts that the individual is unique, while it violates important conventions of markets and prices in the institutional art world.

The tattoo scene is not totally fictional to the extent that tattooing does appear in a few woodblock prints by Utamaro. Among the courtesans of the pleasure quarters of Edo and Osaka, tattoos were love pledges wherein the name of the courtesan's lover would appear on her upper arm or inner thigh. A print by Utamaro shows just such a situation, although in this case we see the woman tattooing her lover, who is wincing with pain.[35] By inserting himself in the tattooing process as the creator of an image to be used later by the tattooist (who sits nearby in awe of Tagasode's perfectly white skin), Utamaro goes against his own art, for woodblock printing, just like the cinema, is based on mechanical reproduction. Thus the artist works against his own medium of representation in order to get to something new. This is why, on his way to the tattoo room, Utamaro defiantly declares to Take that he will become involved in this forbidden activity at the cost of dying, that is, of becoming a ghost.

The quasireligious atmosphere and the dim lighting of the spacious room used for the tattoo scene summon the magical origins of this folk art, which was also deployed in the context of initiation rituals. Precisely because tattooing was taboo during the Edo period, its practice applied to special and to marginal people who wanted either to define themselves as anticonformist or to protest against the strict regulations of the shogun.[36] Most important, the tattoo scene helps us to explain why the director's style in *Utamaro* is based on a denial of visibility. Except for the episode in which Utamaro paints Kintoki and Yama Uba on Tagasode's back (fig. 58), the tattoo remains invisible for most of the narrative. We only hear about it, instead of seeing it, when Okita interrogates two men in the countryside, during her search for Shozaburo. At last, the tattoo becomes visible in conjunction with Tagasode's death, as soon as her clothes are moved aside and her skin glares in the darkness, at the bottom margin of the shot.

In fact, the whole idea of turning the body into art and of achieving invisibility through tattooing (fig. 59) derives from a Buddhist legend, which Mizoguchi a few years later staged on the set of *Ugetsu monogatari* during a pause in production. A famous photograph shows Mizoguchi standing by a kainosho painter, who, with a brush in midair, places Zen calligraphy, a form of picture writing, on the wide back of Mori Masayuki, *Ugetsu*'s male

FIGURE 58. *Utamaro paints the body, in* Five Women around Utamaro
(directed by Kenji Mizoguchi, 1946). Film Stills Archive, The Museum of Modern Art, New York.

FIGURE 59. *Painting the body and becoming invisible, in* Ugetsu monogatari
(directed by Kenji Mizoguchi, 1953). Film Stills Archive, The Museum of Modern Art, New York.

protagonist. As the ending "-osho" suggests, the kainosho, besides being an artist, is also a Buddhist priest. His double identity matches the character of an immensely popular Japanese folk tale that functions as the transgressive subtext of *Utamaro*. To my knowledge there is no statement by Mizoguchi on this specific legend, but he must have known it, since the story of Mimi-Nashi-Hoichi is as popular in Japan as Little Red Riding Hood is in the Western world.

Unable as I am to locate specific and direct statements by Mizoguchi on tattooing or on Mimi-Nashi-Hoichi, I am here coming up against a question of intent. I can attempt to circumvent this issue only by pointing out that since *Utamaro* is a film about the life of an artist, the connection between him and Mizoguchi is so obvious that intent exists in the mode of identification with the Japanese cultural tradition. As a result of this overpowering congruence between the artist in the film and the author of the film, we can feel free to look outside the text, into the collective unconscious of the national culture to which the legend of Mimi-Nashi-Hoichi belongs.

According to the tradition,[37] a blind artist named Hoichi, famous for his skill in recitation and in playing the biwa,[38] lived in the temple of the Amidaji, where a Buddhist priest was very fond of poetry and music. At one point the priest was called away to perform a service at the house of a dead parishioner, so the blind Hoichi remained alone in the temple. During the night the biwa player unknowingly followed a ghost, who brought Hoichi to the palace of his lord and asked him to perform. It was only when the priest returned to the temple that Hoichi's contact with the evil ghost became apparent, for the servants discovered him playing the biwa all night long among the tombs of the Heike. Everything the blind man had imagined was a mere illusion, except for the calling of the dead.

To protect Hoichi from this evil, nocturnal ghost, the priest turned to his writing brushes and covered Hoichi's body with a holy spell called Hannya-Shin-Kyo, or the Heart Sutra, a text in Chinese script that describes, through the Doctrine of the Emptiness of Forms, the unreal character of all things. The sutra goes as follows:

Form is emptiness; and emptiness is form. Emptiness is not different from form; form is not different from emptiness. What is emptiness that is form. . . . Perception, name, concept, and knowledge are also emptiness. . . . There is no eye, ear, nose, tongue, body, and mind. . . . But when the envelopment of consciousness has been annihilated, then he (the seeker) becomes free from all fear, and beyond the reach of change, enjoying final Nirvana.[39]

By turning Hoichi's body into an artistic text, the priest made the biwa player invisible to the evil ghost. Unfortunately, the priest's assistant forgot to paint Hoichi's ears, so during the next nocturnal visit the ghost was able to pull this part of Hoichi's body away, leaving the blind man bleeding and mutilated for some time, until he eventually healed.

The story of Earless Hoichi accounts for Mizoguchi's decision to put the kainosho to work on Masayuki's back, since the protagonist of *Ugetsu* is an artist, a potter, who falls in love with a female ghost. Mizoguchi's passion for ceramics and pottery is well known, and once again the director used a fictional character to explore his artistic self.

In *Utamaro*, the centrality of the tattoo scene, by virtue of its spaciousness, clarity, and intensity, makes even more emphatic the claustrophobic, distancing, and antianthropomorphic quality of the scenes in the rest of the film. In other words, the director's cinematic style strives to achieve the spell of invisibility cast by the Buddhist priest on Hoichi's body. Furthermore, the biwa player's blindness can be said to be in line with Mizoguchi's downplaying of the spectacle of the female body and with his elision of sensual art-historical citations.

Mizoguchi relies on the tattoo scene to confront his sexual as well as his family ghosts through art, precisely because the tattoo, by being inseparable from the body, can function as a mental expansion of one's own psychic energy, for the tattooed body is the visible, breathing, and indelible image of all sorts of desires and fears that individuals carry on themselves, inside themselves, and can never ignore.

Besides invoking the legend of Earless Hoichi, tattooing recalls one of the most violent experiences in Mizoguchi's contact with women. In 1925 he fell in love with a Kyoto waitress and began living with her. The relationship lasted only two months before the woman attacked him with a razor and, staging a veritable scenario of castration, slashed his back while he was sitting in a bathtub. Years later, when he first showed his scar to his screenwriter and friend Yoshikata Yoda, he admonished, "Yoda, women are terrifying." Torn between his anxieties about castration and his desire to rebel against paternal authority, Mizoguchi spoke in favor of his mistress during the trial, forgave her, quit work, and went looking for her again. They were reconciled, and he lived off her income as a maid in a Japanese inn until an acquaintance warned him he was wasting his artistic talent. Eventually

Mizoguchi pursued his filmmaking with a vitality that had been lacking before the woman's violent gesture. Meanwhile the mistress he had left behind disappeared into prostitution.

It is easy to see how the plot of *Utamaro* has an autobiographical flavor, since it is Okita's violence that stimulates the artist's creativity.[40] Were we to read Mizoguchi's experience in real life in the light of the legend of Earless Hoichi, we could conclude that *Utamaro*, as a film, is more than a meditation on the revolutionary as well as oppressive aspects of the cinema, which parallel the double-edged nature of woodblock printing as rebellion against the traditional system of the arts and as commerce instrumental to a mercantile class aspiring to improve its status. In fact *Utamaro* is also an attempt to redefine the cinema through tattooing in a way that turns castration anxiety upside down and transforms its haunting connotations into positive, artistic production, for it is only this reversal that can free Mizoguchi of his paranoia about paternal authority and masculine power.

When he applies his brush to Tagasode's back, Utamaro is Mizoguchi, who becomes the woman who inflicted a terrible wound on him. Even if Utamaro keeps saying to his female model of the moment, "I want your body," this is really a film about the male body, the director's wound. Thus, in painting Tagasode's back, Mizoguchi chooses a difficult strategy to maintain, and it is this untenable approach that might explain the unresolved flavor of the film's ending. The director adopts simultaneously the position of object and subject, of victim and attacker, a feminine persona and the role of the artist-priest.

Such an argument begins to find confirmation in the absence of the female body in Japanese art. Although Utamaro produced highly erotic prints and did not hesitate to show his sitters' sexual organs, the whole genre of the female nude as a fantasy of desire or allegory of truth, offered by the male artist to the male viewer, does not exist in Japanese art the way it does in the West. As a reminder of castration, the female body, in *Utamaro*, has to remain invisible, while its absence is echoed by the director's lack of interest in the seductive power of art-historical citations.

If *Utamaro* is a film about the male body, it is also and most of all an attempt to overcome the pain of sexual difference. This is why the crossing of the boundary, or of the difference, between male and female, which is implied in castration, reappears in two minor, comic characters of *Utamaro*. Take, Utamaro's assistant, is effeminate, emotional, and docile. He is a caricature of the tradition of the weak, passive male (nimaime) that Japanese melodrama derives from Buddhism and Confucianism, two religions notorious for encouraging passivity. Oshin, Take's future wife, is strong, aggressive, and muscular. Yet her physical prowess and ultimate obedience to Take do not buy her the same quality of inner freedom achieved by Okita through violence and death. While Oshin is free to marry Take because her debt to the teahouse has been satisfied, her future as a traditional Japanese wife, under Utamaro's benevolent auspices, is more comparable to a revised state of being rather than to a radical change of position. Finally, the iconography of the film reasserts the idea that the passage from life to death chosen by Okita as a result of her jealousy is not just one more manifestation of women's suffering, but a transgression that reverberates with potentially positive connotations across two sites: the huge gate marking the entrance at Yoshiwara, while the credits roll on the screen, and the bridge Tagasode and Shozaburo walk on during their elopement in the countryside.[41]

To sum up, the director's argument for the Americans, that *Utamaro* would be a film about an artist of the people, barely scratches the surface of this complex text, which would like to solve the plight of Japanese women through Buddhist religious philosophy. Utamaro's tied wrists bear witness to Mizoguchi's frustrating search for a new way of working between Hollywood and Japan, in a rapidly changing society, right after the war. Just as Okita goes so far as to redefine love through death, Mizoguchi turns to the national culture of the past to raise questions about the achievement of freedom and the perpetuation of oppression through the cinema, a medium whose split vocation matches Utamaro's contradictory roles of benevolent father and destructive influence. In this respect Tadao Sato's insight that Mizoguchi did not create anything new, but his artistic genius resided in an ability to deepen an ancient tradition through a modern sensibility, is quite on the mark.[42] While comparing his own medium to other arts—such as woodblock printing and tattooing—through a distancing film style and an elision of art-historical citations, Mizoguchi creates his own sutra in which the equivalence of form with emptiness wards off the evil ghost of sexual difference.

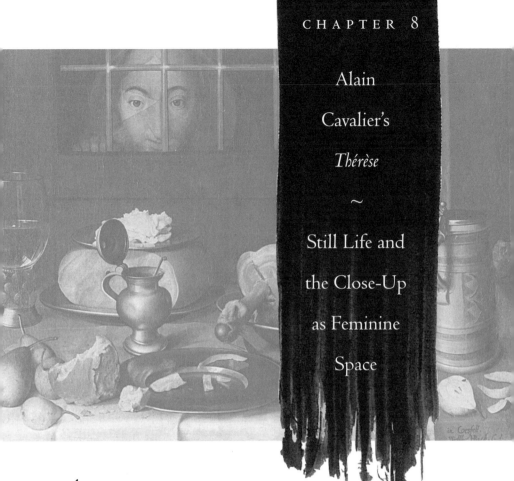

CHAPTER 8

Alain

Cavalier's

Thérèse

~

Still Life and

the Close-Up

as Feminine

Space

*A*s the title barely suggests, *Thérèse* (1986) by Alain Cavalier is a film about the life of Thérèse Martin, a Carmelite nun who died in 1897, at the age of twenty-four, and was canonized in 1925. The simplicity of the title indicates that Cavalier's film, although based on archival photographs and the young woman's diary, *Histoire d'un âme,* is not a celebratory portrait.[1] In fact, it is hardly a biography at all, for many events may remain obscure unless the film viewer is willing to reach beyond the boundaries of the screen and read more about the famous French saint.[2] In other words, it is the film's elliptical quality that is meant to convey the greatness of Thérèse's life, whose achievements, however, completely reject the scale of public history or of a full framing from head to toe through literature or painting.

The daughter of a clockmaker, Thérèse grew up in a religious family; three of her older sisters—Marie, Pauline, and Céline—had already joined the Carmelite order. According to most biographers, Thérèse's decision to step outside lay society originated in one crucial, traumatic experience: the death of her mother when she was a young child. It is as if the convent enabled Thérèse to turn upside down the pain of losing her mother so that a life based on confinement and abstinence transformed itself into an endless source of joy.[3] The film in turn seems to derive its energy from the experience of absence, reduction, separation, for the elision of any reference to the mother's death matches the progression of the narrative through a series of autonomous but all the more poignant tableaux that remind us of the diorama's magic.

Thanks to an agile and unconventional script written by Cavalier's daughter, Camille de Casabianca, as many as sixty episodes of Thérèse's life, from the discovery of her vocation to her death of tuberculosis, are chronicled through disjunctive but evocative close-ups of faces and hands. The time of Cavalier's film, the late nineteenth century, coincides with the invention of cinema. Along with photography, this new technology set the stage for the diffusion of the close-up, a major narrative device that has been associated with a detached, dissecting medical gaze. By making visible small or humble things in Thérèse, such an optical scale brings to mind the impulse behind "a hystophysiology of passions,"[4] the study of hysteria carried out at La Salpetrière, a Parisian hospital for women. There Jean-Martin Charcot (1825–1893), an artist (interior decorating) who turned to science and one of Freud's precursors, conducted his photographic research on the physiognomies and the postures, the spasms and the twists, of hysteric women. In this scientific climate, at the height of the so-called Positivist period, even Gian Lorenzo Bernini's serpentine baroque outline for Saint Teresa of Avila, the great mystic, was considered to be a hysteric symptom, hence an artistic manifestation worthy of clinical attention and microscopic examination. No longer a site for divine "transverberation," the hysteron was the irrational, which modern science tried to explain away.[5]

Yet the more Charcot's photographers tried to explore every curve and every twitch of the female body to solve the mysteries of hysteria, the less they actually discovered.[6] Instead of seeing more by looking at less, enlargement only accelerated the recession of the object under the doctor's intensified vision. Having already defied science at La Salpetrière, in Thérèse the close-up fails once again to dissect, penetrate, and analyze; instead, it expresses, transfigures, and suggests. By turning the human face into a quasilunar landscape and by registering every palpitation of the soul beneath the surface of the skin, Cavalier shifts our attention from asceticism to eroticism, from scientific inquiry to religious faith.

Cavalier's extensive use of close-ups does not in any way reinforce a medical gaze. By contrast, his images achieve a corporeal density, even a sensuous glow, which counteracts the scientific tendency to rely on a cold eye rather than on an affectionate touch. Instead of referring to the doctor's magnifying lens, Cavalier's close-ups evoke the mother's breast, as seen and felt by the nursing child, and also celebrate the fusion of self and other, of the saint with the divine.[7] Were we to expand upon the well-known theory that "the cinema apparatus may be likened to the mother not only in its replication of a dream/womb state but in its presentation of a surface for imagery—like the maternal breast on which the dozing infant once projected its fantasies,"[8] we could conclude that Cavalier's close-ups of faces and hands refer back to the infant's experience of the mother's expression and touch, before the acquisition of language, of autonomous identity, and of social awareness, so that the regression of Cavalier's spectator is based not only on the rejection of context and history but also on the recovery of a heightened level of perception, of an amplified sensitivity, as if the close-up could reinstate for a moment the pleasure of tactile, oral, and visual contact with the mother. This is why Cavalier's mise-en-scène, although sparse and removed from the arena of public life, is all the more vibrant and nearly sensuous. In short, through the close-up, Cavalier invokes a return to the mother-infant bond, a blissful state of fusion between self and other that only a mystic can parallel by becoming one with God.

Besides using the close-up to suggest the infant's bond with the mother, Cavalier in *Thérèse* confines himself to the exploration of a uniquely feminine space: the convent. By definition this area is removed from the hustle and bustle of the world, just as the kitchens or the domestic interiors depicted in Dutch and Spanish seventeenth-century genre paintings continue to exist outside the public square, the market, and the harbor, for those are spaces reserved to and controlled by men. Thus Cavalier combines the maternal connotations of the close-up with allusions to this tradition devoted to women's silent work, whose exclusion from history Norman Bryson has underlined. According to the art historian, it is as if the still-life component of these indoor scenes—Diego Velázquez's *Black Servant* (circa 1620), *Woman Cooking Eggs* (1618), *Christ in the House of Mary and Martha* (1618)—replete with menial objects and the debris of daily life, had replaced once and for all the bodies of heroes and political events.[9] Although this genre ranks below history painting, the kitchen scenes of centuries ago endow the women in the convent with the power to stand up against the constraints of public space for the sake of a feminine sensibility.

While the links between the maternal sphere and the close-up speak of the plenitude of childhood, the female body is negatively implied in the mixed aura of ordinariness and otherwordliness that lingers over so many genre paintings with still life. In order to explain this strange conjunction of familiarity and mystery, which evokes a threatening but also alluring female presence, a nurturing but also castrating "mother," Bryson invokes Freud's notion of the uncanny, or *unheimlich*. In referring to home, *Heim* does describe a well-known, reassuring place, which, however, by virtue of its involvement with the lowest levels of daily life, has become most unappealing and confining. By casting a negative aura of anonymity on the kitchen, the uncanny points to the ambivalent relation adult males entertain with the womb. For Bryson, this place men long for but can no longer inhabit has propelled the development of domestic genre paintings with still life.

Through the use of the close-up as a trope of erotic bliss and maternal longing, Cavalier dispels the problematic connotations associated with women and still life in genre paintings. Put another way, Cavalier's film is not about the sexual repression experienced by women in convent life; rather it explores how, in representing an alternative to the patriarchal order, the convent fosters the expression of feminine desire. By establishing a conceptual continuum between the close-up and still life, Cavalier is able to shift the aim of the close-up from a clinical gaze to a mystical experience and to show that still life, the genre of humble objects handled by women, threatens the centrality of the male body in historical painting. Thus, in *Thérèse*, a film made of close-ups, still life is no longer the setting for a disturbing female presence but the stage for the positive feminization of masculine figures, such as Jesus and Thérèse's own father. In the end, Cavalier's pictorial style brings to fruition the attributes attached to the protagonist's name after her canonization: Saint Thérèse of the Holy Face and the Infant Jesus.

All Is Loss, Loss Is All

Cavalier's *Thérèse* is a ninety-minute film in which the humblest details, partial views of the body, and religious objects neither go by unnoticed nor fall by the wayside as sheer debris, for their decontextualization, amplification, and fragmentation are exactly what enables them to absorb undercurrents of amorous longing and spiritual intensity. The extensive use of the close-up favors the elimination of anything that is not essential, so what is left acquires an unparalleled degree of potency. Yet an even more radical principle underpins the film's austere but charged visual style. Thérèse's approach to sainthood coincides with a statement made by Cavalier during an interview: "Less is not more, less is all."[10] Both the director and his protagonist believe that perfection lies in taking out; Cavalier exemplifies this credo in his film's acting and language, architecture and props, color and costuming.

Cavalier's strategy of subtraction applies, first of all, to acting. In contrast to Charcot's habit of using professional actresses to imitate hysterical behavior, Cavalier hires nonprofessional performers—namely, two dozen women who lived near the studios of Billancourt, where the film was shot with a small budget. If the well-trained actresses of La Salpetrière were helping the doctors to stage their scientific claims in the most persuasive manner possible, Cavalier's ladies from the neighborhood, thanks to their lack of formal training, enable the director to reveal the playful component at the heart of the mystical experience.

This group of untrained women (except for Catherine Mouchet, the professional who takes the role of Thérèse) constitutes most of Cavalier's total cast of thirty-three people. In *Thérèse*, the male gender is represented only by a few authority figures, such as physicians and high church officials. These priests and doctors compete with each other to secure a monopoly on women's souls and, on a smaller scale, to influence Thérèse's life. Just as the doctors believe more in their therapies than in women's prayers, the priests Thérèse has to consult in order to be accepted by the convent invoke various circumstantial reasons to deny her request. In the end, Thérèse prevails over the church bureaucracy and is hardly intimidated by the medical profession. Called in to diagnose the young woman's illness, one doctor expresses his condemnation of convent life: "They ought to burn this place down!" Behind the grille, with her face veiled—hence resisting the gaze of science—the Mother Superior proudly answers, "We are the salt of the earth!" As for Thérèse, she makes fun of one young doctor's stout build by puffing up her cheeks while he, unaware, examines her lungs.

Close-ups of Renée Falconetti's face in *La passion de Jeanne d'Arc* (1928), by Carl-Theodor Dreyer, enhance "the plenitude of Jeanne's character as a focusing unity,"[11] but in Cavalier's *Thérèse* the close-up magnifies faces and hands while making them anonymous or, better, assigning them to a collective, extended maternal body. Thus, the close-up does not individualize the character, but rather it detaches acting from the idea of a personal, distinctive performance. Acting is reinscribed onto a religious community built around a shared, mystic body whose anonymity evokes the nameless women of domestic genre paintings with still life. This reduction of acting to a common denominator of magnified faces and hands is taken even farther in the disappearance of the performers' bodies through a highly introspective use of clothing (fig. 60). As the Italian feminist writer Elisabetta Rasy has explained,

> The dress, every dress, has its own self-evident geometry, openings and closings which are certain and well-established, it produces a reliable map. The slippery vulnerable precarious undefined human body is infinitely inferior. Furthermore religious clothing, for Thérèse, does something more. . . . It can transform her into pure gaze. . . . The rigidity of the corset, its flat extension, the candor of the collar, something hard, smooth, insurmountable. Then the wide sleeves, comforting refuge for the hands, and also precipice or simple interstice ready to widen in the contact with something unknown. Then the skirt. The foldings do not deceive, and conform to a sense of expansion, an endless field of the imagination, womb and tomb.[12]

In contrast to an abstract play of openings and foldings in the cloth containing an infinitude of possibilities, the nuns' bodies shrink, in Thérèse's own words, to "a grain of sand which casts no shadows"—a pure, perfect nondimensional geometric point.

The elimination of acting goes hand in hand with Cavalier's narrowing of casual dialogue. Except for a few playfully irreverent remarks about love and Jesus exchanged by Thérèse and other nuns, and some brief conversations that allow the narrative to take off, inside the convent complete silence, whispering, or the formal recitation of prayers prevails over spontaneous, ordinary language. This linguistic void well applies to the preverbal condition shared by mysticism, childhood, and the close-up. More specifically, as "a mute soliloquy,"[13] the close-up seems to absorb the screen into its orbit, so that very little movement can occur and each visual element acquires a hieratic quality enhanced by the frontal approach of the camera. In addition, this way of looking straight at the characters' faces greatly reduces the possibility of shadows.

The nuns cherish the words of the Song of Songs, a key erotic text in mystical literature. The Bible text's sensuous images of fruit and wine are

FIGURE 60. *Introspective clothing, in* Thérèse *(directed by Alain Cavalier, 1986). Film Stills Archive, The Museum of Modern Art, New York.*

FIGURE 61. *Candles, in* Thérèse. *Film Stills Archive, The Museum of Modern Art, New York.*

enacted in the way the nuns' hands linger over and lovingly touch the few objects allowed in their lives: candles (fig. 61), a bunch of daisies, a notebook, a huge jug. Likewise, in the Martin household, Thérèse and Céline drink water as if it were ambrosia out of glasses with a greenish glow typical of the tableware Pieter Claesz painted in his still lifes.

When Thérèse tells her father of her desire to leave him for Carmel, their dialogue is replaced by close-ups of their faces, which are full of love for each other. Their lips do not move; the close-up of each expression is accompanied by words in voice-over. This alternation of address would seem to set up a shot–reverse shot pattern, which is often used to film an exchange in which language comes between two people. However, the dialogue takes place literally face to face, beyond the barrier of words. The close-up shots abstract the faces from normal physical interaction, so that Thérèse and her father *commune* in these shots.[14]

Like acting and spontaneous dialogue, architecture, too, is hardly present. In *Thérèse* there are no doors, no windows, no stairways, no walls, no separate rooms, no corners. On the whole, the convent looks like a prehistoric, amorphous space where Plato's cave, the archetypal movie theater, meets the womb. The elimination of interior architecture matches the ruling out of public buildings. Even though the filmmaker's style refers to the invention of photography, to protocinematic images, historical context is clearly absent. In *Thérèse*, acting itself refers only to the present tense, thus giving the characters very little historical background: for example, we hear only a few, half-whispered allusions to the gossip that blames Thérèse for her father's madness. In a sense, the convent closes in upon itself like a loose-fitting garment, or like a nun's veil—which in turn represents the interface between Carmel and the outside world reduced to a minimum.[15]

Without a doubt, this cloistered handling of space recalls the confinement of women in the kitchen away from the street that is typical of Velázquez's genre paintings with still life. Yet a more positive reading is also possible. The rejection of architecture as history implies a distrust of the marketplace, a fear of the agora. Hence the space of the convent is feminine; it is an agoraphobic place that the nuns inhabit not because they are unable to enter the public square but because they wish to entertain an alternative economy of desire. When compared with the options available to women in the late nineteenth century—La Salpetrière or uncontrolled childbearing— the convent begins to resemble a refuge, if not an oasis. Furthermore, when Lucie, Thérèse's closest companion, leaves Carmel, she climbs down an external wall in blackest night. Thus the setting of Lucie's flight into history hardly fulfills her cosmopolitan fantasy of escape: a dream in which she trades a violin for a train ticket to Paris. Ironically, in this scenario, the technology of the train replaces the music of the violin, science supplants art, hysteria prevails over mysticism. In her escape from the convent, Lucie uses a twisted sheet as a rope, but it even looks like an umbilical cord, perhaps a negative reminder of that maternal womb, or *Heim*, which, in line with the patriarchal world outside, she is eager to sever.

Questions of social class and market economy, like those of history, remain external to the convent. We learn from the Mother Superior that the nuns have no money to pay taxes, and the doctors do not charge them fees. In *La fable mystique*, Michel de Certeau has addressed the subversive potential of what may seem to be only socioeconomic underprivilege: "This condition of being at the fringe is a powerful factor in pushing the mystics towards another scene, an elsewhere of which they try to articulate the Otherness."[16] Were we to graft this state of marginalization onto Cavalier's belief that "less is not more, but less is all," we would begin to understand that Thérèse, as one film critic said, "transmits life,"[17] and even transmits love, but she does so "outside the system of reproduction," or outside an economy in which more always leads to more, in which an investment must produce a profit. Thérèse's sainthood is as aberrant as an unproductive expenditure, or as inexplicable as savings transformed into waste, a loss turned into a source of fulfillment. This is the case because female mysticism—desire without a body, love without an object, surplus without a measure—cannot fit what first Georges Bataille and later Jacques Lacan have referred to as the "inherently (re)productive purposefulness of 'normal' male sexuality and pleasure."[18] Thérèse escapes patriarchy's demand for reproduction: instead of having children, shortly before her death she herself becomes a child whom Jesus will be able to hold in his arms. This process of infantilization is marked by an attachment to sweets: Thérèse asks for a pastry, an éclair, wondering whether this might be too expensive a treat. This hesitation about price underlines how the rules of the market outside the convent threaten the nuns' innocent pleasures.

Cavalier's agoraphobic space expresses the ambition of a female community to do everything with nothing, and so does the nuns' relationship to food. Like many other women mystics, Thérèse practices anorexia not as a form of self-torture but as a way of gaining control over her own life, of becoming the subject rather than the object of desire.[19] By refusing to drink the hot milk offered by one of her sisters, Thérèse makes the Carmelite regime even more rigid for herself with the happy single-mindedness of an athlete in training. As a mystic, Thérèse does avoid food but still revels in the body, in the warmth of human touch: she gives a warm kiss to an older nun and nudges her nurse's cheek with the tip of her foot. It is only when Thérèse temporarily feels lost in the face of death that a hysterical blockage defeats her anorexic strength, and her body ceases to be the tool of her will. Already devastated by tuberculosis, she chokes upon the communion wafer.

Although Cavalier's film eliminates architecture (as solid mass, public space, history), it is also true that the convent's agoraphobic space houses one crucial architectural element, the grille, which—along with a dark curtain, a kind of huge veil—separates the nuns from their visitors. The grille allows outsiders to glimpse into Carmel, while it enables the nuns to define their separation from the rest of the world. By its very structure—both vertical and horizontal, both temporal and spatial, both centripetal and centrifugal—the grille stands for an antagonism, not only between inside and outside but also, as Rosalind Krauss explains, "between the values of science and spiritualism,"[20] whose rift becomes absolute from the nineteenth century onward. Thus the grille in *Thérèse* becomes the appropriate figure for the dialectic of hysteria and mysticism, in which each term holds the potential to reverse itself into the other. Cavalier expresses this circularity by repeatedly avoiding the shot–reverse shot, which is bound to a 180-degree semicircle, and by choosing instead to show people and objects from either side of the grille within the rotation of a 360-degree space.

Except for the striking visual pattern of the grille, Cavalier's decor is so modest that it reminds us of how theatrical staging tends to concentrate upon essential elements more than cinematic space does. His set for *Thérèse* amounts to a few indispensable beds and cots, kitchen tables and small desks, a few chairs, and two armchairs with strikingly beautiful, brightly flowered upholstery. Because Cavalier uses red so sparingly, we cannot help but look for it and notice it when it appears: in the lobster Thérèse and Lucie have to boil, in the caps and belts of church dignitaries, and, most of all, in the blood that hemorrhages from Thérèse's lungs onto the white bedsheets.

Although Cavalier's props are limited—perhaps because they are limited—they acquire a huge power. In maximizing texture and form, Cavalier lends ordinary objects a hyperreality. Through this estrangement of the object, the filmmaker directs attention to it. Cavalier's props are both abstract and primitive; their pristine clarity suggests that they are outside history and born anew out of the abyss of time; they point to another space, they channel the nuns toward another condition, they hover on the edge of eternity.

Cavalier builds a whole episode out of a tin cup that has fallen to the ground. Thérèse's nurse comments on the waste of precious water from Lourdes. Here what is valueless, a tin cup, has become as priceless as a holy token, and vice versa—strange to say—something that is cheap or free (water) becomes expensive because it is holy.[21] When Thérèse irons a handkerchief she has received from her father, she seems to explore, stroke after stroke, a strange continent, possibly the place where absence is sweet. In the laundry room, wet, stretched-out bedsheets become empty canvases, free spaces inviting the mystic's mind to wander or slide away from the earth to the sky, from casual language to prayer and poetry, from the body to the soul.

Along with a highly selective use of red, Cavalier's Manet-like deployment of blank backgrounds in gray, green, blue, and brown tones transforms simplification into concentration.[22] In Edouard Manet's paintings, a woman with a parrot (fig. 62) or a drinker of absinthe stands in isolation, without context, while details of clothing and posture acquire an unusual density that hovers between the documentary and the decorative, in a way somewhat reminiscent of Gustave Flaubert's taste for the telling but also superfluous detail.[23] Using backdrops as passageways or thresholds,[24] the director transports us into a world free of routine perceptions, where eye and ear can awaken to a sense of their powers and nourish the mystic's desire for a heightened, disembodied sensibility. This is why the nuns spend their time walking, walking, walking. On the night of Lucie's escape from the convent, Cavalier dwells on her feet in close-up, answering, so to speak, the exploratory movements of Thérèse's feet painfully scraping the floor. Through death, Thérèse walks into a new state of being; this is why the film ends with a close-up of her shoes, reminiscent of Vincent van Gogh's *Shoes* (1888; fig. 63).

In contrast to Cavalier's belief that "less is all," for many nuns struggling with a life of renunciation, all is loss. It is as if they were "mired in a sort of limbo," a void that they secretly try to fill.[25] An old sister treasures a forbidden portrait of her husband, who died before she entered the convent; Thérèse cherishes the tear gathered on a scrap of cloth from a dead nun's cheek; another sister, sensing Thérèse's saintliness, rushes to acquire

FIGURE 62. Woman with a Parrot (1866), *by Edouard Manet. The Metropolitan Museum of Art (Gift of Erwin Davis, 1889), New York.*

FIGURE 63. Shoes *(1888)*, *by Vincent van Gogh. The Metropolitan Museum of Art (The Annenberg Foundation Gift, 1992), New York.*

relics from her: a bit of fingernail, a lock of hair. Lucie flees the convent after acquiring as many as possible of Thérèse's belongings: the silver-paper shoe of armor Thérèse wore for a photograph in the role of Joan of Arc, the bouquet of flowers she held during the wedding with Christ, the ivory checkers Céline and Thérèse used to play with. Anguished by the departure of his favorite child, Thérèse's father tries to fill the gap separating him from his Carmelite daughters by sending over to the convent two huge jars of jam, a few sardines, a freshly baked pear tart.

During the Christmas party, the rigid dictum of poverty is overturned, for the span of a waltz by Offenbach, with a plethora of microscopic gifts: candleholders, embroidery, cards, decorations. The nuns dance, handing around a life-size wooden figure of the baby Jesus that has been delivered to the convent by a huge local worker. This exchange of gifts and festive atmosphere indicate that underneath a facade of barrenness, life in the convent thrives on love, which is also to say that mysticism does prevail over hysteria. Significantly, in the outside world, at a social gathering, Céline's legs refuse to move; she cannot dance with a man. In fact, the nuns' graceful dance replaces the paralytic postures and uncontrolled convulsions performed by Charcot's patients, while the worker's exclamation "Vive la République" reminds us that the enemies of the monarchy and the supporters of progress greatly admired the work of doctors at La Salpetrière.[26]

Like her companions, Thérèse too experiences the negative pull of empty space. There, the self risks drowning in nothingness, or as Thérèse explains to her confessor, it runs up against a high, insurmountable wall beyond which shine the stars. The dematerialization of a nun's body into a shadow behind the grille, with a curtain in between, frightens the young girl pleading to be accepted into Carmel. Furthermore, during her wedding to Christ, Thérèse steps into a dark area outside the halo of candles. This brief absorption into the unknown conveys the excitement as well as the danger of such a lifelong choice. Thérèse is repeatedly about to leap into a place beyond, and risks hurting herself, just like the panting green frog a visiting sister holds in her palm next to Thérèse's deathbed.

It is also true, however, that in contrast to the other Carmelites, Thérèse becomes a saint precisely because she thrives on the small things that punctuate a life based on absence. This is why her method for sainthood came to be known as "the little way." For a few moments we see the young woman removing a lace collar as she stands in front of a reflecting glass surface. The collar is a metonymy for Thérèse's mother, Zéline, who was a lacemaker. Thérèse's gesture of removal doubles itself on the glass, thus revealing that the mirror image, too, becomes richer, the more barren its source is. The loss of the mother not only kindles Thérèse's passion for renunciation but also burns all the seams, links, and relays in Cavalier's films, in which each tableau seems to surface miraculously out of the black night preceding the invention of the cinema.[27]

Cavalier's rejection of continuity and frequent use of blackouts between images eloquently conveys the thrill of doing without in Thérèse's life and in the mystic's ability to do everything with nothing, to commune with God and achieve fulfillment, without the presence of a sexual other. For Bèrènice Reynaud, Cavalier's juxtaposition of light and darkness is comparable to "the analyst's interruptions in a patient's stream of consciousness, just as the latter is falling in love with his or her own discourse, being drowned in a bliss of signifiers. The analyst, then, marks a stop, breaks the garrulous stream of signifiers, and enables the patient to realize what is hidden in the folds of his or her discourse: the presence of the unconscious."[28]

As the subject of her own discourse on the unconscious and as the producer of her own desiring self, Thérèse, too, can perform the role of the analyst and wallow in the breakdown of her speech just as a child would. Referring to her journal, Thérèse compares this dissolution of language to automatic writing or "fishing," thus reminding the viewer of the scene in which she gutted fish with Lucie. Of course, the subtext of this activity, typical of kitchen scenes in genre paintings, is the mystical "transverberation" of Saint Teresa of Avila. In fact, the famous saint experienced an unearthly pleasure when an angel with a flaming spear reached into her entrails.

Still Life and the Close-Up

Cavalier's simple images acquire the richness of painting because the absence of complex actions allows the spectator's vision to linger over their surfaces. Furthermore, Cavalier's use of flooding light "separates visual from tactile form, and offers the eye—alone—a spectacle immaculately self-contained."[29] In a mise-en-scène without architecture, the screen's frame is the only point of reference, just as a painting's frame regulates the composition from within. Cavalier's space is not a slice of a world that continues beyond the frame; rather, it announces itself as a self-contained area the spectator can only look at, and never penetrate. As Rossana Di Fazio observes, "The performers . . . do not explore the depth of the scene (measuring tridimensional space), but more often they move sideways, so that their actions do not protrude toward the spectator. All these behaviors acknowledge the virtual barrier of representation, even in the extreme close-ups."[30] As a film, *Thérèse* is a sensuous but also highly abstract kind of painting, evocative of the period right before the arrival of the Lumières' train, when, after the invention of photography, art was just beginning to be more about its own procedures and less about the world.

While all these observations point to the pictorial nature of Cavalier's film style, the fact remains that the director cites a range of art-historical references well beyond the tradition of domestic genre painting with a still-life component. The use of the close-up, of course, is meant to rescue daily objects from a negative view of femininity by linking sainthood with a prehistorical realm and mothering with mysticism. Yet it is the references in Cavalier's film to the historical context of Thérèse's life—the late nineteenth century—or to the iconography of convent life that make all the more apparent how the young girl's choice to enter the convent was deeply radical, for in shutting history out, she overcame her exclusion from it.

Film critics, for instance, have compared Cavalier's tableaux of nuns holding a crown of thorns, an hourglass, or a cross to canvases by Philippe de Champaigne, in which faces and hands interrupt the austerity of the cloth with an almost magic candor or ineffable contentment. In addition to the allusions to Champaigne's portraits, it is indeed possible to speculate on a few more art-historical references in Cavalier's film. When Lucie escapes from Carmel, for example, she climbs down a wall using a rope, just as Jean de la Croix did in innumerable images depicting his departure from the monastery. A vase of flowers set toward one side of the table links the Martin household to Impressionist painting, in which the placement of objects is full of meaning: the rejection of well-centered compositions points to women's attempts to deviate from norms they cannot identify with.[31] In the same way that the vase of flowers risks falling off the table, Thérèse defies social conventions and escapes, so to speak, from the center of paternal authority. An off-center vase of flowers also reappears on a small altar Thérèse leans against, as she places her open palm on a portrait of Jesus' face. While emphasizing the tactile nature of the female gaze, the image summarizes how a return to Jesus as mother through the close-up is clearly in conflict with the patriarchal ideology of the world outside the convent.

Thérèse's rebellious behavior defines her as a hysteric whose anorexic body stages her exclusion from history. Yet this self-annihilation, in that it rejects traditional female activities, is also the other side of the women's movement, which was gathering force at the turn of the century. Thérèse disobeys and reads the newspaper while her father is asleep. A lover of risks, she pushes her vocation to the edge by praying for Pranzini, a notorious killer of helpless women. Cavalier links Thérèse to Pranzini by dwelling with his camera on their necks: his hair is cut before the execution, just as her auburn curls fall under the nuns' scissors before she puts on the full Carmelite dress. Something transgressive associated with Pranzini seems to be stored in the soul of Thérèse, who communicates with the criminal by sheer force of prayer. Perhaps touched by Thérèse's willful energy, which inevitably brings to mind the psychic powers attributed to hysterics, Pranzini kisses a cross before dying.

Despite these pictorial allusions, *Thérèse* is a film based primarily on old photographs, many of which were taken by Céline. Thérèse's sister brought

FIGURE 64. *Thérèse as Joan of Arc, in* Thérèse. *Film Stills Archive, The Museum of Modern Art, New York.*

a camera into the convent, just as Thérèse left home with one souvenir, a pencil box. There is another reason why photography is as important a source as painting in Cavalier's film. Even though the director gives us a glimpse of a nun standing by her canvas behind a group of sisters, the Carmelite order, because of its strict rule of modesty and seclusion, has always been hostile to admitting portrait painters coming in from the outside.[32] To underline this interdiction, Cavalier shows us Thérèse seated near the nun-painter, threading brightly colored glass beads—an artistic activity much more suitable to the scale of genre painting with a domestic rather than a historical setting.

With their emphasis on individuality and the body, portraits do not fit the collective and self-effacing atmosphere of the convent, where art-making is replaced by washing, sweeping, and sewing. To be sure, the negative aura surrounding portraiture constitutes the subject of a whole episode in Cavalier's film. After dressing Thérèse up as Joan of Arc, Céline stands behind the camera ready to take a picture of her sister. With its mixture of strength and weakness, Thérèse's costume, armor made of paper, does remind us that mystics and hysterics alike turn their marginality into a source

FIGURE 65. The Young Virgin (c. 1632–33), by *Francisco de Zurbarán.*
The Metropolitan Museum of Art (Fletcher Fund, 1927), New York.

of power. Although the presence of a veil-like cloth hanging in front of the camera eye may seem to link Céline's photographic apparatus to the convent's space, great hostility must exist between this machine and Thérèse, since she unexpectedly faints (fig. 64). Thérèse's collapse echoes the movement of the camera's shutter, and it can also be compared to the blackouts pacing the whole film. In the role of photographer Céline can be seen as an alter ego for the film director. Still, the meaning of this episode remains at once elusive and poignant. Portraiture, photography, death, all these elements accumulate into a heightened awareness of Thérèse's corporeal weight. It takes three nuns to lift her inanimate body from the ground and carry her to bed. It is as if the photographic portrait had made visible all her mortality. Considering that photography was one of Charcot's favorite art forms, it is not surprising that the snapping of a picture affects Thérèse in the same painful way as her dissection by a cold, medical eye.

Cavalier punctuates the convent's space with linen baskets, scissors, cups, flowers, books—in a word, all the objects used by the nuns near Thérèse, and by Carmelites across the centuries. The objects refer all the way back to the religious scenes with still life painted by Francisco de Zurbarán (1598–1664), such as *Virgin and Christ in the House of Nazareth* (1630) and *The Young Virgin* (fig. 65), in which this very same iconography spells out a paradigm of grace and purity. In addition to this choice of objects, two scenes in particular are suffused with the atmosphere of domestic genre painting with still life. A few old nuns sitting around a rough, broad kitchen table sort through heaps of lentils; they exhibit the silent concentration of Velázquez's female servants poaching an egg or staring at a bowl. Finally, the episode of Lucie and Thérèse gutting fish is dominated by a mysterious red lobster, an animal dear to Northern European artists for the way in which it combines opulent color with domestic connotations. Perhaps this animal from the ocean's depth, with the color of blood and passion, a bizarre but also primitive form, embodies the feminine desire that the convent nourishes and society condemns.

At first it may seem that still life in genre painting and the cinematic close-up are two incommensurable entities, between which it is impossible to establish any relation. But both still life and the close-up concern themselves with what Norman Bryson calls "the overlooked." In other words, they make visible what is either too humble or too small to be looked at. Furthermore, by calling attention to unnoticed aspects of daily life, of physiognomy and decor, the close-up and still life rearrange scales of values and challenge hierarchies built into the act of looking. By questioning the meaning of smallness and largeness, Cavalier draws on his awareness that Thérèse became the patron saint of French soldiers in the trenches of World War I, a conflict that altered forever all proportions and relationships.[33]

Still life and the close-up seem to share one more characteristic: the menial objects of domestic genre painting spell out women's marginalization, while the close-up imposes on them a strictly male gaze. In fact, the close-up can be said to present "a partial object, detached from a set . . . of which it forms a part."[34] Thus psychoanalysis and linguistics respectively have linked the close-up to an unconscious structure of the image, namely castration, and to a constitutive procedure of language, synecdoche.

Instead of reading the close-up as castration, Gilles Deleuze celebrates the antihistorical vocation of the close-up, which tears "the image away from spatio-temporal coordinates in order to call forth the pure affect as the expressed."[35] As an "affection-image," Deleuze continues, the close-up is no scientific tool, because it "is not an enlargement and, if it implies a change of dimension, this is an absolute change."[36] Here Deleuze echoes Jean Epstein, who once said that insofar as the close-up is a magnification, it "transforms" rather than "confirms."[37] By leaving history outside his film, Cavalier seems to align himself with Deleuze's understanding of the close-up as that which can release women's affect.

Within this perspective, the nuns' holy relics are not painful reminders of incompleteness or inadequacy just because they are fragments severed from a whole. Rather, the nuns' intense identification with these little articles suggests that they store within them a special promise of completeness and transcendence. Were we to accept and continue to think about this positive reading of the close-up in relation to women and relics, we would soon realize that still-life painting has much to offer to the Carmelites as well. In still life, objects are by far more important than bodies. The genre in which the body dominates the scene is historical painting, and there the scale is macroscopic, and the subjects are heroic men and great events. Furthermore, while it is true that still life represents women as anonymous beings on the edges of public life, its emphasis on objects over bodies makes it potentially more radical than the female nude, a genre in which a woman may be at the center of the scene, but she is there only as the projection of a male fantasy. Hence it is as if, in his use of domestic genre paintings with still life for *Thérèse*, Cavalier had sensed the subversive vocation of this genre, its hidden drive to produce an alternative order. This is why, in line with still life's radical shift of emphasis from bodies to objects, Cavalier uses the close-up to decenter even further the masculine subject.

That Cavalier employs the close-up to valorize mothering and mysticism over history and science and to revise from negative to positive the inscription of women in domestic genre painting is further confirmed by the reversals that *Thérèse* is built on. Cavalier flouts the conventions of mainstream or commercial cinema: it is not the woman but the man, an absent

FIGURE 66. Christ the Redeemer, *by Quirizio da Murano. Galleria dell'Accademia, Venice.*

Other, Jesus, who assumes shifting personae—child, father, spouse, lover. If Jesus is absent as a body, he is vividly present in the nuns' imagination. He is an absent presence Thérèse can sense so acutely that she fans a little crucifix placed on her pillow. Likewise, the nuns have no trouble accepting that a wooden statue of baby Jesus can cry.

The gender role reversal that prevails in *Thérèse*—in which women no longer play various parts for men's pleasure, but Jesus is the ever-changing object of female desire—explains the feminine behavior of Thérèse's father, who surrenders his position as authoritarian patriarch and, in Céline's words, becomes a helpless baby. This transformation becomes most apparent when, like his daughters, Monsieur Martin takes on the veil—a metonymy of the convent's agoraphobic and feminine space—by placing a piece of cloth over his face. Thérèse's father puts on one more female trait when, in an extreme reaction to his daughter's departure for the convent, he clutches the leg of a table with all the pain and intensity of hysterical blockage.

Finally, the feminization of Thérèse's father goes hand in hand with a painterly tradition that depicts Jesus as a mother. An oblique reference to this idea emerges from the episode in which Lucie drinks Thérèse's infected sputum. On the one hand, Lucie's behavior can be easily linked to the disgust that the hysteric typically feels toward the body, after realizing that "it is an accumulation of corruptible flesh."[38] Yet according to the medievalist Caroline Walker Bynum, the drinking of pus was a common practice among women mystics; by doing so, they reminded themselves of the nourishing powers of Christ's open, bleeding wounds.[39] The motif of blood as nurturing milk is well-established in medieval art in which Jesus offers his breast for the *lactatio* of the faithful (fig. 66).

While Thérèse's father acts like a good mother (he warms up his children's beds every night), the bad mother of domestic genre painting with still life reappears in the character of the Mother Superior. According to Thérèse's biographers—and as shown in a few but crucial lines in the film script—the Mother Superior, Marie de Gonzague, had many reasons to dislike Thérèse: she was one of four Martin sisters who had joined the order, and this little group had become a political force within the small boundaries of Carmel at Lisieux. In fact, by virtue of their influence, the Martin sisters were able to support the election of Pauline, Marie de Gonzague's rival, to the highest office in the convent. Apparently, the Mother Superior so disapproved of Thérèse that she denied the young girl medicine during her struggle with tuberculosis (fig. 67).

The reversal of gendered identities in *Thérèse* does not simply underpin Cavalier's visual style, in which less is all, but it also becomes the subtext of a dialogue between Lucie and the young saint. "We are too tiny to have great thoughts," says Lucie, thus echoing Bryson's account of Sir Joshua Reynolds's (1723–1792) condemnation of still life.[40] For the eighteenth-century aesthetician, this genre thrived too much on sensuous detail and

FIGURE 67. *Catherine Mouchet as Thérèse falling ill, in* Thérèse. *Film Stills Archive, The Museum of Modern Art, New York.*

FIGURE 68. Woman Looking at a Table, *by Wolfgang Heimbach (1613–1678). Staatliche Kunstsammlungen, Kassel.*

was incapable of representing the grand, abstract concepts explored by historical painting. Hence Lucie speaks from the side of hysteria, feeling at once inferior to and resentful of the gigantic aspirations of artists who depict public history. As we have seen, however, smallness for Thérèse was the necessary condition for sainthood. In antithesis to Lucie's condemnation of mysticism, Thérèse's lines "I love the wide-open spaces, I love the gigantic pine trees" suggest that the magnifying power of the close-up can make explicit the greatness of humility, the eloquence of microscopic vision, and thus overturn the negative relation traditionally established, on one hand, between women and medical science and, on the other, between women and the genre of waste, debris, filth.

After Cavalier's *Thérèse*, no domestic genre painting with still life will ever be the same. Let us reconsider, for example, Wolfgang Heimbach's (1613–1678) *Woman Looking at a Table* (fig. 68). In this painting the remnants of a hearty meal—ham, bread, fruit, pie, and different kinds of drinking vessels—occupy the foreground; the background shows a woman's face staring from behind a window with a grid and her barely visible hands clutching the window frame right beneath her chin. The disorder of the objects on the table—silver casually laid down, an unfolded napkin, and crumbs, along with table scraps overflowing from a pewter dish in the center—suggests the pleasures of men consuming food in an affluent society in which waste has become the legitimate reward of productivity. The opulence of the foreground, however, is not accessible to the woman behind the grid, who has already broken the rules by becoming a voyeuse intruding upon a masculine space. In his film *Thérèse*, Alain Cavalier rearranges and transforms the key elements of Heimbach's painting. The director adopts a poor, austere table. He renounces the opportunity for voyeurism built into bourgeois life by windows and dividing thresholds. He transports the action into a convent, whose values are antithetical to the world outside and to history. Through the close-up, Cavalier releases an abstract, invisible image of feminine desire, one that is somewhat different from the eroticism men attribute to women. He must have become aware of it for the first time in childhood, when he was being educated by nuns:

> It is the emotion of a man in front of a group of women. It is an emotion
> which has nothing erotic about it. It is a sort of profound subtlety for a
> filmmaker. Film is so capable of transmitting erotic waves, especially
> feminine ones, that it may seem it has been invented only for this purpose.

When a filmmaker films a woman, he films an erotic emotion. And then, all of a sudden, you find yourself in front of women who transmit, I wouldn't quite say something else, but something so fine, so delicate, such a subtle image of life.[41]

Without a doubt, Cavalier's use of cinema to rewrite art history is an act of dangerous tightrope walking, one that competes with the painful doubts and restless expectations that beset Thérèse at night, before she enters the convent. Thus Cavalier's images are charged with an immense anxiety and a daring quality, a combination that captures all the ambiguities surrounding the double-sided configuration of mysticism and hysteria.

~

Notes

~

(Translations of quotations from foreign sources are my own.)

INTRODUCTION
A Thematic and Intertextual Approach

1. Hollander, *Moving Pictures.*
2. Aumont, *L'occhio interminabile.*
3. Brooks, *Melodramatic Imagination.*
4. Bonitzer, *Décadrages,* and Leutrat, *Kaleidoscope.*
5. *Incorporating Images: Film and the Rival Arts.*

CHAPTER 1
Vincente Minnelli's *An American in Paris:* Painting as Psychic Upheaval

1. The flip side of the French glorification of Hollywood is the French under-estimation of American art. Serge Guilbaut explains that between 1935 and 1941, "America, according to the French, is Hollywood. Thus it should come as no surprise that American films were prized and honored in dithyrambic terms. . . . America at the time was also seen as New York and its skyscrapers, so there were laurels for American architecture. Along with cinema and architecture, it was in-dustrial art that was said to be representative of this modern civilization, oppres-sive and brutal of course and yet endlessly fascinating. For the French this was all that America could be. Laudable though its efforts in painting might be, they were really not to be taken seriously. For true painting depended on the aesthetics, the

taste, and the standards of a long cultural tradition. Painting, in short, could only be done in France" (*How New York Stole the Idea of Modern Art*, p. 42).

2. Harvey, *Directed by Vincente Minnelli*, p. 15.

3. Naremore, *Films of Vincente Minnelli*, p. 20.

4. Harvey, *Directed by Vincente Minnelli*, p. 20.

5. Marchelli, *Vincente Minnelli*, p. 41.

6. Naremore reports that Minnelli's "first ambition was to paint, but he worked by turns as a department store decorator, an assistant to a portrait photographer, and a designer of stage settings for the Balaban and Katz chain of movie palaces. . . . Essentially a bricoleur, he kept files of clippings showing different styles of paintings or illustrations, which he liked to go through for inspiration" (*Films of Vincente Minnelli*, p. 2).

7. On Pollock and Surrealism, see Landau, *Jackson Pollock*, p. 14. On Minnelli and Surrealism, see Casper, *Vincente Minnelli and the Film Musical*, p. 116. In *Films of Vincente Minnelli*, Naremore writes, "Like many commercial artists, he [Minnelli] particularly admired the surrealists and was among the first Hollywood directors to use their motifs in a self-conscious way" (p. 2).

8. Knox, *Magic Factory*, p. xi.

9. Casper, *Vincente Minnelli and the Film Musical*, p. 70.

10. On money in the Hollywood musical, see Altman, *American Film Musical*, p. 155.

11. Naremore usefully comments on Minnelli's sexuality: "By his own account, he was a heterosexual who disliked crude American notions of masculinity. His films tend to confirm this attitude, although he worked in a milieu where 'backstage' homosexuality was fairly common, and his best pictures—all of them made during the most restrictive era of the Production Code—are marked by the sort of 'excess' that could not speak its name" (*Films of Vincente Minnelli*, p. 7).

12. On Maurice Chevalier and collaboration, see Harding, *Maurice Chevalier*, and Freedland, *Maurice Chevalier*.

13. Casper, *Vincente Minnelli*, p. 106.

14. Naremore, *Films of Vincente Minnelli*, p. 33.

15. Casper, *Vincente Minnelli*, p. 74.

16. Alley, *Henri Rousseau*, pp. 36–37.

17. Waldman, "The Childish, the Insane, and the Ugly."

18. Guilbaut, *How New York Stole the Idea of Modern Art*, p. 56.

19. Ibid., p. 200.

20. Landau, *Jackson Pollock*, pp. 13–14.

21. Collins, "*Life* Magazine and the Abstract Expressionist."

22. Method acting was based on Stanislavsky's teachings. On this topic, see Moore, *Stanislavsky System*, and Vineberg, *Method Actors*.

23. Roger Copeland, "Merce Cunningham and the Politics of Perception," in *What's Dance?* ed. Copeland and Cohen, p. 309.

24. Landau, *Jackson Pollock*, pp. 11–12.

25. Ibid., p. 14.

26. On Minnelli and Kirk Douglas, Naremore writes, "The actor with whom he [Minnelli] had the richest, most impressive collaboration was Kirk Douglas. In certain ways Douglas prefigured the Method stars, who were somewhat scary, oscillating between morose anguish and extreme violence" (*Films of Vincente Minnelli*, p. 41).

27. Ibid., p. 22.

28. Foster, *Understanding the Beats*, p. 14.

29. Altman, *American Film Musical*, p. 78.

30. Keller, *Toulouse-Lautrec*, p. 66.

31. Knox, *Magic Factory*, p. 141.

32. On movement in Degas and in Toulouse-Lautrec, see Bernheimer, *Figures of Ill Repute*, pp. 157–199.

33. Casper, *Vincente Minnelli*, p. 52.

34. Knox, *Magic Factory*, p. 158.

35. Dufy's use of French national colors is most striking in *Decorated Street, Le Havre* (1906).

36. Marchelli, *Vincente Minnelli*, p. 61.

37. Examples of Delaunay's abstract Paris are *Eiffel Tower with Trees* (1910), *Window on the City #4* (1910), *The City* (1911).

38. Altman, *American Film Musical*, pp. 55 and 57.

39. Ibid., p. 198.

40. Campari, *Vincente Minnelli*, p. 49.

41. Marin, "Disneyland," pp. 54–55. Emphasis added. According to Donald Preziosi, the concept of the "limit" in its most negative formulation is operative in *Lust for Life:* "Boundaries are suggested beyond which artistic vision dissolves into madness and arouses social opprobrium" (*Rethinking Art History*, p. 24).

42. Marin, "Disneyland," p. 53.

43. Lang, *American Film Melodrama*, p. 171.

44. Casper, *Vincente Minnelli*, p. 77.

45. Ibid., p. 100.

CHAPTER 2

Michelangelo Antonioni's *Red Desert:* Painting as Ventriloquism and Color as Movement

1. Tinazzi, *Antonioni*, p. 5.

2. Prédal, *Michelangelo Antonioni*, p. 152.

3. The economic boom took off thanks to the discovery of natural gas and oil. At the head of an industrial consortium heavily supported by the government (Ente Nazionale Idrocarburi, created in 1953), Enrico Mattei supervised the industrial development between the Po Valley and the harbor of Ravenna. By 1963, however, the recession had already set in.

4. Leprohon, *Michelangelo Antonioni*, p. 97.

5. Hughes, *Shock of the New*, p. 225.

6. Aristarco, *Su Antonioni*, p. 92.

7. Leprohon, *Michelangelo Antonioni*, p. 93.

8. Ibid., p. 100.

9. Tinazzi, *Antonioni*, pp. 9–10. At the 1960 Cannes Film Festival, Antonioni also remarked, "There is today a very serious split between science on the one hand—completely projected toward the future and ready each day to repudiate its past if by so doing it can conquer even the smallest fraction of its future—and, on the other hand, a static rigid morality, to which Man, fully aware of its obsolescence, nevertheless continues to cling" (quoted in Roud, "Red Desert," pp. 76–77).

10. Arrowsmith, "Antonioni's *Red Desert*," p. 313.

11. Leprohon, *Michelangelo Antonioni*, p. 100.

12. Prédal, *Michelangelo Antonioni*, p. 32.

13. Arrowsmith, "Antonioni's *Red Desert*," p. 335.

14. Spackman, *Decadent Genealogies*, p. 58.

15. De Chirico, "Meditations of a Painter," p. 397.

16. Brooks, *Melodramatic Imagination*, p. 16.

17. In "History and Culture in the Post-War Era, 1944–1968," Stuart Woolf writes, "The creation of the European Economic Community in 1957 accelerated the pace of growth and after the . . . "economic miracle" of 1958–63, the triumph of rampant capitalism, exempt from public control and prone to stock market manipulations, seemed complete. The 1960s witnessed the spectacular emergence of a domestic market based on middle-and-working-class demand, in southern as well as northern central Italy: 425,000 cars were registered in 1951, 2,449,000 in 1961, 9,173,000 in 1969. Yet as the labour supply began to dry up for the first time in Italian history, and the international economy faltered, the trade unions regained bargaining power. Against this background of alternating struggle and crises, the 1960s were marked by labour conflict" (in *Italian Art in the Twentieth Century*, ed. Emily Braun, p. 277).

18. Brooks, *Melodramatic Imagination*, p. 56.

19. Wollen, "Baroque and the Neo-Baroque," pp. 9–10.

20. Branzi, *Learning from Milan*, p. 32. On the history of industrial design in Italy, see Sparke, *Italian Design*. On the intellectual climate concerning industrial design and the release of *Red Desert*, Albera and Monti write, in *Italian Modern* (p. 14), "The 13th Triennale (1964) was just as anachronistic with its focus on the theme of 'leisure time,' considering the economic boom was over and recession had begun. In fact, after 1963, Italy's economy not only failed to expand at its 1950 rhythm, but actually dropped below the levels it had already reached. . . . The accent was on the notion of physical environment in all its complexity and on the designer's task to attempt to regulate the relationship that each object has with the rest of reality. The idea of environmental control was a point of issue, though

nothing guaranteed that the sum of individually well-designed products could in any way help to resolve the problem of a degrading environment."

21. Branzi, *Learning from Milan*, p. 34.

22. Greene, *Pier Paolo Pasolini*, p. 120.

23. Arrowsmith, "Antonioni's *Red Desert*," p. 320.

24. In *Michelangelo Antonioni* (p. 97), Leprohon cites the director, "I prefer vertical rather than horizontal movements." On Antonioni's vertical orientation in relation to Eisenstein's intellectual montage, see Ranieri, *Amor vacui*.

25. I owe this insight to P. Adams Sitney's analysis of *Red Desert* in his book *Vital Crises in Italian Cinema*.

26. Deleuze, *Cinema 2*, p. 205.

27. Ferzetti, "La fotografia nei film di Antonioni," p. 61.

28. Piero Manzoni (1933–1963) is famous for his "Achromes," works made of polystyrene pellets in various shapes and forms.

29. Bonitzer as cited in Deleuze, *Cinema 1*, p. 119.

30. Barthes, "Quella traccia del senso che si chiama destino," pp. 163–164.

31. Critics have compared Antonioni's characters standing in the winter fog to Giacometti's *City Square* (1949). It is also well known that Antonioni visited Mark Rothko in his studio in 1966. During this meeting the director remarked that both he and the painter were interested in depicting intangible things. Just as fog and smoke, mists and gases, envelop Antonioni's figures in *Red Desert*, in Rothko's flat panels, color floats toward the viewer as if the canvas had surrendered its gravitational pull on the paint. On Antonioni and Rothko, see Gilman, "About Nothing," p. 11, and Seldes, *Legacy of Mark Rothko*, p. 64.

32. Andrew, "Stature of Objects in Antonioni's Films," p. 46.

33. Campari, "Da *Deserto rosso*."

34. Roud, "Red Desert," p. 79.

35. Barthes, "Quella traccia del senso che si chiama destino," p. 163.

36. In contrast to my reading, Anne Hollander has argued that the back of Monica Vitti's head is comparable to the turned female figures of Dutch painting, where the absence of a frontal view enhances the emotional atmosphere of a domestic scene. (*Moving Pictures*, p. 140).

37. Tinazzi, *Antonioni*, p. 4.

38. In 1957 Fiat invaded the market with the 500, a type of car every average Italian could hope to own.

39. Italo Calvino: "In Mondrian's obsessive desire for order and purity, in Kandinsky's inventive nervousness, there was a subjective impetus that was striving for pure expression, while avoiding any confrontation with the objective world. Pollock's and Wols' paintings are, instead, based on an identification with the outside, with a multi-comprehensive, undifferentiated ego—cosmos, natural world, and mechanical fever of the modern city, all these elements enclosed in the same sign. Thus, what was driving the avant-garde of the first forty years of the century

has reversed its direction. At first we had an inarrestable flow of subjectivity—Joyce, expressionism, surrealism seemed about to flood everything, while challenging man's citizenship in an objective world, in order to make him sail on the endless river of the inner monologue or of the automatic unconscious. Now it is the opposite: it is objectivity that is drowning the self; the volcano out of which the magma erupts is no longer the poet's soul, rather the poet is about to jump into the boiling crater of alterity" ("Il mare dell'oggettivitá," in *Su Antonioni*, ed. Aristarco, p. 139).

40. Benayoun, "Le nevada de l'eros blasé," p. 11.

41. Campari, "Da *Deserto rosso*," p. 164. Emphasis added. On the problem of influence also see Manceaux quoting Antonioni: "In any case, these questions of influences aren't really very important. All artists owe something to somebody. This 'somebody' is an element in the work, but it's only the work itself that finally counts" ("In *The Red Desert*," p. 119).

42. A Franciscan aura surrounds Burri's "Sacks," whose poverty reminds us of Italy in the days of Vittorio de Sica's *Shoeshine* (1946), of Jacopone da Todi's Umbria (Burri's native region), and of Roberto Rossellini's *Flowers of Saint Francis* (1949).

43. Barthes: "The most fragile aspect of an artist is this one: he lives in a world that is changing, but he also changes; this may sound banal, but for the artist, it is truly like a vertigo; this is so because he never knows whether the work that he proposes, is produced as a result of changes in the world, or as a result of changes in himself" ("Quella traccia del senso che si chiama destino," p. 164).

44. Prédal, *Michelangelo Antonioni*, p. 150. On Antonioni's and Goethe's color theory, which informed Matisse's thinking, see Tinazzi, *Antonioni*, p. 5. Also, on Béla Balázs and color as experience see Carlo, *Michelangelo Antonioni: Il "Deserto rosso*," p. 22.

45. Benayoun, "Un cri dans le désert"; Tailleur, "Le désert jusqu'à plus soif." On Italian Art Informel, see Barilli, *L'arte in Italia nel secondo dopoguerra*; Vescovo, "L'informale in Antonioni come fonte di realismo," pp. 44–48.

46. In 1949 during a stay in Paris, Burri visited a big show by Dubuffet at the Galerie Drouin.

47. On Dubuffet and Antonioni, see Carlo, *Michelangelo Antonioni: Il "Deserto rosso*," pp. 17–24. In this essay Carlo refers explicitly to Dubuffet.

48. Weiss, *Shattered Forms*, p. 21.

49. Davis, "Most Controversial Director."

50. On Antonioni and music, see Tinazzi, *Antonioni*, p. 6.

51. Arrowsmith, "Antonioni's *Red Desert*," p. 319.

52. On a cyclical view of the historical process and Italian cinema, see Dalle Vacche, *Body in the Mirror*, where I refer to Giambattista Vico's philosophy of history. On Vico's ambivalent stance toward modernity, also see Lilla, *G. B. Vico*. Lilla's book might stimulate further research on the baroque and melodramatic sensibility at the heart of Italian cinema as a whole.

CHAPTER 3
Eric Rohmer's *The Marquise of O:*
Painting Thoughts, Listening to Images

• 1. Matthew Arnold, as cited in Praz, *Mnemosyne and the Visual Arts*, p. 59.

2. Aldo Tassone, "Incontro con Eric Rohmer," in Rohmer, *Eric Rohmer*, p. 16.

3. Rohmer, *L'organization de l'espace dans le Faust de Murnau*, p. 17.

4. Crisp, *Eric Rohmer*, p. 4.

5. Jacques Aumont, "Les couleurs et le goût," in Rohmer, *Eric Rohmer*, pp. 51–62.

6. Crisp, *Eric Rohmer*, p. 12. The statement first appeared in *Amis du film et de la télévision* 178 (March 1971).

7. Monaco, *New Wave*, p. 292.

8. Hammond and Pagliano, "Eric Rohmer on Film Scripts and Film Plans," p. 223.

9. Crisp, *Eric Rohmer*, p. 2.

10. Ibid., p. 3.

11. Hazelton, *Blaise Pascal*, p. 125.

12. Ibid., p. 134.

13. Crisp, *Eric Rohmer*, p. 5.

14. Hammond and Pagliano, "Eric Rohmer on Film Scripts and Film Plans," p. 211.

15. In *"Le Journal d'un Curé de Campagne* and the Stylistics of Robert Bresson," Bazin uses the term "refraction" in a way comparable to my discussion of Rohmer's adaptation: "The aesthetic pleasure we derive from Bresson's film, while the acknowledgement for it goes, essentially, to the genius of Bernanos, includes all that the novel has to offer plus, in addition, its refraction in the cinema" (p. 143). While Bazin's use of the term "refraction" suggests a dialectical relation between Bernanos and Bresson, literature and film, an in-depth analysis of Bresson's use of art history has never been done, except for Schrader's *Transcendental Style of Film.* Schrader discusses Bresson's images in relation to Byzantine aesthetics. In this respect my use of the term "refraction" is broader than Bazin's, for as I have explained in the first part of my essay, Rohmer's dialectic of word and image encompasses the director's views on other art forms (literature, theater, architecture, painting) in relation to the cinema.

16. Borchardt, "Eric Rohmer's *Marquise of O*," p. 132.

17. Spiegel, *Marquise of O*, p. 136.

18. One possible source for the representation of Giulietta as a painter is Constance Marie Charpentier's *Portrait of Mademoiselle Charlotte du Val d'Ognes* (date unknown), in which a woman with a high-waisted neoclassical gown sits by a window with a canvas on her lap, while a pristine light floods the room. Little is known about Charpentier, who was probably a student of David, or the circumstances and the meaning of this beautiful painting, which captures, however, the

atmosphere of the encounter between mother and daughter in an indoor scene Rohmer stages on the Marquise's estate. On this hypothesis, see Sullivan, *"Marquise of O."*

19. Kleist, *"Die Marquise von O,"* p. 95. Translation mine.

20. About this painting, see Powell, *Fuseli.*

21. Bonitzer, *Décadrages,* pp. 31–32.

22. Herbst, "Coloring Word," p. 204.

23. Rohmer, *Taste for Beauty,* p. 21. Emphasis added.

24. Ibid., p. 19.

25. Gerlacn, "Rohmer, Kleist, and *The Marquise of O,"* p. 90.

26. Grignaffini, *La Pelle e l'anima,* p. 43. Translation mine.

27. Borchardt, "Eric Rohmer's *Marquise of O,"* p. 134 n. 2.

28. Fried, *Absorption and Theatricality.*

29. Spiegel, *Marquise of O,* p. 136.

30. Ibid., p. 125.

31. On color Rohmer writes, "Modern painting's great idea is to have given color a life of its own, or at least to have made it the absolute ruler of the canvas, the supreme value" (*Taste for Beauty,* p. 69).

32. Rohmer, "Le Siècle des Peintres."

CHAPTER 4
Jean-Luc Godard's *Pierrot le Fou:*
Cinema as Collage against Painting

1. Williams, *Republic of Images,* p. 380.

2. Sorlin, *European Cinemas, European Societies,* p. 187.

3. Perloff, "Invention of Collage," p. 42.

4. Jean-Louis Leutrat, "Declension," in *Jean-Luc Godard,* ed. Bellour, p. 27.

5. Leutrat, *Kaleidoscope,* p. 90. Translation mine.

6. Elie Faure is Godard's authority in matters of art history, and he is also used in *Le Mépris* (1964). Godard's choice of Faure, however, may have something to do with the art historian's attendance, at the beginning of the century, of intellectual soirees organized by Ricciotto Canudo, an aesthetician of the cinema, until this contact led Faure himself to write a whole book about film, entitled *Cineplastics.* On Faure, film, and the French avant-garde, see Brender, "Functions of Film"; Désanges, *Elie Faure;* Sarrazin, *A la recontre d'Elie Faure;* Strand, "Polemics and Provocation in Paris."

7. Laura Mulvey, "The Hole and the Zero: The Janus Face of the Feminine in Godard," in *Jean-Luc Godard,* ed. Bellour, p. 84.

8. Whitehead, *Pierrot le Fou,* p. 24. All further citations of the film's dialogue are from this edition of the script. Compare Faure's text on Velázquez with the art historian's complete discussion in *History of Art,* pp. 124–136.

9. Roud, *Jean-Luc Godard,* p. 92.

10. Deleuze, "Three Questions about *Six fois deux*," in *Jean-Luc Godard*, ed. Bellour, p. 41.

11. Cerisuelo, *Jean-Luc Godard*, p. 119.

12. Roud quotes the director as saying, "The cinema is something between art and life. Unlike painting and literature, the cinema both gives life and takes from it, and I try to render this concept in my films" (*Jean-Luc Godard*, p. 13).

13. Ibid., p. 24.

14. Païni, "Detour for the Gaze," p. 6.

15. Christine Poggi, "Mallarmé, Picasso, and the Newspaper as Commodity," in *Collage*, ed. Hoffman, p. 187.

16. "Pierrot mon ami," in Godard, *Jean-Luc Godard par Jean-Luc Godard*, p. 267.

17. Barthes, "That Old Thing, Art," in *Pop Art*, ed. Mahsun, pp. 233–240.

18. Donald B. Kuspit, "Collage: The Organizing Principle of Art in the Age of the Relativity of Art," in *Collage*, ed. Hoffman, p. 39.

19. Perloff, "Invention of Collage," p. 35.

20. Guarner, *Films of Jean-Luc Godard*, p. 102.

21. These observations come from Lehman, "Analysis of Jean-Luc Godard's *Pierrot le Fou*," pp. 28–29.

22. Stam, *Reflexivity in Film and Literature*, p. 148.

23. Whitehead, "Let's Talk about *Pierrot*: Interview with Jean-Luc Godard," in *Pierrot le Fou*, p. 5.

24. On *Pierrot* and painting in relation to color, see Leutrat, *Kaleidoscope*, p. 89.

25. Barthes, "That Old Thing, Art," p. 238.

26. Louis Aragon, "What Is Art, Jean-Luc Godard?" in Brown, *Focus on Godard*, pp. 139–140.

27. Janet Bergstrom, "Violence and Enunciation," in *Jean-Luc Godard*, ed. Bellour, p. 52.

28. Kuspit, "Collage," in *Collage*, ed. Hoffman, p. 40.

29. Perloff, "Invention of Collage," p. 25

30. Kline, *Screening the Text*, p. 212.

31. Ibid., p. 205.

32. Whitehead, *Pierrot le Fou*, pp. 15–16.

33. Lehman, "Analysis of Jean-Luc Godard's *Pierrot le Fou*," p. 26.

34. I owe this formulation to Kline, *Screening the Text*, p. 217.

35. Barthes, "That Old Thing, Art," pp. 234–235. Emphasis added.

36. Poggi, "Mallarmé, Picasso, and the Newspaper as Commodity," in *Collage*, ed. Hoffman, p. 184.

37. Kuspit, "Collage," in *Collage*, ed. Hoffman, p. 46.

38. Lehman, "Analysis of Jean-Luc Godard's *Pierrot le Fou*," p. 29.

39. Kuspit, "Collage," in *Collage*, ed. Hoffman, p. 43.

40. Guarner, *Films of Jean-Luc Godard*, pp. 99–100.

CHAPTER 5
Andrei Tarkovsky's *Andrei Rublev:*
Cinema as the Restoration of Icon Painting

1. Tarkovsky, *Sculpting in Time*, p. 64.

2. Anna Lawton, "Art and Religion in the Films of Andrej Tarkovsky," in Brumfield and Velimorovic, eds. *Christianity and the Arts in Russia*, p. 152.

3. Mikhail Romadin, "Film and Painting," in Tarkovskaya, ed., *About Andrej Tarkovsky*, p. 148.

4. Pallasmaa, "Tarkovsky's *Nostalgia*," p.16.

5. Borin, *Il cinema di Andrej Tarkovsky*, p. 24.

6. Bazin, *What Is Cinema?* p. 15.

7. Pallasmaa, "Tarkovsky's *Nostalgia*," p. 15.

8. Ibid.

9. Carroll, *Philosophical Problems of Classical Film Theory*, p. 169.

10. Tarkovsky, *Sculpting in Time*, p. 120.

11. Ibid., p. 37.

12. Gerhard, *World of Icons*, p. 203.

13. Galavaris, *Icon in the Life of the Church*, p. 4.

14. Baggley, *Doors of Perception*, p. 83.

15. Lasareff and Demus, *USSR*, p. 20.

16. Tatiana Vladyshevskaia, "On the Links between Music and Icon-Painting in Medieval Russia," in Brumfield and Velimorovic, eds., *Christianity and the Arts in Russia*, p. 18.

17. Ibid., p. 20.

18. Billington, *Horizon Book of the Arts in Russia*, p. 74.

19. Sutherland, "What We Do with the Dream," p. 89.

20. Ciofi Degli Atti, "Le icone," p. 18.

21. Lawton, "Art and Religion in the Films of Andrej Tarkovsky," in Brumfield and Velimorovic, eds., *Christianity and the Arts in Russia*, p. 161.

22. On Eisenstein and montage, see Bordwell, *Cinema of Eisenstein*, and Aumont, *Montage Eisenstein.*

23. Tarkovsky, *Sculpting in Time*, p. 106.

24. On the relation of word and image, see Kearney, "Mirror of History": "The artist can no longer testify to his time in language. So he must testify in images. . . . The icon-frames stand empty and the church walls bare. Word is bereft of image and image of word. . . . Sound seeks out sight and sight sound. In the final sequence Rublev finally meets the young bell-maker who has, through a courageous act of faith, rediscovered the secret art of 'sounding the word' (bell-making) buried with his deceased father. Rublev becomes his spiritual father and both father and son vow to unite their arts—sound and image—to re-create the 'third person of the Trinity': the spirit. The final images show a resplendent icon of the Trinity. . . . Tarkovsky is here referring to the traditional Russian Orthodox doc-

trine of 'cosmic perichoresis': the Spirit can only be made fully incarnate in an historical kingdom when Father (image) and Son (sound) are at last united" (p. 7).

25. Petric, "Tarkovsky's Dream Imagery," p. 30.

26. Betz, "Icon and Russian Modernism," p. 39.

27. Baggley, *Doors of Perception*, pp. 80–81. Emphasis added.

28. Misler, "Nella tradizione dell'arte russa," p. 47.

29. Grande, "Andrej Rublev," p. 12.

30. Strick, "Releasing the Balloon," p. 36.

31. Pallasmaa, "Tarkovsky's *Nostalgia*," p. 19.

32. Misler, "Nella tradizione dell'arte russa," p. 50.

33. Lawton, "Art and Religion in the Films of Andrej Tarkovsky," in Brumfield and Velimorovic, eds., *Christianity and the Arts in Russia*, p. 156.

34. Michael Bird, "Film as Hierophany," in May and Bird, eds., *Religion in Film*, p. 21.

35. Strick, "Releasing the Balloon," p. 34.

36. Misler, "Nella tradizione dell'arte russa," p. 48.

37. Waldman, "Kasimir Malevich," p. 28.

38. On slow motion see Epstein, "Photogénie and the Imponderable": "Nothing before cinematography had even allowed us to extend the variability of intimate psychological time, however limited, to external reality, to modify experimentally the temporal coordinate of the perspective of phenomena, or to guess that one would thus come to know other prodigious forms of the universe. Slow motion and fast motion reveal a world where the kingdoms of nature know no boundaries. Everything is alive" (p. 189).

39. The best discussion of water in Tarkovsky can be found in Baecque, *Andrej Tarkovsky.*

40. Le Fanu, *Cinema of Andrej Tarkovsky*, p. 49.

41. Tarkovsky, *Sculpting in Time*, p. 50.

42. Pallasmaa, "Tarkovsky's *Nostalgia*," p. 20.

43. Betz, "Icon and Russian Modernism," p. 38.

CHAPTER 6
F. W. Murnau's *Nosferatu:*
Romantic Painting as Horror and Desire in Expressionist Cinema

1. Kracauer, *From Caligari to Hitler.* There are several versions of *Nosferatu.* My analysis is based on the video produced in 1991 by Kino International Corporation, New York.

2. Eisner, *Haunted Screen.*

3. Jack Kerouac called *Nosferatu* a "horribly perverted" love story. On Kerouac and *Nosferatu*, see Barlow, *German Expressionist Film*, p. 91. Charles Jameux, Gilberto Perez Guillermo, Judith Mayne, and Robin Wood have also proposed interesting readings of *Nosferatu*, but I feel that Kerouac's comment is the most incisive formu-

lation of how horror and desire are the two key elements of the film in relation to its reworking of the Romantic tradition.

4. In "Social Mobility and the Fantastic," Elsaesser writes, "The Romantic project—the transformation of history into inwardness, inwardness into phenomenological and sensuous immediacy of contemplation—has been accomplished by the cinema, but with a vengeance. For it shows this transformation to have been an act of repression, and history returns in the form of the uncanny and the fantastic. Romanticism wedded to technology has produced a wholly fetishized, reified form of immediacy" (p. 24).

5. In *Apocalyptic Vision*, Levine explains, "The ultimate goal of Expressionism was literally to 'lose its own mind,' to seek an identification with forms of precognitive existence as a manifestation of its collective desire to reenter the world of 'unconscious consciousness,' the world in which all life proceeds on the most primitive, the most instinctual of levels" (p. 3).

6. Ibid., p. 13.

7. The best source of information about Murnau's life and the making of *Nosferatu* is Eisner, *Murnau.*

8. The Franco-Prussian War of 1870 had created bitter feelings between the two nations.

9. Levine, *Apocalyptic Vision*, p. 9.

10. Koerner, *Caspar David Friedrich*, pp. 64–65.

11. Riegl, *Problems of Style*, p. xxvii. On the careers and ideas of Wölfflin and Wörringer, see Devine, ed., *Thinkers of the Twentieth Century*, pp. 625–629.

12. On the disagreements between Wölfflin and Meier-Graefe, see Gaehtgens, "Les rapports de l'histoire de l'art."

13. Böcklin reached his peak of fame in 1897, when his work was exhibited in Berlin.

14. The University of Heidelberg has kindly sent me transcripts of all the classes taken by Murnau as a student. In addition to Romantic German literature, Shakespeare, and German art history, the future director studied the following subjects: Introduction to Old English, Explanation of Monuments, the Nibelungenlied, Readings in Carlyle, Basic Questions of Ethics, Public Speaking, and two semesters dealing with Luther, Gottsched, and Lessing. Murnau's teacher in art history, Carl Neumann (1860–1934), produced several books on Rembrandt. My claim that Heidelberg's history of art department had a Wölfflinian orientation is supported by the fact that Neumann had a Wölfflinian colleague, Henry Thode (1857–1920), who wrote about Giotto, Correggio, Mantegna, and Michelangelo. Thode's art-historical library can be consulted by visiting Gabriele D'Annunzio's lavish mansion on Lake Garda in northern Italy. The Italian poet, in fact, bought Il Vittoriale from the art historian for a modest sum shortly after World War I.

15. Fritz Bürger (1877–1916) was another important theoretician for the avant-garde. More research on Bürger, Berlin, Murnau, and the Expressionists is certainly in order; hardly any work in English has been done on Bürger.

16. For instance, the Expressionist Emil Nolde proudly proclaimed himself a "German" artist. Ironically, in 1933 Hitler denounced Expressionism as "degenerate art." For a definition of Expressionism, see Levine, *Apocalyptic Vision:* "It is a subjective rather than objective art, not relying for its themes upon the visible world of nature but seeking instead to reveal aspects of a hidden, unobservable world, relating to the unconscious or subconscious responses of the artist to his environment. . . . It is an art that seeks to project 'emotional needs, psychological pressures, and private obsessions'" (p. 2).

17. Elsaesser, "Secret Affinities," p. 35. On the limitations of the Expressionist label, also see Aumont, "Forma e deformazione, espressione e espressionismo," *L'occhio interminabile: Cinema e pittura* (Venice: Marsilio, 1991), pp. 132–149.

18. The locations used for *Nosferatu* are the Baltic ports of Rostock, Wismar, and Lubeck, and Transylvania is the High Tatras of Czechoslovakia. Murnau's outdoor realism and poetic treatment of landscape is, of course, linked to Scandinavian cinema (Sjöstrom, Stiller, Gad, Christensen).

19. Jameux, *Murnau*, pp. 32–33.

20. Ibid., p. 17.

21. Koerner, *Caspar David Friedrich*, p. 97. Emphasis added.

22. Ibid., pp. 97–98.

23. On Alfred Kubin, see Eisner, *Haunted Screen*, p. 18; Bouvier and Leutrat, *Nosferatu*, p. 323. Finke, *German Painting from Romanticism to Expressionism:* "In his illustrative drawings and compositions Kubin (1877–1959) took up the fantastic tradition of Brueghel, Bosch, Redon, and Munch. . . . 'I don't see the world like that,' he wrote, 'but in strange, semi-conscious moments I am amazed to espy metamorphoses, which are often almost unnoticeable, so that they can seldom be perceived clearly at first sight but have to be nosed out gradually. . . . My realms are those neither of nature nor of my head, and yet they do exist, in the borderlands of twilight'" (p. 199).

24. On industrialization in Germany, see Mann, *History of Germany since 1789:* "Total German industrial production overtook that of France in the seventies, caught up with the British around 1900 and surpassed it substantially by 1910; by this time it was second only to the Americans. Around 1830 four-fifths of the German population lived on the land and earned their living in agriculture; in 1860 the number had fallen to three-fifths, in 1882 to two-fifths and in 1895 it was barely one-fifth. The second greatest source of energy in the world was established within a period of forty years, in the state which had been thought incapable of possessing even the force of industrial organization shown by France" (p. 201).

25. According to the theories by Edmund Burke, published in *Philosophical Enquiry into the Origins of Our Ideas of the Sublime and the Beautiful* (1757), the sublime stressed limitlessness and infinitude, obscurity and strength of expression, in opposition to the beautiful, which was a closed, orderly, and definitive system. In Burke's wake, Immanuel Kant was the first to situate the sublime in the beholder, rather than in the objects of the world. Unable to find itself in relation to the objects of the world, the subject experiences a glimpse into something otherworldly

and incommensurable, which in turn reflects the subject's ability to fabricate divine and demonic things, and experience horror as well as desire.

26. Koerner, *Caspar David Friedrich*, p. 89.

27. Ibid., p. 212.

28. In *Caspar David Friedrich*, Koerner provides a history and a definition of the Rückenfigur: "The *Rückenfigur* is not Caspar David Friedrich's invention, having a long if not quite coherent history in European painting before the nineteenth century. Already in Giotto turned figures sometimes feature in the foreground of a composition, establishing an imaginary fourth wall in the picture's cube of space. These structuring bodies, though, rarely function strictly as viewers within the painted scene. And although Leon Battista Alberti in his treatise *On Painting* (1435–36) instructs artists to people their pictures with 'someone who admonishes and points out to us what is happening there,' Italian pictorial practice favored to this end figures gazing out of the picture at the viewer, rather than *Rückenfiguren* looking in. . . . With the further development of landscape painting in the sixteenth to eighteenth centuries, the *Rückenfigur* took its place within the stock repertoire of staffage which might ornament a panorama's foreground and determine the over-all character and message of the scene. In the 'view-painting' or *veduta*, a turned figure could establish the vista's scale, enhancing its monumentality and marking off the whole pictorial field as something 'worth seeing.' In one popular variant, the *Rückenfigur* is an artist who sits at the margin of the scene, sketching the land-scape we see. . . . Friedrich's *Rückenfiguren* are perhaps closest to this conceit, al-though the event they dramatize is never the actual labor of making, but rather the originary act of experience itself" (pp. 162–163).

29. Rosenblum, *Modern Painting and the Northern Romantic Tradition*, p. 14.

30. Koerner, *Caspar David Friedrich*, p. 16.

31. Rosenblum, *Modern Painting*, p. 28.

32. Wörringer was crucial for the Expressionists because he argued for the existence and continuity of a nonclassical Northern tradition of spiritual unrest expressing itself by distorting reality.

33. Rosenblum, *Modern Painting*, p. 158.

34. Koerner, *Caspar David Friedrich*, p. 93.

35. In *Philosophy of Horror*, Carroll deals with two fundamental questions about knowledge and pleasure: How can anyone be frightened by what they know does not exist? Why would anyone ever be interested in horror, since being horrified is so unpleasant?

36. Roger Dadoun, "Fetishism in the Horror Film," in Donald, *Fantasy and the Cinema*, p. 55.

37. Levine, *Apocalyptic Vision*, p. 6.

38. Guillermo, "Shadow and Substance," p. 150.

39. Barlow, *German Expressionist Film*, 86.

40. Elsaesser, "Secret Affinities," p. 36. In *Murnau*, however, Eisner says that *Nosferatu* was produced on a shoestring budget by Prana Film (p. 118).

41. Rosenblum, *Modern Painting*, p. 139. In *Philosophy of Horror*, Carroll comments on the mixing of categories (human and animal, for instance), which is typical of the horror genre: "As discussed in an earlier section concerning the definition of horror, many cases of impurity are generated by what . . . I call interstitiality and categorical contradictoriness. Impurity involves a conflict between two or more standing cultural categories. Thus, it should come as no surprise that many of the basic structures for representing horrific creatures are combinatory in nature" (p. 43).

42. Watts, *Music*, p. 67.

43. Jameux, *Murnau*, p. 43. Translation mine.

44. Gordon, *Expressionism*, p. 140.

45. Eisner, *Murnau*, p. 98. On the perception of racial and sexual otherness, see Lloyd, *German Expressionism.*

46. Bergstrom, "Sexuality at a Loss," p. 199. On Murnau and homosexuality, *Nosferatu* and gender, also see Wood, "Murnau's Midnight and *Sunrise.*"

47. *The Desire to Desire: The Woman's Film of the 1940s.*

48. Bergstrom, "Sexuality at a Loss," pp. 200–201.

49. On traveling, windows, and mirrors, see Judith Mayne, "Dracula in the Twilight: Murnau's *Nosferatu* (1922)," in Rentschler, ed., *German Film and Literature*, pp. 25–29.

50. Cardullo, "Expressionism and *Nosferatu*," p. 31.

CHAPTER 7
Kenji Mizoguchi's *Five Women around Utamaro:*
Film between Woodblock Printing and Tattooing

1. Morris, *Kenji Mizoguchi*, p. 13.

2. McDonald, *Mizoguchi*, p. 74.

3. Hirano, *Mr. Smith Goes to Tokyo*, pp. 154–165.

4. Lane, *Images from the Floating World:* "The only real offenses in the eyes of the law were publication of seditious matter and publication without the censor's seal of approval. The publication of pornography as such was not considered a very serious crime, and as late as Koryiusai in the 1770s, artists often signed their true names to their erotica. When at last Utamaro did run into difficulties with the authorities, . . . it was not for his erotica, but for some uncensored historical prints depicting the sixteenth-century Shogun Hideyoshi, whose heir had been deposed by the current Tokugawa regime and about whom the governors naturally felt the pangs of a guilty conscience" (p. 141).

5. Mizoguchi shot *Forty-Seven Ronin*, a tale in two parts of collective suicide (seppuku) in the name of a samurai's honor, between 1941 and 1942. The film is absolutely stunning and worth seeing. In *Mr. Smith Goes to Tokyo*, Hirano remarks, "Many prewar film versions of *Forty-Seven Ronin* were banned from the Japanese screen until the end of the occupation, although stage production of the story had reappeared by November 1947" (p. 66).

6. Hirano, *Mr. Smith Goes to Tokyo*, pp. 44–45.

7. Andrew and Andrew, *Kenji Mizoguchi*, p. 15.

8. Rosenbaum, "Utamaro o meguru gonin no onna," p. 262.

9. Bordwell, "Mizoguchi and the Evolution of Film Language," p. 113.

10. The official ban on prostitution went into effect in 1956.

11. Kirihara, *Patterns of Time*, p. 70.

12. Sato, *Currents in Japanese Cinema*, p. 185.

13. Bock, *Japanese Film Directors*: "Mizo was 'unusual in the extent to which he suffered at the hands of women. He hated women: he was contemptuous of women. On the other hand, when he fell in love, it was with the sincerity of a little boy'" (p. 40). Here Bock is quoting Tadao Sato.

14. Bock, *Japanese Film Directors*: "When she went insane in 1941 due to 'hereditary syphilis' in Mizoguchi's words, he had her institutionalized for the rest of her life. After the Pacific War, he took his wife's widowed sister and her two daughters into his home out of pity. He lived with his sister-in-law as a wife, but proposed marriage to his leading actress, Kinuyo Tanaka, around 1947. She refused him and from 1953 on would have nothing further to do with him because he tried to prevent her from directing her first film" (p. 40).

15. Mahayana Buddhism is a form of mainstream religion in Japan.

16. Ehrlich, "Artist's Desire," p. 2.

17. Andrew, *Film in the Aura of Art*, p. 183.

18. Barrett, *Archetypes in Japanese Films*, p. 120.

19. Let us set this scene against Hirano's research in *Mr. Smith Goes to Tokyo*: "The first public striptease show was staged in November 1947 in a small theater in Tokyo, and was received enthusiastically. It was produced by the Toho Theatrical Company in a 'frameshow' format, in which young women posed on the stage behind a large frame, imitating famous Western and Japanese seminude paintings and thus imparting an artistic, pseudosophisticated flair to the show" (p. 163).

20. Burch, *To the Distant Observer*, p. 243.

21. Hillier, *Utamaro*: "Edo was the capital of . . . a police state, with many of the evils we have come to associate with totalitarianism—repressions, secret police, rigid censorship, and banishments. . . . The years 1780 to 1792 are noted in the annals of Japan as a period of starvation and misery" (pp. 28–29).

22. Webber, *Japanese Woodblock Prints*: "The making of the traditional Japanese woodblock print involved several individuals in the process—the artist, the wood carver, the printer, and the publisher" (p. 7).

23. *Feminine Image: Women of Japan*, p. 23.

24. Hillier, *Utamaro*: "Until the seventeenth century, painting was an art largely performed and enjoyed by the restricted circle of the aristocracy, but it was widely appreciated within that circle. Appreciation of painting was one of the accomplishments that every man of breeding was expected to possess, along with the ability to write an artistic hand, and to compose a neat verse extempore" (p. 11).

25. Murase, *Tales of Japan:* "Utamaro is known to have studied painting with Toriyama Sekien (1712–1788), an artist trained in the Kano School who was also an illustrator of books" (p. 219). In *Utamaro*, Hillier observes, "In landscape—usually, with Utamaro, only the background to his prints—he often shows the Kano touch, and when, in an interior, he depicts a painted screen or kakemono, . . . it is invariably in the Kano manner" (p. 16).

26. Cohen, "Mizoguchi and Modernism": "In most of Mizoguchi's films, there are characters who function as go-betweens within the stories. They either mediate between other characters or manipulate the action by themselves. This figure has a real counterpart in Japanese society (formalized in arranged marriages or informal industrial mediation) and it is a permanent fixture of consensus democracy" (p. 18).

27. Fister, *Japanese Women Artists:* "Because of the relative freedom of behavior in the pleasure quarters, the ukiyo-e world was more receptive to women painters than were traditional workshops. The more liberal view toward women was reflected in the popular fiction of the day which often depicted women as daring and brazen, not the meek creatures praised in Confucian texts" (p. 47).

28. Bonitzer, "Violence et lateralité," p. 30. Translation mine.

29. On Mizoguchi's *Utamaro* and censorship, see Hirano in *Mr. Smith Goes to Tokyo:* "Murders were objectionable if they were presented without any moral judgements. On seeing Kenji Mizoguchi's *Utamaro and Five Women* (1947), George Gercke of CIE opined that showing a character killing to avenge his failure in love was not desirable because it could influence young people harmfully" (p. 75).

30. In his book *In Praise of Shadows* (possibly a source for Barthes's *Empire of Signs*), Tanizaki writes, "We find beauty not in the thing itself but in the patterns of shadows, the light and the darkness, that one thing against another creates" (p. 30).

31. Hillier, *Utamaro:* "Portraiture, 'a likeness in the Western manner, was hardly ever attempted by Japanese artists: there were rare exceptions, such as the occasional portraits of a priest or a memorial portrait of some personage of note, posthumously painted and probably quite unreliable. . . .' Utamaro, however, did produce many half-length 'portraits' of women especially between 1791–1793, but these images have to do more with mood and not so much with individuality" (p. 70).

32. Murase, *Tales of Japan*, p. 220.

33. Ehrlich, "Artist's Desire," p. 4. In *Eros and Massacre*, Desser writes, "Romantic love in Mizoguchi's films is therefore closer to the classic mother-son relationship that critics of Japanese culture see as so crucial" (p. 111).

34. In my reading I am, therefore, assuming that Mizoguchi remains closer to the original myth of Yama Uba or Yamamba as mountain witch and seductress. By contrast, Utamaro, according to an unpublished paper by Meera Viswanathan, a specialist in Japanese literature teaching at Brown University, makes the myth of Yamamba reverberate with an unconventional kind of eroticism that seems to

ignore incest and happily exist beyond transgression in an aura of bliss between the highly sexualized figures of mother and son: the woman suckling the toddler and the child fondling the mother's breast.

35. The picture I have in mind here is *Azamino of Onitsutaya Tattooing Gontaro*, at the Boston Museum of Fine Arts.

36. Rubin, ed., *Marks of Civilization:* "In tracing the history of the Edo tattoo, it is essential to recognize that this practice was harshly sanctioned by the authorities. . . . At the highest economic level of society, merchants were constantly being criticized for extravagance and ostentatious display. More on the level that includes groups likely to indulge in tattooing, there were frequent restrictions, even prohibitions, on cultural forms such as the kabuki drama, ukiyo-e woodblock prints, and various types of popular literature" (pp. 119–120). Two other books have helped me to develop ideas on tattooing. See Martelli, *Il Tatuaggio come arte*, and Sanders, *Customizing the Body.*

37. Hearn, "Story of Mimi-Nashi-Hoichi." A few words about Hearn's biography are necessary. Born in Ireland, Lafcadio Hearn (1850–1904) settled in Japan, where his wife, Setsuko Koizumi, helped him to gather old Japanese folk tales. As a journalist and as a writer Hearn poured out book after book about the land of his adoption. Through his stories and folklore, Hearn is widely known to young and old in Japan. His work was influenced by Irish folklore, writings, and ghost stories that he heard and read in his formative years in Ireland.

38. The biwa, a kind of four-stringed lute, is chiefly used in musical recitative. Formerly the professional minstrels who recited the *Heike-monogatari*, and other tragic histories, were called biwa-hoshi, or lute priests. The origin of this appellation is not clear, but it may refer to the lute players' practice of shaving their heads.

39. Hearn, "Story of Mimi-Nashi-Hoichi," p. 326 n. 7.

40. Bock, *Japanese Film Directors:* "The raging jealous woman would be a part of the realism of Mizoguchi's later films, notably in 1946 *Utamaro and His Five Women* which Yoda wrote using Mizo as the real life model for Utamaro" (pp. 38–39).

41. The motif of lovers walking across the Floating Bridge of Dreams, a metaphor for the insubstantial beauty of life, often reappears in Utamaro's prints.

42. Sato, "On Mizoguchi": "Kenji Mizoguchi lived in a tradition of the old Japanese esthetic, yet he was an artist who succeeded in adding something modern to the heart of that tradition" (p. 15). This essay by Sato has been translated by Paul Andrew and it appears with an introduction by Dudley Andrew.

CHAPTER 8
Alain Cavalier's *Thérèse:*
Still Life and the Close-Up as Feminine Space

1. For Cavalier's photographic sources, see Sainte-Marie, *Photo Album of St. Thérèse.* The Library of the Museum of Modern Art owns a copy of this book, which contains reproductions of archival materials Alain Cavalier must have consulted directly at Lisieux.

2. For a good biography on Thérèse, see Furlong, *Thérèse of Lisieux.*
3. This interpretation appears throughout Furlong's biography.
4. Epstein, "Magnification and Other Writings," p. 11.
5. Mazzoni, "Virgin Births."
6. In Cavalier's film, the illness of Thérèse is tuberculosis, an equivalent of hysteria in turn-of-the-century novels by the Goncourt brothers and Gabriele D'Annunzio.
7. On the close-up and the maternal, also see Eberwein, "Reflections on the Breast": "The infant at the breast in the oral world stage of its development knows no words, only states of being, a condition somewhat akin to that described by mystics explaining their sense of oneness with God. Lewin cites passages from St. Teresa and St. Francis de Sales to illustrate the parallel. From the latter we hear: 'the soul is like a little child still at the breast, whose mother, to caress him whilst he is still on her arm, makes her milk distill into his mouth without his even moving his lips.' That is, the most intense perception of ultimate reality for the mystic is here figured with reference to the earliest nutritive experience" (p. 52).
8. Lucy Fisher, *Shot/Countershot,* p. 78.
9. Bryson, *Looking at the Overlooked,* pp. 136–178.
10. For Cavalier's formula "Less is all," see Kauffmann, "Stanley Kauffmann on Films."
11. Bordwell, *Films of Carl-Theodor Dreyer,* p. 85.
12. Rasy, *La prima estasi,* p. 50.
13. Balázs, *Theory of Film,* p. 63.
14. I owe this insight to my student Polly La Barre.
15. On anorexia and architecture, see Seidenberg and Crow, *Women Who Marry Houses;* Brown, "Anorexia, Humanism, and Feminism." For a completely different reading of both the veil and the close-up, see Doane, *Femmes Fatales.*
16. Mazzoni, "Virgin Births," p. 33.
17. O'Brien, "Success in Small Things," p. 691.
18. Mazzoni, "Virgin Births," p. 71.
19. Bynum, *Holy Feast and Holy Fast,* pp. 272–273.
20. Krauss, *Originality of the Avant-Garde,* p. 13.
21. I owe this insight to my student Polly La Barre.
22. For Cavalier's reference to Manet, see Bonitzer and Toubiana, "La petite voie," p. 7.
23. For Cavalier's reference to Flaubert, see ibid., p. 61.
24. For Cavalier on transitions, passages, and thresholds, see Ramasse, "Entretien avec Alain Cavalier sur *Thérèse,*" p. 26.
25. Milne, "*Thérèse,*" p. 69.
26. On the antimonarchic orientation of French positivism, see Pierrot, *The Decadent Imagination.*
27. On Cavalier's backdrops, see Philippon, "L'enfance de l'art": "Ces fondus sont beaucoup plus nombreux, et beaucoup plus rapprochés, au tout début du film

que dans son déroulement ultérieur: comme s'il s'agissait d'abord, pour le film, de sortir à tâtons de la nuit d'avant le cinéma, d'apprivoiser l'image qui va le caractériser de bout en bout, tant cette image est neuve, inédite, virginale" (p. 5).

28. Reynaud, "New York Film Festival," p. 20.

29. Bryson, *Looking at the Overlooked*, p. 76.

30. Di Fazio, "Al cinema," p. 80.

31. On this use of flowers in Impressionist painting and in Germaine Dulac's *Smiling Mme Beudet* (1923), see Abel, *French Cinema*, p. 342.

32. Thérèse's sister, Céline, was a self-taught painter who relied on the most disparate popular, religious imagery for her own mediocre work. On painting in the convent, see Saint-Marie, *Photo Album of St. Thérèse*, pp. 15–20.

33. Rasy, *La prima estasi*, p. 56.

34. Deleuze, *Cinema 1*, p. 95.

35. Ibid., p. 96.

36. Ibid., p. 95.

37. Epstein, "Magnification and Other Writings," p. 13.

38. Mazzoni, "Virgin Births," p. 58.

39. Bynum, *Holy Feast and Holy Fast*, pp. 272–273.

40. Lucie's remark echoes Sir Joshua Reynolds's condemnation of still life as described by Bryson: "Still life, unable to abstract itself from its entanglement in detail, and incapable of producing mental as opposed to merely sensuous pleasure, is crushed by Reynolds' megalographic doctrine, that great art can exist only when particulars are shed and art achieves the level of 'general ideas'" (*Looking at the Overlooked*, p. 175).

41. Ramasse, "Entretien avec Alain Cavalier sur *Thérèse*," p. 28.

~

Bibliography

~

INTRODUCTION
A Thematic and Intertextual Approach

Aumont, Jacques. *L'occhio interminabile: Cinema e pittura.* Venice: Marsilio, 1991.
Bonitzer, Pascal. *Décadrages: Cinéma et peinture.* Paris: Editions de l'Etoile, 1985.
Brooks, Peter. *The Melodramatic Imagination: Balzac, Henry James, Melodrama, and the Mode of Excess.* New York: Columbia University Press, 1984.
Hollander, Anne. *Moving Pictures.* New York: Knopf, 1989.
Leutrat, Jean-Louis. *Kaleidoscope.* Lyons: Presses Universitaires de Lyons, 1988.
Peucker, Brigette. *Incorporating Images: Film and the Rival Arts.* Princeton: Princeton University Press, 1995.

CHAPTER I
Vincente Minnelli's *An American in Paris:*
Painting as Psychic Upheaval

Alley, Ronald. *Henri Rousseau: Portrait of a Primitive.* Secaucus, N.J.: Chartwell Books, 1978.
Altman, Rick. *The American Film Musical.* Bloomington: Indiana University Press, 1989.
Anderson, Lindsay. "Minnelli, Kelly, and *An American in Paris.*" *Sequence* 14 (1952): 36–38.
Aprá, Adriano. "Solitudine di Vincente Minnelli." *Filmcritica*, no. 134 (1963): 343–350.
Bernheimer, Charles. *Figures of Ill Repute: Representing Prostitution in Nineteenth-Century France.* Cambridge: Harvard University Press, 1989.

Bitsch, Charles, and Jean Domarchi. "Entretien avec Vincente Minnelli." *Cahiers du Cinéma*, no. 74 (1957): 4–15.

Campari, Roberto. *Vincente Minnelli.* Florence: La Nuova Italia, 1977.

Casper, Joseph Andrew. *Vincente Minnelli and the Film Musical.* New York: S. A. Barnes & Co., 1977.

Chaumeton, Etienne. "L'oeuvre de Vincente Minnelli." *Positif,* no. 12 (1954): 36–45.

Collins, Bradford R. "*Life* Magazine and the Abstract Expressionists, 1948–1951: A Historiographic Study of a Late Bohemian Enterprise." *Art Bulletin* 73 (June 1991): 283–308.

Copeland, Roger, and Marshall Cohen, eds. *What's Dance? Readings in Theory and Criticism.* New York: Oxford University Press, 1983.

Delamater, Jerome. *Dance in the Hollywood Musical.* Ann Arbor, Mich.: UMI Research Press, 1981.

Domarchi, Jean, and Jean Douchet. "Rencontre avec Vincente Minnelli." *Cahiers du Cinéma*, no. 128 (1962): 3–14.

Foster, Edward Halsey. *Understanding the Beats.* Columbia: University of South Carolina Press, 1992.

Freedland, Michael. *Maurice Chevalier.* New York: Morrow, 1981.

Genné, Beth Eliot. "Vincente Minnelli's Style in Microcosm: The Establishing Sequence of *Meet Me in St. Louis.*" *Arts Journal* 43, no. 3 (1983): 247–254.

Grob, Jean. "Vincente Minnelli." *Image et Son,* no. 149 (1962): 12–13.

Guilbaut, Serge. *How New York Stole the Idea of Modern Art: Abstract Expressionism, Freedom, and the Cold War.* Translated by Arthur Goldhammer. Chicago: University of Chicago Press, 1983.

Harcourt-Smith, Simon. "Vincente Minnelli." *Sight and Sound* 21, no. 3 (1952): 115–199.

Harding, James. *Maurice Chevalier: His Life, 1888–1972.* London: Secker & Warburg, 1982.

Harvey, Stephen. *Directed by Vincente Minnelli.* New York: Museum of Modern Art, Harper & Row, 1989.

Johnson, Albert. "The Films of Vincente Minnelli: Part 1 and Part 2." *Film Quarterly* 12, no. 2 (1958): 25–35, and no. 3 (1959): 32–42.

Keller, Horst. *Toulouse-Lautrec: Painter of Paris.* New York: Harry N. Abrams, 1968.

Knox, Donald. *The Magic Factory: How MGM Made "An American in Paris."* Foreword by Andrew Sarris. New York: Praeger Publishers, 1973.

Landau, Ellen. *Jackson Pollock.* New York: Harry N. Abrams, 1989.

Lang, Robert. *American Film Melodrama: Griffith, Vidor, Minnelli.* Princeton: Princeton University Press, 1989.

Lassaigne, Jacques. *Toulouse-Lautrec e la Parigi dei cabarets.* Milan: Fratelli Fabbri, 1969.

Le Pichon, Yann. *The World of Henri Rousseau.* Translated by Yoachim Neugroschel. New York: Viking Press, 1982.

Marchelli, Massimo. *Vincente Minnelli.* Milan: Edizioni il Formichiere, 1979.

Marin, Louis. "Disneyland: A Degenerate Utopia." *Glyph, Johns Hopkins Textual Studies*, no. 1 (1977): 50–66.

Moore, Sonia. *The Stanislavsky System.* New York: Penguin Books, 1984.

Naremore, James. *The Films of Vincente Minnelli.* Cambridge: Cambridge University Press, 1993.

Preziosi, Donald. *Rethinking Art History: Meditations on a Coy Science.* New Haven: Yale University Press, 1989.

Tietze, Hans. *Toulouse-Lautrec.* New York: Beechurst Press, n.d.

Torok, Jean-Paul, and Jacques Quincey. "Vincente Minnelli ou le peintre de la vie rêvée." *Positif,* nos. 50–52 (1963): 54–74.

Vineberg, Steve. *Method Actors: Three Generations of an American Acting Style.* New York: Schirmer Books, 1991.

Waldman, Diane. "The Childish, the Insane, and the Ugly: The Representation of Modern Art in Popular Films and Fiction of the Forties." *Wide Angle* 5, no. 2 (1983): 52–65.

Wallace, Philip Hope. "*An American in Paris.*" *Sight and Sound* 21, no. 2 (1951): 77–78.

Werner, Alfred. *Raoul Dufy.* New York: Harry N. Abrams, 1987.

CHAPTER 2

Michelangelo Antonioni's *Red Desert:*
Painting as Ventriloquism and Color as Movement

Albera, Giovanni, and Nicolas Monti. *Italian Modern: A Design Heritage.* New York: Rizzoli, 1989.

———. "*Deserto rosso.*" *Cahiers du Cinéma,* no. 159 (1964): 14.

———. *Le montagne incantate.* Milan: Electa, 1983.

Andrew, Dudley. "The Stature of Objects in Antonioni's Films." *TriQuarterly,* no. 11 (1968): 40–59.

Aristarco, Guido. "La donna nel deserto di Antonioni." *Cinema Nuovo,* no. 173 (1965): 12–15.

———. *Su Antonioni: Materiali per una analisi critica.* Rome: La Zattera di Babele, 1988.

Arrowsmith, William. "Antonioni's *Red Desert:* Myth and Fantasy." In *The Binding of Proteus.* Edited by Marjorie W. McCune, Tucker Orbison, and Philip M. Withim, 312–337. Lewisburg, Pa.: Bucknell University Press, 1980.

Ballo, Guido. *La linea dell'arte italiana.* Rome: Edizioni Mediterranee, 1964.

Barilli, Renato. *Dubuffet matériologue.* Bologna: Alfa, 1963.

———, ed. *L'Arte in Italia nel secondo dopoguerra.* Bologna: Il Mulino, 1979.

Barilli, Renato, and Franco Solmi, eds. *L'Informale in Italia.* Milan: Mazzotta, 1983.

Barthes, Roland. "Quella traccia del senso che si chiama destino." In *Su Antonioni: Materiali per una analisi critica.* Edited by Guido Aristarco. Rome: La Zattera di Babele, 1986.

Benayoun, Robert. "Le nevada de l'eros blasé." *L'Avant-Scène du Cinéma,* no. 49 (1969): 11.

————. "Un cri dans le désert." *Positif,* no. 66 (1965): 43–59.

Biarese, Cesare. *I film di Michelangelo Antonioni.* Rome: Gremese, 1985.

Bigongiari, Piero. "Nicholas De Staël: Il pittore del primo giorno della creazione." *La Biennale di Venezia,* no. 41: 9–23.

Boatto, Alberto. "Lo spazio del presente." *Metro,* no. 13 (1968): 33–38.

Borden, Diane M. "Antonioni and Architecture." *Mise-en-scéne* 2 (1980): 23–26.

Branzi, Andrea. *Learning from Milan: Design and the Second Modernity.* Cambridge: MIT Press, 1988.

Braun, Emily, ed. *Italian Art in the Twentieth Century.* Munich and London: Prestel-Verlag, 1989.

Brooks, Peter. *The Melodramatic Imagination: Balzac, Henry James, Melodrama, and the Mode of Excess.* New York: Columbia University Press, 1984.

Bruno, Eduardo. *"Deserto rosso." Filmcritica,* no. 146 (1964): 350–360.

Calvesi, Maurizio. *Le due avanguardie: Dal futurismo alla Pop Art.* Milan: Laterza, 1966.

Cameron, Jan, and Robin Wood. *Antonioni.* New York: Praeger, 1971.

Campari, Roberto. "Da *Deserto rosso:* Il colore." In *Michelangelo Antonioni: Identificazione di un autore.* Vol. 2. Parma: Pratiche 1983–1985.

Carlo, Carlo di, ed. *Michelangelo Antonioni: Il "Deserto rosso."* Bologna: Cappelli, 1978.

Cassou, Jean. "Evolution de l'art de Soulages." *Art International* 8, no. 7 (1964): 34–36.

Celant, Germano. *Arte povera.* New York: Praeger, 1969.

————. "The Italian Complexity." *Il Modo Italiano* (January–February 1984) Regione Piemonte LAICA 1983: 15–52.

Chatman, Seymour. *Antonioni: The Surface of the World.* Berkeley: University of California Press, 1985.

Chipp, Herschel B., ed. *Theories of Modern Art: A Source Book by Artists and Critics.* Berkeley: University of California Press, 1968.

Colpart, Gilles. "Le *désert rouge." Téléciné,* no. 211 (1976): 14.

Cooper, Douglas. *Nicolas de Staël.* New York: W. W. Norton & Co., 1961.

Costa, Antonio. *"Deserto rosso."* In *Tradizione e innovazione nel cinema degli autori Emiliano Romagnoli.* Modena: Comune di Modena, 1976.

Cowie, Peter. *Antonioni, Bergman, Resnais.* London: Tantivey Press, 1963.

Cuccu, Lorenzo. *Antonioni: Il discorso dello sguardo, da "Blow Up" a "Identificazione di una donna."* Pisa: ETS, 1990.

————. *La visione come problema: Forme e svolgimeno del cinema di Antonioni.* Rome: Bulzoni, 1973.

Dalle Vacche, Angela. *The Body in the Mirror: Shapes of History in Italian Cinema.* Princeton: Princeton University Press, 1992.

Davis, Melton S. "Most Controversial Director." *New York Times Magazine,* 15 November 1964.

De Chirico, Giorgio. "Meditations of a Painter." In *Theories of Modern Art: A Source Book by Artists and Critics,* edited by Herschel B. Chipp. Berkeley: University of California Press, 1968.

De Launay, Marc. "*Le désert rouge.*" *Image et Son/Revue du Cinéma*, no. 269 (1973): 71–78.

Deleuze, Gilles. *Cinema 1: The Movement-Image.* Translated by Hugh Tomlinson and Barbara Habberjam. Minneapolis: University of Minnesota Press, 1986.

———. *Cinema 2: The Time-Image.* Translated by Hugh Tomlinson and Robert Galeta. Minneapolis: University of Minnesota Press, 1989.

Dell'Arco, Maurizio Fagiolo. *Rapporto 60: Le arti oggi in Italia.* Rome: Bulzoni, 1966.

———. *Michelangelo Antonioni.* Rome: Bianco e Nero, 1964.

Dorfles, Gillo. *Il disegno industriale e le sua estetica.* Bologna: Cappelli, 1963.

Eco, Umberto. "L'opera aperta nelle arti visive." In *Opera Aperta: Forma e indeterminazione nella poetiche contemporanee.* Milan: Bompiani, 1962.

Ferzetti, Fabrizio. "La fotografia nei film di Antonioni." In *Michelangelo Antonioni: Identificazione di un autore.* Vol. 2. Parma: Pratiche, 1983–1985.

Fink, Guido. "*Deserto rosso:* La réalité acceptée." *Etudes Cinématographiques*, nos. 36–37 (1964): 92–97.

Fossati, Paolo. *Il design in Italia.* Turin: Einaudi, 1972.

Giaomielli, A. M., and J. Saitta. *Crisi dell' uomo e della societá nei film di Visconti e di Antonioni.* Alba: Edizioni Paoline, 1972.

Giaume, Joelle Mayet. *Michelangelo Antonioni: Le fil intérieur.* Brussels: Editions Yellow Now, 1990.

Gilman, Richard. "About Nothing—with Precision." *Theater Arts* 46, no. 7 (1962): 10–12.

Godard, Jean-Luc. "Jean-Luc Godard Interviews Michelangelo Antonioni." Translated by Elizabeth Kingsley-Rowe from a tape-recording. *Movie*, no. 12 (1965): 31–34.

Goldmann, Annie. *Cinéma et société moderne, le cinéma de 1958 à 1968: Godard, Antonioni, Resnais, Robbe-Grillet.* Paris: Editions Anthropos, 1971.

Greene, Naomi. *Pier Paolo Pasolini.* Princeton: Princeton University Press, 1990.

Grenier, Jean. "Du noir en général chez Soulages." *XXe Siècle*, no. 13 (1959): 67–73.

Hollander, Anne. *Moving Pictures.* New York: Knopf, 1989.

Houston, Beverley, and Marsha Kinder. "*Red Desert.*" In *Self and Cinema: A Transformalist Perspective.* Pleasantville, N.Y.: Redgrave Publishing, 1980.

Houston, Penelope. "The Landscape of the Desert." *Sight and Sound* 34 (Spring 1965).

Hughes, Robert. *The Shock of the New: Art and the Century of Change.* London: Thames & Hudson, 1980.

Jenkins, Paul, and Esther Jenkins, eds. *Observations of Michel Tapié.* N.p.: Paul Jenkins, 1956.

Kauffmann, Stanley. "The Artist Advances." In *Renaissance of the Film,* edited by Julius Belloni, 211–217. New York: Collier Books, 1950.

Leprohon, Pierre. *Michelangelo Antonioni: An Introduction.* Translated by Scott Sullivan. New York: Simon & Schuster, 1963.

Lilla, Mark. *G. B. Vico: The Making of an Anti-Modern.* Cambridge: Harvard University Press, 1993.

Lyons, Robert Joseph. *Michelangelo Antonioni's Neorealism: World's View*. New York: Arno Press, 1976.

Madrignani, Carlo A. "Il mestiere di vivere in Antonioni." *Belfagor* 40 (30 September 1985): 597–606.

Manceaux, Michèle. "In *The Red Desert*." *Sight and Sound* 33 (Summer 1964): 118–119.

Mancini, Michele, and Perella Giuseppe. *Michelangelo Antonioni: Architetture della visione*. Rome: Coneditor, 1986.

Mechini, Pietro, and Roberto Salvadore. *Rossellini, Antonioni, Buñuel*. Padova, Venice: Marsilio, 1973.

Perry, Ted. *Michelangelo Antonioni: A Guide to References and Resources*. Boston: G. K. Hall, 1986.

Prédal, René. *Michelangelo Antonioni: La vigilance du désir*. Paris: Editions du Cerf, 1991.

Raimondi, Giuseppe. "Jean Dubuffet: Pratico delle natura." *La Biennale di Venezia*, no. 38 (1960): 18–24.

Ranieri, Nicola. *Amor vacui: Il cinema di Michelangelo Antonioni*. Chieti: Metis, 1990.

Rifkin, Ned. *Antonioni's Visual Language*. Ann Arbor, Mich.: UMI Research Press, 1982.

Rohdie, Sam. *Antonioni*. London: British Film Institute, 1990.

Roud, Richard. "*The Red Desert*." *Sight and Sound* 34 (Spring 1965): 76–80.

Sanna, Jole de. "Renovating the New: The Art of Lucio Fontana." *Artforum* 26 (November 1987): 108–113.

Schmalenbach, Werner. *Kurt Schwitters*. New York: Harry N. Abrams, 1967.

Seldes, Lee. *The Legacy of Mark Rothko*. New York: Holt, Rinehart & Winston, 1978.

Sitney, P. Adams. *Vital Crises in Italian Cinema: Iconography, Stylistics, Politics*. Austin: University of Texas Press, 1995.

Spackman, Barbara. *Decadent Genealogies: The Rhetoric of Sickness from Baudelaire to D'Annunzio*. Ithaca: Cornell University Press, 1989.

Sparke, Penny. *Italian Design*. London: Thames & Hudson, 1988.

Sutton, Denys. Introduction to *Nicholas de Staël*. Milan: Fabbri, 1966.

Tailleur, Roger. "Le désert jusqu'à plus soif . . ." *Positif*, nos. 67–68 (1965): 81–92.

Tailleur, Roger, and Paul-Louis Thirard. *Antonioni*. Paris: Editions Universitaires, 1963.

Tapié, Michel. *Un art autre: Il s'agit de nouveaux dévidages du réel*. Paris: Gabriel-Giraud et Fils, 1952.

Taylor, Stephen. "The *Red Desert*: Neurosis à la mode." *Hudson Review* 18 (1965): 252–259.

Tazzi, Pier Luigi. "Michelangelo Antonioni." *Artforum* 22 (January 1984): 88.

Thirard, Paul-Louis. "Michelangelo Antonioni." In *Premier Plan 15*. Lyons: Serdoc, 1960.

Tilliette, Xavier. "*Deserto rosso*: Le mirage et le désert." *Etudes Cinématographiques*, nos. 36–37 (1964): 98–103.

Tinazzi, Giorgio. *Antonioni*. Florence: La Nuova Italia, 1974.

Tomassoni, Italo. *Piet Mondrian*. Florence: Sadea/Sansoni, 1969.

Trini, I. "The Sixties in Italy." *Studio International* 184 (November 1972): 165–170.

Il Verri: L'Informale. Milan: Rusconi & Paolazzi, 1961. Originally published in *Il Verri* 5, no. 3 (1961).

Vescovo, Marisa. "L'informale in Antonioni come fonte di realismo." *Cinema Nuovo,* no. 209 (1971): 44–48.

Vetrocq, Marcia. "Utopias, Nomads, Critics: From Arte Povera to the Transavanguardia." *Arts* 63 (April 1989): 49–54.

Waldman, Diane. *Collage, Assemblage, and the Found Object.* New York: Harry N. Abrams, 1992.

Weiss, Allen S. *Shattered Forms: Art Brut, Phantasms, Modernism.* Albany: State University of New York Press, 1992.

Wollen, Peter. "Baroque and Neo-Baroque in the Age of Spectacle." *Point of Contact* 3, no. 3 (1993): 9–21.

CHAPTER 3
Eric Rohmer's *The Marquise of O:*
Painting Thoughts, Listening to Images

The Age of Revolution: French Painting, 1774–1830. Detroit: Detroit Institute of Arts; N.Y.: Metropolitan Museum of Art; Paris: Reunion des Musées Nationaux, 1975.

Angeli, Giovanna. *Eric Rohmer.* Milan: Miozzi, 1979.

Bazin, André, "*Le Journal d'un Curé de Campagne* and the Stylistics of Robert Bresson." In *What Is Cinema?* Vol. 1. Berkeley: University of California Press, 1967.

Bonitzer, Pascal. *Décadrages: Cinéma et peinture.* Paris: Editions de l'Etoile, 1985.

———. "Le plan-tableau." *Cahiers du Cinéma,* no. 370 (1985): 18.

Borchardt, Edith. "Eric Rohmer's *Marquise of O* and the Theory of the German Novella." *Literature/Film Quarterly* 12, no. 2 (1984): 129–135.

Briganti, Giuliano. *Pittori dell'immaginario: Arte e rivoluzione psicologica.* Milan: Electa, 1977.

Bruteau, Beatrice. "The Immaculate Conception: Our Original Face." *Cross Currents* 39 (Summer 1989): 181–95.

Capretz, Pierre J. "Eric Rohmer et *La Marquise d'O* . . . : Ironie et sentiment." *French Review* 50 (April 1977).

Charney, Hanna. "Dream Gaps in Cinematic Language: Rohmer's *The Marquise of O* . . . and Resnais' *Providence.*" *New York Literary Forum* 8–9 (1981): 257–266.

Clurman, Harold. "*The Marquise of O.*" *Nation,* 6 November 1976, 475.

Cohn, Dorritt. "Kleist's *Marquise von O* . . . : The Problem of Knowledge." *Monatshefte* 67 (1975): 129–144.

Connolly, John. "Ingres and the Erotic Intellect." In *Woman as Sex Object: Studies in Erotic Art, 1730–1970,* edited by Thomas B. Hess and Linda Nochlin. Vol. 38 of *Art News Annual.* New York: Newsweek, 1972.

Crisp, Colin G. *Eric Rohmer: Realist and Moralist.* Bloomington: Indiana University Press, 1988.

D'Ancona, Mirella Levi. *The Iconography of the Immaculate Conception in the Middle Ages and Early Renaissance.* New York: College Art Association, Art Bulletin, 1957.

De Nanteuil, Luc. *Jacques-Louis David.* New York: Harry N. Abrams, 1990.

Dyer, Denys. *"Die Marquise von O."* In *The Stories of Kleist: A Critical Study.* London: Duckworth, 1977.

Eder, Richard. "Eric Rohmer." *New York Times,* 22 October 1976.

Eitner, Lorenz. "Neoclassicism and Romanticism, 1750–1850: Sources and Documents." In *Twilight of Humanism.* Vol. 2. Englewood Cliffs, N.J.: Prentice-Hall, 1970.

Ellis, John M. *Heinrich von Kleist: Studies in the Character and Meaning of His Writings.* Chapel Hill: University of North Carolina Press, 1979.

Fried, Michael. *Absorption and Theatricality: Painting and Beholder in the Age of Diderot.* Chicago: University of Chicago Press, 1980.

Gerlacn, J. "Rohmer, Kleist, and *The Marquise of O . . .*" *Literature/Film Quarterly* 8, no. 2 (1980): 84–91.

Graham, Ilse. *Heinrich von Kleist: Word into Flesh, a Poet's Quest for the Symbol.* New York: Walter de Gruyter, 1977.

Grignaffini, Giovanna. *La Pelle e l'anima: Intorno alla nouvelle vague.* Florence: La Casa Usher, 1984.

Grisolia, Raoul. "La forma dello spazio nel cinema di Rohmer." *Cinema Nuovo,* July–October 1983: 13–14.

Hammond, Robert, and Jean-Pierre Pagliano. "Eric Rohmer on Film Scripts and Film Plans." *Literature/Film Quarterly* 10, no. 4 (1982): 219–225.

Harrigan, Renny. *"Effi Briest, The Marquise of O:* Women Oppressed." *Jump Cut,* no. 51 (1977): 3–5.

Hazelton, Roger. *Blaise Pascal: The Genius of His Thought.* Philadelphia: Westminster Press, 1974.

Herbst, Hildburg. "Coloring Word: Rohmer's Film Adaption of Kleist's Novella *The Marquise of O."* *Literature/Film Quarterly* 16, no. 3 (1988): 201–209.

Huff, Steven. "Kleist and Expectant Virgins: The Meaning of the 'O' in *Die Marquise von O."* *Journal of English and German Philology* 81, no. 3 (1982): 367–375.

Janson, Horst W. "Fuseli's Nightmare." *Arts and Sciences* 2 (Spring 1963): 1.

Johnson, William. "Review of *The Marquise of O."* *Film Quarterly* 30, no. 3 (1977): 50–53.

Kleist, Heinrich von. *"Die Marquise von O . . ."* In *Erzählungen.* Munich: Deutscher Taschenbuch Verlag, 1970.

Lessing, Gottfried. *Laocoön: An Essay on the Limits of Painting and Poetry.* Translated by Edward A. McCormick. Library of Liberal Arts, vol. 78. Indianapolis: Bobbs-Merrill, 1962.

Mancini, Michele. *Eric Rohmer.* Florence: La Nuova Italia, 1982.

Milesi, Maurizio. "Nei film di Rohmer le immagini transmettono pensiero scritto." *Cineforum*, no. 183 (1979): 190–199.

Monaco, James. *The New Wave: Truffaut, Godard, Chabrol, Rohmer, Rivette.* New York: Oxford University Press, 1980.

Noel, Bernard. *David.* New York: Crown Publishers, 1989.

Powell, Nicolas. *Fuseli: The Nightmare.* New York: Viking Press, 1972.

Praz, Mario. *Mnemosyne and the Visual Arts.* Princeton: Princeton University Press, 1970.

Rhiel, Mary Elizabeth. "Re-Viewing Kleist: The Construction of Authorial Subjectivity in West German Kleist Films." *Dissertation Abstracts International* 49, no. 12 (1989): 3739A.

Richardson, E. P. "Fuseli's *Nightmare.*" *Art Bulletin, Detroit Institute of Art* 34, no. 1. (1954).

Rohmer, Eric. *Eric Rohmer: Un hommage du Centre Culturel Français de Turin.* Milan: Fabbri, 1988.

———. "*La Marquise d'O . . .* : Annotazioni sulla regia." *Filmcritica* 28 (March 1977): 95/9-6.

———. *L'organisation de l'espace dans le Faust de Murnau.* Paris: Union Générale d'Editions, 1977.

———. "La référence picturale dans mes films, communication d' Eric Rohmer aux rencontres sur 'Peinture et Cinéma." *Quimper*, March 1987.

———. "Le siècle des peintres." *Cahiers du Cinéma* 9, no. 49 (1955): 12–13.

———. *The Taste for Beauty.* Translated by Carol Volk. Cambridge: Cambridge University Press, 1989.

Rohmer, Eric, and H. W. Janson. *Nineteenth-Century Art.* New York: Harry N. Abrams, 1984.

Rosenblum, Robert. *The International Style of 1800: A Study in Linear Abstraction.* New York: Garland, 1976.

Saviane, Renato. *Kleist.* Florence: Leo S. Olschki, 1989.

Schrader, Paul. *Transcendental Style of Film: Ozu, Bresson, Dreyer.* Berkeley: University of California Press, 1972.

Silz, Walter. *Heinrich von Kleist: Studies in His Works and Literary Character.* Philadelphia: University of Pennsylvania Press, 1961.

Spector, Jack J. *Delacroix: The Death of Sardanapalus.* New York: Viking Press, 1974.

Spiegel, Alan. *"The Marquise of O": Film by Eric Rohmer, Novella by Heinrich von Kleist.* New York: Ungar Publishing, 1985.

Sullivan, Victoria. "*The Marquise of O:* Rohmer Changes His Erotic Formula." *Wide Angle* 1, no. 4 (1977): 61–63.

Swales, Erika. "The Beleaguered Citadel: A Study of Kleist's *Die Marquise von O . . .*" *DVLG* 51 (1977): 129–147.

Tinazzi, Giorgio. "Ritratti critici di contemporanei: Eric Rohmer." *Belfagor* 43, no. 5 (1988): 519–530.

Wallach, Martha. "Ideal and Idealized Victims: The Lost Honor of the Marquise von O, Effi Briest, and Katharina Blum in Prose and Film." *Women in German Yearbook* 1 (1985): 51–75.

Walsh, Michael. "Structured Ambiguity in the Films of Eric Rohmer." *Film Criticism*, no. 2 (1976): 130–36.

Westerback, Colin. "*The Marquise of O.*" *Commonweal*, 17 December 1976, 817.

CHAPTER 4
Jean-Luc Godard's *Pierrot le Fou:*
Cinema as Collage against Painting

Achard, Maurice. *Vous avez dit Godard: J'm'appelle pas Godard.* Paris: Editions Libre-Hallier, 1980.

Allegri, Luigi. *Ideologia e linguaggio del cinema contemporaneo: Jean-Luc Godard.* Parma: Universitá di Parma, Centro Studi e Archivio della Comunicazione, 1976.

Amaya, Mario. *Pop Art . . . and After.* New York: Viking Press, 1965.

Anchisi, Pietro. "*Pierrot le Fou,* Jean-Luc Godard." In *Cinema e Film.* Vol. 1. Rome: Garzanti, 1967.

Bann, Stephen. "Collage: The Poetics of Discontinuity." *Word and Image* 4, no. 1 (1988): 353–363.

Bellour, Raymond, ed. *Jean-Luc Godard: Son and Image, 1974–1991.* Museum of Modern Art. New York: Harry N. Abrams, 1992.

Boatto, Alberto. *Pop Art.* Roma: Laterza, 1983.

Bormiche, Roger. *Le Gang: [L'histoire de* Pierrot le Fou*].* Paris: Fayard, 1975.

Brender, Richard. "Functions of Film: Léger's Cinema on Paper and on Cellulose, 1913–1925." *Cinema Journal* 24, no. 1 (1984): 41–64.

Brown, Royal S., ed. *Focus on Godard.* Englewood Cliffs, N.J.: Prentice-Hall. 1972.

Caen, Michel. "L'oeil du cyclone." *Cahiers du Cinéma,* no. 174 (1965): 74.

Cerisuelo, Marc. *Jean-Luc Godard.* Paris: L'Hermivier: Editions de Quatre-Vents, 1989.

Collet, Jean. *Godard.* New York: Crown, 1970.

Crispoti, Enrico. *La Pop Art.* Milan: Fabbri, 1966.

Davenport, Russell W., and Winthrop Sargeant. "A *Life* Round Table on Modern Art." *Life,* October 1948, 78.

Désanges, Paul. *Elie Faure.* Paris: Editions Universitaires, 1966.

Delahaye, Michel. "Jean-Luc Godard and the Childhood of Art." *Cahiers du Cinéma* (English), no. 10 (1967): 18–29.

Delamater, Jerome H. "Jean-Luc Godard's *Pierrot le Fou.*" *Film Heritage* 10, no. 3 (1975): 5–12.

Dumont, Pascal. "*Pierrot le Fou* et Jean-Luc Godard." *Cinétélé Supplément à Cinéma,* nos. 319–320 (1985): 1.

Ehrenstein, David. "Other Inquisitions: Jean-Luc Godard's *Pierrot le Fou.*" In *Jean-*

Luc Godard, edited by Tony Mussman, 221–231. New York: E. P. Dutton & Co., 1968.

Farassino, Alberto. *Jean-Luc Godard*. Florence: La Nuova Italia, 1974.

Farber, Manny. "Each New Movie Is Primarily about Film in Relation to an Idea." *Artforum* 7, no. 2 (1968): 58–61.

———. "White Elephant Art versus Termite Art." *Film Culture*, no. 27 (1962–1963): 9–13.

Faure, Elie. *The Art of Cineplastics*. Translated by Walter Pach. Boston: Four Seasons Co., 1923.

———. *History of Art: Modern Art*. Translated by Walter Pach. New York and London: Harper & Bros., 1924.

———. *The Spirit of Forms*. Translated by Walter Pach. New York: Garden City Publishing, 1937.

Giannetti, Louis D. *Godard and Others: Essays on Film Form*. Rutherford, N.J.: Fairleigh Dickinson University Press, 1974.

Gilliatt, Penelope. "Humanism Breaks Camp." *New Yorker*, 14 July 1975, 93–95.

"Jean-Luc Godard." *Camera Obscura*, nos. 8–10 (1982), special triple issue.

Godard, Jean-Luc. *Godard on Godard: Critical Writings*. Edited by Jean Narboni and Tom Milne. Introduction by Richard Roud. New York: Viking Press, 1972.

———. *Jean-Luc Godard par Jean-Luc Godard*. Edited by Alain Bergala. Paris: Editions de l'Etoile, 1985.

———. *Pierrot le Fou*. Adapted by Jonathan Weld. Performed at Ice and Fire Theater at the Circus, New York, 24 September 1973.

Guarner, José-Luis. *The Films of Jean-Luc Godard*. New York: Praeger, 1970.

Guegan, Gérard. "Décollages." *Cahiers du Cinéma* (English), no. 163 (1965): 56–57.

Hoffman, Katherine, ed. *Collage: Critical Views*. Ann Arbor, Mich.: UMI Research Press, 1989.

Jay, Martin. *Downcast Eyes: The Denigration of Vision in Twentieth-Century French Thought*. Berkeley: University of California Press, 1993.

Kline, T. Jefferson. *Screening the Text: Intertextuality in the New Wave French Cinema*. Baltimore: Johns Hopkins University Press, 1992.

Kreidl, John Francis. *Jean-Luc Godard*. Boston: Twayne Publishers, 1980.

Lefevre, Raymond. *Jean-Luc Godard*. Paris: Edilig, 1983.

Lehman, Peter. "An Analysis of Jean-Luc Godard's *Pierrot le Fou*." *Velvet Light Trap*, no. 9 (1973): 23–39.

Lesage, Julia. *Jean-Luc Godard: A Guide to References and Resources*. Boston: G. K. Hall, 1979.

Leutrat, Jean-Louis. *Kaleidoscope*. Lyons: Presses Universitaires de Lyons, 1988.

Lippard, Lucy. *Pop Art*. New York: Praeger, 1966.

Mahsun, Carol Anne, ed. *Pop Art: The Critical Dialogue*. Ann Arbor, Mich.: UMI Research Press, 1989.

Mancini, Michele. *Godard*. Rome: Trevi, 1969.

Monaco, James. *The New Wave: Truffaut, Godard, Chabrol, Rohmer, Rivette.* New York: Oxford University Press, 1976.

Païni, Dominique. "A Detour for the Gaze: The Painted Portrait in Film." Actes du Colloque tenu au Musée du Louvre les 5 et 6 April 1991. *Iris* 14–15:3–6.

Perloff, Marjorie. "The Invention of Collage." *New York Literary Forum* 10–11 (1983): 5–47.

"*Pierrot le Fou.*" *L'Avant-Scène du Cinéma,* nos. 171–172 (1976): 71–111.

Pinto, Sandra. "All'ombra delle pompe di benzina: Momenti dell'ideologia popolare nell'arte d'oggi." *Metro,* no. 13 (1968): 39–47.

Richetin, René. "Notes sur la couleur au cinéma." *Cahiers du Cinéma,* no. 182 (1966): 60–67.

Roud, Richard. *Jean-Luc Godard.* Garden City, N.J.: Doubleday, 1968.

————. *The Films of Jean-Luc Godard: A Lecture.* Presented at the Museum of Modern Art, New York, 31 January 1968.

Sarrazin, Hélène. *A la rencontre d'Elie Faure: Première approche et tentative de compréhension.* Periguese: P. Fanlac, 1982.

Sorlin, Pierre. *European Cinemas, European Societies, 1939–1990.* New York: Routledge, 1991.

Stam, Robert. *Reflexivity in Film and Literature: From Don Quixote to Jean-Luc Godard.* Ann Arbor, Mich.: UMI Research Press, 1985.

Strand, John. "Polemics and Provocation in Paris: The Art Magazine Comes of Age." *Art International,* no. 5 (1988): 24–34.

Thevoz, Michèle. "Collages." *Cahiers du Cinéma* (English), no. 3 (1966): 52–56.

Vincentanne, Stephane. *La bande à "Pierrot le Fou."* Paris: Champ Libre, 1970.

Whitehead, Peter. *"Pierrot le Fou": A Film by Godard.* English translation and description of action. New York: Simon & Schuster, 1969.

Williams, Alan. *Republic of Images: A History of French Filmmaking.* Cambridge: Harvard University Press, 1992.

CHAPTER 5
Andrei Tarkovsky's *Andrei Rublev:*
Cinema as the Restoration of Icon Painting

Agel, Henri. "Andrej Tarkovsky." In *Le visage du Christ à l'écran.* Paris: Desclée, 1985.

Alberta, François. "Eisenstein et Tarkovsky: Au delà des images." *Rectangle,* March–April 1988: 32–33.

Alcala, Manuel. "Andrej Tarkovsky: Maestro del cine religioso y metafisico." *Razon y Fe: Revista Hispanoamericana de Cultura* 211 (February 1985): 155–169.

Amengual, Barthelemy. "I filtri della rappresentazione e le allegorie staliniste." *Cinema Nuovo,* September–December 1975: 384–402.

————. "Tarkovsky: Ribelle o restauratore." *Cinema Nuovo* 30, no. 273 (1981): 29–35.

Aumont, Jacques. *Montage Eisenstein.* Translated by Lee Hildrath, Constance Penley, and Andrew Ross. Bloomington: Indiana University Press, 1987.

Baecque, Antoine de. *Andrej Tarkovsky.* Paris: Editions de l'Etoile, *Cahiers du Cinéma,* 1989.

———. "L'homme de terre." *Cahiers du Cinéma,* no. 386 (1986): 23–25.

Baggley, John. *Doors of Perception: Icons and Their Spiritual Significance.* London and Oxford: Mowbray, 1987.

Bazin, André. "Cinema and Theology." *South Atlantic Quarterly* 91, no. 2 (1992): 393–408.

———. *What Is Cinema?* Vol. 1. Translated by Hugh Gray. Berkeley: University of California Press, 1967.

Bedouele, Guy. *Du spirituel dans le cinéma.* Paris: Les Editions du Cerf, 1985.

Betz, Margaret. "The Icon and Russian Modernism." *Artforum* 15, no. 10 (1977): 38–45.

Billington, James H. *The Horizon Book of the Arts in Russia.* New York: American Heritage Publishing, 1970.

Bini, Luigi. "Andrej Tarkovsky: Il cinema della coscienza." *Letture: Libro e Spettacolo Mensile di Studi e Rassegne* 39, no. 411 (1984): 789–818.

Bonitzer, Pascal. "L'idée principale." *Cahiers du Cinéma,* no. 386 (1986): 12–13.

———. "Quelques jours, quelques films." *Cahiers du Cinéma,* no. 385 (1986): 28–32.

Bordwell, David. *The Cinema of Eisenstein.* Cambridge: Harvard University Press, 1993.

Borelli, Sauro. *Il cinema dei desideri.* Modena: Ufficio Cinema Modena, 1982.

———. "Tarkovsky: Le cifre della poesia." *Bianco e Nero* 47 (October–December 1986): 62–77.

Borin, Fabrizio. *Il cinema di Andrej Tarkovsky.* Roma: Jouvence, 1989.

Bresson, Robert. *Notes on Cinematography.* Translated by Jonathan Griffin. New York: Urizen Press, 1977.

Brumfield, William C., and Milos M. Velimorovic, eds. *Christianity and the Arts in Russia.* Cambridge: Cambridge University Press, 1993.

Bruno, Edoardo. "Tra la terra e il cielo." *Filmcritica* 37, nos. 365–366 (1986): 234–236.

Carroll, Noël. *Philosophical Problems of Classical Film Theory.* Princeton: Princeton University Press, 1988.

Ciofi degli Atti, Fabio. "Le icone." In *Antiche icone dai Musei Sovietici: La pittura in Russia e in Ucraina dal XV al XVIII secolo.* Palazzo Strozzi, Florence, 20 December 1984–10 March 1985. Milan: Electa, 1984.

Clements, Robert J. "Brueghel's *Fall of Icarus:* Eighteen Modern Literary Readings." *Studies in Iconography* 7–8 (1981–1982): 253–268.

Cohen, Louis H. *The Cultural-Political Traditions and Development of the Soviet Cinema: 1917–1972.* New York: Arno Press, 1974.

Cormack, Robin. *Writing in Gold: Byzantine Society and Its Icons.* New York: Oxford University Press, 1985.

Dempsey, Michael. "Lost Harmony: Tarkovsky's *The Mirror* and *The Stalker.*" *Film Quarterly* 35, no. 1. (1981): 12–17.

Donadeo, Suor Maria. *Le icone: Immagini dell'invisibile.* Brescia: Morcelliana, 1981.

Epstein, Jean. "Photogénie and the Imponderable." In *French Film Theory and Criticism: A History-Anthology,* Vol. 1, 1907–1929, edited by Richard Abel, 188–192. Princeton: Princeton University Press, 1988.

Estève, Michel, ed. *Andrei Tarkovsky.* Etudes Cinématographiques, nos. 135–138. Paris: Lettres Modernes, Minard, 1983.

Fedotov, G. P. *The Russian Religious Mind.* Cambridge: Harvard University Press, 1946.

Frezzato, Achille. "Protagonista di un'epoca." *Cineforum* 27, no. 265 (1987): 74–80.

—————. *Tarkovski.* Florence: La Nuova Italia, 1977.

Galavaris, George. *The Icon in the Life of the Church.* Leiden: E. J. Brill, 1981.

Gerhard, H. P. *The World of Icons.* New York: Harper & Row, 1971.

Gordeyev, Sergei. *Vladimir: A Guide.* Moscow: Radya Publishers, 1983.

Grande, Maurizio. "Andrej Rublev: Il senso della terra." *Filmcritica* 27 (January–February 1976): 10–12.

Kearney, Richard. "A Mirror of History." *Film Directions* 1, no. 3 (1978): 4–8.

—————. Revisualizing Times Past. *Studies: An Irish Quarterly Review* 71, no. 281 (1982): 85–93.

Kennedy, Harlan. "Midsection: Tarkovsky." *Film Comment* 23 (May–June 1987): 44–46.

Kirchman, Milton. "Leonardo da Vinci on Creative Processes in Art." *Liberal and Fine Arts Review* 2, no. 2 (1982): 22–46.

Lasareff, Victor, and Otto Demus. *USSR: Early Russian Icons.* New York: New York Graphic Society, UNESCO, 1958.

Le Fanu, Mark. "Ahead of Us?" *Sight and Sound* 55, no. 4 (1986): 284–285.

—————. "Bresson, Tarkovsky, and Contemporary Pessimism." *Cambridge Quarterly,* Summer 1984.

—————. *The Cinema of Andrej Tarkovsky.* London: British Film Institute, 1987.

Liehm, Mira, and Antonin Liehm. *The Most Important Art: East European Film after 1945.* Berkeley: University of California Press, 1945.

Magny, Joël. "Le mystère des limites." *Cahiers du Cinéma,* no. 385 (1986): 14–17.

Martin, Michael. "Itineraire d'un demiurge: Andrej Tarkovsky." *Revue du Cinéma,* no. 366 (1981): 77–88.

May, John R., and Michael Bird, eds. *Religion in Film.* Knoxville: University of Tennessee Press, 1982.

Misler, Nicoletta. "Nella tradizione dell'arte russa." *Per Andrej Tarkovsky.* Atti del convegno del 19 Gennaio 1987. Rome: Centro Sperimentale di Cinematografia, 1987.

Mitchell, Tony. "Andrej Tarkowski and *Nostalgia.*" *Film Criticism* 11, nos. 1–2 (1987): 101–110.

Montagu, Ivor. "Man and Experience: Tarkovsky's World." *Sight and Sound* 42, no. 2 (1973): 89–94.

Muratov, P. P. *Les icônes russes.* Paris: J. Schiffrin, Editions de la Pléiade, 1927.

Musatti, Cesare. "Pioggia e acquitrino nella *Nostalgia* di Tarkovsky." *Cinema Nuovo* 34, no. 293 (1985): 5–6.

Pallasmaa, Juhani. "Tarkovsky's *Nostalgia*: Notes on the Phenomenology of Architecture in Cinema." *Focus* (Helsinki University of Technology, Faculty of Architecture Yearbook), 1991–1992: 13–24.

Passek, J. L., ed. *Le cinéma russe et soviétique.* Paris: Centres Georges Pompidou, 1981.

Petric, Vlada. "Tarkovsky's Dream Imagery." *Film Quarterly* 43, no. 2 (1989–1990): 28–34.

Petrie, Graham, and Ruth Dwyer, eds. *Before the Wall Came Down: Soviet and East European Film-Makers Working in the West.* Lanham, Md.: University Press of America, 1990.

Popescu, Nicolae. "La très orthodoxe demeure d'Andrej Tarkovsky." *Liberté* 185 (October 1989): 16–22.

Radcliff-Umstead, Douglas, ed. *Holding the Vision.* Introduction by Jerry Bloedow. Kent, Ohio: Kent State University, International Film Society, 1983.

Ratschewa, Maria. "The Messianic Power of Pictures: The Films of Andrej Tarkovsky." *Cineaste* 13, no. 1 (1983): 27–29.

Rice, David Talbot. *Russian Icons.* London and New York: King Penguin Books, 1947.

Ross, Bruce. "Nostalgia and the Child 'Topoi': Metaphors of Disruption and Transcendence in the Work of Joseph Brodsky, Marc Chagall, and Andrej Tarkovsky." *Analecta Husserliana* 28 (1990): 307–323.

Salvestroni, Simonetta. *Semiotica dell'immaginazione: Dalla letteratura fantastica russa alla fantascienza sovietica.* Venice: Marsilio, 1984.

Salvestroni, Simonetta, and Robert M. Philmus. "The Science-Fiction Films of Andrej Tarkovsky. *Science-Fiction Studies* 14, no. 3 (1987).

Schrader, Paul. *Transcendental Style of Film: Ozu, Bresson, Dreyer.* Berkeley: University of California Press, 1972.

Sendler, Egon S. J. *L'icône: Image de l'invisible.* Paris: Deselée de Bronner, 1981.

Stoil, Michaeljon. *Cinema beyond the Danube: The Camera and Politics.* Metuchen, N.J.: Scarecrow, 1974.

———. "Releasing the Balloon, Raising the Bell." *Monthly Film Bulletin* 58, no. 685 (1991): 34–37.

———. "In the Picture: Tarkovsky's Translation." *Sight and Sound* 50, no. 3 (1981): 152–153.

———. "Offret." *Monthly Film Bulletin* 54, no. 636 (1987): 7–8.

Sutherland, Fraser. "What We Do with the Dream: Gaston Bachelard and the Materials of the Imagination." *Canadian Fiction Magazine* 39 (1981): 87–96.

Tarkovskaya, Marina, ed. *About Andrej Tarkovsky.* Translated by Maureen Ryley. Moscow: Progress Publishers, 1990.

Tarkovsky, Andrei. *Sculpting in Time: Reflections on the Cinema.* Translated by Kitty Hunter Blair. Austin: University of Texas Press, 1989.

————. "Andrei Rublëv." Translated by Kitty Hunter Blair. Introduction by Philip Strick. London: Faber & Faber, 1991.

Trubetskoi, E. N. *Speculation in Colors: The Question of the Meaning of Life in Ancient Russian Religious Painting.* Paris: YMCA Press, 1965.

Truppin, Andrea. "And Then There Was Sound: The Films of Andrej Tarkowski." In *Sound Practice,* edited by Charles F. Altman, 235–248. New York: Routledge, 1992.

Turovskaya, Maya. *Tarkovsky: Cinema as Poetry.* Translated by Natasha Ward. London: Faber and Faber, 1989.

Valmarana, Paolo. "Andrej Rublëv." *Doppio Schermo.* Torino: ERI, 1987.

Waldman, Diane. "Kasimir Malevich: The Supremacy of Pure Feeling." *Arts Magazine* 48, no. 3 (1973): 24–29.

Wierzewski, W. "The Artist and His Age." *Young Cinema and Theatre,* no. 3 (1973): 26–34.

Zakharchenko, Vasili. "Science Fiction Painting." *Soviet Literature* 2, no. 431 (1984): 180–184.

Zamperini, Paolo, ed. *Il fuoco, l'acqua, l'ombra.* Florence: La Casa di Usher, 1989.

CHAPTER 6
F. W. Murnau's *Nosferatu:*
Romantic Painting as Horror and Desire in Expressionist Cinema

Annau, David. *Cinefantastic: Beyond the Dream Machine.* London: Lorrimer, 1974.

Aumont, Jacques. *L'occhio interminabile: Cinema e pittura.* Venice: Marsilio, 1991.

Barlow, John D. *German Expressionist Film.* Boston: Twayne Publishers, 1982.

Barsacq, Léon. *Caligari's Cabinet and Other Grand Illusions: A History of Film Design.* Translated by Michael Bullock. Revised and edited by Elliott Stein. Boston: New York Graphic Society, 1976.

Bergstrom, Janet. "Sexuality at a Loss: The Films of F. W. Murnau." *Poetics Today* 6, nos. 1–2 (1985): 185–203.

Blin, Roger. "Murnau: Ses films." *La Revue du Cinéma* 25 (July 1931): 24–34.

Borde, Raymond, Freddy Bauche, François Courtade, Marcel Tariol. *Le cinéma réaliste allemand.* Lausanne: La Cinémathéque Suisse, 1959.

Bouvier, Michel, and J. L. Leurat. *Nosferatu.* Preface by Julien Gracq. Paris: Gallimard, 1981.

Burke, Edmund. *Philosophical Enquiry into the Origins of Our Ideas of the Sublime and the Beautiful.* Edited by James T. Boulton. Notre Dame, Ind.: Notre Dame University Press, 1968.

Buttigieg, Joseph. "Wörringer among the Modernists." *Boundary 2: A Journal of Postmodern Literature and Culture* 8, no. 1 (1979): 359–366.

Cardullo, Bert. "Expressionism and *Nosferatu.*" *San José Studies* 11, no. 3 (1985): 25–33.

Carroll, Noël. *The Philosophy of Horror: Paradoxes of the Heart.* New York: Routledge, 1990.

Chiarini, Paolo. *L'espressionismo Tedesco: Storia e struttura.* Rome: Laterza, 1985.

Clark, John R. "Expressionism in Film and Architecture." *Art Journal* 34 (Winter 1974–1975): 115–122.

Coates, Paul. *The Gorgon's Gaze: German Cinema, Expressionism, and the Image of Horror.* Cambridge: Cambridge University Press, 1991.

Collier, Jo Leslie. *From Wagner to Murnau: The Transposition of Romanticism from Stage to Screen.* Ann Arbor, Mich.: UMI Research Press, 1988.

————. *Marine Painting in England, 1700–1900.* New York: Clarkson N. Potter, 1973.

Courtade, Francis. *Cinéma expressionniste.* Paris: Cinémathèque de Toulouse, Henri Veyrier, 1984.

Delevoy, Robert L. *Symbolists and Symbolism.* Translated by Barbara Bray, Elizabeth Wrightson, and Bernard C. Swift. New York: Rizzoli, 1982.

Detlev, J. K. Penkert. *The Weimar Republic: The Crisis of Classical Modernity.* New York: Hill & Wang, 1992.

Devine, Elizabeth, ed. *Thinkers of the Twentieth Century: A Biographical, Bibliographical, and Critical Dictionary.* Detroit: Gale Research Co., 1983.

Doane, Mary Ann. *The Desire to Desire: The Woman's Film of the 1940s.* Bloomington: Indiana University Press, 1987.

Domarchi, Jean. "Présence de F. W. Murnau." *Cahiers du Cinéma* 21 (March 1953): 3–11.

Donald, James, ed. *The Fantastic, the Sublime, and the Popular: What's at Stake in Vampire Films.* London: British Film Institute, 1989.

————, ed. *Fantasy and the Cinema.* London: British Film Institute, 1989.

Dyrness, William. "Caspar David Friedrich: The Aesthetic Expression of Shleiermacher's Romantic Faith." *Christian Scholar's Review* 14, no. 4 (1985): 335–346.

Eichner, Hans. "The Rise of Modern Science and the Genesis of Romanticism." *PMLA* 97 (1982): 8–30.

Eisner, Lotte. *The Haunted Screen: Expressionism in German Cinema and the Influence of Max Reinhardt.* Translated by Roger Graves. Berkeley: University of California Press, 1977.

————. *Murnau.* Berkeley: University of California Press, 1973.

Elsaesser, Thomas. "Secret Affinities." *Sight and Sound* 58 (Winter 1988–1989): 33–39.

————. "Social Mobility and the Fantastic: German Silent Cinema." *Wide Angle* 5, no. 2 (1982): 14–25.

————. "Film History and Visual Pleasure: Weimar Cinema." In *Cinema Histories, Cinema Practices,* edited by Patricia Mellencamp and Philip Rosen, 47–84. Frederick, Md.: University Publications, 1984.

Exertier, Sylvain. "F. W. Murnau: La lettre oubliée de *Nosferatu.*" *Positif,* no. 228 (1980): 47–51.

Finke, Ulrich. *German Painting from Romanticism to Expressionism.* Boulder, Colo.: Westview Press, 1975.

Fisher, Peter S. *Fantasy and Politics: Visions of the Future in the Weimar Republic.* Madison: University of Wisconsin Press, 1991.

Gaehtgens, Thomas W. "Les rapports de l'histoire de l'art et de l'art contemporain en Allemagne á l'époque de Wölfflin et de Meier-Graefe." *La Revue de l'Art* 88 (1990): 31–38.

Gay, Peter. *Weimar Culture: The Outsider as Insider.* New York: Harper & Row, 1968.

Gordon, Donald E. *Expressionism: Art and Idea.* New Haven: Yale University Press, 1987.

Grant, Barry Keith, ed. *Planks in Reason: Essays on the Horror Film.* Metuchen, N.J.: Scarecrow, 1984.

Grignaffini, Giovanna, and Leonardo Quaresima. *Cultura e cinema nella Republica di Weimar.* Venice: Marsilio, 1978.

Guillermo, Gilberto Perez. "F. W. Murnau: An Introduction." *Film Comment* 7, no. 2 (1971): 13–15.

———. "Shadow and Substance: Murnau's *Nosferatu.*" *Sight and Sound* 36, no. 3 (1967): 150–159.

Hernand, Jost. "Unity within Diversity? The History of the Concept 'Neue Sachlichkeit.'" In *Culture and Society in the Weimar Republic,* edited by Keith Bullivant, 166–182. Manchester: Manchester University Press, 1977.

Himmelhaber, Georg. *Biedermeier, 1815–1835: Architecture, Painting, Sculpture, Decorative Arts, Fashion.* Munich: Prestel, 1989.

Hyde, Thomas Dewitt. "A Study of Authorial Vision in the German Films of F. W. Murnau." *Dissertation Abstracts International* 50, no. 4 (1989): 813A.

Jameux, Charles. *Murnau.* Paris: Editions Universitaires, 1965.

Jelavich, Peter. *Berlin Cabaret.* Cambridge: Harvard University Press, 1993.

Kallier, Jane. *Alfred Kubin: Visions from the Other Side.* New York: Galerie St. Etienne, 1983.

Koerner, Joseph Leo. *Caspar David Friedrich and the Subject of Landscape.* New Haven: Yale University Press, 1990.

Kracauer, Siegfried. *From Caligari to Hitler: A Psychological History of the German Cinema.* Princeton: Princeton University Press, 1947.

Levine, Frederick S. *The Apocalyptic Vision: The Art of Franz Marc as German Expressionism.* New York: Harper & Row, 1979.

Lloyd, Jill. *German Expressionism: Primitivism and Modernity.* New Haven: Yale University Press, 1991.

Longyear, Rey M. *Nineteenth-Century Romanticism in Music.* Englewood Cliffs, N.J.: Prentice-Hall, 1988.

Luhr, William. "*Nosferatu* and Postwar German Film." *Michigan Academician* 14, no. 4 (1982): 453–458.

Mann, Golo. *The History of Germany since 1789.* New York: Praeger, 1968.

Manvell, Roger. Introduction to *Masterworks of the German Cinema: "The Golem," "Nosferatu," "M," "The Threepenny Opera."* New York: Harper & Row, 1973.

Monaco, Paul. *Cinema and Society: France and Germany during the Twenties.* New York: Elsevier, 1976.

Mori, Phil. "Il testamento di Murnau." *Bianco e Nero* 4 (1951): 12–19.

Norman, Geraldine. *Biedermeier Painting, 1815–1848: Reality Observed in Genre, Portrait, and Landscape.* London: Thames & Hudson, 1987.

Pétat, Jacques-Jean, and Roy-Dominique Païni. "De Murnau à Herzog: L'eternel retour de Nosferatu le vampire." *Cinéma* (Paris), no. 243 (1979): 5–15.

Potts, Alex. "A German Art History." *Burlington Magazine* 127 (December 1985): 900–903.

Prawer, Siegbert Salomon. *Caligari's Children: The Film as Tale of Terror.* New York: Oxford University Press, 1980.

Rabinach, Anson. "Between Enlightenment and Apocalypse: Benjamin, Bloch, and Modern German Jewish Messianism." *New German Critique: An Interdisciplinary Journal of German Studies* 34. (Winter 1985): 78–124.

Rentschler, Eric, ed. *German Film and Literature: Adaptations and Transformations.* New York: Methuen, 1976.

Richard, Lionel. *Phaidon Encyclopedia of Expressionism.* Oxford: Phaidon Press, 1978.

Riegl, Alois. *Problems of Style: Foundations for a History of Ornament.* Translated by Evelyn Kain. New Jersey: Princeton University Press, 1992.

Romer, Richard Ira. *The Cinematic Treatment of the Protagonists in Murnau's "Nosferatu," Browning's "Dracula," and Whale's "Frankenstein."* Dissertation Abstracts International 46, no. 1 (1985): 2A–3A.

Rosenblum, Robert. *Modern Painting and the Northern Romantic Tradition: Friedrich to Rothko.* New York: Harper & Row, 1975.

Roth, Lane. "Dracula Meets the Zeitgeist: *Nosferatu* (1922) as Film Adaptation." *Film Literature Quarterly* 7, no. 4 (1979): 309–313.

Schafer, R. Murray. *E. T. A. Hoffmann and Music.* Toronto: University of Toronto Press, 1975.

Schrade, Hubert. *German Romantic Painting.* New York: Harry N. Abrams, 1977.

Schrader, Bärbel, and Jürgen Schebera. *The Golden Twenties: Art and Literature in the Weimar Republic.* New Haven: Yale University Press, 1988.

Scognamillo, Giovanni. "F. W. Murnau." *Bianco e Nero* 6 (1953): 10–26.

Siegel, Linda. *Caspar David Friedrich and the Age of German Romanticism.* Boston: Branden Press, 1978.

Tone, Pier Giorgio. *Friedrich Wilhelm Murnau.* Florence: La Nuova Italia, 1977.

Vaughan, William. *German Romantic Painting.* New Haven: Yale University Press, 1980.

Vienna in the Age of Schubert: The Biedermeier Interior, 1815–1848. London: Ebron Press, 1979.

Vines, Elisabeth Lee. "Landscape through Literature: Caspar David Friedrich and Three German Romantic Writers." *Dissertation Abstracts International* 48, no. 4 (1987): 931A.

Waite, Geoffrey C. W. "Wörringer's Abstraction and Empathy: Remarks on Its Reception and on the Rhetoric of Criticism." *The Turn of the Century: German Literature and Art, 1890–1915,* edited by Hans H. Schulte. Bonn: Bonvier, 1981.

Waller, Gregory. *The Living and the Undead: From Stoker's "Dracula" to Romero's "Dawn of the Dead."* Urbana: University of Illinois Press, 1985.

Warren, Paul. "La paternité revisitée de F. W. Murnau et de Fritz Lang." *Etudes Littéraires* 18, no. 1: 157–181.

Watts, Pauline. *Music: The Medium of the Metaphysical in E. T. A. Hoffmann.* Amsterdam: Rodopi NV, 1972.

Weinstein, Joan. *The End of Expressionism: Art and the November Revolution in Germany, 1918–1919.* Chicago: University of Chicago Press, 1990.

Willett, John. *Art and Politics: The New Sobriety, 1917–1933.* New York: Pantheon Books, 1978.

Wollenger, H. H. *Fifty Years of German Film.* London: Falcon Press, 1948.

Wood, Robin. "Burying the Undead: The Use and Obsolescence of Count Dracula." *Mosaic* 16, nos. 1–2 (1983): 175–187.

———. "Murnau's Midnight and *Sunrise.*" *Film Comment* 12, no. 3 (1976): 4–9.

Young, Vernon. *On Film: Unpopular Essays on a Popular Art.* New York: Quadrangle, New York Times Book Co., 1972.

Youssef, Ishaghpour. "Le pays que le soleil parcourt pendant la nuit." *Cahiers du Cinéma,* no. 327 (1981): 54–55.

CHAPTER 7
Kenji Mizoguchi's *Five Women around Utamaro:*
Film between Woodblock Printing and Tattooing

Addiss, Stephen. *The Art of Zen: Painting and Calligraphy by Japanese Monks, 1600–1925.* New York: Harry N. Abrams, 1989.

Allombert, Guy. "Cinq femmes autour d'Utamaro." *Revue du Cinéma,* no. 288–289 (1974): 62–3.

Andrew, Dudley. *Film in the Aura of Art.* Princeton: Princeton University Press, 1984.

———. "Mizoguchi: A Brief Introduction." Mizoguchi: The Master. Japan Film Center, May 1–June 28. Brochure.

Andrew, Dudley, and Andrew, Paul. *Kenji Mizoguchi: A Guide to References and Resources.* Boston: G. K. Hall, 1981.

Baecque, Antoine de. "Eaux profondes." *Cahiers du Cinéma,* no. 394 (1987): 28–30.

Barr, Stephen H. "Reframing Mizoguchi." *Film Criticism* 8, no. 1 (1983): 79–85.

Barrett, Gregory. *Archetypes in Japanese Films: The Sociopolitical and Religious Significance of the Principal Heroes and Heroines.* London: Associated University Press, 1989.

Barthes, Roland. *Empire of Signs.* Translated by Richard Howard. New York: Hill & Wang, 1982.

Belton, John. *Cinema Stylists.* London: Scarecrow Press, 1983.

Benedict, Ruth. *The Chrysanthemum and the Sword: Patterns of Japanese Culture.* London: Routledge, 1967.

Bianchi, Pietro. *Maestro del cinema.* Milan: Garzanti, 1972.

Blouin, Claude. *Dire l'éphémère.* Quebec: Hurtbuise, HMH, 1983.

Bock, Audie. *Japanese Film Directors.* New York: Kodansha International–USA, Harper & Row, 1978.

Bonitzer, Pascal. "Violence et latéralité" *Cahiers du Cinéma*, no. 319 (1981): 26–34.

Bordwell, David. "Mizoguchi and the Evolution of Film Language." In *Cinema and Language*, edited by Stephen Heath and Patricia Mellencamp. Frederick, Md.: University Publications of America, 1983.

Bowie, Henry P. *On the Laws of Japanese Painting*. New York: Dover Publications, 1952.

Burch, Noel. *To the Distant Observer: Form and Meaning in the Japanese Cinema*. London: Scholar Press, 1979.

Il cinema di Kenji Mizoguchi. Venice: La Biennale di Venezia, 1980.

Cohen, Robert. "Mizoguchi and Modernism: Structure, Culture, Point of View." *Sight and Sound* 42, n. 2 (1978): 110–118.

————. "Textual Poetics in the Films of Kenji Mizoguchi: A Structural Semiotics of Japanese Narrative." Dissertation, University of California, Los Angeles, 1983.

Creekmur, Corey K. "Mizoguchi and Desire: *Osaka Elegy* and *Sisters of the Gion*." In *Purdue University Seventh Annual Conference on Film*, edited by Marshall Deutelbaum and Thomas P. Adler. West Lafayette, Ind.: Dept. of English, Purdue University, 1983.

Dale, Peter M. *The Myth of Japanese Uniqueness*. London: Random House, 1986.

Delarue, Jacques. "Florescence and Decay of the Tattooer's Art." *Graphics* (Zurich) 7, no. 35 (1951): 182–187.

Demonsablon, Philippe. "La splendeur du vrai." *Cahiers du Cinéma*, no. 95 (1959): 1–3.

Desser, David. *Eros and Massacre: An Introduction to the Japanese New Wave Cinema*. Bloomington: Indiana University Press, 1988.

Douchet, Jean. "Connaissance de Kenji Mizoguchi." *Cinéma*, nos. 236–237 (1978): 93–114.

Ehrlich, Linda C. "The Artist's Desire: Reflections on the Films of Kenji Mizoguchi." *East-West Film Journal* 4, no. 2 (1990): 1–13.

————, and David Desser. *Cinematic Landscapes: Observations on the Visual Arts and Cinema of China and Japan*. Austin: University of Texas Press, 1994.

Eisenstein, S. M. *Cinématisme: Peinture et cinéma*. Brussels: Editions Complex, 1980.

The Feminine Image: Women of Japan. Honolulu: Honolulu Academy of the Arts, 1985.

Fister, Pat. *Japanese Women Artists, 1600–1900*. Lawrence: Spencer Museum of Art, University of Kansas, 1988.

Hearn, Lafcadio. "The Story of Mimi-Nashi-Hoichi." In *Writings from Japan*, edited by Francis King, 319–328. New York: Viking Penguin, 1985.

Hillier, Jack Ronald. *Utamaro: Colour Prints and Paintings*. Oxford: Phaidon, 1979.

Hirano, Kyoko. *Mr. Smith Goes to Tokyo: Japanese Cinema under the American Occupation, 1945–1952*. Washington, D.C.: Smithsonian Institution Press, 1992.

Iwazaki, Akira. "Kenji Mizoguchi." *Anthologie du Cinéma*, no. 3 (1968): 441–488.

Kasza, Gregory J. *The State and Mass Media in Japan, 1918–1945*. Berkeley: University of California Press, 1988.

Kirihara, Donald. "Kabuki, Cinema, and Mizoguchi Kenji." In *Cinema and Language*, edited by Stephen Heath. Frederick, Md.: University Publications of America, 1983.

―――. "Three Kinds of Space in the *Downfall of Osen*." In *Purdue University Seventh Annual Conference on Film*, edited by Marshall Deutelbaum and Thomas P. Adler. West Lafayette, Ind.: Dept. of English, Purdue University, 1983.

―――. *Patterns of Time: Mizoguchi and the Nineteen Thirties*. Madison: University of Wisconsin Press, 1992.

Lane, Richard. *Images from the Floating World: The Japanese Print*. New York: Putnam, 1978.

Leach, Jane. "Mizoguchi and Ideology: Two Films from the Forties." *Film Criticism* 8, no. 1 (1983): 66–78.

Manceau, Jean-Louis. "Kenji Mizoguchi." *Cinéma*, no. 394 (1987): 2–3.

Martelli, Plinio. *Il Tatuaggio come arte*. Padua: Mastrogiacomo, 1980.

Mascia-Lees, Frances E., and Patricia Sharpe. *Tattoo, Torture, Mutilation, and Adornment: The Denaturalization of the Body in Culture and Text*. Albany: State University of New York Press, 1992.

McDonald, Keiko. *Cinema East: A Critical Study of Major Japanese Film*. Rutherford, N.J.: Fairleigh Dickinson University Press, 1993.

―――. *Mizoguchi*. Boston: Twayne Publishers, 1984.

―――. "Thematic Conflict and Mode of Representation in Mizoguchi's *Street of Shame*." In *Holding the Vision: Essays on Film*, edited by Douglas Radcliff-Umstead. Kent, Ohio: Kent State University, International Film Society, 1983.

Mellen, Joan. *The Waves at Genji's Door: Japan through Its Cinema*. New York: Pantheon Books, 1976.

Mesnil, Michel, ed. *Mizoguchi Kenji*. Cinéma d'aujourd'hui, vol. 31. Paris: Editions Seghers, 1965.

Mizoguchi, Kenji. "Trois interviews." *Cahiers du Cinéma*, no. 116 (1961): 15–21.

Morris, Peter. *Kenji Mizoguchi*. Ottawa: Canadian Film Institute, 1967.

Murase, Miyeko. *Tales of Japan: Scrolls and Prints from the New York Public Library*. New York: Oxford University Press, 1986.

Perkins, Dorothy. *Encyclopedia of Japan: Japanese History and Culture from Abacus to Zori*. New York: Roundtable Press, 1991.

Pictorial Encyclopedia of Japanese Culture: The Soul and Heritage of Japan. Tokyo: Gakken, 1987.

Richie, Donald, and J. L. Anderson. "Kenji Mizoguchi." *Sight and Sound* 25, no. 2 (1955): 76–81.

―――. *Japanese Cinema: An Introduction*. Hong Kong and New York: Oxford University Press, 1990.

―――. *Japanese Cinema: Film Style and National Character*. Garden City, N.Y.: Doubleday, 1971.

Rijksmuseum (Netherlands). Rijksprentenkabinet. *The Age of Harunobu: Early Japanese Prints, c. 1700–1800*. Amsterdam: 1977.

————. Rijksprentenkabinet. *The Age of Utamaro: Japanese Prints, c. 1780–1800.* Amsterdam: 1979.

Rivette, Jacques. "Mizoguchi vu d'ici." *Cahiers du Cinéma* 14, no. 81 (1958): 28–30.

Ronan, Sean G., and Toki Koizumi. *Lafcadio Hearn (Koizumi Yakumo): His Life, Work, and Irish Background.* Dublin: Ireland-Japan Association, 1991.

Rosenbaum, Jonathan. "Review of Keiko McDonald's *Mizoguchi.*" *Quarterly Review of Film Studies* 10, no. 1 (1985): 75–76.

————. "Utamaro o meguru gonin no onna." *Monthly Film Bulletin* 43 (December 1976): 262–263.

Rubin, Arnold, ed. *Marks of Civilization: Artistic Transformation of the Human Body.* Los Angeles: Museum of Cultural History, UCLA, 1988.

Sanders, Clinton R. *Customizing the Body: The Art and Culture of Tattooing.* Philadelphia: Temple University Press, 1989.

Sato, Tadao. "Mizouchi et la 'love romance'." *La Revue du Cinéma*, no. 384 (1983): 73–78.

————. *Currents in Japanese Cinema.* Translated by Gregory Barrett. New York: Kodansha International–USA, Harper & Row, 1982.

————. "On Mizoguchi." *Film Criticism* 4, no. 3 (1980): 2–16.

Serceau, Daniel. *Mizoguchi: De la révolte aux songes.* Paris: Cerf, 1983.

Simsolo, Noël. "Notes sur Kenji Mizoguchi." *Image et Son*, no. 337 (1979): 51–80.

Tanizaki, Junichiro. *In Praise of Shadows.* Translated by Thomas J. Harper and Edward G. Seidensticker. N.p.: Leete's Island Books, 1977.

Tessier, Marc. "Mizoguchi Kenji." *Dossiers du Cinéma*, series 2 (February 1971): 117–123.

Webber, Lucille R. *Japanese Woodblock Prints: The Reciprocal Influence between East and West.* Provo, Utah: Brigham Young University Press, 1979.

Wood, Robin. "Mizoguchi: The Ghost Princess and the Seaweed Gatherer." *Film Comment* 19, no. 2 (1973): 32–40.

Vê-Hô. *Mizoguchi.* Paris: Editions Universitaires, 1963.

CHAPTER 8
Alain Cavalier's *Thérèse:*
Still Life and the Close-Up as Feminine Space

Abel, Richard. *French Cinema: The First Wave, 1915–1929.* Princeton: Princeton University Press, 1984.

Almendros, Nestor. "Landscape of the Face." *Screen Actor* 27 (1988): 16–21.

Amiel, Vincent. "Trois cinéastes sur le bord des planches: Cavalier, Deville, Resnais." *Positif*, no. 308 (1986): 20–22.

Ansen, David. "A Natural's Simple Path to Sainthood." *Newsweek*, 19 January 1987, 61.

Balázs, Béla. *Theory of the Film: Character and Growth of a New Art.* Translated by Edith Boone. New York: Dover Publications, 1970.

Berger, Joseph. "Some Films Are Finding Saints as Compelling as Sinners." *New York Times*, 4 January 1987.

Bonitzer, Pascal. "Quelques jours, quelques films." *Cahiers du Cinéma*, no. 385 (1986): 28–32.

Bonitzer, Pascal, and Serge Toubiana. "La petite voie: Entretien avec Alain Cavalier." *Cahiers du Cinéma*, no. 387 (1986): 7–9.

Blake, Richard A. "Film: The Face of a Saint." *America*, 24 January 1987, 55–56.

Bordwell, David. *The Films of Carl-Theodor Dreyer*. Berkeley: University of California Press, 1981.

Borden, Diane M. "Bergman's Style and the Facial Icon." *Quarterly Review of Film Studies* 2, no. 1 (1977): 42–51.

Brown, Gillian. "Anorexia, Humanism, and Feminism." *Yale Journal of Criticism* 5, no. 1 (1991): 189–215.

Bryson, Norman. *Looking at the Overlooked: Four Essays on Still Life Painting*. Cambridge: Harvard University Press, 1990.

Bynum, Caroline Walker. *Holy Feast and Holy Fast*. Berkeley: University of California Press, 1987.

Camy, Gérard. "*Thérèse*." *Jeune Cinéma*, no. 175 (1986): 18.

Canby, Vincent. "Film Festival: *Thérèse*, a Little Flower of Jesus." *New York Times*, 17 December 1986.

Cardullo, Bert. "Film Chronicle: Sid, Nancy, and Thérèse." *Hudson Review* 40, no. 1 (1987): 121–130.

Cavalier, Alain. "Filmography." *Sequences*, no. 126 (1986): 26–30.

————. "Lettre d'Alain Cavalier à Michel Boujut." *Avant-Scène*, no. 364 (1987): 10.

Chevassu. François. "*Thérèse*." *Revue du Cinéma*, no. 418 (1986): 24.

Chevrie, Marc. "Quoi? La Grâce." *Cahiers du Cinéma*, nos. 383–384 (1986): 22–24.

Corliss, Richard. "Cinema: What She Did for Love." *Time* 5 January 1987, 75.

Cormier, Raymond J. "Rohmer's Grail Story: Anatomy of a French Flop." *Stanford French Review* 5, no. 3 (1981): 391–396.

Deleuze, Gilles. *Cinema 1: The Movement-Image*. Translated by Hugh Tomlinson and Barbara Habberjam. Minneapolis: University of Minnesota Press, 1986.

Denby, David. "Movies: Shrieks and Whispers." *New York* 12 January 1987, 51–52.

Detassis, Piera. "*Thérèse*." *Cineforum* 27, no. 264 (1987): 71–74.

Di Fazio, Rossana. "Al cinema: Ri-vedere la pittura." *Cinema e cinema* 16, nos. 54–55. (1989): 73–84.

Doane, Mary Ann. "Veiling over Desire: Close-ups of the Woman." In *Femmes Fatales: Feminism, Film Theory, Psychoanalysis*. New York: Routledge, 1991.

Donohue, John W. "*Thérèse*: A Second Opinion." *America* 14 February 1987.

Eberwein, Robert T. "Reflections on the Breast." *Wide Angle* 4, no. 3 (1981): 48–53.

Emond, Cécile. *L'iconographie carmélitaine dans les anciens Pays-Bas méridionaux*. Brussels: Paleis der Academien, 1961.

Epstein, Jean. "Magnification and Other Writings." Translated by Stuart Liebman. *October*, no. 3 (1977): 9–25.

Estève, Michel. "L'univers de la sainteté." *Esprit* 10, no. 119 (1986): 99–100.

Fisher, Lucy. *Shot/Countershot: Film Tradition and Women's Cinema.* Princeton: Princeton University Press, 1989.

Furlong, Monica. *Thérèse of Lisieux.* New York: Pantheon Books, 1987.

Harvey, Stephen. "The Twenty-fourth New York Film Festival." *Film Comment* 2 (December 1986).

Holden, Stephen. "An Enigma: Rigorous in Her Craft." *New York Times,* 26 December 1986.

Insdorf, Annette. "*Thérèse:* A Simple Movie That Wins Accolades." *New York Times,* 28 December 1986.

Kael, Pauline. "The Current Cinema: At Fifteen." *New Yorker,* 26 January 1987, 73–75.

Kauffmann, Stanley. "Stanley Kauffman on Films: A Bride." *New Republic,* 29 December 1986, 24–25.

Kelleher, Ed. "Cavalier's Immaculate *Thérèse* Explores Innocence, Madness." *Film Journal* 89 (December 1986).

Krauss, Rosalind F. *The Originality of the Avant-Garde and Other Modernist Myths.* Cambridge: MIT Press, 1985.

Lynch, J. D. "Love in Action and Contemplation." *Christian Century* 104 (1987): 360–361.

Magli, Ida. *Santa Teresa di Lisieux.* Milan: Rizzoli, 1984.

Martin, Adrian. "Confessions of a Mask." *Cinema Papers* (Australia), no. 68 (1988): 18–21.

Mazzoni, Cristina Maria. "Virgin Births and Hysterical Pregnancies: Neurosis and Mysticism in French and Italian Literature at the Turn of the Century." Dissertation, Comparative Literature, Yale University Press, 1991.

Milne, Tom. "*Thérèse.*" *Sight and Sound* 56, no. 1 (1986–1987): 69–70.

Nugent, Christopher. "The Face as Theology." *Theology Today* 41 (October 1984): 314–320.

O'Brien, Tom. "Screen: Rites of Passage." *Commonweal,* 26 December 1986, 690–692.

———. "Success in Small Things: An Interview with Film Director Alain Cavalier." *Commonweal,* 26 December 1986.

Pierrot, Jean. *The Decadent Imagination, 1880–1900.* Translated by Derek Coltman. Chicago: University of Chicago Press, 1981.

Philippon, Alain. "L'enfance de l'art." *Cahiers du Cinéma,* no. 387 (1986): 10–11.

Ramasse, François. "Entretien avec Alain Cavalier sur *Thérèse.*" *Positif,* no. 308 (1986): 23–29.

Rasy, Elisabetta. *La prima estasi.* Milan: Mondadori, 1985.

Reynaud, Bérénice. "The New York Film Festival: Questions of Framing." *Afterimage* 14 (January 1987): 19–20.

Sainte-Marie, Father François de. *The Photo Album of St. Thérèse of Lisieux.* New York: P. J. Kenedy & Sons, 1962.

Santo, Vincenzo. "L'immagine dell'occhio." *Segnocinema*, no. 31 (1988): 6–9.

Sarris, Andrew. "About Faces." *American Film* 4 (June 1979): 54–61.

Seidenberg, Robert, and Karen Crow. *Women Who Marry Houses: Panic and Protest in Agoraphobia.* New York: McGraw Hill, 1983.

Shaffer, Lawrence. "Reflections on the Face in Film." *Film Quarterly* 8, no. 2 (1977–1978): 31–32.

Steele, Bruce C. "Saints, Spectacle, Sensuality." *Columbia Film View* 5, no. 2. (1986–1987): 14–17.

Tassone, Aldo. "Alla scoperta di Alain Cavalier." *Segnocinema*, no. 29 (1987): 3–4.

"*Thérèse* d'Alain Cavalier." *L'Avant-Scène*, no. 364 (1987): 19–87.

Tobin, Michael. "Thérèse de Lisieux and Bernanos' First Novel." *French Forum* 10, no. 1 (1985): 84–96.

Toubiana, Serge, and Pascal Bonitzer. "Les dix premières secondes: Entretien avec Catherine Mouchet." *Cahiers du Cinéma*, no. 387 (1986).

Tournés, Andrée. "*Thérèse.*" *Jeune Cinéma*, no. 177 (1986): 43–46.

~

Index

~

Illustrations in *italic*

Abstract Expressionism. *See* Expressionism
adaptations, of literary texts for screen,
85–93, 161
African art, 31
Albera, Giovanni, 250n.20
Alberti, Leon Battista, 259–260n.28
Alley, Ronald, 24
Almendros, Nestor, 97
Altman, Rick, 33
American in Paris, An: art, love and money
in, 16–18; as atypical musical, 16–18;
ballet in, 3, 16, 19–22, 27, 41;
childhood in, 39; and Dufy, 22–23,
29; music in, 19, 33–35, 38; national
identity in, 19–21, 36, 38; painter and
painting in, 15, 20–35, 41, 42; Paris as
Disneyland in, 35–42; plot of, 16–17;
and Pollock, 27–32, *32*; primitivism
in, *30*, 31–32; psychic upheaval in, 2,
5, 16, 35–42; and Renoir, 23–24, *25*;
and Rousseau, 24–27, *25*, *26*; scenes
from, *25*, 28–30, *33*; sexual identity
in, 18, 19–21, 35; and Toulouse-
Lautrec, 33–35
Ames, Preston, 22

Andrei Rublev: animals in, 152–153, 156–
157; architecture in, 150–152; dialogue
in, 146–147; divinity in, 138, *139,*
140–144, *142,* 148, *151,* 153, 159; doors
and windows in, 146–150; flight in,
153–154, 155–157; historical process
in, 144–146; human faces in, 141–
144; icon painting in, *139,* 140–144,
142, 146, 147, *151,* 158–160; narrative
of, 140–141; pictorial devices in, 136–
138, 146–150, 156–157; psychical
experience in, 136, 157–158; reaction
versus action in, 144–146; restoration of tradition in, 157–160; Soviet
censorship of, 159; water in, 136–137,
158
Andrew, Dudley, 63, 202
Angelico, Fra, 135
animals, 152–153, 156–157, 187
Annunciation, The, 151
anticinema, 205
Antonioni, Michelangelo: characters of,
compared to Giacometti's *City
Square,* 251n.31; color used by, 9–10,
43–44, 62, 68–69, 252n.44; as
director of *Red Desert,* 2, 3, 5, 6, 7, 9–

10, 43–80, 250n.20; on directorship, 46, 78; feminine vision and, 48–49; films of, 48; on influences on artists, 252n.41; and neorealism, 44, 45, 50–51; relations with actors, 78, 79; and Rothko, 251n.31; on science and morality, 250n.9; on settings, 45–47; shooting techniques of, 46–47, 64–67; vertical orientation, 251n.24. *See also Red Desert*
Aragon, Louis, 122
Arcangeli, Franco, 72
architecture and architectural space: in Antonioni's cinema, 3, 60, 65–66; in Cavalier's cinema, 228–230, 234; in Godard's cinema, 110; in Rohmer's cinema, *91*, *92–106*, *95*, *96*, *98–102*; in Tarkovsky's cinema, 150–152
Arnold, Matthew, 81, 82
Arrowsmith, William, 49
Art Informel, 69, 70, 72, 73, 76
artist, and relationship to works, 252n.42
Art Nouveau, 15
Astruc, Alexandre, 83, 86
Atget, Eugene, 24
Aumont, Jacques, 9–12
avant-gardism, 27–28, 68, 154, 162, 164, 165, 194, 251n.39, 254n.6, 258n.15

Bachelard, Gaston, 144
Baggley, John, 143, 147, 148
Balázs, Béla, 252n.44
Balla, Giacomo, 55
ballet, 3, 16, 18–23, 27, 31, 33, 35, 41
Balthus, 159
Balzac, Honoré de, 118, 129
Barlow, John, 186–187
baroque, 51–52, 70
Barthes, Roland, 63, 64, 116, 120, 127, 252n.43
Bataille, Georges, 229
Baudelaire, Charles, 49

Bazin, André, 45, 84, 94, 137, 138, 140, 145, 253n.15
Belmondo, Jean-Paul, 107, 109, *115*, 117, 124, 133
Benayoun, Robert, 69, 72
Bergstrom, Janet, 122, 190, 192
Berlin, Irving, 31
Bernini, Gian Lorenzo, 222
Betz, Margaret, 159
Bianco e Nero, 46
Biedermeier art, 182–184
Bismarck, Chancellor Otto von, 164
Bizet, Georges, 109
Blow-Up, 63
Böcklin, Arnold, 164, 165, 169, *169*, 170, 258n.13
body painting. *See* tattooing
Bogart, Humphrey, 127
Bonitzer, Pascal, 12, 62, 63, 89
Borckhardt, Edith, 87, *91*
Bordwell, David, 201
Borges, Jorge Luis, 126
Bosch, Hieronymus, 53, 135, 149
Boucher, François, 97
Brando, Marlon, 5, 28, 30
Branzi, Andrea, 55
Braque, Georges, 63, 154
Braudel, Fernand, 55
Breathless, 120, 127
Brecht, Bertolt, 14
Bresson, Robert, 253n.15
Brigadoon, 15
Brodsky, Isaak, 160
Brooks, Peter, 10, 50, 51, 52
Brown, Gerard Baldwin, 32
Brueghel, Pieter, the Elder, 136
Bryson, Norman, 223, 224, 266n.40
Buddhism, 203, 204, 220, 262n.15
Buñuel, Luis, 15
Buoninsegna, Duccio di, 135
Burch, Noel, 205
Bürger, Fritz, 258n.15
Burke, Edmund, 259n.25

Burri, Alberto, 68–69, 68, 252n.42, 252n.46

Bynum, Caroline Walker, 240

Byron, George Gordon, 100, 101

Cabinet of Doctor Caligari, 167

Café Flaubert, 31, 32, 33

Calvino, Italo, 251n.39

Campari, Roberto, 14, 39, 63

Canudo, Ricciotto, 254n.6

Cardullo, Bert, 195

Carmen, 109–110

Caron, Leslie, 16, 17, 24, 33

Carpaccio, Vittore, 135

Casabianca, Camille de, 222

Casper, Joseph Andrew, 17, 41

Cavalier, Alain: artistic credo of, 225; close-ups in films of, 222–226, 235, 240; as director of *Thérèse*, 2, 5, 8, 9, 221–245; divinity as theme of, 223, 234, 236, 238, 240, 243; on filmmakers, 245; props in films of, 230–231, 265n.27; shooting techniques of, 223–226, 231, 240, 245, 265n.7; still life in films of, 9, 235–245. *See also Thérèse*

Céline, Louis-Ferdinand, 118

censorship, 159, 200, 201, 207, 209, 210, 212, 261n.4, 261n.5, 263n.29

Certeau, Michel de, 229

Chagall, Marc, 15, 153

Charcot, Jean-Martin, 222, 225

Charpentier, Constance Marie, 253n.18

Chevalier, Maurice, 19

Chionetti, Carlo, 45

City Square, 251n.31

Claesz, Pieter, 228

Clift, Montgomery, 5, 28, 30

close-ups, 222–226, 235, 240, 265n.7

Cocteau, Jean, 15

Cohan, George M., 36

collage, 10–11, 108–109, 111–113, 123, 126–130, 132, 134

Confucianism, 204, 220, 263n.27

Copeland, Roger, 30

critics. *See* specific film critics

Cubism, 31, 108, 166

Dada, 68–69, 108

Dadoun, Roger, 179

Dalí, Salvador, 15

dance. *See* ballet

D'Annunzio, Gabriele, 49, 258n.14, 264–265n.6

Dante Alighieri, 50

Darwin, Charles, 187

da Todi, Jacopone, 252n.42

David, Jacques-Louis, 94–97, 95, 253n.18

David, Jean-Jacques, 102

Dean, James, 28, 128

death: in Japanese cinema, 202, 204, 220, 263n.29; in Murnau's cinema, 194–195. *See also* suicide

De Chirico, Giorgio, 49–50, 53, 54, 55, 169, 170

Degas, Edgar, 35

Degele, Hans Ehrenbaum, 165

Delacroix, Eugène, 100, 102, 102, 122, 135

Delaunay, Robert, 37, 38

Deleuze, Gilles, 62, 63, 239

Depero, Fortunato, 55

Der Blaue Reiter, 166, 167, 168, 171

Descartes, René, 83, 84

De Sica, Vittorio, 44, 252n.42

Designing Woman, 15

Deutsches Theater, 168

Diderot, Denis, 97

Die Brücke, 166, 167

directors. *See* specific directors

divinity: in Cavalier's cinema, 223, 234–236, 238, 240, 243; in Godard's cinema, 126; in Murnau's cinema, 174–175, 178; in Rohmer's cinema, 85; in Tarkovsky's cinema, 138–144, 139, 142, 148, 151, 153, 160

Doane, Mary Ann, 191
Domarchi, Jean, 13
doppelgänger theme, 127–128
Dostoyevsky, Fyodor Mikhailovich, 180
Douchet, Jean, 13
Douglas, Kirk, 248n.26
Dovzshenko, Alexander, 154
Dracula, 161, 182, 261n.40
Dreyer, Carl-Theodor, 225
Dubuffet, Jean, 69, 71, 72, 77,
    252nn.46–47
Duchamp, Marcel, 15
Dufy, Raoul, 22–24, 29, 35, 38, 120
Dürer, Albrecht, 164
Duvivier, Julien, 127

Eakins, Thomas, 15
editing. See film editing
Ehrlich, Linda, 203, 214
Eisenstein, S. M., 138–140, 145, 154,
    251n.24
Eisner, Lotte, 162, 166, 169, 189
Elsaesser, Thomas, 162, 167, 169, 187,
    257n.4
Enlightenment, the, 94, 126
Epstein, Jean, 239
Ernst, Max, 15
eroticism. See sexual desire
Escher, M. C., 135
Expressionism: and Art Informel, 69;
    definition of, 258–259n.16; goal of,
    258n.5; Hitler's denunciation of,
    258n.16; as label, 166; limitations of,
    and Murnau, 4, 8, 162, 164–168, 180–
    187, 190, 191, 193, 194, 196; and
    Pollock's avant-gardism, 27–28, 31,
    36, 42

Face of Christ Not Made by Human Hands,
    142
Falconetti, Renée, 225
Faure, Elie, 109, 122, 254n.6
Fautrier, Jean, 69, 72, 73

Fauvism, 120, 166
Fazio, Rossana Di, 235
female body, 112, 205
femininity: in Antonioni's cinema, 47–
    48, 65, 66; in Cavalier's cinema, 223;
    in Godard's cinema, 122; in
    Minnelli's cinema, 20, 27, 31; in
    Mizoguchi's cinema, 202–203; in
    Murnau's cinema, 191–193. See also
    gender roles; sexual identity
film editing: in Mizoguchi's cinema,
    206, 209, 210, 212; in Murnau's
    cinema, 188, 193
Filonov, Pavel, 154
Five Women around Utamaro: censorship of,
    199, 207, 210, 263n.29; and cinema as
    popular medium, 206–214; critics'
    views of, 200; death in, 202, 204,
    220, 263n.29; jealousy in, 203,
    264n.40; love in, 202, 263n.29,
    264n.41; plot of, 198–199; scene
    from, 216; shooting techniques in,
    205–206, 209–210; suicide in, 199,
    202, 204, 207, 219, 261n.5; tattooing
    in, 7, 199, 209, 214–220; and
    woodblock printing, 7, 199, 200,
    206–207, 211; Yoshikata Yoda as
    scriptwriter of, 200
Flaubert, Gustave, 231
Flowers of Evil, The, 111
Flowers of Saint Francis, 252n.42
Foch, Nina, 17
Forty-Seven Ronin, 261n.5
Fragonard, Jean-Honoré, 97, 98, 99, 100
Freud, Sigmund, 86, 187, 191, 222, 224
Friedrich, Caspar David, 100, 100, 162,
    163, 165, 170–172, 172, 174, 175, 177,
    178, 182, 184, 185, 259–260n.28
Fuller, Samuel, 109, 111, 123, 133
Fusco, Giovanni, 54
Fuseli, Henry, 89, 90, 91, 101, 103, 105
futurism, 31, 52, 55, 80, 166

Gabin, Jean, 127
Galeen, Henrick, 165
Garland, Judy, 14
Gauguin, Paul, 164
gender roles: in Antonioni's cinema, 6, 57–61; battle of sexes in *Red Desert*, 51, 57–61; in Cavalier's cinema, 8, 225, 240–245; in cinema, 4, 6, 7; in Godard's cinema, 120–126; in Murnau's cinema, 189–194
Gercke, George, 263n.29
Géricault, Théodore, 135
Gershwin, George, 21, 22, 31, 35, 36, 38
Gershwin, Ira, 22
Giacometti, Paolo, 251n.31
Gigi, 14
Giotto, 258n.14, 259–260n.28
God. *See* divinity
Godard, Jean-Luc: and collage, 10–11, 108–109, 111–113, 123, 126–130, 132, 134; as director of *Pierrot le Fou*, 2, 5–11, 107–134, 255n.24; films of, 109–110, 112, 120, 126, 254n.6; separate poles of films of, 134, 254n.12; shooting techniques of, 110–111, 122–124. *See also Pierrot le Fou*
Godfrey, Peter, 38
Goerits, Mathias, 76
Goethe, Johann Wolfgang von, 252n.44
Gogh, Vincent van, 31, 126, 164, 231, 233
Gordon, Donald, 188
Gothic art, 175, 179
Goya, Francisco, 97, 103
Graham, Martha, 30
Grande, Maurizio, 150
Grau, Albin, 165, 183
Greenaway, Peter, 8
Greuze, Jean-Baptiste, 96–97, 98
Grünewald, Matthias, 164
Guarner, José-Luis, 117
Guetary, Georges, 17
Guilbaut, Serge, 247n.1

haiku, 145
Hardy, Oliver, 128
Harris, Richard, 45
Harvey, Stephen, 14
Hazelton, Roger, 85
Hearn, Lafcadio, 264n.37
Heimbach, Wolfgang, 243, 244
Hirano, Kyoko, 261n.5, 262n.15, 263n.29
Hitchcock, Alfred, 46
Hitler, Adolf, 258n.16
Hofmannsthal, Hugo von, 164
Holbein, Hans, 164
Hollander, Anne, 9, 12, 251n.36
Home from the Hill, 14
horror, 162, 167, 178–180, 187–196, 260n.35, 260–261n.41
Hypothesis of a Stolen Canvas, 8

Ibsen, Henrik, 180
icon painting, 139, 140–144, 142, 146, 147, 151, 158–160, 256n.16
Impressionism, 15, 163, 203
industrial design, 67, 250n.20
industrialization, 60, 69, 259n.24
International Style, 46–47

Jameux, Charles, 167, 188
Japan: U. S. occupation of, 197, 198, 261n.5; appreciation of painting in, 262n.24; ban on prostitution in, 261n.10; cinema and American censorship, 198, 207; film industry in, 198, 200; immediate post–World War II period, 197–198; publication of pornography in, 261n.5; totalitarianism in, 262n.21
jealousy, 202, 203, 264n.40
Joan of Arc, 225, 231, 237, 237
Joyce, James, 118

Kandinsky, Vassily, 154, 251n.39
Kant, Immanuel, 188, 259n.25
Karina, Anna, 107, 109, 111, 115, 120, 124, 131, 133

Kaulbach, 183
Keller, Horst, 34, 35
Kelly, Gene, 16, 17, 24, 25, 28–30, 33, 33, 35, 36, 41, 42
Kerouac, Jack, 257n.3
Kersting, Georg Friedrich, 96, 96, 191, 192
Kirchner, Ludwig, 175, 176
Kirihara, Donald, 202
Kleist, Heinrich von, 81, 82, 85–90, 92, 103, 171
Kline, T. Jefferson, 123, 126
Koerner, Joseph Leo, 163, 168, 259–260n.28
Kracauer, Siegfried, 162, 187
Krauss, Rosalind, 230
Kubin, Alfred, 170, 259n.23
Kunieda, Kanji, 200
Kuspit, Donald, 117, 129, 132

La Bruyère, Jean de, 84
Lacan, Jacques, 229
La Chienne, 127
Lang, Robert, 40
La Notte, 48
La Rochefoucauld, François de, 84
Lasker-Schüler, Else, 164
Last Year at Marienbad, 93
La Tour, Georges de, 101
Laurel, Stan, 128
Lawton, Anna, 135
Le Amiche, 48
Le Corbusier, 46
Le Fanu, Mark, 157
Lehman, Peter, 129
Le Mépris, 254n.6
Lenin, Vladimir Ilich, 160
Leonardo da Vinci, 45, 142
Lessing, Gottfried, 81, 82
Leutrat, Jean-Louis, 109
Levant, Oscar, 17
Levine, Frederick S., 258n.5
Lichtenstein, Roy, 121

Liebknecht, Karl, 193
Liehm, Mira, 68
Life of Oharu, 209
Lindner, Robert, 31
Lipps, Theodor, 188
literary texts, adapted for screen, 85–90, 92, 161
love: in Five Women around Utamaro, 202, 263n.29, 263n.33; in Godard's cinema, 113–115; in Minnelli's cinema, 15, 16–18; in Utamaro's prints, 264n.41. See also sexual desire
Lumière brothers, 235
Lust for Life, 15, 249n.41
Luxemburg, Rosa, 193

MacArthur, Douglas, 197–198
Malevich, Kazimir, 152, 154, 155, 156
Manet, Édouard, 21, 231, 232
Manguin, Henri-Charles, 120
Mann, Thomas, 164
Ma nuit chez Maud, 83, 84
Manzoni, Piero, 62, 251n.28
Marc, Franz, 162, 165, 169, 187, 192
Marin, Louis, 39, 40
Marinetti, F. T., 55, 123
Marquet, Pierre-Albert, 120
Marquise of O, The: architectural space in, 104–110; characters' evolution in, 88, 90, 92, 97, 100; conflicts between mind, senses, and emotion in, 83, 88, 90, 92–93; dialectic of word and image in, 81, 83–85; female eroticism in, 90; Kleist novella, based on, 81, 82, 85–93; pictorial, architectural, and filmic space in, 92–106; psychoanalysis in, 90, 92, 97; rape of Marquise in, 89–92, 100; Rohmer's approach to adaptation in, 88–93, 106; scenes from, 91, 99, 101; silence and absence of music in, 103–104
Martin, Thérèse. See Teresa of Avila, Saint

Mary Poppins, 39

Masculin/Féminin, 109

masculinity, 31, 47, 66. *See also* sexual identity

maternity, 223–224, 228–229, 241, 243, 263nn.33–34, 265n.7

Matisse, Henri, 63, 69, 105, 106, 118, 125, 126, 252n.44

Mattei, Enrico, 249n.3

Meet Me in St. Louis, 15

Meier-Graefe, Julius, 164, 168, 180, 258n.12

melodrama: in Antonioni's cinema, 10, 50–52, 55, 70, 78, 79; in Minnelli's cinema, 40–41; and Mizoguchi, 202, 220

men. *See* gender roles; masculinity; sexual desire; sexual identity

Metro-Goldwyn-Mayer (MGM), 6, 14, 16, 18, 21, 23, 42

Mies van der Rohe, Ludwig, 46

Mimi-Nashi-Hoichi, 217–218, 264n.37

Minnelli, Vincente: critics' opinions of, 14, 16, 17, 31, 41, 248n.7, 248n.26; as director of *An American in Paris*, 2, 3, 5, 6, 13–42; filmic style of, 13–16; films of, 14, 15, 249n.41; and Hollywood, 14, 15, 18, 21, 34, 39–40, 42; interest in painting, 14–15, 248n.6; and Pollock, 15, 16, 27–32; sexuality of, 248n.11; shooting techniques of, 20; use of art-historical sources by, 15, 72; use of sources about Paris, 24, 26, 27, 35–36. *See also American in Paris, An*

Miró, Joan, 15, 38

Misler, Nicoletta, 148, 152, 154

Mizoguchi, Kenji: censorship in cinema of, 207, 209, 212, 263n.29; characters in cinema of, 263n.26; and cinema as popular medium, 206–214; as director of *Five Women around Utamaro*, 2, 4, 5, 6, 7, 8, 197–220; as director

of *Ugetsu monogatari*, 209, 215, 216, 217–218; and film editing, 206, 209, 210, 212; films of, 209, 261n.5; and melodrama, 202; relationships with women, 202–203, 218–219, 262nn.13–14; self-censorship by, 200–201; shooting techniques of, 205–206, 209–210; traditional esthetic of, 264n.42; visual style of, 200–201. *See also Five Women around Utamaro*

modernism, 15–16, 51

Modigliani, Amedeo, 15, 126

Mondrian, Pieter Cornelius, 64, 104, 154, 251n.39

Monet, Claude, 144

money and love, 15, 16–18

Monroe, Marilyn, 127

Monti, Nicolas, 250n.20

Mouchet, Catherine, 225, 242

Mulligan, Jerry, 30, 31

Mulvey, Laura, 109

Munch, Edvard, 165, 180

Murano, Quirizio da, 241

Murnau, F. W.: as director of *Faust*, 82, 92, 171; as director of *Nosferatu: A Symphony of Horror*, 2, 4, 5, 7, 8, 161–196; editing by, 188, 193; education of, 163–166, 190, 258n.14; and Expressionism, 4, 8, 162, 164–168, 180–187, 190, 191, 193, 194, 196; and Friedrich, 171–178, 187; and German national identity, 168–171; links to Scandinavian cinema, 259n.18; and Romanticism, 4, 8, 162, 166–180, 184, 189, 196, 257n.3; and science and technology, 7, 170–171, 186–187, 195; sexuality of, 189–191; shooting techniques of, 186–187. *See also Nosferatu*

music: in Antonioni's cinema, 54–55; in Cavalier's cinema, 233; in medieval Russia, 256n.16; in Minnelli's cinema, 19, 31, 33, 34, 35, 38; in

Mizoguchi's cinema, 217, 263n.38;
and Murnau, 187–188. *See also* ballet
musicals, 14, 16–18, 29–30, 34, 38–39

Naniwa Bushi, 202
Naremore, James, 14, 31, 248n.26,
248nn.6–7
national identity, 19–21, 36, 168–171
neoclassicism, 81, 103
neorealism, 44, 45, 50–51
Neumann, Carl, 164, 258n.14
Newman, Paul, 28
Nietzsche, Friedrich Wilhelm, 170, 190
Noh, 202
Nolde, Emil, 171, 258n.16
Nosferatu: animals in, 187; divinity in,
174–175, 178; double as theme in,
189–190; Expressionism in, 4, 8,
166–168, 180–187, 190–196; and
Friedrich, 171–178, 187; gender roles
in, 7, 189–194; and German national
identity, 168–171; and Gothic art,
175, 179; horror as theme of, 162, 167,
178–180, 187–196; locations for,
259n.18; and music, 187–188;
Romanticism in, 4, 8, 162, 166–180,
184, 189, 193, 196, 257n.3;
Rückenfigur in, 172, 178; scenes
from, *173, 176, 177, 183, 185, 195*;
spectatorship in, 187–191; vampires
in, 7, 161, 162, 171, 179–182, 187–195
Nouveau Realism, 76

Offenbach, Jacques, 233
Oldenburg, Claes, 66
Oliver, 39
oriental art, 7, 63, 156, 199, 200, 202,
204, 206–207, 211, 217–218

painting. *See* specific painters and art
movements
Pallasmaa, Juhani, 136
Pascal, Blaise, 82, 84, 85, 94

Pasolini, Pier Paolo, 48, 49, 57
Passion, 11
Pépé le Moko, 127
Perloff, Marjorie, 108, 117
Peucker, Brigitte, 12, 247n.5
Picasso, Pablo, 117, 122, *124*, 126, 128,
130, 154
Pick-Up on South Street, 111
Pierrot le Fou: collage in, 10–11, 108–109,
111–113, 123, 126–130, 132, 134; color
and line in, 117–123, *124, 125*, 130–131,
255n.24; compared with *Carmen*,
109–110; doppelgänger theme in,
127–128; narrative structure of, 113–
117, 127; and Pop Art, 108, 112, 116,
127; scenes from, *115, 131*; sexual
difference in, 109, 111, 112–113, 120–
126; storyline of, 108–109; word and
image in, 10–11, 111–112, 123–126, 130–
134
Poe, Edgar Allan, 127
Pollock, Jackson, 5, 15, 16, 27–32, *32*, 36,
42, 248n.7, 251n.39
Pop Art, 66, 108, 112, 116, 120, 127, 205,
205–207
pornography, 261n.4
Porter, Cole, 31
Positivism, 222
Post-Impressionism, 31, 166
prehistoric art. *See* Primitivism
Prénom Carmen, 109–110
Preziosi, Donald, 249n.41
Primitivism, 15–16, *30*, 31–32, 59, 105
props, in Mizoguchi's cinema, 211

Rasy, Elisabeta, 226
Red Desert: architecture and painting in,
3, 56, 62–76, *67, 68, 70, 71, 73–75*;
artistic creativity of characters in,
46, 48, 50–51, 60; battle of sexes in,
51, 57–61; color in, 9–10, 43–44, 68–
69; convalescence in, 49–50; and De
Chirico, 53; historical change in, 10,

43, 44, 46, 47, 53–57, 79–80; melodrama in, 10, 50–52, 55, 70, 78, 79; modernism versus baroque in, 51–52; music in, 54–55; oppositional elements in, 47–48, 79–80; scenes from, 52, 59, 61, 76; science, technology, and industry, 53, 55–56, 59, 60, 63, 64, 76; sculpture in, 76; shooting techniques in, 46–47, 64–67; theme of, 44, 47, 50, 52, 56, 79–80; ventriloquism in, 10, 48–49, 51, 62, 78; word and image in, 77–80
Reinhardt, Max, 164, 168
religion. *See* Buddhism; Confucianism; divinity
Rembrandt, 135, 170, 258n.14
Renaissance, 147, 148, 149
Renoir, Jean, 127, 209, 210
Renoir, Pierre-Auguste, 20, 23, 25, 120, 126, 130, 132, 133
Resnais, Alain, 93
Reynolds, Sir Joshua, 244, 266n.40
Riegl, Alois, 164, 165
Rimbaud, Arthur, 113, 114, 119
Rodia, Simon, 69
Rohmer, Eric: approach to Kleist's text, 85–92, 106; artistic identity of, 84; as "auteur-in-absentia," 105–106; color theory of, 254n.31; as director of *Ma nuit chez Maud*, 83, 84; as director of *The Marquise of O*, 2, 5, 6, 7, 81–106; interest in painting, 82, 84, 94–95, 105–106; on Matisse, 105–106; pictorial, architectural, and filmic space in cinema of, 92–106; shooting techniques of, 88, 104–105; on verbal cinema, 83, 84. *See also Marquise of O*,
Romadin, Mikhail, 135
Romanticism, 4, 8, 122, 162, 164–180, 184, 189, 193, 196, 257n.3, 257–258n.4
Rosai, Ottone, 67
Rossellini, Roberto, 84, 252n.42
Rothko, Mark, 66, 251n.31

Rouault, Georges, 126
Roud, Richard, 63, 112
Rousseau, Henri, 20, 24, 25, 26–27, 26, 34, 36, 39
Rubens, Peter Paul, 135
Rückenfigur, 172, 178, 259–260n.28
Ruiz, Raoul, 8

Saint George, 139
Sansho the Bailiff, 209
Sarris, Andrew, 16, 17
Sartre, Jean Paul, 128
Sato, Tadao, 220, 262n.13, 264n.42
Schwind, Moritz von, 170
Schwitters, Kurt, 68, 69
science and technology: in Antonioni's cinema, 53, 55, 56, 60; and Murnau, 7, 170–171, 186–187, 195; in Rohmer's cinema, 7, 95
Seberg, Jean, 120, 123
Sennet, Mack, 128
Senso, 116, 130, 131
sexual desire: in Cavalier's cinema, 224, 229, 240–245, 244; eroticism in Mizoguchi's cinema, 200; female eroticism in *The Marquise of O*, 90; and mother-son relationship, 263nn.33–34; in Murnau's cinema, 179–180, 189–194
sexual identity: in Antonioni's cinema, 76; in cinema, 4, 6; in Godard's cinema, 108, 111, 112–113, 120–126; in Minnelli's cinema, 18, 19–21; in Mizoguchi's cinema, 214, 219–220; in Murnau's cinema, 189–194; in Rohmer's cinema, 100; in Tarkovsky's cinema, 189–194. *See also* femininity; gender roles; masculinity
Shakespeare, William, 164
Sharaff, Irene, 22
Shindo, Kaneto, 200
Shoeshine, 252n.42
Simmel, Georg, 163

Sinténis, Renée, 164
Sironi, Mario, 67, 67
Solaris, 136
Some Came Running, 14
Sorlin, Pierre, 108
Soulages, Pierre, 69, 73, 75
Spiegel, Alan, 87
Spitzweg, Carl, 169
Staël, Nicholas de, 69, 73, 74
Stam, Robert, 119
still life, 9, 181, 235–245, 266n.40
Stoker, Bram, 161, 182
Strauss, Johann, 19
Strick, Philip, 151
Strindberg, August, 180
suicide: in Godard's cinema 110, 131; in
    Japanese cinema, 199, 202, 204, 207,
    219, 261n.5, 263n.5. See also death
Suprematism, 154
Surrealism, 15, 23, 108, 122, 248n.7,
    251n.39

Tailleur, Roger, 69, 72
Tanaka, Kinuyo, 203
Tanguy, Yves, 15
Tarkovsky, Andrei: on cinema, 135; as
    director of Andrei Rublev, 2, 5, 7, 8,
    135–160; divinity as theme of, 136,
    138, 140–144, 148, 153; filmic image
    of, 137–141, 148, 156–157; films of,
    135, 136; and four natural elements,
    136–137, 158; and icon painting, 139,
    140–141, 142, 143, 146, 147, 151, 156,
    158–160; and oriental art, 156;
    pictorial devices in cinema of, 136,
    146–150, 156–157; psychical experi-
    ence in cinema of, 136, 157–158; and
    relation of word and image, 256n.24;
    shooting techniques of, 141–142,
    147–148, 257n.38. See also Andrei Rublev
Tatlin, Vladimir, 154
tattooing, 7, 199, 209, 214–220, 263–
    264nn.35–36

technology. See science and technology
Teresa of Avila, Saint, 221–222, 224,
    234, 235
Thérèse: acting and dialogue in, 225–226,
    228; close-ups in, 222–226, 235, 240;
    diary and photographic sources of,
    221, 235–239; divinity as theme of,
    223, 234–236, 238, 240, 243; gender
    roles in, 8, 225, 240–245; maternity
    in, 223–224, 228–229, 241, 243,
    265n.7; music in, 233; scenes from,
    227, 237; shooting techniques of,
    223–226, 231, 240, 245; space in,
    228–230, 234; still life in, 9,
    235–245; strategy of subtraction in,
    224–235
Thode, Henry, 258n.14
Tingueley, Jean, 76
Toulouse-Lautrec, Henri de, 20, 21, 33–
    36, 33, 42, 164
Tsutaya, Juzaburo, 206
Two Mrs. Carrolls, The, 38

Ugetsu monogatari, 209, 215, 216, 217–218
Umberto D, 44
Utamaro, Kitagawa: difficulties with
    the authorities, 201, 261n.4;
    iconographic details of prints of,
    200, 212, 262n.25; An Oiran, 213;
    portraiture by, 263n.31; woodblock
    prints of, 199, 206, 262n.22, 262n.25,
    263–264n.36, 264n.41
Utrillo, Maurice, 24, 28

vampires, 7, 161, 162, 171, 179–182, 187–
    195. See also Dracula
Van Gogh. See Gogh, Vincent van
Velázquez, Diego, 109, 110, 122, 126, 223,
    228, 254n.8
ventriloquism, 10, 48–49, 51, 62, 78
Vico, Giambattista, 252n.52
Visconti, Luchino, 116, 130, 131
Viswanathan, Meera, 263n.34

Vitti, Monica, 10, 44–48, 51, 60–64, *61,* 76, 79, 251n.36

Vivre sa vie, 112

Vladyshevskaia, Tatiana, 143

Voltaire, 126

Wagner, Fritz Arno, 165

Waldman, Diane, 27–28, 38, 39

Warhol, Andy, 66, 127

Welles, Orson, 209, 210

Whistler, James McNeill, 29, 30

Wiene, Robert, 167

Williams, Alan, 107–108

Wölfflin, Heinrich, 164, 165, 168, 171

Wols, 69, 70, 251n.39

women. *See* female body; femininity; gender roles; sexual desire; sexual identity

woodblock printing, 7, 199, 200, 204, 206–207, 211, 262n.22, 262n.25, 263–264n.36

Woolf, Stuart, 250n.17

World War I, 171, 180, 239

World War II, 4, 19, 28, 197, 198, 261n.5

Wörringer, Wilhelm, 165, 188, 194

Wyler, William, 209, 210

Yama Uba myth, 214, 263n.34

Yoda, Yoshikata, 200

Zurbarán, Francisco de, 238, *238*

This book is set in Monotype Centaur.

Printed on 60 lb Finch Opaque
and bound by Edwards Brothers,
Ann Arbor, Michigan.

Designed and composed by
Ellen McKie on a Macintosh
in Pagemaker 5.0 for the
University of Texas Press.